The Zohar

by
Rav Shimon bar Yochai
From The Book of Avraham

with
The Sulam Commentary

by
Rav Yehuda Ashlag

The First Ever Unabridged
English Translation with Commentary

Published by
The Kabbalah Centre International Inc.
Dean Rav S. P. Berg Shlita

Edited and Compiled by
Rabbi Michael Berg

Copyright © 2003

Published by
The Kabbalah Centre International Inc.

155 E. 48th St., New York, NY 10017
1062 S. Robertson Blvd., Los Angeles, CA 90035

Director Rav Berg

First Printing 2001
Revised Edition 2008

Printed in USA

ISBN: 1-57189-156-0

To my beloved son Louis, who showed me the way of the Light
by passing away at 19 years old. May God bless him forever.

APPLYING THE POWER OF THE ZOHAR

The Zohar is a book of great mystical power and wisdom. It is Universally recognized as the definitive work on the Kabbalah – and it is also so Much more.

The Zohar is a wellspring of spiritual energy, a fountainhead of metaphysical power that not only reveals and explains, but literally brings blessing, protection, and well-being into the lives of all those who read or peruse its sacred texts. All that is required is worthy desire, the certainty of a trusting heart, and an open and receptive mind. Unlike other books, including the great spiritual texts of other traditions, The Zohar is written in a kind of code, through which metaphors, parables, and cryptic language at first conceal but ultimately reveal the forces of creation.

As electrical current is concealed in wire and cable before disclosing itself as an illuminated light bulb, the spiritual Light of the Creator is wrapped in allegory and symbolism throughout the Aramaic text of the Zohar. And while many books contain information and knowledge, the Zohar both expresses and embodies spiritual Light. The very letters on its pages have the power to bring spiritual wisdom and positive energy into every area of our lives.

As we visually scan the Aramaic texts and study the accompanying insights that appear in English, spiritual power is summoned from above – and worlds tremble as Light is sent forth in response.

It's primary purpose is not only to help us acquire wisdom, but to draw Light from the Upper Worlds and to bring sanctification into our lives. Indeed, the book itself is the most powerful of all tools for cleansing the soul and connecting to the Light of the Creator. As you open these pages, therefore, do not make understanding in the conventional sense your primary goal.

Although you may not have a knowledge of Aramaic, look first at the Aramaic text before reading the English. Do not be discouraged by difficulties with comprehension. Instead, open your heart to the spiritual transformation the Zohar is offering you.

Ultimately, the Zohar is an instrument for refining the individual soul – for removing darkness from the earth – and for bringing well being and blessing to our fellow man.

Its purpose is not only to make us intellectually wise, but to make us spiritually pure.

Torah

Also known as the Five Books of Moses, the Torah is considered to be the physical body of learning, whereas the Zohar is the internal soul. The literal stories of the Torah conceal countless hidden secrets.` The Zohar is the Light that illuminates all of the Torah's sublime mysteries.

Beresheet	Genesis
Shemot	Exodus
Vayikra	Leviticus
Bemidbar	Numbers
Devarim	Deuteronomy

Prophets

Amos	Amos
Chagai	Haggai
Chavakuk	Habakkuk
Hoshea	Hosea
Malachi	Malachi
Melachim	Kings
Michah	Micah
Nachum	Nahum
Ovadyah	Obadiah
Shmuel	Samuel
Shoftim	Judges
Tzefanyah	Zephaniah
Yechezkel	Ezekiel
Yehoshua	Joshua
Yeshayah	Isaiah
Yirmeyah	Jeremiah
Yoel	Joel
Yonah	Jonah
Zecharyah	Zechariah

Writings

Daniel	Daniel
Divrei Hayamim	Chronicles
Eicha	Lamentations
Ester	Esther
Ezra	Ezra
Nechemiah	Nehemiah
Iyov	Job
Kohelet	Ecclesiastes
Mishlei	Proverbs
Rut	Ruth

Sir Hashirim	Songs of Songs
Tehilim	Psalms

The Ten Sfirot – Emanations

To conceal the blinding *Light* of the Upper World, and thus create a tiny point into which our universe would be born, ten *curtains* were fabricated. These ten *curtains* are called Ten Sfirot. Each successive Sfirah further reduces the emanation of *Light*, gradually dimming its brilliance to a level almost devoid of *Light* – our physical world known as *Malchut*. The only remnant of Light remaining in this darkened universe is a *pilot light* which sustains our existence. This Light is the life force of a human being and the force that gives birth to stars, sustains suns and sets everything from swirling galaxies to busy ant hills in motion. Moreover, the Ten Sfirot act like a prism, refracting the Light into many *colors* giving rise to the diversity of life and matter in our world.

The Ten Sfirot are as follows:

Keter	Crown
Chochmah	Wisdom
Binah	Understanding
Da'at	Knowledge
Zeir Anpin	Small Face,
	(includes the next six Sfirot):
Chesed	Mercy (Chassadim - plural)
Gvurah	Judgment (Gvurot - Plural)
Tiferet	Splendor
Netzach	Victory (Eternity)
Hod	Glory
Yesod	Foundation
Malchut	Kingdom

The Partzufim - Spiritual forms

One complete structure of the Ten Sfirot creates a *Partzuf* or Spiritual Form. Together, these forces are the building blocks of all reality. As water and sand combine to create cement, the Ten Sfirot combine to produce a Spiritual Form [Partzuf]. Each of the Spiritual Forms below are therefore composed of one set of Ten Sfirot.

These Spiritual Forms are called:

Atik	Ancient
Atik Yomin	Ancient of Days
Atika Kadisha	Holy Ancient
Atik of Atikin	Anceint of Ancients
Aba	Father
Arich Anpin	Long Face
Ima	Mother
Nukva	Female
Tevunah	Intelligence
Yisrael Saba	Israel Grandfather
Zachar	Male

These names are not meant to be understood literally. Each represents a unique spiritual force and building block, producing a substructure and foundation for all the worlds make up reality.

The Five Worlds

All of the above Spiritual Forms [Partzufim] create one spiritual world. There are Five Worlds in total that compose all reality, therefore, five sets of the above Spiritual Forms are required.

Our physical world corresponds to the world of: Asiyah – Action

Adam Kadmon	Primordial Man
Atzilut	Emanation
Briyah	Creation
Yetzirah	Formation
Asiyah	Action

The Five Levels of the soul

Nefesh	First, Lowest level of Soul
Ruach	Second level of Soul
Neshamah	Third level of Soul
Chayah	Fourth level of Soul
Yechidah	Highest, fifth level of Soul

Names of God

As a single ray of white sunlight contains the seven colors of the spectrum, the one Light of the Creator embodies many diverse spiritual forces. These different forces are called *Names of God*. Each Name denotes a specific attribute and spiritual power. The Hebrew letters that compose these Names are the interface by which these varied Forces act upon our physical world. The most common Name of God is the Tetragrammaton (the four letters, *Yud Hei Vav Hei* יהוה.) Because of the enormous power that the Tetragrammaton transmits, we do not utter it aloud. When speaking of the Tetragrammaton, we use the term *Hashem* which means, *The Name.*

Adonai, El, Elohim, Hashem, Shadai, Eheyeh, Tzevaot, Yud Hei Vav Hei

People

Er	The son of Noach
Rabbi Elazar	The son of Rabbi Shimon bar Yochai
Rabbi Shimon bar Yochai	Author of the Zohar
Shem, Cham, Yefet	Noach's children
Shet	Seth
Ya'akov	Jacob
Yishai	Jesse (King David's father)
Yitzchak	Isaac
Yosef	Joseph
Yitro	Jethro
Yehuda	Judah

Angels

Angels are distinct energy components, part of a vast communication network running through the upper worlds. Each unique Angel is responsible for transmitting various forces of influence into our physical universe.

Adriel, Ahinael, Dumah (name of Angel in charge of the dead), Gabriel, Kadshiel, Kedumiel, Metatron, Michael, Rachmiel,

Glossary of Hebrew words

Raphael, Tahariel, Uriel

Nations

Nations actually represent the inner attributes and character traits of our individual self. The nation of Amalek refers to the doubt and uncertainty that dwells within us when we face hardship and obstacles. Moab represents the dual nature of man. Nefilim refers to the sparks of Light that we have defiled through our impure actions, and to the negative forces that lurk within the human soul as a result of our own wrongful deeds.

Amalek, Moab, Nefilim

General

Aba	Father
	Refers to the male principle and positive force in our universe. Correlates to the proton in an atom.
Arvit	The Evening prayer
Chayot	Animals
Chupah	Canopy (wedding ceremony)
Et	The
Avadon	Hell
Gehenom	Hell
Sheol	Hell
	The place a soul goes for purification upon leaving this world.
Ima	Mother
	The female principle and minus force in our universe. Correlates to the electron in an atom.
Kiddush	Blessing over the wine
Klipah	Shell (negativity)
Klipot	Shells (Plural)
Kriat Sh'ma	The Reading of the Sh'ma
Mashiach	Messiah
Minchah	The Afternoon prayer
Mishnah	Study
Mochin	Brain, Spiritual levels of Light
Moed	A designated time or holiday
Negev	The south of Israel
Nukva	Female

Partzuf	Face
Shacharit	The Morning prayer
Shamayim	Heavens (sky)
Shechinah	The Divine presence, The female aspect of the Creator
Tefilin	Phylacteries
The Dinur river	The river of fire
Tzadik	Righteous person
Zion	Another name for Jerusalem
Yisrael	The land of Israel
	The nation of Israel or an individual Israelite
Zohar	Splendor

The Hebrew vowels

Chirik א, Cholam אׁ א, Kamatz אָ, Patach א, Segol א, Sh'va א, Shuruk אּ א, Tzere א.

The Twelve Tribes

Asher, Dan, Ephraim, Gad, Issachar, Judah, Levi, Menasheh, Naphtali, Reuben, Shimon, Zebulun

Jewish Holidays

Rosh Hashanah	The Jewish New Year
Yom Kippur	Day of Atonement
Sukkot	Holiday of the Booths
Shmini Atzeret	The day of Convocation
Simchat Torah	Holiday on which we dance with the Torah
Pesach	Passover
Shavout	Holiday of the Weeks

כרך ד

פרשת חיי שרה, תולדות

Vol. IV

Chayi Sara, Toldot

A Prayer from The Ari

To be recited before the study of the Zohar

Ruler of the universe, and Master of all masters, The Father of mercy and forgiveness, we thank You, our God and the God of our fathers, by bowing down and kneeling, that You brought us closer to Your Torah and Your holy work, and You enable us to take part in the secrets of Your holy Torah. How worthy are we that You grant us with such big favor, that is the reason we plead before You, that You will forgive and acquit all our sins, and that they should not bring separation between You and us.

And may it be your will before You, our God and the God of our fathers, that You will awaken and prepare our hearts to love and revere You, and may You listen to our utterances, and open our closed heart to the hidden studies of Your Torah, and may our study be pleasant before Your Place of Honor, as the aroma of sweet incense, and may You emanate to us Light from the source of our soul to all of our being. And, may the sparks of your holy servants, through which you revealed Your wisdom to the world, shine.

May their merit and the merit of their fathers, and the merit of their Torah, and holiness, support us so we shall not stumble through our study. And by their merit enlighten our eyes in our learning as it stated by King David, The Sweet Singer of Israel: "Open my eyes, so that I will see wonders from Your Torah" (Tehilim 119:18). Because from His mouth God gives wisdom and understanding.

"May the utterances of my mouth and the thoughts of my heart find favor before You, God, my Strength and my Redeemer" (Tehilim 19:15).

CHAYEI SARAH

Names of Articles

1. "So they took up Jonah, and cast him into the sea"

A synopsis

Here Rabbi Yosi explains the hidden meaning of the biblical story of Jonah and the whale, and the nature of the symbols used in the story. We learn that the soul is judged each night while we sleep, and that this judgment is twofold. People are not judged according to the evil that they are destined to commit, but rather for the good that they have and will go on to do. The question of whether The Creator takes pleasure in punishing the wicked is then raised. In answer, it is pointed out that all human beings have a predetermined amount of evil they are allowed to commit. Once this limit passed, there is pleasure at their demise.

The Relevance of this Passage

The universal law of cause and effect is deeply embedded into our reality. For every negative action there is an equal negative reaction. The concept of time, however, creates a separation between cause and effect in our physical world. When man commits a negative deed, *time* delays the inevitable consequences. Repercussions from wrongful actions appear at a later date, creating the illusion that these repercussions are random events. Our negative inclination then tempts us to point the finger of blame at God because the original cause – our negative action – is forgotten and hidden somewhere in the past. A reading of this section makes us more keenly aware of our actions and the judgments they invariably bring, arousing a stronger intention to ardently walk the path of righteousness.

1. וַיִּהְיוּ חַיֵּי שָׂרָה מֵאָה שָׁנָה וְעֶשְׂרִים שָׁנָה וְשֶׁבַע שָׁנִים. רַבִּי יוֹסֵי, פָּתַח וְאָמַר, וַיִּשְׂאוּ אֶת יוֹנָה וַיְטִלֻהוּ אֶל הַיָּם וַיַּעֲמֹד הַיָּם מִזַּעְפּוֹ. הָכָא אִית לְאִסְתַּכְּלָה, מ"ט, אַרְעִישַׁת יַמָּא, עֲלֵיהּ דְּיוֹנָה, וְלָא אַרְעִישַׁת עֲלֵיהּ אַרְעָא, כֵּיוָן דַּהֲוָה אָזִיל, בְּגִין דְּלָא תִשְׁרֵי עֲלֵיהּ שְׁכִינְתָּא, יַמָּא אֲמַאי אָחִיד בֵּיהּ, כַּד הֲוָה אָזִיל.

1. "And Sarah's life was a hundred year and twenty year and seven years" (Beresheet 23:1). Rabbi Yosi opened the discussion with the verse, "So they took up Jonah, and cast him into the sea, and the sea ceased from its raging" (Yonah 1:15). We have to examine this text carefully. Why did the sea rage upon Jonah and not the earth, NAMELY THE NUKVA CALLED EARTH? He was leaving the land, so that the Shechinah would not hover above him. IN

OTHER WORDS, HE WAS RUNNING AWAY FROM THE LAND OF YISRAEL – FROM THE SECRET OF THE NUKVA. If so, why did the sea seize him when he went away, AND NOT THE LAND FROM WHICH HE RAN?

‫2. אֶלָּא, וַדַּאי מִלָּה בְּאַתְרֵיה הֲוָה. יַם, תְּנַן, יַם דַּמְיָא לִרְקִיעַ, וּרְקִיעַ לְכִסֵּא הַכָּבוֹד, וּבְגִין כָּךְ, יַמָּא אָחִיד בֵּיה וּנְטַל לֵיה, מִקַּמֵּי יַמָּא עָרַק.‬

2. RABBI YOSI ANSWERS THAT the verse was accurate, for the sea resembles the firmament, and the firmament resembles the Throne of Glory. For that reason, the sea grabbed him and received him in its midst. He was fleeing from the sea, NAMELY FROM THE PROPHECY THAT IS DRAWN FROM THE MOCHIN OF THE NUKVA, WHICH IS AN ASPECT OF THE SEA. THUS, THE SEA RAGED UPON HIM, NOT THE LAND. HE WAS CAST INTO THE SEA TO RETURN HIM TO THE PROPHECY FROM WHICH HE WAS FLEEING.

‫3. וַיִּשְׂאוּ אֶת יוֹנָה וַיְטִלֻהוּ אֶל הַיָּם. אוֹלִיפְנָא, כַּד הֲוָה נָטְלֵי לֵיה וְטָבְעֵי יַרְכוֹי בְּיַמָּא, הֲוָה יַמָּא שָׁכִיךְ, זָקְפִין לֵיה, אִתְרְעִישׁ יַמָּא, כָּל מַה דְּטָבְעֵי לֵיה, הָכֵי אִשְׁתְּכֵיךְ יַמָּא, עַד דְּאִיהוּ אָמַר, שָׂאוּנִי וַהֲטִילֻנִי אֶל הַיָּם, מִיַּד וַיִּשְׂאוּ אֶת יוֹנָה וַיְטִלֻהוּ אֶל הַיָּם.‬

3. "So they took up Jonah, and cast him into the sea." We learned that when they cast him into the sea and immersed him to his knees, the sea calmed. When they lifted him, the sea raged. The deeper they immersed him, the calmer the sea became, until he said, "Take me up, and cast me into the sea" (Yonah 1:12). Immediately, "they took up Jonah, and cast him into the sea."

‫4. כֵּיוָן דְּאִתְרְמֵי בַּיָּם פָּרְחָה מִנֵּיה נִשְׁמָתֵיה וְסָלְקָא עַד כָּרְסְיָיא דְמַלְכָּא, וְאִתְדָּנַת קַמֵּיה, וְאַהֲדָרַת לֵיה נִשְׁמָתֵיה, וְעָאל בְּפוּמָא דְהַהוּא נוּנָא, וּמִית נוּנָא לְבָתַר אִתְקַיַּים הַהוּא נוּנָא, וְאוֹקְמוּהָ.‬

4. When he was thrown into the sea, his soul soared and ascended to the King's throne to be judged. When his soul was returned to him, he entered the mouth of that fish, which died and later came back to life.

‫5. תָּא חֲזֵי, בְּשַׁעֲתָא דְּבַר נָשׁ סָלֵיק בְּעַרְסֵיה, כָּל לֵילְיָא וְלֵילְיָא נִשְׁמָתֵיה נָפְקַת מִנֵּיה, וְאִתְדָּנַת קַמֵּי בֵּי דִינָא דְמַלְכָּא, אִי זַכָּאָה‬

לְאִתְקַיְּימָא, אִתְהַדְּרַת לְהַאי עָלְמָא.

5. Come and behold: When a man goes to sleep each night, his soul leaves him to be judged before the King's court. If it merits life, his soul is returned to this world.

6. וְדִינָא הוּא בִּתְרֵין גְּוָונִין, דְּהָא לָא דָיְינִין לֵיהּ לְבַר נָשׁ, עַל בִּישִׁין דְּאִיהוּ עָתִיד וְזַמִּין לְמֶעְבַּד, דִּכְתִיב כִּי שָׁמַע אֱלֹהִים וְגוֹ' בַּאֲשֶׁר הוּא שָׁם. וְלָא תֵימָא, דְּדָנִין לֵיהּ עַל טָבִין דְּעָבֵיד לְחוֹד, אֶלָּא לְאוֹטָבָא לֵיהּ עַל אִינּוּן טָבִין דְּהַשְׁתָּא, כְּמָה דְּאִתְּמַר, וְדָנִין לֵיהּ עַל זַכְיָין דְּאִיהוּ זַמִּין לְמֶעְבַּד, וּבְגִינַיְיהוּ אִשְׁתְּזִיב, אע"ג דְּאִיהוּ הַשְׁתָּא חַיָּיבָא. בְּגִין דְּקוּדְשָׁא בְּרִיךְ הוּא עָבֵיד טִיבוּ, עִם כָּל בִּרְיָין, וְכָל אָרְחוֹי דְּאִיהוּ עָבֵיד, לְאוֹטָבָא לְכֹלָּא, וְלָא דָאִין לב"נ, עַל בִּישִׁין דְּאִיהוּ זַמִּין לְמֶעְבַּד, וּבְגִין כָּךְ אִתְדָּן בַּר נָשׁ, קַמֵּי קוּדְשָׁא בְּרִיךְ הוּא.

6. The judgement is twofold, for man is not judged for the evil he is destined to commit. "For Elohim has heard the voice of the lad where he is" (Beresheet 21:17) is written, NOT IN THE FUTURE TENSE. You should not say that man is judged only for the good he has already done, rather he is rewarded for his present good as was said above, and he is also judged for the good he will do in the future. He is saved for their sake, as they said, even though he is now wicked. The Holy One, blessed be He, does good with all people and does everything to benefit all, therefore He does not sentence man for the evil he is about to do. Hence, man is judged before the Holy One, blessed be He, WHO KNOWS THE FUTURE.

7. תָּא חֲזֵי, כֵּיוָן דְּאַטִּילוּ לֵיהּ לְיוֹנָה בְּיַמָּא, מַה כְּתִיב, וַיַּעֲמֹד הַיָּם מִזַּעְפּוֹ. הַיָּם עִלָּאָה, מַאי וַיַּעֲמֹד, דְּקָאֵים בְּקִיּוּמֵיהּ, כִּדְקָא יָאוֹת, בַּעֲמִידָה אִיהוּ, כַּד רוֹגְזָא שָׁכִיךְ, בְּשַׁעְתָּא דְּדִינָא שַׁרְיָא בְּעָלְמָא, הַהוּא בֵּי דִינָא, אִיהוּ כְּאִתְּתָא דְּמִתְעַבְּרָא, וְקַשְׁיָא לְאוֹלָדָא, וְכַד אוֹלִידַת שָׁכִיךְ רוּגְזָא. הָכֵי נָמֵי, כַּד דִּינָא שַׁרְיָא בְּעָלְמָא לָא שָׁכִיךְ וְלָא נָח, עַד דְּאִתְעֲבֵיד דִּינָא בְּחַיָּיבַיָּא, כְּדֵין הוּא נַיְיחָא דִּילֵיהּ, לְמֵיקַם בְּדוּכְתָּא שְׁלִים, וּלְמֵיקַם בְּקִיּוּמֵיהּ, הה"ד וּבַאֲבֹד רְשָׁעִים רִנָּה. וְהָא אוּקְמוּהָ.

7. Come and behold. Once they cast Jonah into the sea, it is written: "And the sea ceased (lit. 'stood') from its raging." THIS IS the supernal sea, THE NUKVA. It stood where it was, for when anger calms down, it stands. When judgement is passed upon the world, that court, NAMELY THE NUKVA, is like a pregnant woman experiencing severe labor pains. When she gives birth, the panic ceases. Similarly, when judgement is passed upon the world, it does not calm or rest until justice is administered to the wicked. Then it rests, wholly standing in its place and perfectly maintained. This is what the verse meant by the words: "But when the wicked perish, there is jubilation" (Mishlei 11:10). This has already been explained.

8. בַּאֲבֹד רְשָׁעִים רִנָּה. וְהָכְתִיב הֶחָפֹץ אֶחְפֹּץ מוֹת הָרָשָׁע. וְהָא לֵית נַיְיחָא קַמֵּי קוּדְשָׁא בְּרִיךְ הוּא, כַּד אִתְעֲבֵיד דִּינָא בְּרַשִׁיעַיָּיא. אֶלָּא, כָּאן קוֹדֶם דְּאִשְׁתְּלֵים קִיסְטָא, כָּאן לְבָתַר דְּאִשְׁתְּלֵים קִיסְטָא.

8. HE THEN ASKS ABOUT THE VERSE, "But when the wicked perish, there is jubilation." Is it not written, "Have I any pleasure at all that the wicked should die" (Yechezkel 18:23)? This would mean that there is no pleasure for the Holy One, blessed be He, when judgement is administered to the wicked. HE ANSWERS, Before their measure was filled, THE HOLY ONE, BLESSED BE HE, DID NOT HAVE PLEASURE THAT THE WICKED SHOULD DIE. But now, after the measure is full, "WHEN THE WICKED PERISH, THERE IS JUBILATION."

2. And Dumah rises, and receives the reckoning

A synopsis

The Zohar describes disturbing details concerning the fate awaiting the wicked at the time of the Resurrection of the Dead, emphasizing the urgent need for all of us to replace our bad deeds with good ones immediately.

The Relevance of this Passage

Intellectual blockages in our consciousness prevent us from completely accepting and beholding the truth of the World to Come and the gravity of our erring actions. Though we might accept the notion of a Creator and other spiritual principles on a purely intellectual level, internalizing and living these truths is a much more difficult task, and the basis of our spiritual work. The intent of this passage is to remove impediments and doubts, opening our eyes to spiritual truths and stimulating greater awareness. As we become more devout in our pursuit of righteousness, replacing the bad we have done in this world becomes an intrinsic part of our nature. And this process is furthered by the Light emanating from this portion.

תּוֹסֶפְתָּא

9. וַיִּהְיוּ חַיֵּי שָׂרָה. גּוּפָא דְמַתְנִיתִין, אֲנַן קְרֵיבִין הֲוֵינָא, שְׁמַעְנָא קָלָא מִתְהַפֵּךְ מֵעֵילָא לְתַתָּא, אִתְפַּשְּׁטַת בְּעַלְמָא, קָל מְתַבַּר טוּרִין, וּמְתַבַּר טִנָּרִין תַּקִּיפִין, עִלְעוּלִין רַבְרְבִין סָלְקִין, אוּדְנָנָא פְּתִיחָן.

Tosefta (Addendum)

9. "And Sarah's life was..." The body of the Mishnah, NAMELY ITS ESSENCE, WAS LONG AND IS NOW ABRIDGED. We, WHO ARE VERSED IN THE MISHNAH, were close TO THE INNER SIDE OF THE GRADE and heard a voice that travels down from above and expands throughout the world. This voice uproots mountains and smashes strong rocks, NAMELY ITS ILLUMINATION UPROOTS AND SMASHES ALL THE KLIPOT. Great spirits rise, and ears are open.

10. הֲוָה אָמַר בְּמַטָלְנוֹי קוּץ קוֹצִיתָא, דְּמִיכָן דְּמִימִין דִּשְׁינָתָא

בְּחוֹרֵיהוֹן, קַיְימִין בְּקִיּוּמֵיהוֹן. מַלְכָּא דִמְמַלְלָא, נָטְרֵי תַּרְעִין, שְׁלִיטָא דְּחַיָלִין סַגִּיאִין, קָם בְּקִיּוּמֵיה.

10. As THE VOICE TRAVELS TO THREE PLACES, it says: cut off a portion, how the still ones, who are still sleeping, maintain their guard and stand in position. The king, NUKVA, guards the gates, as the ruler over many armies stands by his post.

11. כֻּלְּהוּ לָא מַרְגְּשָׁן, וְלָא יָדְעֵי דְּסִפְרָא פְּתִיחַ, וּבִשְׁמָא אִכְתּוֹב, וְדוּמָה קָאִים, וְנָטֵיל בְּחוּשְׁבְּנָא, וְדַיְירֵי עַפְרָא תָּיְיבִין לְבַר, וְקָרֵיב טַב לְאִתְמְנָאָה בְּהוּ, לָא תְּאֵיבִין, גִּלְגוּלָא וְהִפּוּךְ.

11. Nobody notices or knows that the book is open, and is written in by a name, and Dumah rises to receive the reckoning. The dwellers of dust, NAMELY THE WICKED, go back outside. The good part, THE CENTRAL COLUMN, THAT IS YESOD, WHICH IS CALLED GOOD APPROCHES, to be counted among them, but they do not wish for rolling and reversing.

12. נָפְלִין וְלָא קַיְימִין, אִתְמְחוּן חַיָּיבִין מִסִּפְרָא דְדוּמָה, מַאן יִתְבַּע לוֹן, וּמַאן יָתֵיב בְּחוּשְׁבַּנְהוֹן, וַוי לוֹן, וַוי לְחַיֵּיהוֹן, וַוי לְרִגְשֵׁיהוֹן, בְּגִינֵיהוֹן אִתְקְרֵי, יִמָּחוּ מִסֵּפֶר חַיִּים וְגו'.

(עד כאן תוספתא)

12. BECAUSE THEY DO NOT WANT THE ROLLING AND REVERSING, they fall and do not come back to life. THUS, the wicked are wiped from the book of Dumah. Who then shall claim them AT THE TIME OF THE RESURRECTION OF THE DEAD, AS IT IS SAID THAT AT THE TIME OF THE RESURRECTION, THE ANGEL METATRON WILL RECEIVE A NOTE AT THE CEMETERIES FROM DUMAH. BUT WHO WILL CLAIM THOSE WICKED WHO ARE NOT ACCOUNTED FOR IN THE RECKONING OF DUMAH AT THE RESURRECTION? And who will care for their accounts? THIS ALLUDES TO THE HARSH KLIPAH NAMED "SICHON," WHO DOES THE RECKONING AND CORRESPONDS TO "DUMAH", FOR "DUMAH" MEANS SILENCE, WHILE

"SICHON" MEANS CONVERSATION OR TALKING. Woe to them, woe to their lives, woe to their pains. For them, the verse says: "Let them be blotted out of the Book of the Living" (Tehilim 69:29).

End of Tosefta (Addendum)

3. "He who tills a field is a king"

A synopsis

There is a hidden meaning in the mention of Sarah's exact life span in the Torah, for such details are given for no other women – nor does any other woman have a portion of the scriptures devoted to her name, as Sarah does. The symbols employed by passages concerning Sarah are pointed out and explained, along with the meaning of various statements that cannot be unlocked without the key of Kabbalah. We learn that, like Abraham, Sarah did not in any way cling to negative inclinations. This earned supernal life for herself, her husband, and later, her son.

The Relevance of this Passage

Man, on his own, does not possess the inner power necessary to eradicate the dark side of his nature. Scriptural giants like Abraham and Sarah, however, are generators of such spiritual forces. Their existence in this physical realm and their presence in the Torah, serve as a wellspring of this energy, from which all generations can draw. Sarah's grace and godliness, together with the energy of supernal life, reach us through the medium of the Aramaic words comprising this passage.

13. וַיִּהְיוּ חַיֵּי שָׂרָה. מַאי שְׁנָא הָכָא שָׂרָה, דִּכְתִיב מִיתָתָה בְּאוֹרַיְיתָא, מִכָּל נְשֵׁי דְעַלְמָא, דְּלָא כְתִיב הָכֵי מִיתַתְהוֹן בְּאוֹרַיְיתָא. אָמַר רַבִּי חִיָּיא, וְלָאו, וְהָכְתִיב וַתָּמָת רָחֵל וַתִּקָּבֵר בְּדֶרֶךְ אֶפְרָתָה. וּכְתִיב וַתָּמָת שָׁם מִרְיָם וגו'. וּכְתִיב, וַתָּמָת דְּבוֹרָה מֵינֶקֶת רִבְקָה. וּכְתִיב וַתָּמָת בַּת שׁוּעַ אֵשֶׁת יְהוּדָה.

13. "And Sarah's life was…": HE ASKS: Of all the women in the world, Why is Sarah the only one whose death is mentioned in Torah? Rabbi Chiya answered, This is not so, for it is written: "And Rachel died, and was buried in the way to Efrat" (Beresheet 35:19), "and Miriam died there" (Bemidbar 20:1), "and Deborah, Rivkah's nurse, died" (Beresheet 35:8), and "the daughter of Shua, Judah's wife died" (Beresheet 38:12). THE DEATH OF MANY WOMEN IS MENTIONED IN THE TORAH.

14. אָמַר ר' יוֹסֵי, בְּכֻלְּהוּ לָא כְתִיב, כְּמָה דִכְתִיב בְּשָׂרָה, דְּאִתְּמַר, וַיִּהְיוּ חַיֵּי שָׂרָה מֵאָה שָׁנָה וְעֶשְׂרִים שָׁנָה וְשֶׁבַע שָׁנִים שְׁנֵי חַיֵּי שָׂרָה.

דְּהָא בְּכֻלְּהוּ, לָא אִתְמָנוּן יוֹמִין וּשְׁנִין, כְּמוֹ לְשָׂרָה. בְּכֻלְּהוּ לָא כְּתִיב פָּרְשָׁתָא חֲדָא בִּלְחוֹדָהָא, כְּמוֹ לְשָׂרָה. אֶלָּא, רָזָא אִיהוּ, בְּגִין הַהוּא דַּרְגָּא, דְּכָל יוֹמִין וּשְׁנִין דְּבַר נָשׁ, בֵּיהּ תַּלְיָין.

14. Rabbi Yosi responded: But it is not written of them as it is written of Sarah, of whom it is said, "And Sarah's life was a hundred and twenty seven years old: these were the years of Sarah's life" (Beresheet 23:1). No other woman's days and years were specified as they were for Sarah. Furthermore, none of them has a portion of the scriptures devoted to them, as does Sarah. There is an esoteric reason for this. IN THE SCRIPTURES, SARAH'S DAYS AND YEARS ARE SPECIFIED, but the secret is that the days and years of all men depend on this grade. THIS MEANS THAT THE MOCHIN, WHICH IS THE SECRET OF THE LIFE SPAN OF SARAH, IS ALLUDED TO IN THE NUMBER "127 YEARS." FROM THIS, THE LIFE SPAN OF MAN IS ALSO DRAWN.

15. פָּתַח וַאֲמַר, וְיִתְרוֹן אֶרֶץ בַּכֹּל הִיא מֶלֶךְ לְשָׂדֶה נֶעֱבָד. וְיִתְרוֹן אֶרֶץ בַּכֹּל הִיא וַדַּאי, דְּהָא מִתַּמָּן נָפְקִין רוּחִין וְנִשְׁמָתִין, וְתוֹעַלְתָּא לְעָלְמָא. מֶלֶךְ לְשָׂדֶה נֶעֱבָד, מַאן מֶלֶךְ, דָּא קוּדְשָׁא בְּרִיךְ הוּא. לְשָׂדֶה נֶעֱבָד, כַּד אִיהוּ אִתְתַּקַּן כְּדְקָא יָאוֹת. וּמֶלֶךְ, דָּא מֶלֶךְ עִלָּאָה, דְּאִתְחַבַּר לְשָׂדֶה, כַּד אִיהוּ נֶעֱבָד. מַאן שָׂדֶה, דָּא שָׂדֶה אֲשֶׁר בֵּרְכוֹ ה'. דִּכְתִיב כְּרֵיחַ שָׂדֶה אֲשֶׁר בֵּרְכוֹ ה'. דְּכַד אִיהוּ נֶעֱבָד וְאִתְתַּקַּן, בְּכָל מַה דְּאִצְטְרִיךְ לֵיהּ, כְּדְקָא יָאוֹת, כְּדֵין מֶלֶךְ עִלָּאָה אִתְחַבַּר עִמֵּיהּ.

15. He opened with the verse, "Moreover, land has an advantage for everyone: he who tills a field is a king" (Kohelet 5:8). "Moreover, land has an advantage" IS THE NUKVA "for everyone." Certainly, THIS IS THE SECRET OF YESOD OF ZEIR ANPIN, CALLED "All" (Heb. kol). Because FROM YESOD emanate spirits and souls and goods to the world. Of the verse, "He who tills a field is a king," IT IS ASKED, Who is the king? He is the Holy One, blessed be He, who "tills a field" when it is properly cultivated. The King is the supernal King, NAMELY ZEIR ANPIN, who is joined to the field when it is tilled. IT IS ASKED, What is the field? This is a field which Hashem has blessed, NAMELY THE NUKVA, AS IT IS WRITTEN: "Like the smell of a field which Hashem has blessed" (Beresheet 27:27). For when it is tilled and cultivated properly, the supernal King, ZEIR

ANPIN, unites with it.

‏16. רַבִּי אֶלְעָזָר אָמַר, מֶלֶךְ לְשָׂדֶה נֶעֱבָד. כַּמָּה גַווֹנֵי, רָזִין עִלָּאִין הָכָא. מֶלֶךְ: דָּא שְׁכִינְתָּא, דְּלָא שַׁרְיָא בְּבֵיתָא, לְאִתְתַּקְּנָא בָּהּ, אֶלָּא בְּזִמְנָא דְּאִתְנְסִיב בַּר נָשׁ, וְאִזְדַּוַּוג בְּאִנְתְּתֵיהּ, לְאוֹלָדָא וּלְמֶעֱבַד אִיבִין, וְאִיהִי אַפִּיקַת נִשְׁמָתִין, לְאַשְׁרָאָה בָּהּ, וּבְגִין כָּךְ לְשָׂדֶה נֶעֱבָד, וְלָא לְאַחֲרָא.

16. Rabbi Elazar asks: How many mysteries are alluded to in the verse, "He who tills a field is a king"! A king is the Shechinah, which only dwells in a man's house when he is married and mates with his wife to beget children and bear fruit. And she, THE SHECHINAH, brings out souls to dwell in her, which is why THE SHECHINAH IS CONNECTED only to a tilled field.

‏17. דָּבָר אַחֵר, מֶלֶךְ: דָּא אִשָּׁה יִרְאַת ה', כִּדְבָר אַחֵר אִשָּׁה יִרְאַת ה' הִיא תִתְהַלָּל. לְשָׂדֶה נֶעֱבָד, דָּא אִשָּׁה זָרָה, כִּדְבָר אַחֵר לִשְׁמָרְךָ מֵאִשָּׁה זָרָה. בְּגִין דְּאִית שָׂדֶה, וְאִית שָׂדֶה. אִית שָׂדֶה, דְּכָל בִּרְכָאן וְקִדּוּשִׁין, בֵּיהּ שַׁרְיָין, כְּמָה דְאַתְּ אָמַר, כְּרֵיחַ שָׂדֶה אֲשֶׁר בֵּרֲכוֹ ה'. וְאִית שָׂדֶה, דְּכָל חֵירוּב וּמְסָאֲבוּ, וְשֵׁיצָאָה, וְקַטוֹלִין, וּקְרָבִין, בֵּיהּ שָׁרְיָין. וְהַאי מֶלֶךְ, זִמְנִין דְּאִיהוּ נֶעֱבַד לְהַאי שָׂדֶה, דִּכְתִיב, תַּחַת שָׁלֹשׁ רָגְזָה אֶרֶץ וגו', תַּחַת עֶבֶד כִּי יִמְלֹךְ, וגו', וְשִׁפְחָה כִּי תִירַשׁ גְּבִירְתָּהּ. וְהַאי מֶלֶךְ, אִתְכַּסְיָא נְהוֹרֵיהּ וְאִתְחַשָּׁךְ עַד דְּאִתְדְּכֵי, וְאִתְחַבַּר לְעֵילָא.

17. Another explanation: A king is "a woman who fears Hashem," as it is written: "A woman who fears Hashem, she shall be praised" (Mishlei 31:30). THIS IS THE SHECHINAH. A tilled field is a strange woman, NAMELY THE OTHER SIDE, as it is written: "That they may keep you from the strange woman" (Mishlei 7:5). For there is a field, and there is a field. There is a field in which all blessings and holiness dwell, as it is written: "Like the smell of a field which Hashem has blessed," NAMELY THE SHECHINAH. And there is a field, in which destruction and defilement, extinction, killings and war reside, NAMELY THE OTHER SIDE. This king, NAMELY THE SHECHINAH, sometimes tills the second field, THE OTHER SIDE, as it is written: "For three things the earth is disquieted...and a handmaid that is heir to her mistress" (Mishlei 30:21). IN THIS CASE, HEAVEN FORBID, THE FIELD OF THE OTHER SIDE INHERITS THE

SHECHINAH, AND THE LIGHT OF THE SHECHINAH is covered and darkened until it is purified and joins ZEIR ANPIN above.

18. וּבְגִין כָּךְ שָׂעִיר דְּר״ח, בְּגִין דְּאִתְפְּרַשׁ הַהוּא שָׂדֶה מִמַּלְכָּא קַדִּישָׁא, וְלָא שַׁרְיָין בְּהַאי שָׂדֶה בִּרְכָאן, מֵהַאי מֶלֶךְ. וְכַד אִיהוּ נֶעֱבַד לְהַאי שָׂדֶה, כְּדֵין כְּתִיב, כִּי בַשָּׂדֶה מְצָאָהּ וְגוֹ׳. כִּי בַשָּׂדֶה כְּמָה דְאִתְּמַר.

18. This is the purpose of offering the goat on the first day of the month, when no blessings dwell upon the second field, THE OTHER SIDE, as it is separated from the Holy King, THE SHECHINAH. When that field is tilled FOR THE OTHER SIDE, then it is written: "For he found her in the field, AND THE BETROTHED MAIDEN CRIED OUT, BUT THERE WAS NONE TO SAVE HER" (Devarim 22:27), the field is THE OTHER SIDE, as has been explained.

19. תָּא חֲזֵי, אָתַת חַוָּה לְעַלְמָא, אִתְדַּבְּקַת בְּהַאי חִוְיָא, וְאַטִּיל בָּהּ זוּהֲמָא. וְגָרְמָא מוֹתָא לְעַלְמָא, וּלְבַעֲלָהּ. אָתַת שָׂרָה, וְנָחֲתַת וְסָלְקַת, וְלָא אִתְדַּבְּקַת בֵּיהּ, כד״א וַיַּעַל אַבְרָם מִמִּצְרַיִם הוּא וְאִשְׁתּוֹ וְכָל אֲשֶׁר לוֹ. אָתָא נֹחַ לְעַלְמָא, מַה כְּתִיב, וַיֵּשְׁתְּ מִן הַיַּיִן וַיִּשְׁכָּר וַיִּתְגַּל וְגוֹ׳.

19. Come and behold: Eve came into the world and clung to the serpent. He injected impurities into her, and she brought death to the world and to her husband. Sarah then came and went down INTO THE PLACE OF THE OTHER SIDE, BUT she rose again without any KLIPOT clinging to her, as it is written: "And Abram went up out of Egypt, he, and his wife, and all that he had" (Beresheet 13:1). When Noah came to the world, it is written that "he drank of the wine, and was drunk, and he was uncovered within his tent" (Beresheet 9:21).

20. וּבְגִין דְּאַבְרָהָם וְשָׂרָה, לָא אִתְדַּבְּקוּ בֵּיהּ, בְּגִין כָּךְ שָׂרָה זָכְתָה לְחַיִּין עִלָּאִין, לָהּ, וּלְבַעֲלָהּ, וְלִבְנָהָא בַּתְרָאָהּ, הה״ד הַבִּיטוּ אֶל צוּר חֻצַּבְתֶּם וְאֶל מַקֶּבֶת בּוֹר נֻקַּרְתֶּם. וְעַל דָּא, וַיִּהְיוּ חַיֵּי שָׂרָה, דְּזָכְתָה בְּהוֹ בְּכֻלְּהוּ, וְלָא כְּתִיב בְּכֻלְּהוּ נָשֵׁי, וַיִּהְיוּ חַיֵּי חַוָּה, וְכֵן בְּכֹלָּא, הִיא אִתְדַּבְּקַת בַּחַיִּין, וְעַל דָּא דִּילָהּ הֲווֹ חַיִּין.

20. Because Abraham and Sarah did not cling to THE OTHER SIDE, Sarah earned supernal life for herself, her husband, and her son after her. This is the meaning of the verse: "Look at the rock whence you are hewn [ABRAHAM], and to the hole of the pit from which you were dug out [SARAH]" (Yeshayah 51:1). Therefore, it is written: "And Sarah's life was...", for she merited all THE YEARS. It is not so for the rest of the women, FOR IT IS NOT WRITTEN: "And Chavah's life was..." and so on. Sarah clung to life. Therefore, her life was her own.

4. He who is small and he who is great

A synopsis
The inner meaning of Sarah's age, as cited in the Torah, relates to
the importance of approaching life with reverence and humility – for
The Creator delights in those who transcend pride and self-interest,
raising them in stature, whereas He diminishes those who inflate
themselves with self-importance and vanity. Greatness in the world
above is attained by behaving with humility and selflessness here in
the physical realm.

The Relevance of this Passage
When people succumb to the demands of their ego, preoccupying
themselves with affairs in the material world, they receive
immediate, but short-lived gratification and rewards. Their self-love
deepens and their hearts harden. In contrast, spiritual
accomplishments do not gratify the ego. For this reason, humility
and selflessness are more difficult to kindle, though their rewards
are far greater and long-lasting. Kabbalah teaches that the eternal
World to Come is not somewhere in the future, but is readily
attainable here and now, according to our degree of spiritual
transformation. A reading of this section helps us to resist pride
and arrogance by raising our awareness of their consequences in
the physical and spiritual realms.

תּוֹסֶפְתָּא

‏21. זַכָּאָה אִיהוּ, מַאן דְּאַזְעֵיר גַּרְמֵיהּ, בְּהַאי עַלְמָא, כַּמָּה אִיהוּ רַב
וְעִלָּאָה, בְּהַהוּא עַלְמָא. וְהָכֵי פָּתַח רַב מְתִיבְתָּא, מַאן דְּאִיהוּ זְעֵיר,
אִיהוּ רַב. מַאן דְּאִיהוּ רַב, אִיהוּ זְעֵיר. דִּכְתִיב וַיִּהְיוּ חַיֵּי שָׂרָה וְגוֹ'.
מֵאָה, דְּאִיהוּ חוּשְׁבַּן רַב, כְּתִיב בֵּיהּ שָׁנָה, זְעֵירוּ דִּשְׁנִין, חַד, אַזְעֵיר
לֵיהּ. שֶׁבַע דְּאִיהוּ חוּשְׁבַּן זְעֵיר, אַסְגֵּי לֵיהּ וְרַבֵּי לֵיהּ, דִּכְתִיב שָׁנִים. תָּא
חֲזֵי, דְּלָא רַבֵּי קוּדְשָׁא בְּרִיךְ הוּא, אֶלָּא לִדְאָעֵיר, וְלָא אַזְעֵיר, אֶלָּא
לִדְרַבֵּי, זַכָּאָה אִיהוּ, מַאן דְּאַזְעֵיר גַּרְמֵיהּ בְּהַאי עַלְמָא, כַּמָּה אִיהוּ רַב
בְּעָלְוָיָא. לְהַהוּא עַלְמָא (עַד כָּאן).

Tosefta (Addendum)

21. Happy is he who makes less of himself in this world. How great and high he is in the eternal world. The head of the Yeshivah spoke to that effect, saying that whoever is small IN THIS WORLD is great IN THE ETERNAL WORLD. He who is great IN THIS WORLD is small IN THE ETERNAL WORLD, as it is written: "And Sarah's life was a hundred year..." A hundred, which is a large number, is followed by the word "year", FOR IT IS LESSENED TO A YEAR. Seven, WHICH IS A SMALL NUMBER, was greatly increased, for it is followed by the word "years." Come and behold: The Holy One, blessed be He, only makes greater the person who lessens himself. He diminishes only the person who makes himself great. Happy is he who diminishes himself in this world. How great he is above in the eternal world.

End of Tosefta (Addendum)

22. מַאן דְּפָסַק יִתְפְּסַק. מַאן דְּקְצַר, יִתְקַצַּר. מַאן דְּקְצַר, יִתְאָרַךְ. ר"ל, מַאן דְּפָסַק מִלִּין דְּאוֹרַיְיתָא, עַל מִלִּין בְּטֵלִין, יִתְפַּסְקוּן חַיּוֹהִי מֵהַאי עַלְמָא, וְדִינֵיהּ קַיְימָא בְּהַהוּא עָלְמָא. מַאן דְּקְצַר אָמֵן, וְלָא מַאֲרִיךְ גּוֹ נַיְיחָא, יִתְקַצַּר מֵחַיִּין דְּהַאי עָלְמָא. מַאן דְּאָמַר אֶחָד, אִצְטְרִיךְ לְחָטְפָא אָלֶ"ף, וּלְקַצֵּר קְרִיאָה דִּילֵיהּ, וְלָא יְעַכֵּב בְּהַאי אוֹת כְּלָל, וּמַאן דְּיַעֲבֵיד דָּא יִתְאָרְכוּן חַיָּיו.

22. This paragraph does not belong here. It belongs to another portion, where it is explained.

5. "And Sarah's life"

A Synopsis
Sarah's life is connected to the Mochin [another term for Spiritual Light] and the secret of Ten Sfirot that are contained within the dimension of Binah. The number 37 appears frequently here. This was Isaac's age at the time of his binding, for example, and it was because of his binding that Sarah died. The Angel of Death appeared before Sarah and told her that Abraham was about to sacrifice their son. These events convey the various levels of spiritual Light that Sarah's life revealed in this world.

The Relevance of this Passage
The metaphysical forces embodied by Sarah are instilled within us through thoughtful meditation upon these verses.

23. וַיִּהְיוּ חַיֵּי שָׂרָה. אִינוּן חַיִּין, כֻּלְּהוּ לְעֵילָא, מֵאָה שָׁנָה לְעֵילָא. וְעֶשְׂרִים שָׁנָה לְעֵילָא, וְשֶׁבַע שָׁנִים לְעֵילָא, כֻּלְּהוּ הֲווֹ כִּדְקָא יָאוֹת. אָמַר רַבִּי שִׁמְעוֹן, תָּא חֲזֵי, רָזָא דְמִלָּה, מַאי שְׁנָא בְּכֻלְּהוּ, דַּאֲמַר שָׁנָה שָׁנָה, וּבְאִינוּן שֶׁבַע, דַּאֲמַר שָׁנִים. דִּכְתִיב מֵאָה שָׁנָה וְעֶשְׂרִים שָׁנָה וּלְבָתַר שֶׁבַע שָׁנִים.

23. "And Sarah's life was..." All this life is above IN BINAH. A hundred year REFERS TO KETER above. "Twenty year" IS CHOCHMAH AND BINAH above. The seven years ARE THE SEVEN LOWER SFIROT above. THIS IS THE SECRET OF THE FIRST THREE AND THE LOWER SEVEN SFIROT OF BINAH, WHERE SARAH RECEIVED LIFE, WHICH IS MOCHIN. Rabbi Shimon said, Come and look at the secret of all this. Why is the number seven followed by the word "years", while all other numbers are followed by the word "year"?

24. אֶלָּא מֵאָה שָׁנָה, כְּלָלָא דְכֹלָּא תַּמָּן, דְּאִתְכְּלִיל אֲתַר עִלָּאָה, כֹּלָּא כַּחֲדָא, בְּרָזָא דְמֵאָה בִּרְכָאָן, בְּכָל יוֹמָא. וְכֵן עֶשְׂרִים שָׁנָה, דְּאִתְכְּלִיל עִלָּאָה סְתִימָא דְכָל סְתִימִין, וּבְגִין כָּךְ כְּתִיב שָׁנָה רָזָא דְיִחוּדָא, דְּלָא אִתְפְּרַשׁ מַחֲשָׁבָה וְיוֹבְלָא לְעָלְמִין.

24. The "hundred year" includes everything, NAMELY KETER, WHICH INCLUDES ALL TEN SFIROT. EACH SFIRAH COMPRISES TEN, AND

TOGETHER THEY COMPRISE ONE HUNDRED. For there is included the highest and most secret place of all, WHICH IS ARICH ANPIN, with the hundred daily benedictions, MEANING THAT IT DAILY GIVES THE ABUNDANCE OF A HUNDRED BENEDICTIONS UPON MALCHUT FROM THE HUNDRED SFIROT IN IT. ARICH ANPIN IS THE SECRET OF KETER OF ATZILUT. Also, the "twenty year," WHICH ARE CHOCHMAH AND BINAH, INCLUDE ARICH ANPIN, the most concealed of all. For that reason, it is written "year" IN THE SINGULAR, which is the secret of unison, for a thought and a Jubilee (Heb. *yovel*). THE SECRET OF CHOCHMAH AND BINAH never separate from each other, AS THE FIRST THREE SFIROT ARE JOINED TO EACH OTHER AS ONE.

25. שֶׁבַע שָׁנִים: אִלֵּין אִתְפָּרְשָׁן, וְנָפְקָאן מִכְּלָלָא סְתִימָאָה דִּלְעֵילָא. וְאַף עַל גַּב דְּכֹלָּא יִחוּדָא חֲדָא, אֲבָל מִתְפָּרְשָׁן, בְּדִינָא וְרַחֲמֵי, בְּכַמָּה סִטְרִין וְאוֹרְחִין, מַה דְּלָא הֲוֵי הָכִי לְעֵילָא. וּבְגִין כָּךְ כְּתִיב שָׁנָה, רָזָא דְיִחוּדָא, דְּלָא אִתְפְּרַשׁ לְעָלְמִין. וְכֻלְּהוּ אִקְרוּן חַיִּים, וַיִּהְיוּ חַיֵּי שָׂרָה, דַּהֲווֹ מַמָּשׁ, דְּאִתְבְּרִיאוּ וְאִתְקַיְּימוּ לְעֵילָא.

25. But the seven years, WHICH ARE THE SEVEN LOWER SFIROT OF BINAH, are separated from each other and from that which is hidden above, ARICH ANPIN. Although everything is united and all are equal, THE LOWER SEVEN pertain to Judgement and Mercy in many aspects and paths. This is not so IN THE FIRST THREE SFIROT OF BINAH, FOR ARICH ANPIN IS ENCLOTHED IN THEM above THE CHEST, WHERE THERE IS NO JUDGEMENT AT ALL. For that reason, it is WRITTEN "SEVEN YEARS" AND NOT 'SEVEN year', AS WITH THE FIRST THREE SFIROT. THE WHOLE TEN SFIROT, THE FIRST THREE AND LOWER SEVEN, are called life. Therefore it is written: "And Sarah's life was...", for it existed. It was created substantively and existed above, IN THE TEN SFIROT OF BINAH.

26. אֲמַר רַבִּי חִיָּיא, הָא אוּקְמוּהָ, דְּהָא כַּד אִתְעֲקַד יִצְחָק, בַּר תְּלָתִין וְשֶׁבַע שְׁנִין הֲוָה, וְכֵיוָן דְּאִתְעֲקַד יִצְחָק, מִיתַת שָׂרָה, דִּכְתִיב וַיָּבֹא אַבְרָהָם לִסְפֹּד לְשָׂרָה וְלִבְכֹּתָהּ. מֵאַיִן בָּא, מֵהַר הַמּוֹרִיָּה, בָּא מִלְּמֶעְקַד לֵיהּ לְיִצְחָק, וְאִינּוּן תְּלָתִין וְשֶׁבַע שְׁנִין, מִיּוֹמָא דְּאִתְיְילִיד יִצְחָק, עַד שַׁעֲתָא דְּאִתְעֲקַד, אִינּוּן הֲווֹ חַיֵּי שָׂרָה וַדַּאי, כְּחוּשְׁבַּן וַיִּהְיוּ, בְּגִימַטְרִי"א

תְּלָתִין וּשְׁבַע שְׁנִין הֲווֹ, כְּמָה דְּאִתְּמָר, מִדְּאִתְיְלִיד יִצְחָק עַד דְּאִתְעֲקַד.

26. Rabbi Chiya said that it has been explained WHY THE DEATH OF SARAH IS WRITTEN RATHER THAN THAT OF THE OTHER WOMEN. Isaac was 37 years old when he was bound, and because he was bound, Sarah died, as is written: "And Abraham came to mourn for Sarah, and to weep for her" (Beresheet 23:2). From where did he come? From mount Moriyah, where he was binding Isaac. The 37 years from the time that Isaac was born until the time he was bound were the life of Sarah, for "vayihyu (was)" is 37 years in numerical value – the years from Isaac's birth to his binding. IN ORDER TO MENTION THIS, SARAH'S DEATH IS MENTIONED IN THE TORAH.

6. "And the cows took the straight way"

A synopsis

The meaning of this difficult scriptural passage is expounded by Rabbi Yosi. We learn that while they carried the Ark, the cows were able to sing – although this gift vanished as soon as they no longer performed this work. Rabbi Chiya explains that a psalm of David referring to a "new song", refers to a time when the psalm or Holy Spirit or Nukva – that is, our physical world, also known as Malchut – will glow with the light of the sun, which itself is a coded reference to the concept of Messiah. It is after this that the Resurrection of the Dead takes place, a time when the world will be renewed and set free from death's rule.

The Relevance of this Passage

A cow is both a metaphor and physical expression of an intense *desire to receive*. In view of this, cows are seen as powerful tools for attracting spiritual energy. Thus, red meat is a recommended dish for the first meal of the Shabbat, since the internal energy of the meat serves to draw down the Light of the Creator. The Torah's parchment, which functions as an antenna to arouse metaphysical forces, is produced from the skin of a calf. The Zohar, therefore, uses the cow as a symbol for man's own insatiable *desire to receive for the self alone* – and the image of a singing cow reveals a creature rising above its inborn nature. This power emerged the moment the cows began transporting the Ark and the scrolls contained inside. Here the Zohar alludes to the Torah's ability to help overcome innate immoral tendencies and self-seeking desires. When mankind has completely removed all his Evil Inclinations, death will be removed from the landscape of human existence. World peace and fulfillment will be eternally achieved, signified by the Zohar's reference to the light of the sun, which represents Messiah. An ability to hasten a personal and global redemption is awarded to us by means of these verses and their corresponding spiritual influences. We remove the force of death from our lives. Bear in mind the fact that "death" can refer to the demise of a business, the end of an important relationship, or the collapse of our emotional well-being.

27. רַבִּי יוֹסֵי פָּתַח, מִזְמוֹר שִׁירוּ לַה׳ שִׁיר חָדָשׁ כִּי נִפְלָאוֹת עָשָׂה הוֹשִׁיעָה לּוֹ יְמִינוֹ וּזְרוֹעַ קָדְשׁוֹ. הַאי קְרָא, אוֹקְמוּהָ חַבְרַיָּא, דְּפָרוֹת אָמְרוּהָ. כְּמָה דִכְתִיב וַיִּשַּׁרְנָה הַפָּרוֹת בַּדֶּרֶךְ. מַאי וַיִּשַּׁרְנָה, דַּהֲווֹ אָמְרֵי

שִׁירָתָא חַדְתָּא. וּמַאי שִׁירָה אָמְרוּ. מִזְמוֹר שִׁירוּ לַה' שִׁיר חָדָשׁ כִּי נִפְלָאוֹת עָשָׂה.

27. Rabbi Yosi began with the verse, "A psalm, O sing (Heb. *shiru*) to Hashem a new song; for He has done marvelous things: His right hand, and his holy arm have gained Him the victory" (Tehilim 98:1). The friends explained that this was said by cows, as it is written: "And the cows took the straight way (Heb. *vayisharnah*)" (I Shmuel 6:12). The word "vayisharnah" also means that they sang (Heb. *sharu*) a new song. What new song? "A psalm. O sing to Hashem a new song."

28. הָכָא אִית לְאִסְתַּכְּלָא, דְּכָל מַה דְּבָרָא קוּדְשָׁא בְּרִיךְ הוּא בְּעַלְמָא, כֻּלְּהוּ אָמְרֵי תּוּשְׁבְּחָן וְשִׁירָתָא קַמֵּיהּ, בֵּין לְעֵילָּא בֵּין לְתַתָּא, וְאִי תֵּימָא, דְּאִינְהוּ מִגַּרְמַיְיהוּ אָמְרֵי שִׁירָתָא דָּא, הָכֵי הוּא וַדַּאי, דְּרָזָא עִלָּאָה אִיהוּ, אֲבָל הַנֵּי, אֲרוֹנָא הֲוָה עַל גַּבַּיְיהוּ, וְכֵיוָן דַּאֲרוֹנָא אִשְׁתְּקִיל עֲלַיְיהוּ, וְשַׁוְּיוּהּ לְעֵילָּא, אִינּוּן שְׁרִירוּ שִׁירָתָא, דְּהָא כֵּיוָן דְּאִתְנְטִיל מִנַּיְיהוּ אֲרוֹנָא, הֲווֹ גַּעָאן, כְּאוֹרַח שְׁאָר פָּרוֹת דְּעַלְמָא, וְלָא אָמְרוּ שִׁירָתָא, וַדַּאי אֲרוֹנָא דְּעַל גַּבַּיְיהוּ עָבֵיד לוֹן לְזַמְּרָא.

28. We should examine this verse carefully. Everything that the Holy One, blessed be He, created in the world offers praises and songs to Him, either above or below. If you thus say THAT THE COWS sang this song, it is assuredly so, for there is a deep secret here. When they carried the Ark, they sang, but once the Ark was taken from them, they again behaved like other cows in the world and did not sing. Surely, the Ark above them made them sing.

29. מִזְמוֹר. הָא אוֹקִימְנָא וְאִתְּמַר בְּכֹלָּא כְּתִיב, מִזְמוֹר לְדָוִד, אוֹ לְדָוִד מִזְמוֹר, וְהָכָא לָא אֲמַר דָּוִד כְּלָל, אֶלָּא מִזְמוֹר. דְּרוּחַ קוּדְשָׁא, זַמִּין לְזַמְּרָא לֵיהּ לְזִמְנָא דְּיוֹקִים קוּדְשָׁא בְּרִיךְ הוּא לְיִשְׂרָאֵל מֵעַפְרָא, וּכְדֵין שִׁירוּ לַה' שִׁיר חָדָשׁ, כְּדֵין אִיהוּ חָדָשׁ, דְּהָא שִׁירָתָא כְּהַאי, לָא אִתְּמַר מִיּוֹמָא דְּאִתְבְּרֵי עָלְמָא.

29. IT IS WRITTEN: "A psalm" unlike other places, where it is written: 'A psalm of David' or 'David's psalm.' Here David is not mentioned at all, just "a psalm." This is because the Holy Spirit is destined to sing it, when the Holy One, blessed be He, raises Yisrael from the dust. THEREFORE, DAVID IS NOT MENTIONED HERE. Then "O sing to Hashem a new song", for this is a new song that has not been sung since the world was created.

30. אָמַר רִבִּי חִיָּיא, כְּתִיב אֵין כָּל חָדָשׁ תַּחַת הַשֶּׁמֶשׁ. וְהָכָא שִׁירָתָא דָּא, אִיהִי חָדָשׁ, וְאִיהִי תַּחַת הַשֶּׁמֶשׁ, דְּהָא תְּחוֹת שִׁמְשָׁא לֶהֱוֵי, וּמַאי אִיהוּ, דָּא סִיהֲרָא, וּכְדֵין הֲוֵי חָדָשׁ תַּחַת הַשֶּׁמֶשׁ. מַאי טַעְמָא, בְּגִין כִּי נִפְלָאוֹת עָשָׂה. וּמַאן אִינּוּן נִפְלָאוֹת, הַאי דִּכְתִיב הוֹשִׁיעָה לּוֹ יְמִינוֹ וּזְרוֹעַ קָדְשׁוֹ. הוֹשִׁיעָה לּוֹ, לְמַאן לְהַהוּא דַּרְגָּא, דַּאֲמַר שִׁירָתָא דָּא, בְּגִין דִּבְהוֹ אִסְתַּמִּיךְ בִּימִינָא וּבִשְׂמָאלָא. הוֹשִׁיעָה לּוֹ יְמִינוֹ וַדַּאי, לְהַהוּא דַּרְגָּא, דְּהַאי מִזְמוֹר, אֵימָתַי, בְּזִמְנָא דִּיקוּמוּן מֵתֵי עָלְמָא, וְיִתְעָרוּן מֵעַפְרָא, כְּדֵין יְהֵא חָדָשׁ, מַה דְּלָא אִתְעֲבֵיד בְּהַאי עָלְמָא.

30. Rabbi Chiya said that it is written: "There is nothing new under the sun" (Kohelet 1:9), but lo, this song is new and under the sun, for it will be under the sun. What is this NEW SONG? It is the moon, WHICH IS THE NUKVA. For then the moon will be new under the sun, MEANING THAT ITS LIGHT WILL BECOME AGAIN LIKE THE LIGHT OF THE SUN, WHICH IS ZEIR ANPIN. What is meant by the phrase: "IT WILL BE NEW UNDER THE SUN?" IT IS THE MEANING OF THE VERSE: "For He has done marvelous things." What are these marvelous things? They are "His right hand, and His holy arm have gained Him the victory." THIS IS THE SECRET OF HIS RIGHT AND LEFT HANDS, CHESED AND GVURAH, "have gained Him the victory." For whom did they gain victory? For the grade that sang this song, THE HOLY SPIRIT, WHICH IS THE NUKVA. THE NUKVA was supported by right and left, AS IT IS WRITTEN: "HAVE GAINED HIM THE VICTORY." Therefore "His right hand...gained Him victory," the grade called psalm, NAMELY THE HOLY SPIRIT, WHICH IS THE NUKVA, WHOSE LIGHT WILL BE AS THE LIGHT OF THE SUN. When will that be? When the dead of the world rise from the dust, then what has not yet been done in the world will be new.

31. רִבִּי יוֹסֵי אָמַר, בְּזִמְנָא דְּיַעֲבֵיד קוּדְשָׁא בְּרִיךְ הוּא נוּקְמִין בְּעָלְמָא, בְּגִינַיְיהוּ דְּיִשְׂרָאֵל, כְּדֵין יִתְאֲמַר שִׁירָתָא, דְּהָא לְבָתַר יִתְעָרוּן מֵעַפְרָא מֵתֵי עָלְמָא, וְיִתְחַדַּשׁ עָלְמָא, בְּקִיּוּם שָׁלִים, דְּלָא לֶיהֱוֵי כְּקַדְמֵיתָא

דְּשַׁלִּיט מוֹתָא בְּעָלְמָא בְּגִין דְּחִוְיָא גָּרֵים מוֹתָא בְּעָלְמָא לְכֹלָּא, וְאִסְתָּאַב עָלְמָא, וְאִתְחֲשִׁיךְ אַנְפּוֹי.

31. Rabbi Yosi said, When the Holy One, blessed be He, takes revenge on the world for Yisrael, He will sing this new song, NAMELY AT THE COMING OF MESSIAH, WHICH IS NOT THE TIME OF RESURRECTION. For after THE COMING OF MESSIAH, the dead of the world will rise from the dust and the world will be completely renewed. It will be different in that death will not rule the world, as it had since the serpent brought death to all, defiled the world, and darkened the faces of men.

7. "And I will put enmity between you and the woman"

A synopsis

This troublesome phrase, uttered by The Creator in the Garden of Eden, refers to the unbridgeable gulf between the godly and the godless of this world, which will never be made whole as long as the serpent of death retains his power. We also learn how seven of the Sfirot create and sustain the days of man. In spite of all the misery they cause, the wicked are ultimately erased, as if they never existed, while the righteous enjoy eternal life.

The Relevance of this Passage

Without the Light of the Zohar, the inner meaning of the Torah remains obscured by confusion and misunderstanding. The work of deciphering the language of the Torah is itself a step toward spiritual growth. By endeavoring to comprehend the Torah's mysteries, we earn spiritual Light and fulfillment. In particular, the Zohar clarifies the significance of *women* in Torah, whose meaning is always spiritual and never merely literal. Thus, the term *man* refers to the upper spiritual realm and the *desire to share*, while *woman* denotes our physical realm and the *desire to receive*. Spiritual Light arising from the upper world can only illuminate our lower world when our Evil Inclination – termed 'the serpent of death' – is conquered and our character transformed. Man's evil tendencies are the lifeblood of the serpent. As long as our negative aspects remain within us, the Angel of Death will prevail over our physical existence. We must learn to loathe our Evil Inclination; to have enmity for our own *desire to receive for the self alone*. In this particular passage we acquire strength for building a deep aversion toward these negative traits.

32. תָּא חֲזֵי, כְּתִיב וְאֵיבָה אָשִׁית בֵּינְךָ וּבֵין הָאִשָּׁה, מַאי וְאֵיבָה, כְּדִכְתִיב חָלְפוּ עִם אֳנִיּוֹת אֵבֶה. דְּהָא כַּמָּה אַרְבִּין שָׁטָאן גּוֹ יַמָּא רַבָּא, וְאִית אַרְבִּין וּסְפִינָן, מִתְפָּרְשָׁן דָּא מִן דָּא, וְאִינּוּן אַרְבִּין דְּהַאי נָחָשׁ שָׁאט בְּגַוַוייְהוּ, אִקְרוּן אֳנִיּוֹת אֵבֶה.

32. Come and behold: It is written, "And I will put enmity between you and the woman..." (Beresheet 3:15). HE ASKS, What is enmity (Heb. *eyvah*)? He replied that it is as written: "They pass away with swift (Heb. *eveh*) ships" (Iyov 9:26), for among the ships sailing in the great sea, some, called enemy ships, are the ships of the serpent sailing amongst them.

33. בֵּינְךָ וּבֵין הָאִשָּׁה. דָּא אִשָּׁה יִרְאַת ה'. וּבֵין זַרְעֲךָ, אִלֵּין שְׁאָר עַמִּין עעכו"ם. וּבֵין זַרְעָהּ, אִלֵּין יִשְׂרָאֵל. הוּא יְשׁוּפְךָ רֹאשׁ, דָּא קוּדְשָׁא בְּרִיךְ הוּא, דְּזַמִּין לְבַעֲרָא לֵיהּ מֵעָלְמָא, דִּכְתִיב בִּלַּע הַמָּוֶת לָנֶצַח. וּכְתִיב וְאֶת רוּחַ הַטֻּמְאָה אַעֲבִיר מִן הָאָרֶץ.

33. The phrase "between you and the woman" refers to "the woman who fears Hashem" (Mishlei 31:30), MALCHUT. The words "and between your seed" refer to the rest of the heathen nations, THE SEED OF THE SERPENT, WHILE "and her seed", namely Yisrael, MEANS THE SEED OF MALCHUT. "He shall bruise your head" is a reference to the Holy One, blessed be He, who will remove the serpent from the world, as it is written: "He will destroy death forever" (Yeshayah: 25:8) and "also I will cause...the unclean spirit to pass out of the land" (Zecharyah 13:2).

34. רֹאשׁ, דָּא לְזִמְנָא דְּאָתֵי דְּיִתְעָרוּן מֵתַיָּא, דְּהָא כְּדֵין לֶהֱוֵי עָלְמָא רֹא"שׁ, דְּיִתְקַיְּים בְּרֹא"שׁ, דְּאִיהוּ עָלְמָא עִלָּאָה. וְאַתָּה תְּשׁוּפֶנּוּ עָקֵב. דָּא בְּהַאי עָלְמָא, הַשְׁתָּא דְּאִיהוּ עָקֵב, וְלָאו אִיהוּ בְּקִיּוּמָא, וְהַהוּא חִוְיָא נָשִׁיךְ לְעַלְמָא, וְאַחְשִׁיךְ אַנְפּוֹי בִּרְיָין.

34. The word "head" means in the future when the dead will live, for then the world will be maintained by the head. THAT MEANS THE FIRST THREE SFIROT, THE SUPERNAL WORLD, WILL SHINE UPON IT. "and you shall bruise his heel" means now in this world, before all is perfected. The world is not whole as long as the serpent bites the world and darkens the faces of the people.

35. תָּא חֲזֵי, יוֹמִין דְּבַר נָשׁ אִתְבְּרִיאוּ, וְקָיְימוּ בְּאִינּוּן דַּרְגִּין עִלָּאִין, כֵּיוָן דְּמִסְתַּיְּימוּ לְאִתְקַיְּימָא בְּאִינּוּן דַּרְגִּין, דִּכְתִיב יְמֵי שְׁנוֹתֵינוּ בָּהֶם שִׁבְעִים שָׁנָה וְגו', מִכָּאן וּלְהָלְאָה, לֵית דַּרְגָּא לְאִתְקַיְּימָא. וּבְגִין כָּךְ, וְרָהְבָּ"ם עָמָל וָאָוֶן. וְאִינּוּן כְּלָא הֲווֹ.

35. Come and behold: The days of man were created and sustained by the supernal grades, NAMELY THE SEVEN SFIROT–CHESED, GVURAH, TIFERET, NETZACH, HOD, YESOD AND MALCHUT. Once they do not exist by these grades, as it is written: "The days of our years are seventy"

(Tehilim 90:10), there is no other grade by which to be maintained. THE NUMBER SEVENTY CORRESPONDS TO THE SEVEN SFIROT, EACH COMPRISING TEN. For this reason, "their pride is but trouble and wretchedness" (Zecharyah 13:2.), and then it is as if they never existed.

36. אֲבָל אִינוּן יוֹמִין דְּצַדִּיקַיָּא הֲווֹ וְאִתְקַיְּימוּ, כִּדְבָר אָחֳר, וַיִּהְיוּ חַיֵּי שָׂרָה. וְכֵן וְאֵלֶּה יְמֵי שְׁנֵי חַיֵּי אַבְרָהָם. וְאִי תֵּימָא, הָכֵי נָמֵי כְּתִיב בְּיִשְׁמָעֵאל, דִּכְתִיב שְׁנֵי חַיֵּי יִשְׁמָעֵאל. אֶלָּא בִּתְשׁוּבָה אַהֲדַר, וְעַל דָּא קָרֵי בְּיוֹמוֹי, וַיִּהְיוּ.

36. But the days of the righteous are eternal. THEY LIVE LONGER THAN SEVENTY YEARS BECAUSE THEY RECEIVE FROM THE SUPERNAL MAZAL, WHICH ADDS LIFE OVER SEVENTY YEARS, AS MUCH AS THEY WANT. This is as written: "And Sarah's life was..." and "these are the days of the years of Abraham's life which he lived" (Beresheet 25:7). If you say it is also written of Ishmael: "And these are the years of the life of Ishmael" (Zecharyah 13:17), ALTHOUGH HE WAS NOT RIGHTEOUS this is only because he repented. Therefore, it is written "these are" of his days AS OF ABRAHAM.

8. "Your eyes did see my unshaped flesh"

A synopsis

Here we learn how the three prayers recited by a traveler can be embodied in one blessing. Then Rabbi Yehuda teaches that all of our deeds – good and bad – are recorded in a heavenly book. Knowing this reveals the importance of praying before embarking on any action. Rabbi Bo and Rabbi Yitzchak next debate the meaning of "unshaped flesh" and how this bestial state applies respectively to David and Adam. Unshaped flesh refers to the *desire to receive for the self alone*, which is akin to an animal's primal desires. We learn why no one was left who bore a resemblance, even vaguely, to the original Adam. Before the sin, Adam was a being of untold spiritual and physical beauty, which man later attempted to use for negative purposes.

Rabbi Yehuda goes on to explain that the gifts of the Creator are given solely to support spiritual goals. If a man takes pride in his wealth or his children, instead of using them in divine service, he will ultimately be destroyed by them. So it is with the beauty of Adam, which the Creator gives in order that a man can become still more devout and connected to the Law. Those who fail to keep pure what the Creator has given, are soon driven from the world. We are told that each night is divided into three 'shifts', when the soul of man leaves the 'unshaped flesh' of his body to be examined by the Holy One on three separate issues. If the soul fails this test, Rabbi Shimon is quoted by Rabbi Yehuda as saying, it is ejected from this divine realm. Great emphasis is placed on the fact that every single one of our actions is seen and recorded. Therefore, nothing should be done without due care for its consequences.

The Relevance of this Passage

Man's nature is to regard wealth and luxury as prized attributes. All of us are inclined to place more value on physical beauty and external appearances than on the intangible inner qualities of life. Intellectually, we might accept the ideal that the only possessions worth having are those that cannot be bought and sold. But living a life that truly embodies this ideal is a formidable task, for the ego holds sway over all our thoughts and actions. The spiritual intent of this segment is to keep our consciousness focused on the Light of Creator, even during sleep. The spiritual Light that emerges here makes us more cognizant of our actions and their repercussions, and helps us value and appreciate life's real treasures.

מִדְרָשׁ הַנֶּעֱלָם

37. וַיִּהְיוּ, רַבָּנָן פָּתְחֵי בְּהַאי קְרָא, לְכָה דוֹדִי נֵצֵא הַשָּׂדֶה נָלִינָה בַּכְּפָרִים. תָּ"ר, הַיּוֹצֵא לַדֶּרֶךְ, יִתְפַּלֵּל שָׁלֹשׁ תְּפִלּוֹת: תְּפִלָּה שֶׁהִיא חוֹבָה שֶׁל יוֹם. וּתְפִלַּת הַדֶּרֶךְ, עַל הַדֶּרֶךְ שֶׁהוּא עוֹשֶׂה. וּתְפִלָּה, שֶׁיַּחֲזוֹר לְבֵיתוֹ לְשָׁלוֹם. וְלֵימָא לְהוּ לְהָנֵי שְׁלֹשָׁה, אֲפִלּוּ בְּאֶחָד, יָכִיל לְמֶעְבְּדֵיהּ, דְּתָנֵינָן כָּל שְׁאֵלוֹתָיו שֶׁל אָדָם, יָכִיל לְמִכְלָלִינְהוּ, בְּשׁוֹמֵעַ תְּפִלָּה.

Midrash Hane'elam (Homiletical interpretations on the obscure)

37. "And...was" (Beresheet 23:1). Our sages began with the verse, "Come, my beloved, let us go forth into the field; let us lodge in the villages" (Shir Hashirim 7:13). The sages have taught that a person who is traveling should recite three prayers: the obligatory daily prayer; the prayer for protection on the way; and a prayer to return home in peace. THE RECITATION OF THESE PRAYERS does not require three BENEDICTIONS, for it can be done in one BLESSING, as we have learned that everything a man asks can be included within the blessing: "Blessed are you, O Eternal, who hears our prayers."

38. אָמַר רַבִּי יְהוּדָה, כָּל עוֹבָדוֹי דְּבַר נָשׁ, כְּתִיבִין בְּסִפְרָא, הֵן טַב, הֵן בִּישׁ, וְעַל כֻּלְּהוֹן, עָתִיד לְמִיתַּן דִּינָא, דְּתָנֵינָן, אָמַר רַב יְהוּדָה אָמַר רַב, מַאי דִכְתִיב, גָּלְמִי רָאוּ עֵינֶיךָ, אוֹתָם הַדְּבָרִים שֶׁעָשָׂה הַגּוֹלֶם, שֶׁאֵינוֹ מַשְׁגִּיחַ בָּעוֹלָם הַבָּא, כּוּלָם רָאוּ עֵינֶיךָ, שֶׁעִיַּינְתָּ בָּהֶם. וְעַל סִפְרָךְ כּוּלָם יִכָּתֵבוּ, לָתֵן עֲלֵיהֶם דִּין וְחֶשְׁבּוֹן, לָעוֹלָם הַבָּא, הִלְכָּךְ, יַקְדִּים אָדָם תְּפִלָּתוֹ תָּמִיד, וְיוֹעִיל לֵיהּ.

38. Rabbi Yehuda said that all of man's deeds, both good and evil, are written in a book IN THE SUPERNAL WORLD, and that each man will be judged according to them. For we have learned from Rav Yehuda who quoted Rav that the verse suffices which reads, "Your eyes did see my unshaped flesh" (Tehilim 139:16). It means that the shapeless flesh REFERS TO THE BODY, which does not care about the World to Come. "Your eyes did see" everything it did, since You have looked carefully at it. "For in Your book all things are written" (Ibid.) to be judged in the World to Come. Therefore, it behooves man to hasten to pray before he acts, which may bring him good.

39. אָמַר רַבִּי יִצְחָק אֵין אָדָם עוֹשֶׂה עֲבֵרוֹת אֶלָּא מִי שֶׁהוּא גּוֹלֶם וְלֹא אָדָם, וְהַיְינוּ הַהוּא דְּלָא מִסְתַּכֵּל בְּנִשְׁמָתָא קַדִּישָׁא, אֶלָּא כָּל עוֹבָדוֹי, כְּהַאי בְּעִירָא, דְּלָא מַשְׁגַּחַת וְלָא יָדְעַת. אָמַר רַבִּי בָּא, וְכִי גּוֹלֶם, מִתְקְרֵי דָּוִד, דַּאֲמַר הַאי פְּסוּקָא. אָמַר לוֹ רַבִּי יִצְחָק, אָדָם הָרִאשׁוֹן אֲמָרוֹ, גָּלְמִי רָאוּ עֵינֶיךָ, קוֹדֶם שֶׁזָּרַקְתָּ בִּי נִשְׁמָה, רָאוּ עֵינֶיךָ, לְמֶעְבַּד בְּדִיוֹקְנִי, בְּנֵי נָשָׁא דְּדָמוּ לִי. וְעַל סִפְרְךָ כֻּלָּם יִכָּתֵבוּ, מַאן אִינוּן. יָמִים יוּצָרוּ, כְּהַאי צוּרָה דִּידִי. וְלֹא אֶחָד בָּהֶם, דְּלָא אִשְׁתְּאַר חַד מִנְּהוֹן.

39. Rabbi Yitzchak said that a man does not transgress; only he who is a shapeless matter and is not a man transgresses. This is a man who cares not for THE NEEDS OF the holy soul. He behaves like a beast, which does not care or know. Rabbi Bo asks RABBI YITZCHAK, Was David called a shapeless matter, NAMELY HE WHO CARES NOT FOR THE SOUL, BECAUSE it was he who wrote the verse? Rabbi Yitzchak replied that Adam said, "Your eyes did see my unshaped flesh," FOR "UNSHAPED FLESH" MEANS MATTER WHOSE SHAPE IS NOT YET FINISHED. He said that before You gave me my soul, WHEN I WAS STILL UNSHAPED FLESH, Your eyes sought to create men in my image. "For in Your book all things are written," FOR IT WILL BE WRITTEN DOWN who they are IN NAME. "The days also in which they are to be fashioned" (Tehilim 139:16) means that they will be created in his image. The phrase: "And not one of them" means that none survived.

40. אָמַר רַבִּי בָּא, לָמָה. אָמַר לֵיהּ תָּא חֲזֵי, כֻּלְּהוּ דְּדָמֵי לֵיהּ, אוֹ בִּרְמִיזָא דִּילֵיהּ, לָא מֵתוּ בְּמִיתַת נַפְשְׁהוֹן, וְכֻלְּהוּ לָקוּ, בְּהַהוּא עִנְיָינָא מַמָּשׁ. תָּא חֲזֵי, אָמַר רַבִּי יְהוּדָה, דְּיוֹקְנֵיהּ דְּאָדָם הָרִאשׁוֹן, וְשַׁפִּירוּתֵיהּ, הֲוָה כְּזָהֲרָא דִּרְקִיעָא עִלָּאָה, דְּעַל גַּבֵּי שְׁאָר רְקִיעֵי, וּכְהַהוּא נְהוֹרָא, דְּגָנֵיז קוּדְשָׁא בְּרִיךְ הוּא, לְצַדִּיקַיָּיא לְעָלְמָא דְּאָתֵי, וְכָל אִינוּן דַּהֲווֹ רְמִיזָא בֵּיהּ מִדְּיוֹקְנֵיהּ דְּאָדָם הָרִאשׁוֹן, בֵּיהּ לָקוּ וּמִיתוּ.

40. Rabbi Bo ASKS: Why WAS NO ONE LEFT OF THOSE WHO BORE A RESEMBLANCE TO THE IMAGE OF ADAM? He answers, Come and behold: Those who resembled Adam even slightly, THAT IS, VAGUELY, did not die a natural death. All were struck FOR RESEMBLING ADAM. SAMSON'S FORCE FAILED HIM, AS DID SAUL'S NECK, AND SO ON. Come and behold: Rabbi

Yehuda said that the image of Adam and his beauty were as the splendor of the supreme firmament above all the firmaments, as the light that the Holy One, blessed be He, saved for the righteous in the World to Come. Therefore, all who had something of Adam's image were stricken by it and died, AS WILL BE EXPLAINED.

41. דְּכָךְ אוֹרְחוֹי דְּקוּדְשָׁא בְּרִיךְ הוּא, יָהֵיב עוֹתְרָא לְבַר אֵינָשׁ, לְמָה, לְמֵיזַן עֲנָיָין, וּלְמֶעְבַּד פִּקוּדוֹי. לָא עָבֵיד הַאי, וְאִתְגָּאֵי בְּהַהוּא עוֹתְרָא, בֵּיהּ יִלְקֵי, דִּכְתִיב עֹשֶׁר שָׁמוּר לִבְעָלָיו לְרָעָתוֹ. יָהֵיב לֵיהּ בְּנִין, לְמָה, לְמֵילַף לְהוּ אוֹרְחוֹי דְּקוּדְשָׁא בְּרִיךְ הוּא, וּלְמִיטַר פִּקוּדוֹי, כִּדְאָמוּר בְּאַבְרָהָם, כִּי יְדַעְתִּיו לְמַעַן אֲשֶׁר יְצַוֶּה אֶת בָּנָיו וְאֶת בֵּיתוֹ אַחֲרָיו וְשָׁמְרוּ דֶּרֶךְ ה' לַעֲשׂוֹת צְדָקָה וְגוֹ'. לָא עָבֵיד הַאי וּמִתְגָּאֶה בְּהוֹ, בְּהוֹ לָקֵי, דִּכְתִיב לֹא נִין לוֹ וְלֹא נֶכֶד בְּעַמּוֹ וְגוֹ'. וְכֵן כְּהַאי גַוְונָא, כַּד יָהֵיב קוּדְשָׁא בְּרִיךְ הוּא, מִשַּׁפִּירוּתָא טָבָא עִלָּאָה דְּאָדָם הָרִאשׁוֹן לְהוּ, לְמָה, בְּגִין לְמִיטַר פִּקוּדוֹי, וּלְמֶעְבַּד רְעוּתֵיהּ, לָא עָבְדוּ כְּדֵין, אֶלָּא אִתְגָּאוּ בֵּיהּ. בֵּיהּ לָקוּ, בְּהַאי שַׁפִּירוּתָא.

41. These are the ways of the Holy One, blessed be He. If He gives a man wealth, it is for the purpose of sustaining the world and performing His commandments. If man does not do so, but instead takes pride in his wealth, he will be destroyed by it, as it is written: "Riches kept for their owner to his hurt" (Kohelet 5:12). If the Holy One, blessed be He, gives him children, He gives them so they can learn the ways of the Holy One, blessed be He, and to keep His commandments. It is written of Abraham: "For I have known him, that he shall command his children and his household after him, and they shall keep the way of Hashem, to do justice and judgement" (Beresheet 18:19). If he does not do so, but instead takes pride in them, he is hurt by them, as it is written: "No great grandchild has he and no grandchild among his people" (Iyov 18:19). Similarly, when the Holy One, blessed be He, gives the good and supernal beauty of Adam, He gives it to them so they will keep His commandments and abide by His wishes. If they instead take pride in it, they will be hurt by the beauty with which they were blessed.

42. אָמַר רַב יְהוּדָה, כַּד בָּרָא קוּדְשָׁא בְּרִיךְ הוּא, אָדָם הָרִאשׁוֹן, הֲוָה גּוֹלֶם, עַד לָא זָרִיק בֵּיהּ נִשְׁמָתָא, וְקָרָא לְהַהוּא מַלְאָכָא, דְּהוּא מְמוּנֶּה

עַל דְּיוֹקְנָא דִּבְנֵי נָשָׁא, וַאֲמַר לוֹ, עַיֵּין, וְצֹר בְּדִיוֹקְנָא דְּדֵין, שִׁיתָּא בְּנֵי נָשָׁא, הה"ד וַיּוֹלֶד בִּדְמוּתָא כְּצַלְמוֹ וַיִּקְרָא אֶת שְׁמוֹ שֵׁת, כְּלוֹמַר שִׁיתָּא.

42. Rabbi Yehuda said that when the Holy One, blessed be He, first created Adam–while he still was unshaped flesh and had no soul He said to the angel who was assigned over the images of men, "Look, and shape in this form six men: SAMSON, SAUL, ASAEL, JOSIAH, ZEDEKIAH, AND ABSHALOM. This is the meaning of the verse: "And begot a son in his own likeness, after his image and called his name Seth" (Beresheet 5:3). The Aramaic word Seth means six AND REFERS TO THE SIX PEOPLE MENTIONED.

43. אָמַר רַבִּי יִצְחָק, מֵהַהוּא עַפְרָא מַמָּשׁ, דְּאִתְבְּרֵי אָדָם הָרִאשׁוֹן, נְסִיב קוּדְשָׁא בְּרִיךְ הוּא, לְאִתְבְּרָאָה אִלֵּין שִׁיתָּא, וְקָרָא לֵיהּ שֵׁת, שִׁיתָּא, הה"ד וַיּוֹלֶד בִּדְמוּתוֹ כְּצַלְמוֹ, מֵאוֹתָהּ הָעִיסָה, שֶׁנִּבְרָא הַגּוֹלֶם שֶׁלּוֹ, וְעַל כָּךְ נֶאֱמַר, גָּלְמִי רָאוּ עֵינֶיךָ, וְעַיְינַת בּוֹ, לַעֲשׂוֹת דְּדָאמוּ לֵיהּ. וְעַל סִפְרְךָ כֻּלָּם יִכָּתֵבוּ, מַאן אִינוּן, כֻּלְּהוּ דְּלָא נָטְרוּ, מַאי דְּיָהַב קוּדְשָׁא בְּרִיךְ הוּא לוֹן, וְאִתְטָרְדוּ מִן עָלְמָא.

43. Rabbi Yitzchak said that the Holy One, blessed be He, created these six men from the same dust that was used to create Adam. The words: "And called his name Seth" is derived from the Aramaic word "sheeta," which translates as six. IT MEANS THAT HE CREATED SIX MEN. This is the meaning of: "And begot...in his own likeness, after his image" (Ibid.)–from the same dough that his unshaped flesh was created. Therefore, it is written: "Your eyes did see my unshaped flesh," WHICH MEANS that You looked well to create in his image. "For in Your book all are written" means that those who did not keep what the Holy One, blessed be He, gave them were driven from the world.

44. תְּנַן הָתָם, אָמַר רַב יְהוּדָה אָמַר רַב אַשְׁכַּחְנָא, דִּתְלַת מִטְרָן הֲוֵי לֵילְיָא, וְכָל חַד וְחַד, אִית עִנְיָינָא, דְּקוּדְשָׁא בְּרִיךְ הוּא, בְּבַר נָשׁ. כַּד נָפִיק נִשְׁמָתֵיהּ מִנֵּיהּ, וְאִשְׁתְּאַר הַהוּא גּוֹלְמָא נָאִים עַל עַרְסֵיהּ, וְנִשְׁמָתֵיהּ סָלְקָא בְּכָל לֵילְיָא, קַמֵּי קוּדְשָׁא בְּרִיךְ הוּא, אָמַר רַבִּי יִצְחָק,

אִי זַכָּאָה הִיא, חָדָאן עִמָּה, וְאִי לָא דַּחְיָין לָה לְבַר.

44. In relation to this, Rabbi Yehuda quoted Rav as saying that the night is divided into three shifts OF FOUR HOURS EACH. During each shift, the Holy One, blessed be He, has a special matter of interest with man. It is when the soul leaves him and the unshaped flesh, NAMELY THE BODY, remains asleep in his bed. The soul ascends each night before the Holy One, blessed be He, AND HE DEALS WITH IT EVERY SHIFT. Rabbi Yitzchak said those above are happy with it if it has merit; if not, it is pushed out.

9. "To mourn for Sarah, and to weep for her"

A synopsis

Through the rabbis' Kabbalistic discussion of the relationship between soul and body, we explore the allegorical nature of the Torah's stories and characters. For example, Abraham represents the righteous soul after it has departed this world, while Sarah represents the physical body left behind. Next we are informed of what occurs immediately after death: the soul usually revisits and mourns its body for seven days before ascending to the higher world. In the case of a wicked person, however, the soul may find itself bound to the earth and the discarded body for up to a year. But at the death of spiritually advanced people, such as Abraham, the holiness of the body itself merits special protection until the time when all the dead shall rise from their dust. This phenomenon, we discover, explains several otherwise baffling passages of scripture.

The Relevance of this Passage

The Torah's message and the Zohar's mystical insights are intended for the here and now, so that our future may be peaceful and secure. By gathering the forces released through the name *Abraham* and these revered words of wisdom, we elevate our physical body to a higher level of spiritual purity.

45. אָמַר רַב יְהוּדָה אָמַר רַב, מַאי דִכְתִיב הִשְׁבַּעְתִּי אֶתְכֶם בְּנוֹת יְרוּשָׁלַם אִם תִּמְצְאוּ אֶת דּוֹדִי מַה תַּגִּידוּ לוֹ שְׁחוֹלַת אַהֲבָה אָנִי. אָמַר רַבִּי פִּנְחָס אָמַר רַבִּי יְהוּדָה, הִשְׁבַּעְתִּי אֶתְכֶם בְּנוֹת יְרוּשָׁלַם, הַנְּשָׁמָה אוֹמֶרֶת לְאוֹתָם הַנְּשָׁמוֹת, הַזּוֹכוֹת לִיכָּנֵס לִירוּשָׁלַם שֶׁל מַעְלָה, וְהֵם הַנִּקְרָאוֹת בְּנוֹת יְרוּשָׁלַם, עַל שֶׁזּוֹכוֹת לִיכָּנֵס שָׁם, וּלְפִיכָךְ הַנְּשָׁמָה אוֹמֶרֶת לָהֶם, הִשְׁבַּעְתִּי אֶתְכֶם בְּנוֹת יְרוּשָׁלַם אִם תִּמְצְאוּ אֶת דּוֹדִי, דָּא קוּדְשָׁא בְּרִיךְ הוּא. רַב אָמַר, זֶה זִיו אִסְפַּקְלַרְיָאה שֶׁל מַעְלָה. מַה תַּגִּידוּ לוֹ שְׁחוֹלַת אַהֲבָה אָנִי, לֵיהָנוֹת מִזִּיו שֶׁלּוֹ, וּלְהִסְתּוֹפֵף בְּצִלּוֹ. רַב הוּנָא אָמַר, שְׁחוֹלַת אַהֲבָה אָנִי, אוֹתָהּ הַתְּשׁוּקָה, וְהַכִּסּוּף שֶׁכָּסַפְתִּי בָּעוֹלָם עַל הַכֹּל, לְפִיכָךְ אֲנִי חוֹלָה.

45. Rav Yehuda stated that Rav asks, Why is it written, "I charge you, O daughters of Jerusalem, if you find my beloved, that you tell him that I am sick with love" (Shir Hashirim 5:8)? Rabbi Pinchas said that Rabbi Yehuda responded, "I charge you, O daughters of Jerusalem" is what the soul says to the souls who are worthy of entering Jerusalem above. They are called daughters of Jerusalem for having the merit to enter. Therefore, the soul says to them, "I charge you, O daughters of Jerusalem, if you find my beloved", which is a reference to the Holy One, blessed be He. Rav said that this is the splendor of the upper mirror. Tell him that I am sick with love" to rejoice in His splendor and to sit often in His shadow. Rav Huna said, "I am sick with love" because of the passion, the longing I feel for everything in the world, therefore I am sick.

46. רַבִּי יְהוּדָה אָמַר, זוֹ אַהֲבָה, שֶׁאוֹהֶבֶת הַנְּשָׁמָה לַגּוּף, דְּכֵיוָן שֶׁנִּשְׁלַם קִצּוֹ שֶׁל גּוּף, אוֹתָם הַיָּמִים שֶׁנִּגְזְרוּ עָלָיו, כְּמָה דְאַתְּ אָמַר וַיִּהְיוּ חַיֵּי שָׂרָה, מַה כְּתִיב, וַיָּקָם אַבְרָהָם מֵעַל פְּנֵי מֵתוֹ וגו'. אָמַר רַב יְהוּדָה אָמַר רַב, מַה כְּתִיב בְּפָסוּק קוֹדֶם זֶה, דִּכְתִיב וַתָּמָת שָׂרָה בְּקִרְיַת אַרְבַּע הִיא חֶבְרוֹן בְּאֶרֶץ כְּנַעַן.

46. Rabbi Yehuda said that this is the love the soul has for the body. When the body dies, as when "Sarah's life was..." it is written: "And Abraham stood up from before his dead" (Beresheet 23:3). Rav Yehuda said that according to the Rav, it is written in the previous verse: "And Sarah died in Kiryat Arba, that is Hebron, in the land of Canaan" (Ibid. 2).

47. רַבִּי יִצְחָק אָמַר רַבִּי יוֹחָנָן, בָּרָא קוּדְשָׁא בְּרִיךְ הוּא לָאָדָם, וְהִכְנִיס בּוֹ אַרְבָּעָה דְבָרִים, הַנֶּחְלָקִים בַּגּוּף. אָמַר רַבִּי יְהוּדָה, הַמְחוּבָּרִים בַּגּוּף. רַבִּי יִצְחָק אָמַר, הַנֶּחְלָקִים בַּגּוּף, שֶׁהֵם חוֹלְקִים לְהִתְפָּרֵשׁ, כָּל אֶחָד לִיסוֹדוֹ, כְּשֶׁיּוֹצֵא הָאָדָם מִן הָעוֹלָם הַזֶּה. רַבִּי יְהוּדָה אָמַר, הַמְחוּבָּרִים בַּגּוּף, בְּחַיָּיו, מַשְׁמַע מִקְרָא דִכְתִיב, וַתָּמָת שָׂרָה, זֶה הַגּוּף. בְּקִרְיַת אַרְבַּע, אֵלּוּ הָאַרְבַּע יְסוֹדוֹת. הִיא חֶבְרוֹן, שֶׁהָיוּ מְחוּבָּרִים בְּגוּפוֹ, בְּחַיָּיו. בְּאֶרֶץ כְּנַעַן, בָּעוֹלָם הַזֶּה, הַבּוֹחֵר אָדָם בִּזְמַן מוּעָט.

47. Rabbi Yitzchak referred to Rabbi Yochanan as stating that the Holy One, blessed be He, created Adam and then inserted in him four things that are divided in the body. Rabbi Yehuda said, "That are connected to the body," while Rabbi Yitzchak said, "That are divided in the body. Each is

separated to its element when man leaves this world." Rabbi Yehuda said, They are connected to the body during its life, namely as it is written: "And Sarah died", which refers to the body. "In Kiryat Arba (lit. 'city of the four')," these are the four elements. The words: "that is Hebron" mean that they were connected in the body during a person's lifetime (Hebron is derived from the word *chibur*, connected). "In the land of Canaan" means in this world, the world in which man dwells for a short period of time.

48. וַיָּבֹא אַבְרָהָם לִסְפֹּד לְשָׂרָה וְלִבְכֹּתָהּ. הַיְינוּ דִּתְנַן, כָּל שִׁבְעַת הַיָּמִים, נַפְשׁוֹ שֶׁל אָדָם, פּוֹקֶדֶת לְגוּפוֹ, וּמִתְאַבֶּלֶת עָלָיו, הֲדָא הוּא דִּכְתִיב, אַךְ בְּשָׂרוֹ עָלָיו יִכְאָב וְנַפְשׁוֹ עָלָיו תֶּאֱבָל. כְּהַאי גַּוְונָא, וַיָּבֹא אַבְרָהָם לִסְפֹּד לְשָׂרָה וְלִבְכֹּתָהּ. וַיָּבֹא אַבְרָהָם, זוֹ הִיא הַנְּשָׁמָה. לִסְפֹּד לְשָׂרָה, זֶה הַגּוּף.

48. "And Abraham came to mourn for Sarah, and to weep for her" (Beresheet 23:2.). We are taught that the soul of man visits the body for seven days and mourns for it. This is the meaning of: "Only when his flesh is upon him does he feel pain, and while his soul is within him does he mourn" (Iyov 14:22). Similarly, "Abraham came to mourn for Sarah, and to weep for her." "Abraham came" refers to the soul, while "to mourn for Sarah" refers to the body.

49. אָמַר רַבִּי יִצְחָק, בְּשָׁעָה שֶׁהַנְּשָׁמָה זוֹכָה, וְעוֹלָה לִמְקוֹם מַעֲלָתָהּ, הַגּוּף שׁוֹכֵב בְּשָׁלוֹם, וְיָנוּחַ עַל מִשְׁכָּבוֹ, הֲדָא הוּא דִּכְתִיב, יָבֹא שָׁלוֹם יָנוּחוּ עַל מִשְׁכְּבוֹתָם הֹלֵךְ נְכֹחֹה. מַאי הֹלֵךְ נְכֹחֹה. אָמַר רַבִּי יִצְחָק, הַנְּשָׁמָה הֹלֵךְ נְכֹחֹה, לִמְקוֹם הָעֵדֶן, הַגָּנוּז לָהּ. מַאי מַשְׁמַע. אָמַר רַבִּי יְהוּדָה, מֵהַאי מַשְׁמַע, נְכֹחֹה כְּתִיב, בֵּה"א. וּבְשָׁעָה שֶׁאֵינָה זוֹכָה, וְהִיא רְאוּיָה לְקַבֵּל עוֹנָשָׁהּ, הוֹלֶכֶת מְשׁוֹמֶמֶת, וּמְבַקֶּרֶת בְּכָל יוֹם לַגּוּף, וְלַקֶּבֶר.

49. Rabbi Yitzchak said that the body rests in peace and lies in its grave when the soul has merit and rises to its high place. This is referred to in the verse: "He that walks in his uprightness shall enter in peace to them that rest in their graves" (Yeshayah 57:2). Who is it that "walks in his uprightness"? Rabbi Yitzchak says that it is the soul that goes upright to Eden that lies

concealed in wait for it. What does this mean? Rabbi Yehuda says: This is why NECHOCHOH (his uprightness) is written with the letter *Hei*. If it has no merit and deserves punishment, it walks about desolately and visits the body and the grave daily.

50. אָמַר רַבִּי יוֹסֵי, הַאי קוּלִיתָא דְקַרְדִינוּתָא, כַּד אָזִיל בְּסִרְיָחוּתָא לְכָאן וּלְכָאן, אָזַל וּמְבַקֵּר לָהּ לְאַתְרָה, תְּרֵיסַר יַרְחֵי. כָּךְ נִשְׁמָתָא, הַהִיא דְאִתְחֲזִיָא לְקַבְּלָא עָנְשָׁא, אָזְלָה לְבַר בְּעָלְמָא, וּמְפַקֶּדֶת לָהּ לְאַתְרָה, תְּרֵיסַר יַרְחֵי, בְּבָתֵּי קִבְרֵי וּבְעָלְמָא.

50. Rabbi Yosi said that the hard bone, NAMELY THE FEMUR THAT WAS HIT AND DISLOCATED, moves here and there with its stench, coming and visiting its place for twelve months. So does the soul that is worthy of punishment. It goes out in the world, visiting its place in the world and the graveyard for twelve months.

51. אָמַר רַבִּי יְהוּדָה, תָּא חֲזֵי דִּכְתִיב וַיָּקָם אַבְרָהָם מֵעַל פְּנֵי מֵתוֹ וְגו׳, אָמַר רַבִּי אַבָּא, וְהָא תְּנַן, דְּכַד נִשְׁמָתָא הִיא בְּתַשְׁלוּמָא עִלָּאָה, נִתּוֹסָף בָּהּ ה׳ וְנִקְרֵאת אַבְרָהָם, בְּתַשְׁלוּמָא עִלָּאָה. וְהָכָא אַתְּ אָמַר, דְּכַד לֵיתָא זַכָּאָה כָּל כָּךְ, דִּכְתִיב וַיָּקָם אַבְרָהָם. עֲבַדַת מַאן דְּיָתֵיב בְּכָרְסַיָּיא, נָחֵית בְּגוֹ זוּטָר תַּתָּאָה.

51. Rabbi Yehuda said, Come and behold the verse: "And Abraham stood up from before his dead." Rabbi Aba raised A DIFFICULT POINT. We learned that when the soul is in supernal complement, NAMELY IN BINAH, the letter *Hei* joins it, and it is called Abraham in supernal wholeness. Now you hint that he is not that righteous, as it is written: "And Abraham stood up." You cause the one who sits in the great throne to come down to sit in the small and lower THRONE.

52. אֶלָּא הָכֵי גְּזַרְנָא, וַיָּקָם אַבְרָהָם מֵעַל פְּנֵי מֵתוֹ, דְּאָמַר ר׳ בּוֹ אָמַר רַבִּי זְרִיקָא, כְּשֶׁהַנְּשָׁמָה רְאוּיָה לַעֲלוֹת לִמְקוֹם עֶדְנָהּ, קוֹדֶם מַגִּינָה עַל הַגּוּף הַקָּדוֹשׁ, שֶׁיּוֹצֵאת מִשָּׁם, וְאַחַר כָּךְ עוֹלָה, לִמְקוֹם מַעֲלָתָהּ, הה״ד וַיָּקָם אַבְרָהָם מֵעַל פְּנֵי מֵתוֹ, זֶהוּ הַגּוּף.

-36-

52. But I reach a decision WHEN I EXPLAIN THE VERSE: "And Abraham stood up from before his dead." As Rabbi Bo said, Rabbi Zrika said that the soul first protects the holy body from which it came when it is worthy of ascending to Eden. Then it ascends to its elevated place. This is the meaning of: "And Abraham stood up from before his dead," namely the body.

‏53. וַיְדַבֵּר אֶל בְּנֵי חֵת, אֵלּוּ שְׁאָר גּוּפוֹת הַצַּדִּיקִים, שֶׁהֵם חַתָּחְתִּים וְנֶהֱלָמִים בָּעוֹלָם, לְמַעַן יִרְאַת קוֹנָם, חַתִּים עַל שֶׁהֵם שׁוֹכְנֵי עָפָר, וְאַמַּאי צְרִיכָה לְהוּ, אָמַר ר׳ יְהוּדָה, כֹּלָּא בְּמִנְיָינָא כְּתִיבִין, וְעַל דַּהֲוֵי גוּפָא בְּמִנְיָינָא עִמְּהוֹן.

53. The phrase: "And spoke to the sons of Chet" (Yeshayah 57:2) refers to the rest of the bodies of the righteous, who are frightened and beaten in the world for the fear of their Possessor. They are afraid and in terror (Heb. chat) for being dwellers of the dust. HE ASKS: Why does THE SOUL need THE BODIES OF THE RIGHTEOUS? Rabbi Yehuda responded, Because they are all written down in the reckoning, THAT IS, THEY ARE PUT INTO THE ACCOUNTS AND ARE MADE TO COME OUT ACCORDING TO THE RECKONING AT THE RESURRECTION OF THE DEAD. THUS, THE SOUL SPOKE WITH THEM so that the body would be numbered in their lists. THIS IS THE MEANING OF: "AND SPOKE TO THE SONS OF CHET."

‏54. וּמַה אָמַר לוֹ, בְּדֶרֶךְ פִּיּוּס וּבְדֶרֶךְ כָּבוֹד, גֵּר וְתוֹשָׁב אָנֹכִי עִמָּכֶם וְגוֹ׳, דְּהַאי גוּפָא, יֶהֱוֵי בְּמִנְיָינָא חַד עִמְּכוֹן בְּחַבּוּרָא דָא. אָמַר רַבִּי, רְאֵה מַה כְּתִיב וַיַּעֲנוּ בְנֵי חֵת אֶת אַבְרָהָם וְגוֹ׳. כְּמוֹ כֵן, בְּדֶרֶךְ כָּבוֹד, בְּדֶרֶךְ פִּיּוּס הָדָא הוּא דִכְתִיב שְׁמָעֵנוּ אֲדוֹנִי נְשִׂיא אֱלֹהִים אַתָּה בְּתוֹכֵנוּ.

54. What did THE SOUL CALLED ABRAHAM say to them? It said in a conciliatory and respectful manner, "I am a stranger and a sojourner with you" (Beresheet 23:3), MEANING this body will be counted with you in one quorum by this union. Rabbi said, Look at what is written: "And the children of Chet answered Abraham..." (Yeshayah 57:4). They also answered him in a respectful and conciliatory manner. This is the meaning of: "Hear us, my lord, you are a mighty prince among us."

10. Dumah brings them into and out of reckoning

A synopsis

The role of Dumah, angel in charge of graveyards, is discussed. The rabbis agree that he is in charge of all bodies – good and wicked – sorting them into graves according to merit, until the Day of Reckoning. Torah interpretation tells us that Abraham's body was granted a special "treasure of peace and great rest." Also, according to various rabbis, those who have kept the Law, studied Torah, and performed acts of great piety, may inherit either 200 or 400 "worlds in the World to Come."

The Relevance of this Passage

A righteous person is not necessarily one who has attained the same level of spirituality and wisdom as the eminent sages of antiquity or the great Kabbalists cited in the Zohar. We are not expected to reach their level, but we are expected to at least strive for it. Therefore, an individual who consistently endeavors toward high spiritual goals is defined as righteous. More important than the level attained is the degree of change that we achieve through spiritual growth. Hence, we need to awaken loftier aspirations and goals. Moreover, we require inner strength and determination to pursue higher levels of righteousness. These qualities take root within us as we meditatively study this section of Zohar.

55. מַאי נְשִׂיא אֱלֹהִים אַתָּה. אָמַר ר' פִּנְחָס, קוֹדֶם שֶׁיֵּצֵא הַצַּדִּיק מִן הָעוֹלָם, בַּת קוֹל יוֹצֵאת בְּכָל יוֹם, עַל אוֹתָם הַצַּדִּיקִים בְּגַן עֵדֶן, הָכִינוּ מָקוֹם לִפְלוֹנִי שֶׁיָּבֹא לְכָאן. וְעַל כֵּן הֵם אוֹמְרִים, מֵאֵת אֱלֹהִים מִלְמַעְלָה, אַתָּה נָשִׂיא, בְּכָל יוֹם בְּתוֹכֵנוּ, בְּמִבְחַר קְבָרֵינוּ, בְּמִבְחַר הַצַּדִּיקִים, בַּחֲבוּרַת הַצַּדִּיקִים הַמּוּבְחָרִים, מָנָה אוֹתוֹ, הַכְנִיסֵהוּ בְּחֶשְׁבּוֹן עִמָּנוּ, וְאִישׁ מִמֶּנּוּ לֹא יִמְנַע, אֶת הַמִּנְיָן, כִּי כֻּלָּנוּ שְׂמֵחִים בּוֹ, וּמַקְדִּימִים לוֹ שָׁלוֹם.

55. What is meant by the phrase: "You are a mighty prince (or: a prince of Elohim)" (Beresheet 23:5)? Rabbi Pinchas responded that, before the righteous leave the world, a divine voice echoes every day among the righteous in the Garden of Eden to 'prepare a place for so-and-so who will come here'. Therefore, they say, from Elohim above, "You are a prince" every day among us: "in the choicest of our graves" (Ibid.): among the

choicest company of the righteous he should be counted. No one will prevent fulfillment of the quorum, for we all rejoice in him and hasten to greet him.

56. אָמַר רַבִּי יוֹסֵי בֶּן פָּזִי, תָּא חֲזֵי, כֵּיוָן שֶׁהַנְּשָׁמָה פּוֹגַעַת בָּהֶם, וְתָדוּן, לְאַחַר כָּךְ, פּוֹגַעַת לְאוֹתוֹ הַמַּלְאָךְ, הַמְמֻנֶּה עֲלֵיהֶם, דְּתָנָן, מַלְאָךְ מְמוּנֶּה, עַל בָּתֵּי קִבְרֵי, וְדוּמָה שְׁמוֹ, וְהוּא מַכְרִיז בֵּינֵיהֶם, בְּכָל יוֹם, עַל הַצַּדִּיקִים, הָעֲתִידִים לִיכָּנֵס בֵּינֵיהֶם, וּמִיָּד פּוֹגַעַת בּוֹ, כְּדֵי לְשַׁכֵּן הַגּוּף, בְּהַשְׁקֵט, וּבְבִטְחָה, וּבִמְנוּחָה, וּבַהֲנָאָה, הֲדָא הוּא דִכְתִיב, וַיְדַבֵּר אֶל עֶפְרוֹן.

56. Rabbi Yosi ben Pazi said, Come and behold: after the soul meets them, it is sentenced. It meets the angel appointed over them, the angel in charge of the graveyards, named Dumah. He announces among them, every day, the names of the righteous who are about to come among them. It immediately entreats him to lodge the body in tranquillity, safety, rest, and pleasure. This is the meaning of: "And he spoke to Efron" (Yeshayah 57:11).

57. אָמַר רַבִּי יֵיסָא, זֶה הַמַּלְאָךְ הַנִּקְרָא דוּמָה, וְלָמָּה נִתְכַּנֶּה שְׁמוֹ עֶפְרוֹן, עַל שֶׁהוּא מְמוּנֶּה עַל שׁוֹכְנֵי עָפָר, וְהוּפְקְדוּ בְּיָדוֹ, כָּל פִּנְקְסֵי הַצַּדִּיקִים, וַחֲבוּרוֹת הַחֲסִידִים, הַשׁוֹכְנִים בֶּעָפָר, וְהוּא עָתִיד לְהוֹצִיאָם בְּחֶשְׁבּוֹן.

57. Rabbi Yesa asks, Why is the angel Dumah called Efron? He responded, Because he is in charge over the dwellers of dust (Heb. *afar*). All the lists of the righteous and companies of the pious that dwell in the dust were given to him, and he will bring them out according to the reckoning.

58. וְתָאנָא אָמַר רַבִּי אֶלְעָזָר, לֶעָתִיד לָבֹא, כְּשֶׁיִּפְקוֹד הַקוּדְשָׁא בְּרִיךְ הוּא לְהַחֲיוֹת הַמֵּתִים, יִקְרָא לַמַּלְאָךְ הַמְמוּנֶּה עַל הַקְּבָרוֹת, וְדוּמָה שְׁמוֹ וְיִתְבַּע מִמֶּנּוּ מִנְיַן כָּל הַמֵּתִים, הַצַּדִּיקִים וְהַחֲסִידִים, וְאוֹתָם גֵּרֵי הַצֶּדֶק, וְשֶׁנֶּהֶרְגוּ עַל שְׁמוֹ, וְהוּא מוֹצִיאָם בְּחֶשְׁבּוֹן, כְּמוֹ שֶׁנִּטְּלָם בְּחֶשְׁבּוֹן, הֲדָא הוּא דִכְתִיב הַמּוֹצִיא הַמּוֹצִיא בְּמִסְפַּר צְבָאָם וְגו' אִישׁ לֹא נֶעְדָּר.

58. Rabbi Elazar said, When the Holy One, blessed be He, comes to raise the dead in the future, He shall call the angel named Dumah, who is appointed over the graves. He will ask him for an enumeration of all the dead, the righteous and the pious, and all the sincere proselytes killed for the sake of His name. He will bring them out according to the reckoning, the same as he put them into it. This is the meaning of the verse: "That brings out their host by number...not one is missing" (Yeshayah 40:26).

59. וְתָאנָא, אָמַר רַבִּי שְׁמוּאֵל בְּרַבִּי יַעֲקֹב, נַפְשׁוֹת הָרְשָׁעִים, נְתוּנוֹת בְּיָדוֹ שֶׁל מַלְאָךְ זֶה, שֶׁשְּׁמוֹ דוּמָה, לְהַכְנִיסָם בַּגֵּיהִנֹּם, וְלָדוּן שָׁם, וְכֵיוָן שֶׁנִּמְסָרוֹת בְּיָדוֹ, שׁוּב אֵינָן חוֹזְרוֹת, עַד שֶׁיִּכָּנְסוּ לַגֵּיהִנֹּם, וְזֶה יִרְאַת דָּוִד שֶׁנִּתְיָירֵא, כְּשֶׁעָשָׂה אוֹתוֹ עָוֹן, שֶׁנֶּאֱמַר לוּלֵי ה' עֶזְרָתָה לִי כִּמְעַט שָׁכְנָה דוּמָה נַפְשִׁי. אָמַר רַבִּי יֵיסָא, הַנְּשָׁמָה פּוֹגַעַת לוֹ, לְהַכְנִיס אוֹתוֹ גוּף, עִם שְׁאָר גּוּפוֹת הַצַּדִּיקִים, בְּחֶשְׁבּוֹנָם, הֲדָא הוּא דִכְתִיב וַיְדַבֵּר אֶל עֶפְרוֹן וְגוֹ'.

59. In the name of Rabbi Ya'akov, Rabbi Shmuel said that the souls of the evil are in the hands of the angel Dumah, who will send them to Gehenom to be sentenced. Once they are put in Dumah's hands, they do not return again before going to Gehenom. This is what David feared when he committed that sin, as it is written: "Unless Hashem had been my help, my soul had soon dwelt in Dumah" (Tehilim 94:17). Rabbi Yesa said, The soul entreats him to put the body with the bodies of the other righteous and be enumerated in their numbers. This is the meaning of: "And he spoke to Efron..."

60. אָמַר רַבִּי תַּנְחוּם, הַמַּלְאָךְ קוֹדֵם וְאוֹמֵר לוֹ. רְאֵה מַה כְּתִיב לְמַעְלָה, וְעֶפְרוֹן יוֹשֵׁב בְּתוֹךְ בְּנֵי חֵת, שֶׁחָתוּ לִשְׁכּוֹן בֶּעָפָר, וְהוּא מַקְדִּים וְאוֹמֵר לוֹ, לְהַכְנִיס אוֹתוֹ הַגּוּף, בְּחֶשְׁבּוֹן הַצַּדִּיקִים, הה"ד וַיַּעַן עֶפְרוֹן הַחִתִּי אֶת אַבְרָהָם בְּאָזְנֵי בְנֵי חֵת לְכֹל בָּאֵי שַׁעַר עִירוֹ לֵאמֹר. מַאי לְכֹל בָּאֵי שַׁעַר עִירוֹ, רַב נַחְמָן אָמַר, אִינוּן דְּעָאלוּ, בְּכְתָב חוּשְׁבַּן פִּנְקָסֵיהּ דְּאָמַר רַב נַחְמָן, וְהָכִי אִתְגְּזַר, בְּחֶשְׁבּוֹן עַל יְדוֹי דְדוּמָה, עָאלִין בְּבָתֵּי קִבְרֵי, וּבְחוּשְׁבַּן פִּתְקָא, זַמִּין לְאַפְּקָא לוֹן, וְהוּא מְמוּנֶּה עַל דַּיְירֵי

עָפְרָא.

60. Rabbi Tanchum added that the angel first addresses him. Look at what was written before the verse. It is: "And Efron dwelt among the children of Chet" (Beresheet 23:9), who were afraid of dwelling in the dust. He hastens to instruct Dumah to put that body in the reckoning of the righteous. Then the verse reads, "And Efron the Hittite answered Abraham in the ear of the children of Chet, even of all that went in at the gate of his city, saying" (Ibid.). Who went in at the gate of his city? Rabbi Nachman said, Those who were written in the list. As Rabbi Nachman said, and so is was decreed, by the reckoning made by Dumah, they enter, the cemeteries. And by the reckoning he will take them out. And he is in charge of the dwellers of dust.

61. מַהוּ הַשָּׂדֶה נָתַתִּי לָךְ וְהַמְּעָרָה אֲשֶׁר בּוֹ. אָמַר רַבִּי יוֹסֵי, הַפְקָדָא דִּשְׁלָוָה, וּמְנוּחָה רַבָּה. אָמַר ר' שָׁלוֹם בַּר מִנְיוּמֵי, אֵין לְךָ כָּל צַדִּיק וְצַדִּיק מֵאוֹתָם הָעוֹסְקִים בַּתּוֹרָה, שֶׁאֵין לוֹ מָאתַיִם עוֹלָמוֹת וְכִסּוּפִין בִּשְׁבִיל הַתּוֹרָה, הה"ד וּמָאתַיִם לַנּוֹטְרִים אֶת פִּרְיוֹ, וּמָאתַיִם, עַל שֶׁמּוֹסְרִים עַצְמָם בְּכָל יוֹם, כְּאִילוּ נֶהֶרְגוּ עַל קְדוּשַׁת שְׁמוֹ, נִצְחוֹ, כְּהַאי פְּסוּקָא לִמְסוֹר נַפְשׁוֹ עַל קְדוּשַׁת שְׁמוֹ, מַעֲלֶה עָלָיו הַכָּתוּב כְּאִלוּ נֶהֱרַג בְּכָל יוֹם עָלָיו, הה"ד כִּי עָלֶיךָ הוֹרַגְנוּ כָּל הַיּוֹם. אָמַר רַב נַחְמָן, כָּל הַמּוֹסֵר נַפְשׁוֹ בְּהַאי פְּסוּקָא, נוֹחַל אַרְבַּע מֵאוֹת עוֹלָמוֹת לָעוֹלָם הַבָּא. אָמַר רַב יוֹסֵף, וְהָא תְּנַן מָאתַיִם. אָמַר רַב נַחְמָן מָאתַיִם עַל הַתּוֹרָה, וּמָאתַיִם עַל שֶׁמְּמַסֵּר עַצְמוֹ בְּכָל יוֹם, עַל קְדוּשַׁת שְׁמוֹ.

(עַד כָּאן מִדְרָשׁ הַנֶּעֱלָם).

61. What is meant by: "The field I give you, and the cave, that is in it" (Beresheet 5:10)? Rabbi Yosi said that it is a treasure of peace and great rest. Rabbi Shalom ben Manyumi said, There is not one righteous of those who are occupied in Torah, who has not 200 bright worlds for the sake of Torah. It is written, "And those that keep its fruit 200" (Shir Hashirim 8:12), for they renounce themselves daily, as if they are killed to sanctify His name and His eternity. Whoever surrenders his soul to sanctify His name, the scripture says it is as if he were killed daily for His sake, as it is written: "But for your sake are we killed all the day long" (Tehilim 44:23). Rabbi

Nachman said that whoever surrenders his soul according to this verse inherits 400 worlds in the World to Come. Rabbi Yosef said, We were taught that there are 200. According to Rabbi Nachman, it is 200 for Torah and 200 for surrendering every day for the sake of the holiness of His name.

End of Midrash Hane'elam (homiletical interpretations on the obscure)

11. "And Sarah died in Kiryat Arba"

A synopsis

Here the Zohar explores the ways in which people's lives determine the quality and nature of their death. The rabbis also resume a discussion of Sarah's uniqueness among women, now comparing her with Miriam, whose age is not mentioned in scripture. Associated with water, Miriam's death is emblematic of the ancient sins of the children of Yisrael. They, it is explained, owe their happiness and stability solely to the Torah – which is a gift of the Holy One, intended to reveal the true nature and purpose of His creation. Rabbi Yehuda goes on to make an analogy between the effect of a weak king on his kingdom and that of an unrighteous man on his own life. The exploration finally circles back on itself with the assertion that death has no power over someone as pure as Sarah, who died in the place where David was united with the patriarchs. This spiritual locale is the point at which the physical world joins with the spiritual. David represents our material realm, known as Malchut, while the patriarchs signify the spiritual domain. Bridging these two worlds exemplifies the concept of perfection. In this way, the righteousness of the individual soul, the righteousness of the ruler and his people, and the holiness of the land itself, are shown to be one and the same. We learn that as long as a man's soul is nurtured by the Light – which is portrayed here as filtering through the seven lower Sfirot – both his life and his death will remain in harmony with the divine, for a righteous existence alone spares us defilement by the Angel of Death.

The Relevance of this Passage

In practical terms, the Upper World, or the patriarchs, refers to our soul and the *desire to share*. Our physical world of Malchut or David, refers to our material body and the *desire to receive for the self alone*. Our ultimate objective in life is to balance and enjoin these two worlds, creating a new dynamic, known in lay terms as *the desire to receive for the sake of sharing*. When we receive for the sake of imparting to others, we achieve perfect harmony with the sharing nature of the Creator. This assures a life and an afterlife filled with Light. Both the Torah and the Zohar serve to gradually sweeten the trait of *receiving for the self* into *receiving for the purpose of sharing*. Here, the Zohar invokes the 'energy of Sarah' to help achieve this effect, strengthening our resolve whenever the temptation to satisfy our own desires arises.

62. וַתָּמָת שָׂרָה בְּקִרְיַת אַרְבַּע. ר' אַבָּא אָמַר, כְּגַוְונָא דָא, לָא הֲווֹ בְּכָל נְשֵׁי עָלְמָא, דְּהָא אִתְּמַר חוּשְׁבַּן יוֹמָהָא, וּשְׁנָהָא, וְקִיּוּמָהָא בְּעָלְמָא, וְהַהוּא אֲתַר דְּאִתְקַבְּרַת בֵּיהּ. אֶלָּא לְאַחֲזָאָה, דְּלָא הֲוָה כְּשָׂרָה, בְּכָל נְשֵׁי עָלְמָא

62. "And Sarah died in Kiryat Arba" (Beresheet 23:2). Rabbi Aba noted that, of all the women in the world, only for Sarah are the number of her days and years and the time of her life in the world mentioned, as well as the place in which she was buried. This shows that there was no other woman in the world like Sarah.

63. וְאִי תֵימָא הָא מִרְיָם, דִּכְתִיב וַתָּמָת שָׁם מִרְיָם וַתִּקָּבֵר שָׁם. בְּגִין לְאַחֲזָאָה סָרְחָנָא דְּיִשְׂרָאֵל קָא אָתָא, דְּהָא מַיָּיא לָא אַזְלֵי לְהוּ בְּיִשְׂרָאֵל, אֶלָּא בִּזְכוּתָא דְּמִרְיָם. אֲבָל לָא אִתְּמַר בְּמִיתָתָהּ, כְּמָה דְּאִתְּמַר בְּשָׂרָה.

63. If you say that it is written of Miriam: "And Miriam died there, and was buried there" (Bemidbar 20:1) AS IT IS WRITTEN OF SARAH, NOTE THAT THIS WAS WRITTEN only to show that Yisrael sinned, AS SAID IN THE NEXT VERSE: "AND THERE WAS NO WATER FOR THE CONGREGATION: AND THEY GATHERED THEMSELVES TOGETHER" (IBID. 2). Yisrael had no water there without Miriam, and HER DAYS AND YEARS were not specified when describing her death, as was done for Sarah.

64. רַבִּי יְהוּדָה פָּתַח אַשְׁרֵיךְ שֶׁמַּלְכֵּךְ בֶּן חוֹרִים וְשָׂרַיִךְ בָּעֵת יאכֵלוּ, הַאי קְרָא אוֹקְמוּהָ חַבְרַיָּיא, אֲבָל אִית לָן לְאִסְתַּכְּלָא בֵּיהּ, דְּזַכָּאִין אִינּוּן יִשְׂרָאֵל, דְּקוּדְשָׁא בְּרִיךְ הוּא יָהַב לוֹן אוֹרַיְיתָא, לְמִנְדַּע כָּל אוֹרְחִין סְתִימִין, וּלְאִתְגַּלְיָיא לוֹן רָזִין עִלָּאִין.

64. Rabbi Yehuda opened the discussion saying, "Happy are you, O land, that your king is a man of freedom, and your princes eat in due season" (Kohelet 10:17). This verse was explained by the friends. Nevertheless, we have studied that the children of Yisrael are happy because the Holy One, blessed be He, gave them Torah with which to know the hidden ways and reveal the supreme mysteries.

65. וְהָא אִתְּמַר, אַשְׁרֶיךָ אֶרֶץ, דָּא אֶרֶץ הַחַיִּים, בְּגִין דְּמַלְכָּא דִּילָהּ, אַזְמִין לָהּ כָּל בִּרְכָאן, דְּאִתְבָּרְכָא מֵאֲבָהָן עִלָּאִין, רָזָא דְוא״ו, דְּאִיהוּ קַיְּימָא לְאַרְקָא עֲלָהּ בִּרְכָאן תָּדִיר, וְאִיהוּ בֶּן חוֹרִין, בֶּן יוֹבְלָא, דְּאַפֵּיק עָבְדִּין לְחֵירוּ, בְּרָא דְּעָלְמָא עִלָּאָה, דְּאַפֵּיק תָּדִיר כָּל חַיִּין, וְכָל נְהִירוּ, וְכָל מְשַׁח רְבוּת, וְכֹלָּא אִנְגִּיד הַאי בְּרָא בּוּכְרָא, לְהַאי אֶרֶץ, כד״א בְּנִי בְכֹרִי יִשְׂרָאֵל, וּבְגִין כָּךְ, אַשְׁרֶיךָ אֶרֶץ.

65. "Happy are you, O land" refers to the land of the living, NAMELY THE NUKVA, WHICH CLOTHES THE LIVING ELOHIM, IMA, because her king, ZEIR ANPIN, prepared for her all the blessings he had received from the supernal fathers – THE SUPERNAL ABA AND IMA. THAT KING IS the secret of the letter *Vav*, which is always in readiness to pour blessing over her. He is called "a man of freedom", the son of a Jubilee, WHICH IS BINAH, NAMELY YISRAEL-SABA, AND TEVUNAH, THE MOCHIN who liberates slaves and gives them freedom, THE MOCHIN OF THE ILLUMINATION OF CHOCHMAH. He is also a son of the supernal world – THE SUPERNAL ABA AND IMA – who gives generously FROM THEIR EVERLASTING UNION all life and illumination, the oil of greatness, and honor. Thus it is written, "Yisrael is my son, my firstborn" (Shemot 4:22). Therefore, "Happy are you, O land."

66. וּמַה דְּאִתְּמַר אִי לָךְ אֶרֶץ שֶׁמַּלְכֵּךְ נָעַר, כְּמָה דְּאוֹקְמוּהָ, דְּהַאי אֶרֶץ תַּתָּאָה, וְעָלְמָא תַּתָּאָה, לָא יָנְקָא אֶלָּא מִגּוֹ שָׁלְטָנוּתָא דְּעָרְלָה, וְכֹלָּא מֵהַהוּא מַלְכָּא דְּאִקְרֵי נָעַר, כְּמָה דְּאוֹקְמוּהָ. וַוי לְאַרְעָא דְּאִצְטְרִיךְ לִינָקָא הָכֵי.

66. The verse "Woe to you, O land, when your king is a child" (Kohelet 10:16) is explained as follows. This is the nether land, and the nether world draws nourishment from the uncircumcised foreskin alone. All is drawn down only from the king called child, NAMELY METATRON, as was explained. Woe to the world that must nourish this way.

67. תָּא חֲזֵי הַאי נָעַר לֵית לֵיהּ מִגַּרְמֵיהּ כְּלוּם, בַּר כַּד נָטֵיל בִּרְכָאן לִזְמְנִין יְדִיעָן, וְכָל זִמְנִין דְּאִתְמָנְעוּ מִנֵּיהּ, וְאִתְפְּגִים סִיהֲרָא, וְאִתְחֲשָׁךְ, וּבִרְכָאן אִתְמָנְעוּ מִנֵּיהּ, וַוי לְעָלְמָא, דְּאִצְטְרִיךְ לִינָקָא בְּהַהִיא שַׁעְתָּא.

וְעוֹד בְּכַמָּה דִינִין אִתְדָּן הַאי עַלְמָא, עַד לָא יָנְקָא מִנֵּיהּ, דְּכֹלָּא בְּדִינָא אִתְקַיַּים וְאִתְעֲבַד וְאוֹקִמוּהָ.

67. Come and behold this child, METATRON, who has nothing of himself, but the blessings he receives FROM THE NUKVA at appointed times. Each time these blessings are withheld when the moon, NUKVA, is rendered defective and becomes dark. Woe to the world that depends on him for survival. Moreover, the world suffers many judgments before it draws nourishment from him, NAMELY FROM THE KLIPOT, for all is established and maintained through judgments, as has been explained.

68. תָּא חֲזֵי, וַתָּמָת שָׂרָה בְּקִרְיַת אַרְבַּע, רָזָא אִיהוּ, בְּגִין דְּלָא הֲוָה מִיתָתָהּ, עַל יְדָא דְּהַהוּא נָחָשׁ עֲקִימָאָה, וְלָא שָׁלַט בָּהּ כִּשְׁאָר בְּנֵי עָלְמָא. דְּאִיהוּ שַׁלִּיט בְּהוּ, וְעַל יְדֵיהּ, מֵתוּ בְּנֵי עָלְמָא, מִיּוֹמָא דְּגָרֵים לוֹן אָדָם, בַּר מֹשֶׁ"ה וְאַהֲרֹ"ן וּמִרְיָ"ם, דִּכְתִיב בְּהוֹ עַל פִּי ה'. וּבְגִין יְקָרָא דִּשְׁכִינְתָּא, לָא כְתִיב בְּמִרְיָם עַל פִּי ה'.

68. The verse: "And Sarah died..." also contains a secret, which is that she did not die by the tortuous serpent, NAMELY THE ANGEL OF DEATH. It had no power over her, as it has over the people of the world. As a result of Adam's sin, all the people in the world die by the serpent except Moses, Aaron, and Miriam, WHO DIED BY A KISS, as is written: "Upon the mouth of Hashem" (Bemidbar 33:38). In honor of the Shechinah, it is not mentioned of Miriam, "upon the mouth of Hashem," ALTHOUGH SHE, TOO, DIED BY A KISS.

69. אֲבָל בְּשָׂרָה, כְּתִיב בְּקִרְיַת אַרְבַּע, רָזָא דְּקִרְיַת אַרְבַּע, בְּרָזָא עִלָּאָה וְלָא עַל יְדָא אָחֳרָא, בְּקִרְיַת אַרְבַּע וְלָא בְּנָחָשׁ. בְּקִרְיַת אַרְבַּע הִיא חֶבְרוֹן, דְּאִתְחַבַּר דָּוִד מַלְכָּא בַּאֲבָהָן, וְעַל דָּא לָא הֲוָה מִיתָתָהּ בִּידָא אָחֳרָא, אֶלָּא בְּקִרְיַת אַרְבַּע.

69. Yet of Sarah it is written: "And Sarah died in Kiryat Arba" because she died in and by the hands of Kiryat Arba, and not by the serpent. She died by the hands of Kiryat Arba that is Hebron, where David was united with the patriarchs. Therefore she died not by another, but in Kiryat Arba.

70. תָּא חֲזֵי, כַּד יוֹמִין דְּבַר נָשׁ, אִתְקַיְּימוּ בְּדַרְגִּין עִלָּאִין, אִתְקַיַּים בַּר נָשׁ בְּעַלְמָא, כֵּיוָן דְּלָא אִתְקַיַּים בְּדַרְגִּין עִלָּאִין, נָפְקֵי וְנָחֲתֵי לְתַתָּא, עַד דִּקְרִיבוּ לְהַאי דַרְגָּא דְּמוֹתָא שַׁרְיָא בֵּיהּ, וּכְדֵין נָטִיל רְשׁוּ לְאַפֵּיק נִשְׁמָתָא, וְטָאס עַלְמָא בְּזִמְנָא חֲדָא, וְנָטִיל נִשְׁמָתָא, וְסָאִיב לֵיהּ לְגוּפָא, וְאִשְׁתְּאַר מְסָאֲבָא. זַכָּאִין אִינוּן צַדִּיקַיָּא דְּלָא אִסְתָּאֲבוּ, וְלָא אִשְׁתְּאַר בְּהוֹ מְסָאֲבוּתָא.

70. Come and behold: When man's days are maintained by the supernal grades, NAMELY THE SEVEN LOWER SFIROT – CHESED, GVURAH, TIFERET, NETZACH, HOD, YESOD AND MALCHUT – man thrives in the world. If he is not sustained by the supernal grades, MEANING HE HAS LIVED SEVENTY YEARS DRAWN FROM THE SEVEN LOWER SFIROT – CHESED, GVURAH, TIFERET, NETZACH, HOD, YESOD AND MALCHUT – his days come out OF THE SFIROT and beneath THE SFIROT until they approach the level where death dwells. NAMELY, THE ANGEL OF DEATH UNDERNEATH MALCHUT, OF WHICH IT IS SAID, "SIN CROUCHES AT THE DOOR" (BERESHEET 4:7). Then the Angel of Death receives permission to take out the man's soul. He flies through the world in one flight, takes the soul and defiles the body, which remains defiled. Happy are the righteous who were not defiled by him, for no defilement remained in their bodies.

12. The serpent of the firmament

A synopsis

The stars of the Milky Way – called here 'the serpent of the firmament' – perform a special function in the lives of men, assisting both those who wish to be purified, and those who wish to defile themselves.

Rabbi Yitzchak and Rabbi Yosi discuss the evil man, Bilaam, the sorcerer. From their discussion we learn that the primordial serpent is the source of all enchantment and magic. It is in sorcery that the seeds of defilement lie. Those who wish to cast spells draw to themselves the unholy spirit, just as anyone wishing to do good will draw the Light.

The Relevance of this Passage

The stars that glint in the heavens are portals through which spiritual influences enter this material existence. The structure of electricity helps us understand their role: Electrical current can light entire cities. The same current, however, can also cause great destruction. The manner in which we employ the energy, determines its positive or destructive quality, but the nature of the energy never changes. Man was given free will to choose how to draw spiritual energy – via the *desire to receive for the self alone*, or the *desire to receive for the sake of sharing*. This passage summons up forces that awaken us to the dual nature of our desires, impelling us to seek purification rather than defilement.

71. וְתָא חֲזֵי, בְּאֶמְצָעוּת דִּרְקִיעָא, אִתְקַּטַּר חַד אוֹרְחָא קַסְטְרִירָא. וְאִיהוּ חִוְיָא דִּרְקִיעָא, דְּכָל כֹּכְבִין דַּקִּיקִין, כֻּלְּהוּ קְטִירִין בֵּיה, וְקַיְימֵי בֵּיה, תַּלֵּי תַּלִּין, וְאִינוּן מְמַנָּן בִּסְתִירוּ עוֹבְדֵי בְּנֵי עָלְמָא.

71. Come and behold: In the middle of the firmament is a glowing trail. This is the serpent of the firmament THAT ASTRONOMERS CALL THE MILKY WAY. All the small stars are attached to it in groups, THAT IS, THEY ARE GATHERED AND STAND IN IT LIKE COUNTLESS MOUNTAINS. They are in charge of the secret deeds of the inhabitants of the world.

72. כְּגַוְונָא דָא, כַּמָּה חֲבִילֵי טְהִירִין, נָפְקֵי לְעָלְמָא, מֵהַאי חִוְיָא עִלָּאָה קַדְמָאָה, דְּאִתְפַּתָּא בֵּיה אָדָם, וְכֻלְּהוּ מְמַנָּן בִּסְתִירוּ עוֹבְדֵי עָלְמָא, וּבְגִין כָּךְ, אָתֵי בַּר נָשׁ לְאִתְדַּכָּאָה, מְסַיְּיעִין לֵיה מִלְּעֵילָא, וְסִיּוּעָא

דְּמָארֵיהּ סַחֲרָא לֵיהּ, וְאִסְתַּמַּר וְאִקְרֵי קָדוֹשׁ.

72. Similarly, there are bunches of lights of Klipot that come into the world from the supernal primordial serpent that seduced Adam. They are appointed to learn the secret deeds of the world. Therefore when a man wishes to be purified, he receives help from above, and the help of his Master encircles and protects him. He is then called 'holy'.

73. אָתֵי בַּר נָשׁ לְאִסְתָּאֲבָא, כַּמָּה חֲבִילִין טְהִירִין אִזְדַּמְּנוּ לֵיהּ וְכֻלְּהוּ שַׁרְיָין בֵּיהּ, וּמְסַחֲרִין לֵיהּ, וּמְסָאֲבִין לֵיהּ, וְאִקְרֵי טָמֵא, וְכֻלְּהוּ אָזְלֵי, וּמַכְרְזֵי קַמֵּי, טָמֵא טָמֵא, כְּמָה דְאַתְּ אָמַר וְטָמֵא טָמֵא יִקְרָא. וְכֻלְּהוּ קְטִירִין בְּהַהוּא חִוְיָא קַדְמָאָה, וּסְתִירִין בְּכַמָּה עוֹבָדֵי עָלְמָא.

73. If a man wishes to be defiled, several groups of lights of Klipot are waiting for him. They all hover about and around him. They defile him, so he is called unholy. They go before him and proclaim, Unholy, unholy, as it is written: "And shall cry, 'Unclean, unclean'" (Vayikra 17:45). They are all connected to the primordial serpent and are hidden in the deeds of the people of the world.

74. ר' יִצְחָק וְרִבִּי יוֹסֵי, הֲווֹ אָזְלֵי מִטְבֶרְיָא לְלוֹד. אָמַר ר' יִצְחָק, תְּווֹהֲנָא עַל הַהוּא רָשָׁע דְּבִלְעָם, דְּכָל עוֹבָדוֹי דְּהַהוּא רָשָׁע, הֲווֹ מִסִּטְרָא דִּמְסָאֲבָא. וְהָכָא אוֹלִיפְנָא רָזָא חֲדָא, דְּכָל זִינֵי נְחֲשַׁיָּא דְעָלְמָא, כֻּלְּהוֹן מִתְקַטְּרָן וְנָפְקִין, מֵהַהוּא נָחָשׁ קַדְמוֹנִי, דְּאִיהוּ רוּחַ מְסָאֲבָא מְזוּהֲמָא, וּבְגִין כָּךְ, כָּל חָרָשִׁין דְּעָלְמָא, אִקְרוּן עַל שְׁמָא דָא, נְחָשִׁים, וְכֻלְּהוּ מֵהַאי סִטְרָא נָפְקֵי. וּמַאן דְּאִתְמְשַׁךְ בְּהַאי הָא אִסְתָּאַב.

74. Rabbi Yitzchak and Rabbi Yosi were walking from Tiberias to Lod. Rabbi Yitzchak said, I wonder about the evil man Bilaam. All he did was from the side of defilement. Here we learn a secret, which is that all kinds of sorcery and witchcraft of the world are connected and derive from the primordial serpent, which is the impure spirit of defilement. Therefore all enchantment (Heb. *nechashim*) is named AFTER THE PRIMORDIAL SERPENT (HEB. *NACHASH*). They all derive from that side, and anyone who is drawn to that MAGIC is defiled.

75. וְלָא עוֹד, אֶלָּא דְּבָעֵי לְאִסְתָּאֲבָא, בְּגִין לְאַמְשָׁכָא עֲלֵיהּ הַהוּא סִטְרָא דְּרוּחַ מְסָאֲבָא. דְּהָא תָּנִינָן, כְּגַוְונָא דְּאִתְעַר בַּר נָשׁ, הָכֵי נָמֵי אַמְשִׁיךְ עֲלֵיהּ מִלְּעֵילָּא, אִי אִיהוּ אִתְעַר בְּסִטְרָא דִּקְדוּשָׁה, אַמְשִׁיךְ עֲלֵיהּ קְדוּשָׁה מִלְּעֵילָּא וְאִתְקַדָּשׁ. וְאִי אִיהוּ אִתְעַר, בְּסִטְרָא דִּמְסָאֲבָא, הָכֵי אַמְשִׁיךְ עֲלֵיהּ רוּחַ מְסָאֲבָא, וְאִסְתָּאֵב. דְּהָא אִתְּמַר, עַל מַה דְּתָנִינָן, אָתֵי בַּר נָשׁ לְאִסְתָּאֲבָא, מְסָאֲבִין לֵיהּ.

75. Moreover, one should be impure to cast a spell. One has to draw upon oneself that side of the unholy spirit. As man is aroused from below, he draws upon himself from above. If he is aroused below on the side of holiness, he draws upon himself the supernal holiness and is sanctified. If he is aroused below on the side of defilement, he draws upon himself the spirit of defilement and becomes unholy. Upon this, they said that whoever wishes to be defiled is defiled.

76. בְּגִין כָּךְ הַהוּא רָשָׁע דְּבִלְעָם, בְּגִין לְאַמְשָׁכָא עֲלֵיהּ רוּחַ מְסָאֲבָא, מֵהַהוּא נָחָשׁ עִלָּאָה, הֲוָה אִסְתָּאֵב בְּכָל לֵילְיָא בַּאֲתָנֵיהּ, וַהֲוָה עָבֵיד עִמָּהּ עוֹבָדֵי אִישׁוּת, בְּגִין לְאִסְתָּאֲבָא, וּלְאַמְשָׁכָא עֲלֵיהּ רוּחַ מְסָאֲבָא, וּכְדֵין עָבֵיד חֲרָשׁוֹי וְעוֹבָדוֹי.

76. For that purpose, the wicked Bilaam defiled himself nightly by mating with his ass in order to draw upon himself the unholy spirit from the supernal serpent, thereby drawing on himself the spirit of unholiness. Then he cast his spells and enchantments.

77. וְשֵׁירוּתָא דְּעוֹבָדוֹי הֲוֵי, נָטִיל נָחָשׁ, מֵאִינוּן חִוְיָין, וְקָטִיר לֵיהּ קַמֵּיהּ, וּבְזַע רֵישֵׁיהּ, וְאַפֵּיק לִישָׁנֵיהּ וְנָטִיל עִשְׂבִּין יְדִיעָן, וְאוֹקִיד כֹּלָּא, וְעָבֵיד מִנֵּיהּ קְטָרְתָּא חֲדָא, לְבָתַר נָטִיל רֵישָׁא דְּהַהוּא חִוְיָא, וּבְזַע לֵיהּ לְאַרְבַּע סִטְרִין, וְעָבֵיד מִנֵּיהּ קְטָרְתָּא אָחֳרָא.

77. First he took one of the serpents, tied it in front of him, split his head, and removed its tongue. Then he took certain herbs and burned them to incense. He took the serpent's head, cut it into four pieces, and made from it another incense offering.

78. וַעֲבֵיד עֲגוּלָא חַד, וַהֲוָה אֲמַר מִלִּין, וַעֲבֵיד עוֹבָדִין אַחֲרָנִין, עַד דְּאַמְשִׁיךְ עֲלֵיהּ רוּחִין מְסָאֲבִין, וְאוֹדִיעִין לֵיהּ, מַה דְּאִצְטְרִיךְ, וַעֲבֵיד בְּהוּ עוֹבָדוֹי, כְּפוּם מַה דְּאִינּוּן יָדְעֵי, מִסִּטְרָא דְּהַהוּא חִוְיָא דִּרְקִיעָא. מִתַּמָּן אִתְמְשַׁךְ בְּעוֹבָדוֹי וַחֲרָשׁוֹי, עַד דְּאַמְשִׁיךְ עֲלֵיהּ רוּחַ, מֵהַהוּא נָחָשׁ קַדְמָאָה.

78. He drew a circle round himself, uttered words, and performed other deeds until he drew to himself the spirits of defilement, who told him what he needed to know. He acted according to their information, which they knew from the side of that serpent in the firmament.

79. וּמֵהָכָא הֲוָה יָדַע, יְדִיעָן, וַחֲרָשִׁין, וְקוֹסְמִין. וּבְגִין כָּךְ כְּתִיב וְלֹא הָלַךְ כְּפַעַם בְּפַעַם לִקְרָאת נְחָשִׁים, נְחָשִׁים וַדַּאי, וְעִקְרָא וְשָׁרְשָׁא בִּמְסָאֲבוּתָא אִיהוּ, כְּמָה דְּאִתְּמַר, וּלְבָתַר שֵׁירוּתָא דְּכֹלָּא, לָאו אִיהוּ אֶלָּא בְּנָחָשׁ.

79. This is how he acquired his knowledge, enchantments, and spells. For that reason, it is written: "He went not, as at other times, to seek for enchantments" (Bemidbar 24:1), which alludes to real snakes. As has already been explained, the essence and origin of defilement begins with the serpent.

13. All kinds of witchcraft and sorcery abide only in women

A synopsis

When the serpent came upon Eve it injected impurities into her. For this reason, women are more susceptible to the allure of magic and witchcraft than men. Rabbi Yosi asks why this is so, since the children of Israel were cleansed of impurities at Mount Sinai. Rabbi Yitzchak replies that the Torah was only given to males. Furthermore, since women are of the left side, it is more difficult for them to cleanse themselves of defilement. Various kinds of impurity are discussed, and we learn that anything attached to the world – as are unholy spirits – holds the potential to defile.

The Relevance of this Passage

The term *woman* is used as a metaphor for man's Evil Inclination. Kabbalistically, women are on a much higher level of spirituality, as evidenced by their great intuition and heightened sensitivity. Therefore, only the male is required to work at eradicating his Evil Inclination through Torah. When a woman, however, uses her natural gifts for negative purposes, it is referred to as witchcraft. A reading of this section helps men and women subjugate their negative desires.

80. אָמַר רַבִּי יוֹסֵי, אַמַּאי כָּל זַיְינֵי חֲרָשִׁין וְקוֹסְמִין, לָא אִשְׁתַּכָּחוּ אֶלָּא בִּנְשַׁיָּיא. אֲמַר לֵיהּ, הָכֵי אוֹלִיפְנָא, מִדְּאָתָא נָחָשׁ עַל חַוָּה, הַטִּיל בָּהּ זוּהֲמָא בָּהּ אַטִּיל, וְלָא בְּבַעֲלָהּ. אָמַר, הָכֵי הוּא וַדַּאי. אָתָא רַבִּי יוֹסֵי, וּנְשָׁקֵיהּ לְרַבִּי יִצְחָק, אָמַר כַּמָּה זִמְנִין שָׁאִילְנָא הַאי מִלָּה, וְלָא זָכֵינָא בָּהּ, אֶלָּא הַשְׁתָּא.

80. Rabbi Yosi asks why all kinds of witchcraft and sorcery abide only in women. He said that when the serpent came upon Eve, he injected impurities only into her and not into her husband. BECAUSE WITCHCRAFT RADIATES FROM THE POLLUTION OF THE SERPENT, WITCHCRAFT IS THEREFORE IN WOMEN. He said, Assuredly this is so. Rabbi Yosi kissed Rabbi Yitzchak and said, Many times have I asked upon this matter, but never deserved to understand it until now.

81. אֲמַר לֵיהּ, כָּל הַנֵּי עוֹבָדִים וְכָל מַה דְּיָדַע בִּלְעָם, מֵאָן אֲתַר אוֹלִיף לֵיהּ. אֲמַר לֵיהּ, מֵאֲבוֹי. אֲבָל, בְּאִינוּן הָרֲרֵי קֶדֶם, דְּאִיהוּ אֶרֶץ קֶדֶם,

אוֹלִיף כָּל חֲרָשִׁין וְכָל זִינֵי קוֹדְמִין, בְּגִין דִּבְאִינּוּן טוּרֵי, אִינּוּן מַלְאֲכֵי עַזָ"א וַעֲזָאֵ"ל דְּאַפִּיל לוֹן קוּדְשָׁא בְּרִיךְ הוּא מִן שְׁמַיָּא, וְאִינּוּן קְטִירִין, בְּשַׁלְשְׁלָאֵי דְּפַרְזְלָא, וְאוֹדִיעִין חֲרָשִׁין לִבְנֵי נָשָׁא, וּמִתַּמָּן הֲוָה יָדַע בִּלְעָם, כְּמָה דְאַתְּ אָמֵר מִן אֲרָם יַנְחֵנִי בָלָק מֶלֶךְ מוֹאָב מֵהַרְרֵי קֶדֶם.

81. He asks, Where did Bilaam learn everything that he did, NAMELY ALL HIS SORCERY, and all that he knew? He answers, He learned it from his father. But in "the mountains of the east" (Bemidbar 23:7), in the land of the east, he learned MOST OF the enchantments and kinds of magic, for in these mountains abide the angels Aza and Azael, whom the Holy One, blessed be He, caused to fall from heaven BECAUSE THEY DENOUNCED THE CREATION OF MAN. They are tied in chains of iron there and reveal spells to men. This is where Bilaam gained knowledge, as it is written: "Balak the king of Moab has led me from Aram, out of the mountains of the east" (Ibid.), WHERE AZA AND AZAEL ARE.

82. אָמַר לוֹ, וְהָא כְּתִיב וְלֹא הָלַךְ כְּפַעַם בְּפַעַם לִקְרַאת נְחָשִׁים וַיָּשֶׁת אֶל הַמִּדְבָּר פָּנָיו. אָמַר לוֹ, סִטְרָא תַּתָּאָה דְּאַתְיָא מֵרוּחַ מְסָאֲבָא דִּלְעֵילָא, הוּא רוּחַ מְסָאֲבָא, דְּשַׁלִּיט בְּמַדְבְּרָא, כַּד עָבְדוּ בְּנֵי יִשְׂרָאֵל יַת עֶגְלָא, בְּגִין לְאִסְתָּאֲבָא בַּהֲדֵיהּ, דְּאִיהוּ תַּתָּאָה, וּבְכֹלָּא עֲבַד חֲרָשׁוֹי בְּגִין דְּיָכוֹל לְאַעֲקְרָא לוֹן לְיִשְׂרָאֵל, וְלָא יָכִיל.

82. He said, It is written: "He went not, as at other time, to seek for enchantments, but he set his face toward the wilderness" (Bemidbar 24:1), WHICH MEANS THAT HE DID NOT ALWAYS LOOK FOR ENCHANTMENTS (ALSO: 'SNAKES'). Rabbi Yitzchak said that the lower side, which comes from the unholy spirit above, is the unholy spirit that ruled over the wilderness at the time when the children of Yisrael defiled themselves by committing the sin of the golden calf. THEREFORE, "HE SET HIS FACE TOWARD THE WILDERNESS." He cast his spells to all directions in order to uproot the children of Yisrael, but could not do so.

83. אָמַר רְבִּי יוֹסֵי, הַאי דַּאֲמַרְתְּ בְּקַדְמֵיתָא, דְּכַד נָחָשׁ אָתָא עַל חַוָּה אַטִּיל בָּהּ זוּהֲמָא, שַׁפִּיר, אֲבָל הָא תָּנֵינָן, דְּכַד קָאִימוּ יִשְׂרָאֵל, עַל טוּרָא דְּסִינַי, פָּסַק מִנַּיְיהוּ זוּהֲמָא. יִשְׂרָאֵל דְּקַבִּילוּ אוֹרַיְיתָא, פָּסַק

מִנַּיְיהוּ זוּהֲמָא, אֲבָל שְׁאָר עַמִּין עעכו״ם, דְּלָא קַבִּילוּ אוֹרַיְיתָא, לָא פָּסְקָא זוּהֲמָא מִנַּיְיהוּ.

83. Rabbi Yosi said, When you earlier explained why witchcraft abides in women, you said that the serpent came upon Eve and injected impurity into her. This is well, but we have learned that when Yisrael stood by Mount Sinai and received Torah, their impurities were cleansed. But the heathens who did not receive Torah remained impure, SO IMPURITY IS ALREADY GONE FROM WOMEN. THEREFORE, MY QUESTION IS STILL UNANSWERED, WHY IS WITCHCRAFT MOSTLY IN WOMEN?

84. אֲמַר לֵיהּ שַׁפִּיר קָאֲמַרְתְּ, אֲבָל תָּא חֲזֵי, אוֹרַיְיתָא לָא אִתְיְיהִיבַת אֶלָּא לִדְכוּרֵי, דִּכְתִיב וְזֹאת הַתּוֹרָה אֲשֶׁר שָׂם מֹשֶׁה לִפְנֵי בְּנֵי יִשְׂרָאֵל. דְּהָא נָשֵׁי, פְּטִירִין מִפִּקּוּדֵי אוֹרַיְיתָא.

84. He said to him, You spoke well. Nevertheless, come and behold: Torah was given to males only, as it is written: "And this is the Torah which Moses set before the children (lit. 'sons') of Yisrael" (Devarim: 4:44). As women were exempt from the commandments of Torah, NAMELY FROM THE COMMANDMENTS VALID AT A FIXED TIME THEREFORE THEY REMAINED IMPURE AT THE GIVING OF TORAH. FOR THAT REASON, WITCHCRAFT, WHICH DERIVES FROM THE IMPURITY OF THE SERPENT, ABIDES MAINLY IN WOMEN.

85. וְעוֹד, דְּאַהֲדָרוּ כֻּלְּהוּ לְזוּהֲמָתָן כְּקַדְמֵיתָא, בָּתַר דְּחָטוּ, וְאִתְּתָא קַשְׁיָא לְאִתְפָּרְשָׁא זוּהֲמָא מִנָּהּ, יַתִּיר מִגַּבְרָא, וּבְגִין כָּךְ, אִשְׁתַּכָּחוּ נָשִׁין בְּחֳרָשַׁיָא, וּבְזוּהֲמָא דָא יַתִּיר מִגּוּבְרִין. דְּהָא נָשַׁיָא מִסִּטְרָא דִשְׂמָאלָא קָא אַתְיָין וְאִתְדַּבָּקוּ בְּדִינָא קַשְׁיָא, וְסִטְרָא דָא, אִתְדַּבַּק בְּהוֹ, יַתִּיר מִגּוּבְרִין, כְּמָה דְּאִתְּמַר, בְּגִין דְּאַתְיָא מִסִּטְרָא דְּדִינָא קַשְׁיָא, וְכֹלָּא אִתְדַּבַּק וְאָזֵיל בָּתַר זִינֵיהּ.

85. Moreover, everyone became defiled again after the sin, EVEN THE MEN. It is more difficult for women to cleanse impurities from themselves than for men. Thus, women practice sorcery and abide in defilement more so than men. THE REASON WHY IT IS DIFFICULT FOR WOMEN TO BE

CLEANSED FROM DEFILEMENT IS THAT women come from the left side and are attached to the strict Judgment OF THE LEFT. This side cleaves to them more than to men, because they come from strict Judgment. Everything is attached to and follows its own kind.

86. תָּא חֲזֵי, דְּהָכֵי הוּא, כְּמָה דַאֲמֵינָא, דְּבִלְעָם הֲוָה אִסְתָּאַב בְּקַדְמֵיתָא, בְּגִין לְאַמְשָׁכָא עֲלֵיהּ רוּחָא מְסָאֲבָא. כְּגַוְונָא דָא, אִתְּתָא בְּיוֹמֵי דִמְסָאֲבוּ דִילָהּ, אִית לֵיהּ לְבַר נָשׁ לְאִסְתַּמְּרָא מִנָּהּ, בְּגִין דְּבְרוּחַ מְסָאֲבָא אִתְדַּבְּקַת וּבְהַהוּא זִמְנָא, אִי אִיהִי תַּעֲבֵיד חֲרָשִׁין, אַצְלָחוּ בִּידָהָא, יַתִּיר מִזִּמְנָא אָחֳרָא דְּהָא רוּחַ מְסָאֲבָא שַׁרְיָא עִמָּהּ, וְעַל דָּא, בְּכָל מַה דְּקְרֵיבַת אִסְתָּאַב, כָּל שֶׁכֵּן מַאן דְּקָרֵיב בַּהֲדָהּ. זַכָּאִין אִינוּן יִשְׂרָאֵל, דְּקוּדְשָׁא בְּרִיךְ הוּא, יָהִיב לוֹן, אוֹרַיְיתָא, וַאֲמַר לוֹן, וְאֶל אִשָּׁה בְּנִדַּת טֻמְאָתָהּ לֹא תִקְרַב לְגַלּוֹת עֶרְוָתָהּ אֲנִי ה'.

86. Come and behold: As I have said, ENCHANTMENT COMES FROM THE DEFILEMENT OF THE SERPENT, for Bilaam used to defile himself first to draw upon him the unholy spirit. THEN HE PRACTICED SORCERY. Similarly, it behooves man to stay away from a woman during menstruation LEST HE TOUCH HER, because she is attached to the spirit of defilement. If she practices sorcery at that time, she will be more successful that at other times. Whatever she touches is therefore defiled, and all the more so whomever approaches her. Happy are the children of Yisrael, for the Holy One, blessed be He, gave them Torah, and told them, "Also you shall not approach to a woman in the impurity of her menstrual flow, to uncover her nakedness... I am Hashem" (Vayikra 18:19-21).

87. אָמַר לֵיהּ, הַאי מַאן דְּאִסְתַּכַּל, בְּצִפְצוּפוֹי דְּעוֹפֵי, אֲמַאי אִקְרֵי נָחָשׁ. אָמַר לוֹ דְּהָא מֵהַהוּא סִטְרָא קָאָתֵי, דְּרוּחַ מְסָאֲבָא, שַׁרְיָא עַל הַהוּא עוֹפָא, וְאוֹדַע מִלִּין בְּעָלְמָא. וְכָל רוּחַ מְסָאֲבָא, בְּנָחָשׁ אִתְדַּבְּקוּ, וְאַתְיָין לְעָלְמָא, וְלֵית מַאן דְּיִשְׁתְּזִיב מִנֵּיהּ בְּעָלְמָא, דְּהָא אִיהוּ אִשְׁתַּכַּח עִם כֹּלָּא, עַד זִמְנָא, דְּזַמִּין קוּדְשָׁא בְּרִיךְ הוּא לְאַעֲבָרָא לֵיהּ מֵעָלְמָא, כְּמָה דְּאִתְּמָר, דִּכְתִיב בִּלַּע הַמָּוֶת לָנֶצַח וּמָחָה ה' אֱלֹהִים דִּמְעָה מֵעַל כָּל פָּנִים וְגו'. וּכְתִיב וְאֶת רוּחַ הַטֻּמְאָה אַעֲבִיר מִן הָאָרֶץ וְגו'.

87. He asks, Why is it called sorcery if someone uses the chirping of birds TO TELL THE FUTURE? It is because the unholy spirit abides in that bird, which is drawn from this side OF DEFILEMENT. That unholy spirit foretells events. Every defiled spirit, is attached to and comes to the world from the serpent and no one in this world is safe from it, because it is everywhere, until the time when the Holy One, blessed be He, will remove it from the world, as it is written: "He will destroy death for ever" (Yeshayah 25:8) and "I will also cause...the unclean spirit to pass out of the land" (Zecharyah 13:2).

14. The cave of Machpelah (Part one)

A synopsis

Rabbi Yehuda tells us how it was that Abraham recognized the significance of the cave of Machpelah, and that he deserved to be buried there. We learn that an ordinary man sees Adam at the moment of death. Yet Abraham saw him, along with a vision of the Garden of Eden, and still lived. This was because Abraham had been in Eden during his own lifetime, and thus looked upon something he was already merited to see when he was alive. He acquires the cave through spiritual wisdom, not through any form of self-centered desire.

The Relevance of this Passage

Our egocentric desires compel us to covet possessions that provide temporary satisfaction. But there is a downside: chaos and darkness appear when the thrill has ended. The soul, however, is in search of permanent fulfillment, and people who achieve that fulfillment are willing and able to forsake short-term, ego-based pleasures. Abraham exemplifies this principle in the story of the cave of Machpelah. By remaining true to a spiritual path, Abraham sought out the cave through his wisdom, not his ego, and therefore merited the greatest possible fulfillment: the Light of the Garden of Eden. The mystical words of the Zohar allow us to glimpse shards of Light gleaming in the Garden. During our lives, this Light helps us to fulfill the needs of our soul, instead of foolishly catering to our ego.

88. רִבִּי יְהוּדָה אָמַר, אַבְרָהָם יָדַע, בְּהַהִיא מְעַרְתָּא סִימָנָא, וְלִבֵּיה וּרְעוּתֵיה תַּמָן הֲוָה, בְּגִין דְּמִקַּדְמַת דְּנָא עָאל לְתַמָן, וְחָמָא לְאָדָם וְחַוָּה, טְמִירִין תַּמָן. וּמְנָא הֲוָה יָדַע, דְּאִינוּן הֲוֹו. אֶלָּא חָמָא דְּיוֹקְנֵיה, וְאִסְתַּכַּל וְאִתְפַּתַּח לֵיה, חַד פִּתְחָא דְּגִנְתָּא דְּעֵדֶן תַּמָן, וְהַהוּא דְּיוֹקְנָא דְּאָדָם, הֲוָה קָאִים לְגַבֵּיה.

88. Rabbi Yehuda said, Abraham recognized a sign in that cave, NAMELY THE CAVE OF MACHPELAH, and his heart and desire were there. For he had entered it before and seen Adam and Eve interred there. HE ASKS: How did he know it was they, FOR HE DID NOT KNOW THEM? HE ANSWERS, He saw the shape OF ADAM and looked at it. Then a door to the Garden of Eden opened before him AND HE UNDERSTOOD that this was the shape of Adam

before him. HE UNDERSTOOD THAT HE DESERVED TO BE BURIED IN THE
GATE OF THE GARDEN OF EDEN BECAUSE HE HAD BEEN IN THE
GARDEN OF EDEN DURING HIS LIFETIME.

89. וְתָא חֲזֵי, כָּל מַאן דְּאִסְתַּכַּל, בְּדִיּוּקְנָא דְּאָדָם, לָא אִשְׁתְּזִיב לְעָלְמִין
מִמִּיתָה, בְּגִין דְּהָא בְּשַׁעְתָּא דְּבַר נָשׁ אִסְתַּלָּק מֵעַלְמָא, חָמֵי לֵיהּ
לְאָדָם, וּבְהַהוּא זִמְנָא מִית. אֲבָל אַבְרָהָם אִסְתַּכַּל בֵּיהּ, וְחָמָא דִיּוּקְנֵיהּ,
וְאִתְקַיַּים, וְחָמָא נְהוֹרָא דְּנָהֵיר בִּמְעַרְתָּא, וְחַד שְׁרָגָּא דָּלֵיק, כְּדֵין תָּאִיב
אַבְרָהָם, דְּיוּרֵיהּ בְּהַהוּא אֲתַר וְלִבֵּיהּ וּרְעוּתֵיהּ הֲוָה תָּדִיר בִּמְעַרְתָּא.

89. Come and behold: Whoever beholds the shape of Adam cannot escape
death. THAT PERSON HAS TO DIE THAT INSTANT, for man sees Adam the
moment that he dies and passes from the world. But Abraham looked at
him, saw his shape, and lived. He saw a light shining from within the cave
and a candle burning. Then he wanted to dwell in that cave, and his heart
and desire were always there.

90. תָּא חֲזֵי, הַשְׁתָּא אַבְרָהָם בְּחָכְמְתָא עֲבַד בְּזִמְנָא דְּתָבַע קַבְרָא
לְשָׂרָה, דְּהָא כַּד תָּבַע, לָא תָבַע לִמְעַרְתָּא בְּהַהוּא זִמְנָא, וְלָא אָמַר
דְּבָעֵי לְאִתְפָּרְשָׁא מִנַּיְיהוּ, אֶלָּא אָמַר, תְּנוּ לִי אֲחוּזַת קֶבֶר עִמָּכֶם
וְאֶקְבְּרָה מֵתִי מִלְּפָנַי. וְאִי תֵימָא דְּלָא הֲוָה עֶפְרוֹן תַּמָּן, תַּמָּן הֲוָה,
דִּכְתִיב וְעֶפְרוֹן יוֹשֵׁב בְּתוֹךְ בְּנֵי חֵת, וְאַבְרָהָם לָא אָמַר לֵיהּ בְּהַהִיא
שַׁעְתָּא כְּלוּם.

90. Come and behold: Abraham behaved wisely when he asks for a grave
for Sarah, for he did not ask for the cave immediately or say that he wanted
to be separated from them. Instead, he said, "Give me a possession of a
burying place with you, that I may bury my dead out of my sight"
(Beresheet 23:3). HE DID NOT MENTION EITHER EFRON OR THE CAVE. If
you say that Efron was not there, IT IS NOT SO. INDEED he was present, as
it is written: "And Efron dwelt among the children of Chet" (Ibid. 9).
NEVERTHELESS, Abraham said nothing to him for the time being.

91. אֶלָּא מַה דַּאֲמַר לוֹן, אָמַר כְּמָה דִכְתִיב וַיְדַבֵּר אֶל בְּנֵי חֵת וְגו'. וְכִי

סָלְקָא דַעְתָּךְ דְּאַבְרָהָם בָּעָא לְאִתְקַבְּרָא בֵּינַיְיהוּ בֵּין מְסָאֲבִין, אוֹ דְּתִאוּבְתֵּיה הֲוָה עִמְהוֹן, אֶלָּא בְּחָכְמָה עֲבַד.

91. He spoke with them further, as it is written: "And spoke to the sons of Chet" (Ibid. 3). Could you conceive that Abraham wanted to be buried among the defiled or that he wanted to join them, when he said, "Give me a possession of a burying place with you"? But he behaved wisely.

92. וְיַלְפִינָן אוֹרַח אַרְעָא הָכָא, בַּמֶּה דַעֲבַד אַבְרָהָם, דְּהָא בְּגִין דְּתִאוּבְתֵּיה וּרְעוּתֵיה הֲוָה בְּהַהִיא מְעַרְתָּא, אַף עַל גַּב דַּהֲוָה תַּמָּן, לָא בָּעָא לְמִשְׁאַל לֵיה מִיָּד, הַהוּא רְעוּתָא דַּהֲוָה לֵיה בִּמְעַרְתָּא, וְשָׁאִיל בְּקַדְמֵיתָא, מַה דְּלָא אִצְטְרִיךְ לֵיה, לְאִינוּן אַחֲרָנִין, וְלָא לְעֶפְרוֹן.

92. And we learn proper conduct from the way Abraham acted, because he desired and wished for that cave. Although Efron was there, he did not want to ask him immediately. He did not ask for the cave but rather for what he did not want, and asks another, not Efron, AS HE SAID TO THE SONS OF CHET: "GIVE ME A POSSESSION OF A BURYING PLACE WITH YOU…"

93. כֵּיוָן דַּאֲמָרוּ לֵיה, קַמֵּי עֶפְרוֹן, שְׁמָעֵנוּ אֲדֹנִי נְשִׂיא אֱלֹהִים אַתָּה בְּתוֹכֵנוּ וגו', מַה כְּתִיב וְעֶפְרוֹן יֹשֵׁב בְּתוֹךְ בְּנֵי חֵת, יָשַׁב כְּתִיב, מְשִׁירוּתָא דְּמִלִּין דַּאֲמַר אַבְרָהָם, תַּמָּן הֲוָה, בְּדֵין אֲמַר שְׁמָעוּנִי וּפִגְעוּ לִי בְּעֶפְרוֹן בֶּן צֹחַר וְיִתֶּן לִי אֶת מְעָרַת הַמַּכְפֵּלָה אֲשֶׁר לוֹ וגו'. וְאִי תֵימָא בְּגִין יְקָרָא דִּילִי יַתִּיר מִנַּיְיכוּ, אֲנָא עָבֵיד, דְּלָא רָעֵינָא בְּכוֹ, בְּתוֹכְכֶם, בְּגִין לְאִתְקַבְּרָא בֵּינַיְיכוּ, דִּרְעֵינוּ בְּכוֹ, בְּגִין דְּלָא אִתְפְּרַשׁ מִנַּיְיכוּ.

93. Once the sons of Chet said to him in the presence of Efron, "Hear us, my lord, you are a mighty prince among us" (Beresheet 23:5), it is written: "And Efron dwelt (lit. 'dwells') among the children of Chet." 'Dwells' is written without vowels and can be conjugated as 'dwelt', which would mean that Efron was already there as they started talking. Then Abraham said, "Hear me, and entreat for me to Efron, the son of Tzochar, that he may give me the cave of Machpelah, which he has" (Ibid. 8). If you say that since my honor is greater than yours I ASK FOR THE CAVE OF THE MACHPELAH FROM EFRON because I do not want to dwell among you, THIS IS NOT TRUE. But "with you" AND "AMONGST YOU" (IBID. 10) — IN OTHER WORDS, to be interred among you. THIS IS WHAT I MEANT, because I want you, so that I shall not be separated from you.

15. "Four hundred shekels"

A synopsis
The secret of what becomes of the body and soul at death, is explored by Rabbi Yosi bar Yehuda and Rabbi Chiya. When soul and body are parted, the angel Dumah becomes custodian of the body, which must show its worthiness to receive the reward of 400 worlds. According to the rabbis, this worthiness takes the form of a deep longing for purity and righteousness; desiring those qualities makes us worthy. Those who did not feel this yearning will not be resurrected on the Day of Reckoning.

The Relevance of this Passage
The Kabbalists have long taught that the Light of the Creator reveals itself only to genuine seekers of the truth. Through our desire for righteousness, we earn the Light and become active participants in the process of Creation. Many people turn to the Creator only when tragedy or hardship strikes. Longing for the Light is easily kindled during moments of adversity. But when times are good, we tend to forget our spiritual aspirations. And as desire for the Light ceases, periods of prosperity inevitably come to an end. This passage sustains and increases our yearning for the Light so that it illuminates our lives without end.

תּוֹסֶפְתָּא

94. רַבִּי יוֹסֵי ב"ר יְהוּדָה, אָזֵיל לְמֵיחֱמֵי לְר' חִיָּיא, אָמַר לוֹ, לֵימָא מַר, אִי שָׁמַע הַאי פַּרְשָׁתָא, הֵיךְ אָמְרוּ מָארֵי מַתְנִיתָא, דְּפֵרְשׁוּהָ בְּעִנְיָינָא דְנִשְׁמָתָא. אָמַר, זַכָּאָה חוּלָקֵיהוֹן דְּצַדִּיקַיָּא, בְּעָלְמָא דְאָתֵי, דְּכָךְ הִיא אוֹרַיְיתָא בְּלִבְּהוֹן, כְּמַבּוּעָא רַבָּא דְמַיָּא, דְּאַף עַל גַּב דְּמַסְתִּימִין לֵיהּ, מִסְגִּיאוּת מַיָּא, פָּתְחִין מַבּוּעִין דְּנָבְעִין לְכָל עֵיבַר.

Tosefta (Addendum)

94. Rabbi Yosi, the son of Rabbi Yehuda, visited Rabbi Chiya and asks, Sir, have you heard how those who are versed in the Mishnah explained this portion of the scripture as concerning the subject of the soul, ABRAHAM BEING THE SOUL AND SARAH THE BODY? He said, Happy is the fate of the righteous in the World to Come, for Torah in their hearts is like a great stream. Although they block it, the water breaks through and creates smaller

streams in all directions.

95. ת"ש, ר' יוֹסֵי, רְחִימָא אַתְּ, אֲנָא אֵימָא לָךְ בְּהַאי פָּרְשָׁתָא, לְעוֹלָם אֵין גּוּף הָאָדָם נִכְנָס בְּחֶשְׁבּוֹן הַצַּדִּיקִים, עַל יַד דּוּמָה, עַד שֶׁתַּרְאֶה הַנְּשָׁמָה, פִּנְקָס סִימָנָה, שֶׁנּוֹתְנִין לָהּ הַכְּרוּבִים בַּגַּ"ע. אָמַר רָבִּי יוֹסֵי, אֲנָא שְׁמַעְנָא, דְּהָא נִשְׁמָתָא, בָּתַר דְּעָיְילַת תַּמָּן, הִיא אָזְלַת לְסָלְקָא לְאַתְרָא לְעֵילָא, וְלָא לְמֵיחַת לְתַתָּא, אֲבָל קוֹדֶם שֶׁתַּעֲלֶה וְתִכָּנֵס, נַעֲשֵׂית אַפְּטְרוֹפוֹס הַגּוּף, עַל יַד דּוּמָה, וּמַרְאָה לוֹ, שֶׁרָאוּי הוּא, לְקַבֵּל שָׂכָר אַרְבַּע מֵאוֹת עוֹלָמוֹת.

95. Come and listen: Rabbi Yosi, you are beloved. I will tell you about this portion of the scripture. In the reckoning of the righteous, Dumah never enters a man's body after his demise until the soul shows him a letter as a sign that the Cherubs gave it in the Garden of Eden. Rabbi Yosi said, I heard that when the soul enters THE GARDEN OF EDEN it ascends to its place, TO BINAH, and does not descend TO MALCHUT. But before the soul ascends, Dumah makes it a custodian of the body. The soul then shows Dumah that the body is worthy to receive 400 worlds as a reward.

96. אָמַר רָבִּי חִיָּיא, הָא רַבִּי אֶלְעָזָר אָמַר, דְּהָא דּוּמָה יָדַע קוֹדֶם, מִשּׁוּם דְּמַכְרְזֵי עֲלָהּ בְּגִנְתָּא דְעֵדֶן. אֲבָל אֲנָא כָּךְ שְׁמַעְנָא, דִּי בְּעִדָּנָא דְּיָהֲבִין לֵיהּ פִּנְקְסָא, חָזַר עַל גּוּפָא, לְאַעֲיִל לֵיהּ בְּפִתְקָא דְּצַדִּיקַיָּיא, עַל יְדוֹי דְּדוּמָה. הֲדָא הוּא דִכְתִיב, אַךְ אִם אַתָּה לוּ שְׁמָעֵנִי נָתַתִּי כֶּסֶף הַשָּׂדֶה קַח מִמֶּנִּי. מַהוּ כֶּסֶף הַשָּׂדֶה, דָּא כְּסוּפָא דְּעָלְמִין אַרְבַּע מֵאוֹת, דְּיָהֲבִין לֵיהּ לְאַחֲסָנָא.

96. Rabbi Chiya argued, yet Rabbi Elazar said that Dumah knows THAT THE BODY IS WORTHY OF THE 400 WORLDS AS ITS REWARD before THE BODY SHOWS HIM, because it is announced in the Garden of Eden. But I have heard that when the soul is given the letter as a token, it returns to the body to enter it in the reckoning of the righteous at the hands of Dumah. It is written: "But if you will give it, I pray you, hear me: I will give you the price of the field, take it of me" (Beresheet 23:12). The price (Heb. kesef) of the field is the longing (Heb. kisuf) and desire for the 400 worlds given as an heirloom FOR THE BODY.

97. רַב יוֹסֵף, כַּד הֲוָה שָׁמַע פָּרְשָׁתָא דָא, מִמָּארֵיהוֹן דִּמְתִיבְתָּא, הֲוָה אָמַר, מָאן דְּאִיהוּ עַפְרָא, מַאי קָא זָכֵי לְהַאי, מָאן יִזְכֶּה, וּמָאן יָקוּם הֲדָא הוּא דִכְתִיב מִי יַעֲלֶה בְהַר ה' וגו'.

97. When he heard this explained by the heads of the Yeshivah, Rav Yosef said, Whoever is made of dust may merit all this, NAMELY THE 400 BRIGHT WORLDS? Who shall merit it? Who shall stand? It is written: "Who shall ascend into the mountain of Hashem or who shall stand in his holy place?" (Tehilim 24:3).

98. אָמַר רַבִּי אַבָּא, תָּא חֲזֵי, מַאי דִכְתִיב, וַיִּשְׁמַע אַבְרָהָם אֶל עֶפְרוֹן וַיִּשְׁקֹל אַבְרָהָם לְעֶפְרוֹן אֶת הַכֶּסֶף, דָּא הוּא כְּסוּפָא רַבָּתָא, דְּאִינוּן עָלְמִין וְכִסּוּפִין. אַרְבַּע מֵאוֹת שֶׁקֶל כֶּסֶף, אַרְבַּע מֵאוֹת עוֹלָמוֹת, וַהֲנָאוֹת, וְכִסּוּפִין, עוֹבֵר לַסֹּחֵר. רַב נַחְמָן אָמַר, שֶׁיַּעֲבוֹר כָּל שַׁעֲרֵי שָׁמַיִם, וִירוּשָׁלַיִם שֶׁל מַעְלָה וְאֵין מוֹחֶה בְּיָדֶה.

98. Rabbi Aba said, Come and behold, it is written: "And Abraham hearkened to Efron, and Abraham weighed to Efron the silver..." This is the longing for those desirable worlds. The "400 shekels of silver" are the 400 worlds of pleasure and desire. As Rabbi Nachman said, "Current money with the merchant" means that one may pass all the gates of heaven and Jerusalem the terrestrial with it, without being detained.

99. תָּא חֲזֵי, מַה כְּתִיב, וְאַחֲרֵי כֵן קָבַר אַבְרָהָם אֶת שָׂרָה אִשְׁתּוֹ, וְנִמְנֶה, עִם שְׁאָר הַצַּדִּיקִים בַּחֲבוּרָתָם, מִפִּתְקָא דִּמְמַנָּא עַל יְדוֹי דְּרוּמָה. אָמַר רַבִּי יִצְחָק, הָכֵי גְמִירְנָא, כָּל אִינוּן דִּכְתִיבִין בִּידוֹי דְרוּמָה, וּמְמַנָּן עַל יְדוֹי, יְקוּמוּן לְזִמְנָא דְּזַמִּין לְאַחֲיָא דָּיְירֵי עַפְרָא, וַוי לְהוֹן לְרַשִּׁיעַיָּא דְּלָא כְתִיבִין עַל יְדוֹי בְּפִתְקָא, שֶׁיֹּאבְדוּ בַּגֵּיהִנֹּם לְעָלְמִין, וְעַל דָּא נֶאֱמַר וּבָעֵת הַהִיא יִמָּלֵט עַמְּךָ כָּל הַנִּמְצָא כָּתוּב בַּסֵּפֶר.

(עַד כָּאן תּוֹסֶפְתָּא).

99. Come and behold: It is written, "And after this, Abraham buried Sarah

his wife" (Beresheet 18:19). THIS REFERS TO THE BODY, which was numbered in the company of the other righteous by a note of the chieftain Dumah. Rabbi Yitzchak said, So I have learned that all the bodies registered and visited by Dumah will be resurrected when THE HOLY ONE, BLESSED BE HE, revives the dwellers of dust. Woe to the wicked who are not registered by him in writing, for they will be lost in Gehenom forever. Of this, it is said, "And at that time your people shall be delivered, every one who shall be found written in the book" (Daniel 12:1).

End of Tosefta (Addendum)

16. The cave of Machpelah (Part two)

A synopsis

A discussion of the events surrounding Abraham's purchase of the Machpelah cave ensues. We learn that Abraham managed to purchase both the cave and the field it stood in for a reasonable price, because he neither outwardly displayed nor inwardly harbored a desire to own either one. He knew that they were his by right – by virtue of his spiritual effort – and this is something very different from a selfish desire for ownership. Indeed, it is Abraham's spiritual elevation that causes the property to seem like a burden to Efron, its original owner. Rabbi Shimon then recounts what transpired between Adam and Abraham in the cave. Adam at first believes that his original humiliation and sin will be compounded in comparison with Abraham's righteousness. But a remarkable truth is now brought to light, when Abraham agrees to pray for Adam. Both Adam and Eve are said to have lived for Abraham's sake, for he was the first man to become aware and cognizant of the Creator. This startling fact concerning Abraham's connection to Adam and Eve is further illuminated when Abraham restores Eve – for whose sin he has not prayed – to Adam's side, an event paralleled by the burial of Sarah. After questions from Rabbi Shimon's son, Rabbi Elazar, we are then taken deep into the secret of the difference between the field of Machpelah and the cave. This difference exists, ultimately, to show that the Holy One's actions in this world are simply intended to bring the Light and sweetness of the Upper Realms. The differences between the cave and the field is a code, referring to the different frequencies of spiritual Light that are present in the physical realm, like the colors of the spectrum.

The Relevance of this Passage

This section helps explain how right conduct and resistance to our avaricious impulses allow us to receive the infinite delight waiting to pour down from the heavenly realm. In turn, we draw the strength to triumph over these self-seeking whims.

105 רַבִּי אֶלְעָזָר אָמַר, בְּשַׁעְתָּא דְעָאל אַבְרָהָם בִּמְעָרְתָּא, הֵיךְ עָאל. בְּגִין דַּהֲוָה רָהִיט אֲבַתְרֵיהּ דְּהַהוּא עֶגְלָא, דִּכְתִיב וְאֶל הַבָּקָר רָץ אַבְרָהָם וְגו', וְהַהוּא בֶּן בָּקָר, עָרַק עַד הַהוּא מְעָרְתָּא, וְעָאל אֲבַתְרֵיהּ, וְחָמָא מַה דְּחָמָא.

100. Rabbi Elazar asks, How did Abraham enter the cave? WHY DID HE ENTER? HE RESPONDED, He was running after a calf, about which it is written: "And Abraham ran to the herd..." (Beresheet 18:7). This calf ran to the cave. Abraham ran after it and saw what he saw.

101. תּוּ בְּגִין דְּאִיהוּ צַלֵּי כָּל יוֹמָא וְיוֹמָא, וַהֲוָה נָפֵיק עַד הַהוּא חֲקַל, דַּהֲוָה סַלֵּיק רֵיחִין עִלָּאִין, וְחָמָא נְהוֹרָא דְּנָפֵיק מִגּוֹ מְעַרְתָּא, וְצַלֵּי תַּמָּן, וְתַמָּן מַלֵּיל עִמֵּיהּ קוּדְשָׁא בְּרִיךְ הוּא, וּבְגִין כָּךְ בָּעָא לֵיהּ, דְּתִיאוּבְתֵּיהּ הֲוָה בְּהַהוּא אֲתַר תָּדִיר.

101. Another REASON was that Abraham prayed every day. He came out to the field that was fragrant with heavenly perfumes, saw light coming out of the cave, and entered there to pray. There the Holy One, blessed be He, spoke with him. As a result, Abraham wanted the cave and always harbored a desire for it.

102. וְאִי תֵּימָא אִי הָכֵי, אַמַּאי לָא בָּעָא לָהּ עַד הַשְׁתָּא. בְּגִין דְּלָא יַשְׁגְּחוּן עֲלֵיהּ, הוֹאִיל וְלָא אִצְטְרִיךְ לֵיהּ, הַשְׁתָּא דְּאִצְטְרִיךְ לֵיהּ, אֲמַר הָא שַׁעְתָּא לְמִתְבַּע לֵיהּ.

102. You may ask, why did he not seek to buy it until then? HE SAYS: Because he had no need for it, he was afraid that they would check it, UNDERSTAND HIS WISH AND THE IMPORTANCE OF THE CAVE, AND THEN ASK FOR MORE MONEY. OR THEY COULD REFUSE TO SELL IT ALTOGETHER. Now that he needed it, the time had come to ask for it.

103. תָּא חֲזֵי, אִי עֶפְרוֹן הֲוָה חָמֵי בִּמְעַרְתָּא, מַה דַּהֲוָה חָמֵי אַבְרָהָם בָּהּ, לָא יַזְבִּין לָהּ לְעָלְמִין, אֶלָּא וַדַּאי לָא חָמָא בָהּ וְלָא כְלוּם, דְּהָא לֵית מִלָּה אִתְגַּלְיָא, אֶלָּא לְמָארֵיהּ, וּבְגִין כָּךְ, לְאַבְרָהָם אִתְגַּלְיָיא, וְלָא לְעֶפְרוֹן, לְאַבְרָהָם אִתְגַּלְיָיא, דִּילֵיהּ הֲוָה לְעֶפְרוֹן לָא הֲוַת אִתְגַּלְיָא לֵיהּ, דְּלָא הֲוָה לֵיהּ חוּלָקָא בֵּיהּ. וּבְגִין כָּךְ, לָא אִתְגְּלֵי לְעֶפְרוֹן כְּלוּם, וְלָא הֲוָה חָמֵי אֶלָּא חֲשׁוֹכָא, וְעַל דָּא זַבִּין לָהּ.

103. Come and behold: If Efron had seen in the cave what Abraham saw, he would never have sold it. But because Efron saw nothing in it, as nothing is revealed except to its owner, it was revealed to Abraham only and not to Efron. It was revealed to Abraham because it was his, and not Efron's, for Efron had no share in it. Therefore Efron saw nothing of the cave. He saw only darkness and therefore, he sold it.

104. וּמַה דְּלָא תָּבַע אַבְרָהָם בְּקַדְמֵיתָא, דִּיְזַבִּין לֵיהּ זָבִין, דְּהָא אַבְרָהָם לָא קָאמַר, אֶלָּא וְיִתֶּן לִי אֶת מְעָרַת הַמַּכְפֵּלָה אֲשֶׁר לוֹ וְגו', בְּכֶסֶף מָלֵא יִתְּנֶנָּה לִי וְגו', וְאִיהוּ אָמַר הַשָּׂדֶה נָתַתִּי לָךְ וְהַמְּעָרָה אֲשֶׁר בּוֹ לְךָ נְתַתִּיהָ וְגו'. בְּגִין דְּכֹלָּא הֲוָה מָאִיס עֲלֵיהּ דְּעֶפְרוֹן, דְּלָא יָדַע מַה הִיא.

104. Moreover, he also sold him what Abraham did not ask him to sell, because Abraham said only, "That he may give me the cave of the Machpelah...for the full price he shall give it me" (Beresheet 23:8) and did not mention the field. And Efron said, "The field I give you, and the cave that is in it, I give it you" (Ibid. 10), for Efron knew not what it was and found it all loathsome. EVEN THE FIELD, IN WHICH THE CAVE WAS, WAS LOATHSOME TO HIM. THEREFORE HE SOLD THE FIELD TOO, ALTHOUGH ABRAHAM DID NOT ASK FOR IT.

105. וְתָא חֲזֵי, כַּד עָאל אַבְרָהָם בִּמְעַרְתָּא, בְּקַדְמֵיתָא חָמָא תַּמָּן נְהוֹרָא, וְאִתְרְמֵי עַפְרָא קַמֵּיהּ, וְאִתְגְּלֵי לֵיהּ תְּרֵין קִבְרִין, אַדְהָכֵי אִסְתַּלַּק אָדָם בְּדִיוֹקְנֵיהּ, וְחָמָא לֵיהּ לְאַבְרָהָם, וְחַיֵּיךְ, וּבֵיהּ יָדַע אַבְרָהָם, דְּתַמָּן הוּא זַמִּין לְאִתְקַבְּרָא.

105. Come and behold: When Abraham entered the cave for the first time, he saw a light. The dust was removed from before him, revealing two graves. Adam rose from his grave in his rightful form, saw Abraham, and laughed. By that, Abraham knew that he was destined to be buried there.

106. אָמַר לוֹ אַבְרָהָם, בְּמָטוּ מִינָךְ, קוּסְטְרָא קְטִיר אִית הָכָא, אָמַר לֵיהּ, קוּדְשָׁא בְּרִיךְ הוּא טְמָרַנִי הָכָא, וּמֵהַהוּא זִמְנָא עַד הַשְׁתָּא, אִתְטַמַּרְנָא כְּגִילְדָּא דְּקִירְטָא, עַד דַּאֲתֵית אַנְתְּ בְּעָלְמָא, הַשְׁתָּא מִכָּאן וָאֵילָךְ, הָא קִיּוּמָא לִי, וּלְעָלְמָא, הֲוָה בְּגִינָךְ.

106. Abraham said to him, 'If you please, is there an unroofed castle here?' HE ASKS THIS BECAUSE THE CAVE OF THE MACHPELAH IS DERIVED FROM THE WORD DOUBLE, THAT IS, A CAVE WITHIN A CAVE. INSTEAD OF COMPLETE DARKNESS, HE SAW LIGHT THERE, AS ONE WOULD IN AN OPEN HOUSE WITH NO ROOF. ADAM answered him, 'The Holy One, blessed be He, hid me here. From then until now, I have been hidden as a fish in a ditch. Since you came into the world, from now on, I and the world are maintained for your sake.'

107. חֲמֵי מַה כְּתִיב וַיָּקָם הַשָּׂדֶה וְהַמְּעָרָה אֲשֶׁר בּוֹ, קִימָה מַמָּשׁ הֲוָה לֵיהּ, מַה דְּלָא הֲוָה לֵיהּ עַד הַשְׁתָּא. רְבִּי אַבָּא אָמַר, וַיָּקָם הַשָּׂדֶה, וַדַּאי קִימָה מַמָּשׁ, דְּקָם וְאִסְתַּלַּק קַמֵּיהּ דְּאַבְרָהָם, בְּגִין דְּעַד הַשְׁתָּא, לָא אִתְחֲזֵי תַּמָּן כְּלוּם, וְהַשְׁתָּא מַה דַּהֲוָה טָמִיר, קָם וְאִסְתְּלֵיק, וּכְדֵין קָם כֹּלָּא בִּנְמוּסוֹי.

107. Look at what is written: "And the field, and the cave that is in it, were made over (also: 'raised') to" (Beresheet 18:20). The field was truly raised, which had not happened previously. By BEING IN ABRAHAM'S POSSESSION, THE FIELD GAINED IN IMPORTANCE. THEREFORE IT IS WRITTEN, "RAISED." Rabbi Aba said, "And he raised the field" means actual raising, as the field was raised and elevated by Abraham, for nothing was seen there until then. Now, IN THE POSSESSION OF ABRAHAM, all that was hidden was raised and elevated according to its worth, as it should be.

108. אָמַר רְבִּי שִׁמְעוֹן, בְּשַׁעֲתָא דְּעָאל אַבְרָהָם בִּמְעַרְתָּא, וְאָעִיל שָׂרָה תַּמָּן, קָמוּ אָדָם וְחַוָּה, וְלָא קַבִּילוּ לְאִתְקַבְּרָא תַּמָּן, אָמְרוּ וּמַה אֲנַן בְּכִסּוּפָא קַמֵּי קוּדְשָׁא בְּרִיךְ הוּא, בְּהַהוּא עָלְמָא, בְּגִין הַהוּא חוֹבָא דְּגָרֵימְנָא, וְהַשְׁתָּא יִתּוֹסַף לָן כִּסּוּפָא אָחֳרָא, מִקַּמֵּי עוֹבָדִין טָבִין דִּבְכוֹ.

108. Rabbi Shimon said, When Abraham entered the cave and brought Sarah thither, Adam and Eve rose and did not want Sarah to be buried there. They said, It is it not enough for us that we are in disgrace in the world before the Holy One, blessed be He, because of the sin that we committed, but now we will further be put to shame because of your good deeds.

109. אָמַר אַבְרָהָם, הָא אֲנָא זַמִּין קַמֵּי קוּדְשָׁא בְּרִיךְ הוּא, בְּגִינָךְ דְּלָא

תִּכְסִיף קַמֵּיהּ לְעָלְמִין. מִיָּד וְאַחֲרֵי כֵן קָבַר אַבְרָהָם אֶת שָׂרָה אִשְׁתּוֹ,
מַאי וְאַחֲרֵי כֵן. בָּתַר דְּקַבֵּיל אַבְרָהָם עֲלֵיהּ מִלָּה דָא.

109. Abraham said, I am ready to pray for you before the Holy One, blessed
be He, so you shall never be disgraced before Him, NAMELY SO HE WILL
FORGIVE YOU COMPLETELY FOR YOUR SIN. "And after this, Abraham
buried Sarah his wife" (Beresheet 18:19). What is the meaning of: "And
after this"? IT MEANS after Abraham undertook TO PRAY FOR ADAM.

110. אָדָם עָאל בְּדוּכְתֵּיהּ, חַוָּה לָא עָאלַת, עַד דְּקָרֵיב אַבְרָהָם, וְאָעֵיל
לֵהּ לְגַבֵּי אָדָם, וְקַבֵּיל לֵהּ בְּגִינֵיהּ, הה"ד וְאַחֲרֵי כֵן קָבַר אַבְרָהָם אֶת
שָׂרָה אִשְׁתּוֹ, לְשָׂרָה לָא כְּתִיב, אֶלָּא אֶת שָׂרָה, לְאַסְגָּאָה חַוָּה, וּכְדֵין
אִתְיַישְׁבוּ בְּדוּכְתַּיְיהוּ כִּדְקָא יָאוּת, הה"ד אֵלֶּה תּוֹלְדוֹת הַשָּׁמַיִם וְהָאָרֶץ
בְּהִבָּרְאָם, וְתָנִינָן בְּאַבְרָהָם. תּוֹלְדוֹת הַשָּׁמַיִם וְהָאָרֶץ, דָּא אָדָם וְחַוָּה,
אֵלֶּה הַשָּׁמַיִם וְהָאָרֶץ לָא כְּתִיב, אֶלָּא תּוֹלְדוֹת הַשָּׁמַיִם וְהָאָרֶץ, וְלָא
תּוֹלְדוֹת בַּר נָשׁ. וְאִינּוּן אִתְקָיְימוּ בְּגִינֵיהּ דְּאַבְרָהָם. וּמְנָא לָן דְּאִתְקָיְימוּ
בְּגִינֵיהּ דְּאַבְרָהָם. דִּכְתִיב וַיָּקָם הַשָּׂדֶה וְהַמְּעָרָה אֲשֶׁר בּוֹ לְאַבְרָהָם, וְעַד
דְּאָתָא אַבְרָהָם, לָא אִתְקָיְימוּ אָדָם וְחַוָּה בְּדוּכְתַּיְיהוּ, בְּהַהוּא עָלְמָא.

110. Adam returned to his place, but Eve did not, AS SHE HAD MADE ADAM
SIN, AS IT IS WRITTEN: "THE WOMAN WHOM YOU DID GIVE TO BE WITH
ME" (BERESHEET 3:12). SHE WAS AFRAID THAT ADAM WOULD NOT
RECEIVE HER. Then Abraham approached and put her with Adam, who
received her for Abraham's sake. This is the meaning of: "And after this,
Abraham buried Sarah his wife." The particle *Et* before "Sarah" is meant to
add Eve, WHOM ABRAHAM RETURNED TO THE GRAVE, AS WAS SAID.
Then ADAM AND EVE were properly settled in their places, as it is written:
"These are the generations of the heaven and of the earth when they were
created (Heb. *behibar'am*)" (Beresheet 2:4). We learned that *behibar'am*
HAS THE SAME LETTERS AS *beAbraham* (lit. 'by Abraham'), WHICH
INDICATES THAT THEY WERE CREATED FOR HIM. The generations of the
heaven and the earth are Adam and Eve. It is not written 'the heaven and the
earth,' but "the generations of the heaven and of the earth", WHICH REFERS
TO ADAM AND EVE, who were not begotten by man. OF THESE THE
VERSE SAYS they lived for the sake of Abraham. How do we know that they

existed for Abraham? Because it is written: "And the field, and the cave that is in it, were made over (also: 'maintained') to Abraham." Until Abraham came, Adam and Eve did not exist in the world. "THE FIELD AND THE CAVE IN IT" ALLUDE TO ADAM AND EVE, WHO DWELT THERE. THE WORDS "BY ABRAHAM" MEAN FOR ABRAHAM. IT IS SHOWN THAT ADAM AND EVE WERE SUSTAINED FOR ABRAHAM'S SAKE.

111. ר' אֶלְעָזָר שָׁאֵיל לְרִבִּי שִׁמְעוֹן אֲבוֹי, אָמַר הַאי מְעַרְתָּא לָאו אִיהוּ כְּפֵילְתָּא, דְּהָא כְּתִיב מְעָרַת הַמַּכְפֵּלָה וּקְרָא קָרֵי לָה לְבָתַר, מְעָרַת שְׂדֵה הַמַּכְפֵּלָה, מַכְפֵּלָה קָא קָרֵי לֵיהּ לַשָּׂדֶה.

111. Rabbi Elazar asks Rabbi Shimon, his father, if the cave is really the Machpelah, for although it is written: "The cave of Machpelah" (Beresheet 23:8), it is later written "the cave of the field of Machpelah" (Ibid. 19). Thus, the field is called Machpelah AND NOT THE CAVE.

112. אָמַר לֵיהּ, הָכֵי קָאֲרֵי לֵיהּ, מְעָרַת הַמַּכְפֵּלָה, כְּמָה דְאַתְּ אָמַר, וְיִתֶּן לִי אֶת מְעָרַת הַמַּכְפֵּלָה, אֲבָל וַדַּאי, לָאו מְעַרְתָּא אִיהוּ מַכְפֵּלָה, וְלָאו שָׂדֶה אִקְרֵי מַכְפֵּלָה, אֶלָּא הַאי שָׂדֶה וּמְעַרְתָּא, עַל שׁוּם מַכְפֵּלָה אִקְרוּן, שָׂדֵה הַמַּכְפֵּלָה וַדַּאי, וְלָא מְעַרְתָּא, דְּהָא מְעַרְתָּא בְּשָׂדֶה אִיהִי, וְהַהוּא שָׂדֶה קָאֵים בְּמִלָּה אָחֳרָא.

112. RABBI SHIMON replies that indeed it is called the cave of Machpelah, as it is written: "That he may give me the cave of Machpelah" (Beresheet 23:8), but neither the cave nor the field along is Machpelah. It refers instead to the field with the cave, TOGETHER they are called Machpelah. Only the field is of Machpelah, not the cave, WHICH MEANS THAT ONLY THE FIELD BEARS THE NAME OF THE MACHPELAH, NOT THE CAVE, because the cave is in the field, and the field is in something else, AS WILL BE DISCUSSED PRESENTLY.

113. תָּא חֲזֵי, יְרוּשָׁלַם כָּל אַרְעָא דְיִשְׂרָאֵל אִתְכְּפַל תְּחוֹתָהּ, וְאִיהִי קַיְימָא לְעֵילָא וְתַתָּא, כְּגַוְונָא דָא, יְרוּשָׁלַם לְעֵילָא יְרוּשָׁלַם לְתַתָּא, אֲחִידָא לְעֵילָא, וַאֲחִידָא לְתַתָּא, יְרוּשָׁלַם לְעֵילָא אֲחִידַת בִּתְרֵין

סְטְרִין, לְעֵילָא וְתַתָּא, וּבְגִין כָּךְ, כְּפֵלְתָּא הִיא.

113. Come and behold: The whole land of Yisrael is enfolded beneath Jerusalem, WHICH IS THE SECRET OF MALCHUT. It is above and below in the following manner. THERE IS the upper Jerusalem, WHICH IS BINAH, and there is the lower Jerusalem, WHICH IS MALCHUT, for it is held above and held below. The upper Jerusalem is held on two sides – above and below – and, therefore, it is doubled.

114. וְעַל דָּא, הַאי שָׂדֶה מֵהַהִיא כְּפֵלְתָּא אִיהוּ, דְּבֵיהּ שַׁרְיָא. כְּגַוְונָא דָא כְּתִיב כְּרֵיחַ שָׂדֶה אֲשֶׁר בֵּרֲכוֹ ה', לְעֵילָא וְתַתָּא, וּבְגִין כָּךְ שָׂדֶה הַמַּכְפֵּלָה וַדַּאי וְלָא שָׂדֶה כָּפוּל.

114. Thus, the field is of that Machpelah (lit. 'double'), WHICH IS MALCHUT, for it dwells there, as it is written: "See, the smell of my son is like the smell of a field which Hashem has blessed" (Beresheet 27:27), WHICH IS MALCHUT. BECAUSE IT IS DOUBLE, above and below, it is written: "the field of Machpelah" and not "a double field", BECAUSE THIS WOULD ALLUDE TO THE DOUBLE MALCHUT CALLED FIELD.

115. תּוּ, רָזָא דְמִלָּה, שָׂדֶה הַמַּכְפֵּלָה וַדַּאי, מַאן מַכְפֵּלָה, ה' דְּבִשְׁמָא קַדִּישָׁא, דְּאִיהִי מַכְפֵּלָה. וְכֹלָּא קַיְימָא כְּחַד, וּבְגִינֵיהּ קָאֲמַר, בְּאוֹרַח סְתִים, ה' מַכְפֵּלָה, דְּלָא הֲוֵי בִּשְׁמָא קַדִּישָׁא, אָת אָחֳרָא מַכְפֵּלָה, בַּר אִיהִי.

115. Moreover, the secret of the matter relates to the field of Machpelah. What is the Machpelah (double)? It is the *Hei* of the Holy Name, which is double, FOR THERE ARE TWO *HEIS* IN THE NAME YUD HEV VAV HEI, and both are as one. For that reason, the scriptures say vaguely the (=Hei) Machpelah, for this is the only double letter in the Holy Name. AND THE WORD "THE MACHPELAH" WITH THE *HEI* ALLUDES TO THE DOUBLE *HEI*, NAMELY THE LOWER *HEI* OF THE NAME YUD HEV VAV HEI, WHICH IS THE SECRET OF MALCHUT SWEETENED BY BINAH, THE FIRST *HEI* OF YUD HEV VAV HEI.

116. וְאַף עַל גַּב דִּמְעָרְתָּא כְּפֵלְתָּא הֲוָה, וַדַּאי, דְּאִיהִי מְעָרְתָּא, גּוֹ

מְעַרְתָּא, אֲבָל עַל שׁוּם אָחֳרָא, אִקְרֵי מְעָרַת שְׂדֵה הַמַּכְפֵּלָה, כְּמָה דְאִתְּמַר. וְאַבְרָהָם יָדַע, וְכַד אָמַר לִבְנֵי חֵת, כַּסֵּי מִלָּה, וַאֲמַר וְיִתֶּן לִי אֶת מְעָרַת הַמַּכְפֵּלָה, עַל שׁוּם דְּאִיהִי מְעַרְתָּא כְּפִלְתָּא, וְאוֹרַיְיתָא לָא קָרֵי לָהּ, אֶלָּא מְעָרַת שְׂדֵה הַמַּכְפֵּלָה כִּדְקָא יָאוֹת.

116. Although the cave was indeed double, a cave within a cave, it is called the cave of the field of Machpelah for a different reason as we said, AFTER THE SWEETENING OF MALCHUT BY BINAH. Abraham knew that, and when he spoke to the sons of Chet, he concealed it by saying "that he may give me the cave of Machpelah," which was called by that name because it was double. HE DID NOT SAY THE FIELD OF MACHPELAH CALLED AFTER THE SWEETENING BY BINAH. In Torah, though, it is called the cave of the field of Machpelah, as it ought to be called, FOR THE SWEETENING OF MALCHUT BY BINAH WAS ONLY OVER THE FIELD AND NOT IN THE CAVE.

117. וְקוּדְשָׁא בְּרִיךְ הוּא, עָבַד כֹּלָּא לְאִשְׁתַּכְּחָא הַאי עָלְמָא, כְּגַוְונָא דִלְעֵילָא, וּלְאִתְדַּבְּקָא דָּא בְּדָא, לְמֶהֱוֵי יְקָרֵיהּ לְעֵילָא וְתַתָּא, זַכָּאָה חוּלָקֵיהוֹן דְּצַדִּיקַיָּא, דְּקוּדְשָׁא בְּרִיךְ הוּא אִתְרְעֵי בְּהוֹ, בְּהַאי עָלְמָא וּבְעָלְמָא דְאָתֵי.

117. The Holy One, blessed be He, does everything so whatever is in this world, MALCHUT, will resemble what there in above, in BINAH. AS A RESULT, they are connected, and His glory is established above and below. Happy is the portions of the righteous that the Holy One, blessed be He, desires them in this world and in the World to Come.

17. "And Abraham was old, advanced in age"

A synopsis

Using Abraham and David as examples, Rabbi Yehuda explains the difference between the righteousness and contrition. While the soul of a contrite person immediately enters the supernal realm, where it cleaves to the Holy One, merely righteous souls may take many years to acquire such a blessing. Even Abraham and David were unable to enter the world where the truly contrite are made welcome. Rabbi Yosi further adds that a contrite soul is closer to the Creator than all others, drawing down more Light from above, in proportion to its yearning and penitence.

The Relevance of this Passage

The Zohar values a spiritual state of mind far above a religious, dogmatic one. Some people observe the Law, but at the expense of hurting those around them. Righteousness turns to self-righteousness and negative action, all in the name of God. Uninterrupted humbleness and repentance for our misdeeds protects us from this fate. This passage helps us raise our consciousness so we can differentiate our desire for righteousness from our need for penitence. Concentrating on penitence hastens us into the Light, rather than merely flattering our egotistical pride.

118. וְאַבְרָהָם זָקֵן בָּא בַּיָּמִים וַה' בֵּרַךְ אֶת אַבְרָהָם בַּכֹּל. רַבִּי יְהוּדָה פָּתַח, אַשְׁרֵי תִּבְחַר וּתְקָרֵב יִשְׁכֹּן חֲצֵרֶיךָ, הַאי קְרָא אִתְּמַר, אֲבָל זַכָּאָה הוּא בַּר נָשׁ, דְּאוֹרְחוֹי אִתְכַּשְׁרָן קַמֵּי קוּדְשָׁא בְּרִיךְ הוּא וְאִיהוּ אִתְרְעֵי בֵּיהּ, לְקָרְבָא לֵיהּ לְגַבֵּיהּ.

118. "And Abraham was old, advanced in age (lit. 'coming with the days'), and Hashem blessed Abraham in all things" (Beresheet 24:1). Rabbi Yehuda opened with the verse, "Happy is the man You choose, and cause to approach to You, that he may dwell in Your courts" (Tehilim 65:5). This verse has already been explained. Nevertheless, happy is the man whose ways are acceptable to the Holy One, blessed be He, who wants to bring himself nearer to Him.

119. תָּא חֲזֵי, אַבְרָהָם אִתְקְרֵיב לְגַבֵּיהּ, וְתֵיאוּבְתֵּיהּ דִּילֵיהּ הֲוָה כָּל יוֹמוֹי בְּהַאי, וְלָא אִתְקְרֵיב אַבְרָהָם בְּיוֹמָא חֲדָא, אוֹ בְּזִמְנָא חֲדָא, אֶלָּא

עוֹבָדוֹי קָרִיבוּ לֵיהּ בְּכָל יוֹמוֹי, מִדַּרְגָּא לְדַרְגָּא, עַד דְּאִסְתַּלַּק בְּדַרְגּוֹי.

119. Come and behold: Abraham came closer to THE HOLY ONE, BLESSED BE HE. All his days, his desire was TO COME CLOSER TO HIM. Abraham did not come closer through one day or at one time, but his GOOD deeds brought him closer every day as he moved from one grade to another, until his grade was elevated.

120. כַּד הֲוָה סִיב, וְעָאל בְּדַרְגִּין עִלָּאִין כִּדְקָא חָזֵי, דִּכְתִיב וְאַבְרָהָם זָקֵן, וּכְדֵין בָּא בַּיָּמִים, בְּאִינוּן יוֹמִין עִלָּאִין, בְּאִינוּן יוֹמִין יְדִיעָאן בְּרָזָא דִּמְהֵימְנוּתָא. וַה' בֵּרַךְ אֶת אַבְרָהָם בַּכֹּל, דְּמִתַּמָּן נָפְקִין כָּל בִּרְכָאן, וְכָל טִיבוּ.

120. When he was old, he entered the supernal grades as he deserved, as it is written: "And Abraham was old" and then "coming with the days." This refers to the supernal days, the days known by the secret of the faith. "And Hashem blessed Abraham in all," NAMELY BY YESOD OF THE SUPERNAL ABA AND IMA CALLED ALL, where blessings and every goodness come from, AS ITS PLENTY NEVER STOPS FLOWING.

121. זַכָּאִין אִינוּן מָארֵיהוֹן דִּתְשׁוּבָה, דְּהָא בְּשַׁעְתָּא חֲדָא, בְּיוֹמָא חֲדָא, בְּרִגְעָא חֲדָא, קְרֵיבִין לְגַבֵּי קוּדְשָׁא בְּרִיךְ הוּא, מַה דְּלָא הֲוָה הָכֵי אֲפִילוּ לְצַדִּיקִים גְּמוּרִים, דְּאִתְקְרִיבוּ גַּבֵּי קוּדְשָׁא בְּרִיךְ הוּא בְּכַמָּה שְׁנִין. אַבְרָהָם לָא עָאל בְּאִינוּן יוֹמִין עִלָּאִין, עַד דַּהֲוָה סִיב, כְּמָה דְּאִתְּמַר. וְכֵן דָּוִד, דִּכְתִיב וְהַמֶּלֶךְ דָּוִד זָקֵן בָּא בַּיָּמִים. אֲבָל מָארֵיהּ דִּתְשׁוּבָה, מִיָּד עָאל, וְאִתְדַּבַּק בֵּיהּ בְּקוּדְשָׁא בְּרִיךְ הוּא.

121. Happy are the penitent, who in one hour, one day, one moment, get as close to the Holy One, blessed be He, as most righteous come to the Holy One, blessed be He, over several years. Abraham did not come into the supernal days until he was old, as has been explained. Neither did David, as it is written: "Now King David was old, advanced in years (lit. 'coming with the days')" (I Melachim 1:1). But a penitent comes right in and cleaves to the Holy One, blessed be He.

122. ר' יוֹסֵי אֲמַר, תָּנִינָן, אֲתַר דְּמָארֵיהוֹן דִּתְשׁוּבָה קַיְימֵי בֵּיהּ, בְּהַהוּא עַלְמָא, צַדִּיקִים גְּמוּרִים לֵית לוֹן רְשׁוּ לְקַיְימָא בֵּיהּ, בְּגִין דְּאִינּוּן קְרֵיבִין לְמַלְכָּא יַתִּיר מִכֻּלְּהוּ, וְאִינּוּן מָשְׁכֵי עֲלַיְיהוּ בִּרְעוּתָא דְּלִבָּא יַתִּיר, וּבְחֵילָא סַגְיָא לְאִתְקָרְבָא לְמַלְכָּא.

122. Rabbi Yosi said, We learned that the wholly righteous have no permission to be in that place where the contrite stand. They are closer to the King than everyone else and draw plenty from above with a more intent heart and greater force in order to come closer to the King.

18. There are many places for the righteous

A synopsis

The relationship of a man's good deeds to the place allotted to him in the World to Come is expounded by the rabbis. We learn that there are ultimately as many different places in upper world as there are varieties of good deeds in this one. Just as the wicked receive a judgment each night while they are asleep, so the righteous nightly receive a blessing, as their souls ascend to carve out their future path to the supernal realms. The righteous souls also enjoy a dialogue with the angels and saints, who in exchange for information from the lower world, confer gifts of wisdom. It was such wisdom, says Rabbi Chiya, that enabled Abraham to understand, locate, and avoid the sources from which unholy spirits bring defilement and negativity to the unwary and unrighteous in this world.

The Relevance of this Passage

In simplest terms, reality includes two basic realms – the upper world, and our existence in the physical dimension. The upper world is the source of our intuition and the force behind moments of mystical insight. When a dream comes true, for example, contact has been made with the upper worlds. When instinct impelled you to make an illogical decision that brought good fortune, this is another form of connection to the upper world. Unfortunately, these acute moments of insight and clarity are rare. We seem to have no control over how or when we make contact with the supernal realms. When we must make decisions and choices based on the evidence of our physical existence, the result is often turmoil and turbulence. The author of the Zohar understood this difficulty, and prescribed this portion as a remedy. A reading of this passage helps us utilize our sleep as a tool for spiritual enlightenment. The 'energy of Abraham' is summoned forth through these verses, strengthening our powers of judgment in matters that help or hinder the entrance of the Light into our world.

123. תָּא חֲזֵי, כַּמָּה אַתְרִין מְתוּקָנִין לֵיהּ לְקוּדְשָׁא בְּרִיךְ הוּא בְּהַהוּא עָלְמָא, וּבְכֻלְּהוּ בֵּי מוֹתָבֵי לוֹן לַצַּדִּיקִים. כָּל חַד וְחַד לְפוּם דַּרְגֵּיהּ כִּדְקָא חָזֵי לֵיהּ.

123. Come and behold: The Holy One, blessed be He, has several places in that world. In them all, there are apartments for the righteous, each

-76-

according to his deserved grade.

124. כְּתִיב אַשְׁרֵי תִּבְחַר וּתְקָרֵב יִשְׁכֹּן חֲצֵרֶיךָ, דְּקוּדְשָׁא בְּרִיךְ הוּא קָרֵיב לוֹן לְגַבֵּיהּ, דְּסַלְקִין אִינּוּן נִשְׁמָתִין מִתַּתָּא לְעֵילָּא, וּלְאִתְאַחֲדָא בְּאַחְסְנַתְּהוֹן, דְּאִתְתַּקָּן לְהוּ. יִשְׁכֹּן חֲצֵרֶיךָ, אִלֵּין אַתְרִין וְדַרְגִּין לְבַר, וּמַאן אִינּוּן, כְּדָבָר אַחֵר וְנָתַתִּי לְךָ מַהְלְכִים בֵּין הָעוֹמְדִים הָאֵלֶּה. וְהַאי הוּא, דַּרְגָּא בֵּין קַדִּישִׁין עִלָּאִין.

124. It is written, "Happy is the man whom You choose, and cause to approach You, that he may dwell in Your courts" (Tehilim 65:5). This verse refers to those whom the Holy One, blessed be He, causes to approach Him, as these are the souls that ascend to join the inheritance prepared for them. "That he may dwell in Your courts" alludes to the outer halls and the grades outside THE TEMPLE. To whom does it refer? The allusion here is as written: "Then I will give you free access among these who stand by..." (Zecharyah 3:7). This is a specific grade assigned among the celestial holy beings.

125. וּמַאן דְּזַכָּאִין לְדַרְגָּא דָּא, אִינּוּן שְׁלִיחָן דְּמָארֵי עַלְמָא, כְּאִינּוּן מַלְאָכִין, וְעָבְדִין שְׁלִיחוּתָא תָּדִיר בִּרְעוּתָא דְּמָארֵיהוֹן, בְּגִין דְּאִלֵּין תָּדִיר בִּקְדוּשָׁה וְלָא אִסְתָּאֲבוּ.

125. All those who merit this grade are the messengers of the Master of the universe like the angels, FOR THOSE WHO STAND BY ARE MESSENGERS. They always do the errands according to their Master's wish, for they are forever in holiness and are never defiled.

126. כְּגַוְונָא דָּא, מַאן דְּאִסְתְּאַב בְּהַאי עַלְמָא, אִיהוּ מָשִׁיךְ עֲלֵיהּ רוּחַ מְסָאַב, וְכַד נָפַק נִשְׁמָתֵיהּ מִנֵּיהּ, מְסָאֲבִין לֵיהּ, וּמְדוֹרֵיהּ בֵּין אִינּוּן מְסָאֲבִין, וְאִלֵּין אִינּוּן מַזִּיקִין דְּעָלְמָא. כְּמָה דְּאִתְמְשַׁךְ בַּר נָשׁ גַּרְמֵיהּ בְּהַאי עַלְמָא, הָכִי הוּא מְדוֹרֵיהּ, וְאִתְמְשַׁךְ בְּהַהוּא עַלְמָא, וְאִינּוּן רוּחֵי מְסָאֲבֵי מְסָאֲבִין לֵיהּ, וְאַעֲלִין לֵיהּ לַגֵּיהִנֹּם.

126. Similarly, whoever is defiled in this world draws the spirit of unholiness to himself. When his soul leaves him, he is defiled BY THE

OTHER SIDE, and his dwelling is with the unclean, with the fiends of the world. As a man draws upon himself in this world, his dwelling will likewise be determined IN THE ETERNAL WORLD. The defiled spirits defile him and bring him into Gehenom.

127. תָּא חֲזֵי מַאן דְּאִתְקַדַּשׁ, וְנָטֵיר גַּרְמֵיהּ בְּהַאי עַלְמָא, דְּלָא אִסְתָּאַב, מְדוֹרֵיהּ בְּהַהוּא עַלְמָא, בֵּין אִינּוּן קַדִּישִׁין עִלָּאִין, וְעַבְדִּין שְׁלִיחוּתָא תָּדִיר, וְאִלֵּין קַיְימֵי בַּחֲצֵר, כְּמָה דְּאַתְּ אָמֵר אֶת חֲצַר הַמִּשְׁכָּן.

127. Come and behold: Whoever sanctifies himself and is on guard against defilement in this world will find his dwelling in the next world among the celestial holy beings who eternally carry forth the missions OF THE HOLY ONE, BLESSED BE HE. They stand by in the court, as it is written: "The court of the tabernacle" (Shemot 27:9), UPON WHICH THE SCRIPTURES FURTHER STATE, "HAPPY IS HE…THAT HE MAY DWELL IN YOUR COURTS."

128. וְאִית אָחֳרָנִין, דְּאִינּוּן לְגוֹ יַתִּיר, דְּלָאו אִינּוּן בַּחֲצֵר, אֶלָּא בְּבֵיתָא, כד"א נִשְׂבְּעָה בְּטוּב בֵּיתֶךָ. אָמַר דָּוִד, נִשְׂבְּעָה בְּטוּב בֵּיתֶךָ, כֵּיוָן דְּאָמַר יִשְׁכֹּן חֲצֵרֶיךָ, אַמַּאי כְּתִיב נִשְׂבְּעָה בְּטוּב בֵּיתֶךָ, יִשְׂבַּע בְּטוּב בֵּיתֶךָ מִיבָּעֵי לֵיהּ, כְּמָה דִכְתִיב יִשְׁכֹּן. אֶלָּא הָא תָּנִינָן, לֵית יְשִׁיבָה בָּעֲזָרָה, אֶלָּא לְמַלְכֵי בֵּית דָּוִד בִּלְחוֹדַיְיהוּ.

128. Others are in a more inner place, not in the court but in the house, as it is written: "We will be satisfied with the goodness of Your house" (Tehilim 65:5). David said, "We will be satisfied with the goodness of Your house." HE ASKS, if he said "that he may dwell in Your courts," why is it written: "We will be satisfied with the goodness of Your house"? Should it not have been written: 'He will be satisfied', as "he may dwell"? But we learned that sitting in the Temple court is solely for the kings of the house of David. THEREFORE HE SAID, AS SPEAKING FOR HIMSELF, "WE WILL BE SATISFIED WITH THE GOODNESS OF YOUR HOUSE" MEANING HIMSELF AND THE OTHER KINGS, WHO HAVE A PLACE IN THE TEMPLE COURT IN THE SECRET OF THE HOUSE, NAMELY THE TEMPLE.

129. וְאִית אֲתָר לַחֲסִידֵי עֶלְיוֹנִין, דְּעַיְילֵי לְגוֹ, וּמַאי אִינּוּן, כִּדְכְתִיב

וְהַחוֹנִים לִפְנֵי הַמִּשְׁכָּן קֵדְמָה לִפְנֵי אֹהֶל מוֹעֵד מִזְרָחָה מֹשֶׁה וְאַהֲרֹן וּבָנָיו וְגוֹ'. וְכַמָּה מְדוֹרִין עַל מְדוֹרִין, וּנְהוֹרִין עַל נְהוֹרִין, מִתְפָּרְשָׁן בְּהַהוּא עַלְמָא, וְכָל חַד אַכְסִיף מִנְּהוֹרָא דְּחַבְרֵיהּ, כְּמָה דְעוֹבָדִין אִתְפָּרְשָׁן בְּהַאי עַלְמָא, הָכֵי נָמֵי, דּוּכְתִּין וּנְהוֹרִין, מִתְפָּרְשָׁן בְּהַהוּא עַלְמָא.

129. There is a place for the most pious who receive EVEN MORE inward, TO THE ASPECT OF THE TEMPLE. Who are they? They are "those that encamp before the tabernacle toward the east, before the Tent of Meeting eastward, shall be Moses and Aaron and his sons..." (Bemidbar 3:38). OF THEM, IT IS WRITTEN: "YOUR HOLY TEMPLE" (TEHILIM 65:5). Many compartments upon compartments, lights upon lights exist in that world, each different from the other, each feeling ashamed by its fellow's light. For as good deeds are different FROM EACH OTHER in this world, so the places FOR THE COMPARTMENTS and their lights are different in that world.

130. וְתָא חֲזֵי, הָא אִתְּמָר, דַּאֲפִילוּ בְּהַאי עַלְמָא, כַּד בַּר נָשׁ נָאִים עַל עַרְסֵיהּ, וְנִשְׁמָתִין אִצְטְרִיכוּ לְאִתְשׁוֹטְטָא בְּעַלְמָא, וְנָפְקוּ מִגּוֹ גוּפָא, לָאו כָּל נִשְׁמָתָא וְנִשְׁמָתָא, סַלְקָא וְשַׁטְיָא, לְמֶחֱזֵי בִּיקָר סֵבֶר אַפֵּי דְּעַתִּיק יוֹמִין, אֶלָּא כְּמָא דְּאִתְמַשִּׁיךְ תָּדִיר, וּכְפוּם עוֹבָדֵי, הָכֵי נִשְׁמָתֵיהּ סַלְקָא.

130. Come and behold: We have learned that even in this world when man is asleep in his bed and the soul comes out of his body to hover about the world, not every soul rises to see the glory of the face of Atik Yomin. His soul ascends as he generally draws upon himself, and according to his deeds.

131. אִי אִסְתָּאַב, אִיהוּ נָאִים וְנִשְׁמָתָא נָפְקָא, וְכָל אִינּוּן רוּחִין מְסָאֲבִין נָקְטִין לָהּ, וְאִתְדַּבְּקַת בְּהוֹ בְּאִינּוּן דַּרְגִּין תַּתָּאִין דְּשַׁטְיָין בְּעַלְמָא, וְאִינּוּן מוֹדִיעִין לָהּ מִלִּין דְּאִינּוּן קְרֵיבִין לְמֵיתֵי בְּעַלְמָא, וְלִזְמַנִין דְּמוֹדְעִין לָהּ, מִלִּין כְּדִיבָן, וְחָיְיכָן בָּהּ, וְהָא אוּקְמוּהָ.

131. When a defiled person sleeps, his soul leaves and the spirits of defilement seize it. It is attached to the lower grades that hover about the world and tell it things that will happen in the world in the future, THINGS THEY HEARD BEHIND THE CURTAIN. And sometimes they tell it false things and laugh at it, as has already been explained.

132. וְאִי זָכֵי בַּר נָשׁ, כַּד אִיהוּ נָאִים וְנִשְׁמָתֵיהּ סָלְקָא, אָזְלָא וְשָׁטְיָא, וּבָקְעָא בֵּין אִלֵּין רוּחִין מְסָאֲבִין, וְכֻלְּהוּ מַכְרִיזִין וְאָמְרִין פַּנּוּן אֲתַר, פַּנּוּן, לָאו דָּא מִסִּטְרָנָא, וְאִיהִי סָלְקָא בֵּין אִינוּן קַדִּישִׁין, וּמוֹדְעֵי לָהּ מִלָּה חֲדָא דִּקְשׁוֹט.

132. If the man has merit, then his soul ascends when he sleeps. It goes around and paves a way among the spirits of defilement. All say, Make way, make way, this one is not of our side. And it ascends among the saints, who tell accurate information to it.

133. וְכַד נָחֲתָא, כָּל אִינוּן חֲבִילִין טְרִיקִין, בָּעָאן לְאִתְקָרְבָא בַּהֲדָהּ, לְמִנְדַּע הַהִיא מִלָּה, וְאִינוּן מוֹדְעִין לָהּ, מִלִּין אָחֳרָנִין, וְהַהִיא מִלָּה דְּנָטְלָא גּוֹ אִינוּן קַדִּישִׁין, בֵּין אִינוּן אָחֳרָנִין, אִיהוּ כְּעִבּוּרָא גּוֹ תִּיבְנָא. וְהַאי אִיהוּ דְּזָכֵי יַתִּיר, בְּעוֹד דְּאִיהוּ קָאֵים, וְנִשְׁמָתָא קַיְימָא, בְּהַאי עָלְמָא.

133. And when the soul descends again, the mixed legions OF ANGELS, IN WHOM HOLINESS IS MINGLED WITH DEFILEMENT, want to approach the soul in order to learn the information it received. In return, they tell it other things. But what it learned from holy beings compares to what it learned from THE MIXED LEGIONS, as grain compares with straw and chaff. This is the most meritorious reward while one is still among the living – that is, while the soul is still in this world.

134. כְּגַוְונָא דָא כַּד נָפְקִין נִשְׁמָתִין מִגוּפָא מֵהַאי עָלְמָא, בָּעָאן לְסַלְּקָא, וְכַמָּה תַּרְעִין חֲבִילֵי טְהִירִין קַיְימֵי, אִי אִינוּן מִסִּטְרַיְיהוּ, כֻּלְּהוּ אָחֲדִין בְּהוּ, בְּאִינוּן נַפְשָׁאן, וּמָסְרֵי לוֹן בִּידָא דְּדוּמָה, לְאַעֲלָא לוֹן בַּגֵּיהִנֹּם.

134. Similarly, when souls in this world leave their bodies, NAMELY, AFTER THEY DIE, they wish to ascend by passing through gates at which one finds

harmful hordes that seize the souls of their own side and deliver them into the hands of Dumah, so that he may take them to Gehenom.

135. וּלְבָתַר סַלְקָן וְאָחֲדָן בְּהוֹ, וְאִינּוּן נָטְלֵי לְהוֹן, וּמַכְרְזֵי בְּהוֹ, אַלֵּין אִינּוּן דְּעָבְרוּ עַל פִּקּוּדֵי דְּמָארֵיהוֹן, וְכֵן שַׁטְיָין בְּכָל עָלְמָא. וּלְבָתַר מְהַדְרֵי לְהוֹ לַגֵּיהִנֹּם, וְכֵן עַד תְּרֵיסַר יַרְחֵי. לְבָתַר תְּרֵיסַר יַרְחֵי, מִשְׁתַּכְּכֵי, בְּהַהוּא אֲתַר דְּאִתְחֲזֵי לוֹן, אִינּוּן נִשְׁמָתִין דְּזָכוּ, סָלְקֵי לְעֵילָא, כְּמָה דְּאִתְּמָר, וְזַכָּאן בְּדוּכְתַּיְיהוּ.

135. Later, as they ascend from Gehenom, the demons grab the souls and proclaim, These transgressed the precepts of their Master. Then, they travel throughout the world, bringing these souls back to Gehenom. THUS, THEY REPEATEDLY TAKE THE SOULS OUT OF GEHENOM, MAKE THEIR PROCLAMATIONS, AND AGAIN RETURN THEM TO GEHENOM for twelve months. After twelve months appeased, they are quieted and rise to the place that they deserve. Meritorious souls ascend and receive their places, as has already been explained.

136. תָּא חֲזֵי, זַכָּאִין אִינּוּן צַדִּיקַיָּא, דְּאִתְגְּנֵיז לְהוֹ, כַּמָּה טָבִין לְהַהוּא עָלְמָא, וְלֵית אֲתַר פְּנִימָאָה בְּכָל אִינּוּן, כְּאִינּוּן דְּיָדְעֵי רָזָא דְּמָארֵיהוֹן, וְיָדְעֵי לְאִתְדַּבְּקָא בְּהוֹ, בְּכָל יוֹמָא עַל אַלֵּין כְּתִיב עַיִן לֹא רָאָתָה אֱלֹהִים זוּלָתְךָ יַעֲשֶׂה לִמְחַכֵּה לוֹ.

136. Come and behold: Happy are the righteous, for much goodness is put aside for them in that world. The innermost place is reserved for the righteous, those who know the secret of their Master and cleave to Him every day. Of these, it is written: "Neither has the eye seen, that an Elohim, beside you, should do such a thing for him that waits for Him" (Yeshayah 64:3).

137. מַאי לִמְחַכֵּה לוֹ, כִּדְבָר אַחַר חִכָּה אֶת אִיּוֹב בִּדְבָרִים. וְאַלֵּין אִינּוּן דִּדְחֲקִין לְמִלָּה דְּחָכְמְתָא, וְדָיְיקִין לָהּ, וּמְחַכָּאן לָהּ, לְמִנְדַּע בְּרִירָא דְּמִלָּה, וְאִשְׁתְּמוֹדְעָא לְמָארֵיהוֹן, אַלֵּין אִינּוּן דְּמָארֵיהוֹן מִשְׁתַּבַּח בְּהוֹן בְּכָל יוֹמָא, אַלֵּין אִינּוּן, דְּעָאלִין בֵּין עָלָּאִין קַדִּישִׁין, וְאַלֵּין עָאלִין כָּל

תַּרְעֵי דִלְעֵילָא, וְלֵית מָאן דְּיִמְחֵי בִּידֵיהוֹן, זַכָּאָה חוּלָקֵיהוֹן בְּעָלְמָא דֵין, וּבְעָלְמָא דְּאָתֵי.

137. HE ASKS, What is meant by: "For him that waits for Him?" He replies that it is similar to the verse: "waited to speak to Job" (Iyov 32:4). This refers to those who are anxious TO FULLY UNDERSTAND some words of wisdom, thereby better understanding their Master. In them, the Master takes pride daily. They enter the upper gates and come among the supernal saints without meeting any obstacles. Happy is their portion in this world and the World to Come.

138. תָּא חֲזֵי, אַבְרָהָם עָאל לְמִנְדַּע וּלְאִתְדַּבְּקָא בְּמָארֵיהּ כְּדְקָא יָאוֹת, לְבָתַר דְּאַקְדִּים עוֹבָדוֹי בְּקַדְמֵיתָא, וְזָכָה בְּאִינוּן יוֹמִין עִלָּאִין, וְאִתְבָּרַךְ מֵאֲתַר דְּכָל בִּרְכָאן נָפְקֵי מִתַּמָּן, דִּכְתִיב וַה' בֵּרַךְ אֶת אַבְרָהָם בַּכֹּל. מַאי בַּכֹּל. אֲתַר דְּנַהֲרָא, דְּלָא פָּסְקֵי מֵימוֹי לְעָלְמִין.

138. Come and behold: Abraham thus entered to properly know and cleave to his Master. First he performed good deeds to merit the supernal days, and was therefore blessed by the place from where all the blessings derive, as it is written: "And Hashem had blessed Abraham in all" (Beresheet 42:1). What is the meaning of "in all"? It means the dwelling place of the river, in which water never stops flowing, NAMELY YESOD OF THE SUPERNAL ABA AND IMA, WHOSE UNION IS ETERNAL.

139. אָמַר רְבִּי חִיָּיא, תָּא חֲזֵי, דְּאַבְרָהָם לָא בָּעָא לְאִתְעָרְבָא בְּנָשֵׁי עָלְמָא, וּלְאִתְדַּבְּקָא בִּשְׁאָר עַמִּין עכו"ם, בְּגִין דִּנְשַׁיָּיא דִּשְׁאָר עַמִּין עכו"ם, אִינוּן סָאֲבִין, לְגוּבְרַיְיהוּ, וּלְאִינוּן דְּמִתְדַּבְּקִין בְּהוֹן, בְּגִין דְּכַד אַבְרָהָם יָדַע חָכְמְתָא, יָדַע עִקָּרָא וְשָׁרְשָׁא, וּמְאָן אֲתַר נָפְקֵי וְשַׁטְיָין רוּחֵי מְסָאֲבִין בְּעָלְמָא, וְעַל דָּא אוֹמֵי לְעַבְדֵּיהּ, דְּלָא יִסַּב אִתְּתָא לִבְרֵיהּ, מִשְּׁאָר עַמִּין.

139. Rabbi Chiya said, Come and behold that Abraham did not want to mix with the women of the world and cling to the heathen nations because the wives of the heathen nations defiled their husbands and those attached to them. Because Abraham had the knowledge of wisdom, he knew the essence and root of the place from which the unholy spirits come out to hover in the world. Therefore, he made his servant swear not to take a wife for his son from among the other nations.

19. Eden drips upon the garden

A synopsis

The rabbis display their profound and comprehensive knowledge of the scriptures and writings, in a complex discussion of an image in Ezekiel, "Behold one wheel upon the earth…" While replete with the arcane wisdom of gematria (numerology) and Kabbalah, and the profound mystical beauty of Solomon's great 'Song', this debate has a surprisingly straightforward resolution – one that echoes previous sections of the Zohar in its emphasis on the importance of a pure heart and good deeds in this world for bringing mercy and peace in the next. Rabbi Yitzchak concludes with a simple exposition of the reason for mentions of Abraham's age. Abraham, literally, "came into the days"; his soul had reached its high-allotted place, where its great longevity was assured.

The Relevance of this Passage

The Talmud reveals the difference between man and beast. A wild animal, according to Talmudic sages, instinctively knows to flee the raging fire. Man's nature, on the other hand, compels him to jump head first into the fiery blaze. Our natural tendency is to invite chaos and mayhem into our lives. We complicate and intellectualize life and its challenges, and we rationalize our responses to them. We refuse to heed the simple principles that create happiness – good deeds and persistent spiritual development. In reading this passage, we clear away the barriers to knowledge, and recognize that even the most complex mysteries arise from the same simple and eternal issues. Indeed, complexity itself is merely another excuse to avoid the quest to draw down Light. This excuse must be overcome like any other.

מִדְרָשׁ הַנֶּעֱלָם

140. וְאַבְרָהָם זָקֵן בָּא בַּיָּמִים וְגו'. אָמַר רַבִּי אֶלְעָזָר, עַל כָּל פָּנִים כָּךְ הוּא, דְּהָאי מַתְנִיתִין שַׁפִּיר, דְּאִתְעֲבֵיד נִשְׁמָתָא, הַהוּא דִּכְתִיב בֵּיהּ, וְהִנֵּה אוֹפַן אֶחָד בָּאָרֶץ אֵצֶל הַחַיּוֹת לְאַרְבַּעַת פָּנָיו, כִּדְאָמוּר בְּהַהִיא מַתְנִיתָא קַמַּיְיתָא.

Midrash Hane'elam (Homiletical interpretations on the obscure)

140. "And Abraham was old, advanced in age" (Beresheet 24:1). We

-84-

learned in the Mishnah: Rabbi Elazar said, In any case, this Mishnah well EXPLAINS THE VERSE: "Behold one ofan (wheel) upon the earth by the living creatures, with its four faces" (Yechezkel 1:15). It becomes a Neshamah as said in the earlier Mishnah. THUS, ALTHOUGH OFAN (WHEEL) IS ALWAYS A NAME OF THE NEFESH, THE MISHNAH STATES THAT THE OFAN IN THIS VERSE BECAME A NESHAMAH AGAIN. THERE IS NO QUESTION ABOUT THIS FACT, AND THE EXPLANATION IS ACCURATE, BUT THE MISHNAH DOES NOT EXPLAIN WHY.

141. אֲמַר לֵיה רִבִּי אַבָּא, לֵימָא לָן מַר, מֵהַהִיא מַתְנִיתִין, אֲמַר לֵיה, הָכִי אִתְפְּרַשׁ, בִּתְלַת עֶשֶׂר מְכִילָן דְּרַחֲמֵי, בְּפָרְשָׁתָא דִילֵיהּ, אֲבָל הָכָא אִית לָן לְמֵימַר, פָּתַח וַאֲמַר, אַחַת הִיא יוֹנָתִי תַמָּתִי אַחַת הִיא לְאִמָּהּ וְגו'. אָמַר רִבִּי אֶלְעָזָר, מַאי הִיא, דַּאֲנַן קָרֵינָן הָכָא, בְּשִׁיר הַשִּׁירִים, לִישָׁנָא דְנוּקְבְתָא, וְהָתָם בְּאוֹרַיְיתָא, לִישָׁנָא דִּדְכוּרָא.

141. Rabbi Aba responded, Tell us, sir, about this Mishnah. What is it? He replied: THE HIDDEN MEANING OF THE VERSE, "BEHOLD ONE WHEEL UPON THE EARTH," AS EXPLAINED IN THE MISHNAH, IS THAT THE OFAN BECOMES A NESHAMAH. This was also explained in another section – the one about the thirteen divine attributes of mercy. But here we have to explain THIS PORTION. He began with the verse: "My dove, my undefiled is but one; she is the only one of her mother" (Shir Hashirim 6:9), FOR THIS VERSE ALLUDES TO THE NESHAMAH. Rabbi Elazar asks, Why do we refer to it here in Shir Hashirim as a female, NAMELY "MY DOVE, SHE...IS BUT ONE", but in the Torah we refer to it as male, NAMELY ABRAHAM?

142. אֶלָּא אָמַר רִבִּי אֶלְעָזָר, הָכָא בַּתּוֹרָה, נִקְרָא בִּלְשׁוֹן זָכָר, אֵצֶל הַגּוּף, מִפְּנֵי שֶׁהַגּוּף, אֵצֶל הַנְּשָׁמָה, כְּאִשָּׁה אֵצֶל הַזָּכָר, וְהַנְּשָׁמָה לְגַבֵּי מַעְלָה, כִּנְקֵבָה בִּפְנֵי הַזָּכָר, וְכָל אֶחָד מַעֲלָתוֹ יוֹרֵשׁ.

142. Rabbi Elazar said, In Torah, THE SOUL is male in relation to the body because the body to the soul is like a woman to a man. In relation to a higher grade, the soul is as a female to a male. Each receives its grade according to the context. THEREFORE, IN THE SONG OF SONGS, WHEN THE KING THAT PEACE IS HIS TALKS OF THE SOUL, BEING OF A HIGHER GRADE, IT IS THEREFORE CONSIDERED AS A FEMALE AND CALLED, "MY

DOVE, MY UNDEFILED...” BUT IN TORAH, THE SOUL IS IN ITSELF AND IS
THEREFORE REFERRED TO AS A MALE, NAMELY ABRAHAM.

143. תְּנַן הָתָם, בְּאַרְבָּעָה פְּעָמִים בְּשָׁעָה, בְּכָל יוֹם, עֵדֶן מְנַטֵּף עַל הַגָּן,
וְיוֹצֵא מֵאוֹתָם הַטִּפּוֹת נָהָר גָּדוֹל, הַמִּתְחַלֵּק לְאַרְבָּעָה רָאשִׁים, וּשְׁמֹנֶה
וְאַרְבָּעִים טִפּוֹת, מְנַטֵּף בְּכָל יוֹם, וּמִשָּׁם שִׁבְעִים אִילָנֵי הַגָּן, הַהָ"ד
יִשְׂבְּעוּ עֲצֵי ה'. ר' תַּנְחוּם אָמַר מֵהָכָא, מַשְׁקֶה הָרִים מֵעֲלִיּוֹתָיו, אֵיזוֹ
הִיא עֲלִיָּה, זֶהוּ עֵדֶן. וְעֵדֶן בְּאֵיזֶה מָקוֹם הוּא. ר' יְהוּדָה אָמַר, לְמַעְלָה
מֵעֲרָבוֹת הוּא. ר' יוֹסֵי אָמַר בַּעֲרָבוֹת הוּא, דְּהָא תְּנַן, שָׁם גִּנְזֵי חַיִּים
טוֹבִים בְּרָכָה וְשָׁלוֹם, וְנִשְׁמָתָן שֶׁל צַדִּיקִים, הוּא הָעֶלְיוֹן. עֵדֶן לְמַטָּה,
מְכֻוָּן כְּנֶגְדּוֹ גַּן בָּאָרֶץ, וְנוֹטֵל מִמֶּנּוּ שֶׁפַע בְּכָל יוֹם.

143. It was taught in the Mishnah that four times an hour every day, Eden
drips upon the garden. The result of these drops is a river which separates
into four branches. Each day, 48 drops fall on the seventy trees in the
garden, as it is written: “The trees of Hashem have their fill” (Tehilim
104:15). Rabbi Tanchum said, It is written: “He waters the hills from His
upper chambers” (Ibid. 13). What is his upper chamber? It is Eden. And
where is Eden? Rabbi Yehuda said, It is above Aravot (sweet firmament).
Rabbi Yosi said that it is in Aravot, where are treasures of good life,
blessing and peace, and the souls of the righteous, as was taught. This is the
upper chamber, while the Garden of Eden is lower, and an earthly garden is
in apposition and draws from it daily.

144. אָמַר רָבִּי אַבָּהוּ, שְׁמֹנָה וְאַרְבָּעִים נְבִיאִים, עָמְדוּ לָהֶם לְיִשְׂרָאֵל,
וְכָל אֶחָד נָטַל בְּחֶלְקוֹ, תַּמְצִית טִפָּה אַחַת מֵאוֹתָם טִפּוֹת שֶׁל עֵדֶן, שֶׁהֵם
שְׁמֹנָה וְאַרְבָּעִים טִפּוֹת. וּמָה אִם כָּל נָבִיא, שֶׁנָּטַל טִפָּה אַחַת מֵהֶן, הָיְתָה
מַעֲלָתוֹ בְּרוּחַ הַקֹּדֶשׁ, עַל כָּל הַשְּׁאָר, אָדָם הָרִאשׁוֹן, שֶׁהָיָה מְקַבֵּל
מִשְּׁמֹנָה וְאַרְבָּעִים לֹא כָּל שֶׁכֵּן, מִכָּאן אַתָּה לָמֵד, כַּמָּה הָיְתָה חָכְמָתוֹ.

144. Rabbi Abahu said that 48 prophets stood for Yisrael. Each one took his
share, which was the essence of one drop from the drops of Eden. If every
prophet who took one drop had the grade of the holy spirit, this was more
true for Adam, who received the 48 drops. From this, you learn the scope of
his wisdom.

145. רְבִּי בָּא אָמַר רַב כַּהֲנָא, וְכִי מֵאַיִן הָיָה לָהֶם לַנְּבִיאִים, מֵאוֹתָם הַטִּפּוֹת, אֶלָּא הָכֵי תְּנַן, בְּכָל טִפָּה וְטִפָּה, הַיּוֹצֵאת מֵעֵדֶן, רוּחַ חָכְמָה יוֹצֵא עִמּוֹ, וְעַל כֵּן אִתְגְּזַר בְּמַתְנִיתִין, אִית מַיָּא מְגַדְּלָן חַכִּימִין, וְאִית מַיָּא מְגַדְּלָן טִפְּשִׁין, וְאִינוּן מַיָּא דִּמְגַדְּלָן חַכִּימִין, אִינוּן מַיָּא, הֲווֹ מִטְּפִין דְּעֵדֶן.

145. Rabbi Bo said that Rabbi Kahana asks, Where did the prophets get these drops? We learned each drop that comes out of Eden includes the spirit of wisdom. Therefore, it was decreed that there is water that raises wise men and water that raises fools. This water that drops from Eden raises wise ones.

146. דְּאָמַר רָבִּי יוֹסֵי, מַיָּא דְּבֵיהּ טִפִּין יַתְבִין, מִכָּל אִינוּן אַרְבַּע נַהֲרֵי, קַדְמָאָה הוּא, דִּכְתִיב שֵׁם הָאֶחָד פִּישׁוֹן. מַאי שֵׁם הָאֶחָד פִּישׁוֹן. הַמְיוּחָד מִכּוּלָם פִּישׁוֹן, וְהוּא הַנּוֹפֵל בְּאֶרֶץ מִצְרַיִם, וּלְפִיכָךְ, הָיְתָה חָכְמַת מִצְרַיִם יוֹתֵר מִכָּל הָעוֹלָם.

146. Rabbi Yosi said, So the water containing the drops comes from the most ancient of four rivers, as it is written: "The name of the first is Pishon" (Beresheet 2:11). Why is it written: "the name of the first is Pishon?" Pishon is different from the rest because it flows into the land of Egypt. Therefore, the wisdom of Egypt is greater than that of the rest of the world.

147. וּמִשֶּׁנִּגְזְרָה גְּזֵרָה, שֶׁאָבְדָה חָכְמַת מִצְרַיִם, נָטַל קוּדְשָׁא בְּרִיךְ הוּא, אוֹתָם טִפִּין וְזָרַק לוֹן בְּהַהוּא גַּנָּא, בְּהַהוּא נַהֲרָא דְּגִנְתָא דְּעֵדֶן, דִּכְתִיב, וְנָהָר יוֹצֵא מֵעֵדֶן לְהַשְׁקוֹת אֶת הַגָּן. וְזֶה הָיָה מוֹלִיד אַרְבָּעָה אֲחֵרִים, וְהָאֶחָד הַמְיוּחָד, הַנּוֹלַד מִמֶּנּוּ, פִּישׁוֹן הָיָה. מִשֶּׁנִּטְלוּ אֵלּוּ הַטִּפּוֹת שֶׁלֹּא יָצְאוּ מֵהַגָּן, אָבְדָה הַחַכְמָה מִמִּצְרַיִם.

147. When it was decreed that the wisdom of Egypt was lost, the Holy One, blessed be He, took the drops and threw them across the garden into the river of the Garden of Eden, as it is written: "And a river went out of Eden to water the garden" (Beresheet 2:10). AND WHEN THE DROPS, WHICH

REMAIN IN THE GARDEN, WERE TAKEN FROM EGYPT, WISDOM WAS
GONE FROM EGYPT. It separated into four other rivers, of which the most
special was Pishon. Wisdom was thus lost in Egypt when the drops were
taken from Egypt and left in the garden.

148. וּמֵאוֹתוֹ הָרוּחַ שֶׁהָיָה יוֹצֵא מֵעֵדֶן, הִמְצוּ כָּל נָבִיא וְנָבִיא, וְהַיְינוּ
דִּכְתִיב, מִתְהַלֵּךְ בַּגָּן לְרוּחַ הַיּוֹם. וְגָנוּז זֶה בַּגַּן עֵדֶן, לֶעָתִיד לָבוֹא, וְזֶה
הוּא הַנָּהָר, שֶׁרָאָה יְחֶזְקֵאל בִּנְבוּאָתוֹ. וְעַל כֵּן אָמַר הַכָּתוּב כִּי מָלְאָה
הָאָרֶץ דֵּעָה אֶת ה' וגו'. שֶׁאוֹתָם מַיִם, תָּמִיד מְגַדְּלִים הַיְדִיעָה בָּעוֹלָם.

148. Every prophet was sucking from that spirit that came out of Eden. This
is the meaning of "walking in the garden in the breeze of the day"
(Beresheet 3:8). It is stored in the Garden of Eden for the future. This is the
river that Ezekiel saw in his prophecy. Therefore the scripture reads, "For
the earth shall be full of the knowledge of Hashem" (Yeshayah 11:9), as this
water always causes the knowledge in the world to increase.

149. ת"ר, כָּל נִשְׁמָתָן שֶׁל צַדִּיקִים, לְמַעְלָה בְּעֵדֶן הֵן, וּמַה מִּמַּה
שֶׁיּוֹרֵד מֵעֵדֶן, יִשְׂגֵּא הַחָכְמָה בָּעוֹלָם, לָעוֹמְדִים בּוֹ, וְנֶהֱנִין מֵהֲנָאוֹתָיו
וְכִסּוּפָיו, עַל אַחַת כַּמָּה וְכַמָּה.

149. The sages said that the souls of all the righteous are above in Eden, and
wisdom is strengthened in the world because of what descends from Eden.
How much more so for every one of those who stand in it and take their fill
of its pleasure and brightness.

150. אָמַר רַבִּי יִצְחָק כֵּיוָן שֶׁהַנְּשָׁמָה זוֹכָה, לִיכָּנֵס בְּשַׁעֲרֵי יְרוּשָׁלַיִם שֶׁל
מַעְלָה, מִיכָאֵ"ל הַשַּׂר הַגָּדוֹל, הוֹלֵךְ עִמָּה, וּמַקְדִּים לָהּ שָׁלוֹם. מַלְאֲכֵי
הַשָּׁרֵת, תְּמֵהִים בּוֹ, וְשׁוֹאֲלִים עָלֶיהָ, מִי זֹאת עוֹלָה מִן הַמִּדְבָּר. מִי
זֹאת, עוֹלָה בֵּין הָעֶלְיוֹנִים, מֵהַגּוּף הֶחָרֵב, שֶׁדּוֹמֶה לְהֶבֶל, דִּכְתִיב אָדָם
לַהֶבֶל דָּמָה. הוּא מֵשִׁיב וְאוֹמֵר, אַחַת הִיא יוֹנָתִי תַמָּתִי, אַחַת הִיא,
מְיוּחֶדֶת הִיא. אַחַת הִיא לְאִמָּהּ וגו', לְאִמָּהּ. זוֹ הִיא כִּסֵּא הַכָּבוֹד,
שֶׁהִיא אֵם לַנְּשָׁמָה, וִיוֹלֶדֶת לָהּ, שֶׁנִּגְזְרָה מִמֶּנָּה.

150. Rabbi Yitzchak said, If the soul deserves to pass through the gates of the terrestrial Jerusalem, the great angel Michael hastens to greet and walk with it. The ministering angels wonder about this and ask, "Who is that, coming up from the wilderness" (Shir Hashirim 8:5). Who rises to be among the high ones from the destroyed body, which resembles a breath, as is written: "Man is like a breath" (Tehilim 144:4)? He answers by saying, "My dove, my undefiled is but one; she is distinguished she is the only one of her mother" (Shir Hashirim 6:9). Her mother is the Throne of Glory, a mother for the soul that gives it birth, for the soul is derived from her.

151. רָאוּהָ בָנוֹת וַיְאַשְּׁרוּהָ, אֵלּוּ שְׁאָר הַנְּשָׁמוֹת, שֶׁהֵן בְּמַעֲלָתָן לְמַעֲלָה, וְהֵם הַנִּקְרָאוֹת בְּנוֹת יְרוּשָׁלַיִם. אָמַר רַבִּי יוֹסֵי, הָא חֲזַרְנָא עַל מַה דַּאֲמָרָן, אֵלּוּ נִקְרָאוֹת בְּנוֹת יְרוּשָׁלַיִם, וְהָאֲחֵרוֹת נִקְרָאוֹת בְּנוֹת לוֹט. רָאוּהָ בָנוֹת וַיְאַשְּׁרוּהָ, שְׁאָר הַנְּשָׁמוֹת, מְשַׁבְּחוֹת לָהּ, וְאוֹמְרוֹת שָׁלוֹם בּוֹאֵךְ. מְלָכוֹת וּפִלַגְשִׁים וַיְהַלְלוּהָ מְלָכוֹת אֵלּוּ הָאָבוֹת, שֶׁהֵם מְלָכוֹת. וּפִלַגְשִׁים: הֵן גֵּירֵי הַצֶּדֶק, כּוּלָּם מְשַׁבְּחוֹת, וּמְקַלְּסוֹת אוֹתָהּ, עַד שֶׁנִּכְנֶסֶת לְמַעֲלָה, וַאֲזַי הַנְּשָׁמָה בְּמַעֲלָתָהּ, וּמִתְקַיְּימָא אֲרִיכוּת הַיָּמִים, הה"ד, וְאַבְרָהָם זָקֵן בָּא בַּיָּמִים. נִכְנַס בַּאֲרִיכוּת הַיָּמִים, לְעוֹה"ב.

151. "The daughters saw her, and called her happy" (Ibid.). This refers to the other souls, whose rank is high and who are called the daughters of Jerusalem. According to Rabbi Yosi, they are called the daughters of Jerusalem while the other ones are called the daughters of Lot. "The daughters saw her, the rest of the souls praise it and say to it, Come in peace. "The queens and the concubines praised her" (Ibid.). The queens are the Patriarchs that are queens. The concubines are the proselytes. They all praise and laud it until it enters above. Then the soul is in its ascended place, and longevity is maintained, as it is written: "And Abraham was old, advanced in age (lit. 'coming into the days')" (Beresheet 24:1), as he entered longevity in the World to Come.

20. About the resurrection of the dead

A synopsis

In this long and complex section, the rabbis first discuss the nature of souls at the time of the Resurrection. They then examine Torah verses concerning difficult questions on the amount of Light souls will merit from the Throne of the Holy One, based upon the souls' deeds and the role of angels in the body's resurrection. We then hear an account of Rabbi Eliezer's visit to his rabbi, Yochanan ben Zakai, on the day of the new moon. They discuss the 'Secret of Ten' – ten dimensions composing reality – through which the primordial Light functions in this world. We learn that the Light of the soul is greater than the Light of angels. The friends then continue their study of Torah, uncovering hidden meanings in phrases concerning the relationship between soul and body in the story of Abraham.

The Relevance of this Passage

The Light derived from the letters and lessons of this portion hastens the coming of the Resurrection in a merciful manner. The resolve to perform good deeds is also kindled in our hearts, enabling us to overcome the seductive lure of physical impulse, serve the true needs our souls, and merit a share in the World to Come.

152. רַבִּי אַבָּא סָבָא, קָם עַל רַגְלוֹי, וַאֲמַר, מְנוּחָה וְשָׁלוֹם גְּרְמִין יְהֵא לָךְ רַבִּי שִׁמְעוֹן בֶּן יוֹחָאי, דְּהַחְזָרַת עֲטָרָה לְיוֹשְׁנָהּ. דְּתָנִינָן בְּמַתְנִיתָא קַדְמָאָה, דְּכֵיוָן שֶׁהַנְּשָׁמָה הִיא בְּתַשְׁלוּמָהּ, בַּאֲתָר עִלָּאָה, לָא תָבָאת לְגוּפָא אֶלָּא אִתְבְּרִיאָן מִנָּהּ, נִשְׁמֵי אָחֲרָנִין, דְּנָפְקֵי מִנָּהּ, וְאִיהִי אִשְׁתְּאָרַת בְּקִיּוּמָא, עַד דְּאָתָא רַבִּי שִׁמְעוֹן בֶּן יוֹחָאי וְדָרַשׁ, וּמַה אִם בָּעוֹלָם הַזֶּה, שֶׁהוּא הֶבֶל, וְהַגּוּף שֶׁהוּא טִפָּה סְרוּחָה, נִכְנֶסֶת בּוֹ, אוֹתָהּ הַנְּשָׁמָה. לֶעָתִיד לָבֹא, שֶׁיִּצָּרְפוּ כֻּלָּם, וְיִהְיֶה הַגּוּף מוּבְחָר, בְּקִיּוּם וְתַשְׁלוּם יוֹתֵר, אֵינוּ דִין לְהִכָּנֵס אוֹתָהּ הַנְּשָׁמָה בּוֹ, בְּכָל הַתַּשְׁלוּמִין, וְהָעִלּוּיִין שֶׁבָּהּ.

152. Rabbi Aba Saba (the elder) stood up and said, May peace and tranquillity come to you, Rabbi Shimon, the son of Yochai, for restoring the diadem to its former splendor. For we learned in the first Mishnah that since

the soul is perfected in the supernal place, it does not return to the body. It remains in the same condition, but other souls are created and come out of it. Then Rabbi Shimon, the son of Yochai, taught that although this world is vanity and the body is a putrid drop of semen, yet the soul enters it. In the future, when everyone will be refined and the body will be more pure, sustained and complete, there will be no reason for the soul to enter it with all its completeness.

153. אָמַר רַבִּי אֲחָא, אוֹתָהּ הַנְּשָׁמָה מַמָּשׁ, וְאוֹתוֹ הַגּוּף מַמָּשׁ, עָתִיד הַקּוּדְשָׁא בְּרִיךְ הוּא, לְהַעֲמִידָן בְּקִיּוּמָן לֶעָתִיד לָבֹא, אֲבָל שְׁנֵיהֶם יִהְיוּ שְׁלֵמִים, בְּתַשְׁלוּם הַדַּעַת, לְהַשִּׂיג מַה שֶּׁלֹּא הִשִּׂיגוּ בָּעוֹלָם הַזֶּה.

153. Rabbi Acha said, The Holy One, blessed be He, will give the very soul and very body existence in the future, but both will be whole and have completeness of knowledge so they can achieve what they did not achieve in this world.

154. וְאַבְרָהָם זָקֵן בָּא בַּיָּמִים וְגו'. ר' בּוֹ אָמַר רָבִּי יוֹחָנָן, בְּאוֹתוֹ הָעוֹלָם: שֶׁהוּא יָמִים, וְלֹא בָּעוֹלָם הַזֶּה, שֶׁהוּא לַיְלָה. אָמַר ר' יַעֲקֹב, בְּאוֹתָם הָעוֹלָמוֹת, שֶׁהֵם יָמִים, בְּאוֹתָם הַהֲנָאוֹת וְהַכְּסוּפִין, שֶׁהוּא נוֹחֵל. וַה' בֵּרַךְ אֶת אַבְרָהָם בַּכֹּל. בְּאוֹתוֹ הַמִּשְׂרָה שֶׁנָּתַן לוֹ הַקּוּדְשָׁא בְּרִיךְ הוּא מִשְּׁמוֹ, שֶׁהִיא אוֹת ה"א שֶׁבּוֹ נִבְרָא הָעוֹלָם.

154. "And Abraham was old, advanced in age (lit. 'coming with the days')." Rabbi Bo said that, according to Rabbi Yochanan, this refers to the world of days, NAMELY LIGHT, and not to that world which is night. Rabbi Ya'akov said, COMING WITH THE DAYS MEANS THAT HE CAME TO those worlds called days because of all the pleasures and the brightness that he inherits. RABBI YA'AKOV IS NOT DIFFERING FROM RABBI YOCHANAN, HE IS SIMPLY EXPLAINING THE VERSE MORE FULLY. "And Hashem had blessed Abraham in all" (Beresheet 24:1) refers to the office, NAMELY TO THE AUTHORITY that the Holy One, blessed be He, gave him of His name, which is the letter Hei by which the world was created.

155. וְתַנְיָא, אָמַר ר' יוֹחָנָן, מַטַּטְרוֹן שַׂר הַפָּנִים, שֶׁהוּא נַעַר, עֶבֶד מֵרַבּוֹ, הָאָדוֹן הַמּוֹשֵׁל עָלָיו, מְמוּנֶּה עַל הַנְּשָׁמָה, בְּכָל יוֹם, לְהַסְפִּיק

לָהּ, מֵאוֹתוֹ הָאוֹר שֶׁנִּצְטַוָּה, וְהוּא עָתִיד לְמֵיסַב, חוּשְׁבַּן פִּתְקָא, בְּבָתֵּי קִבְרֵי, מִן דּוּמָה, וּלְאַחֲזָאָה לֵיהּ קַמֵּי מָארֵיהּ, וְהוּא זַמִּין, לְמֶעְבַּד חָמִיר, הַהוּא גַּרְמָא, תְּחוֹת אַרְעָא, לְתַקָּנָא לְגוּפַיָּיא, וּלְקַיְימָא לוֹן בִּשְׁלֵימוּתָא דְגוּפָא, בְּלָא נִשְׁמָתָא, דְּקוּדְשָׁא בְּרִיךְ הוּא יְשַׁדַּר לָהּ לְאַתְרָהּ.

155. We learned that Rabbi Yochanan said, Metatron, the great minister, is a boy, a servant whose Rabbi, his master, rules him. He is in charge of the soul and gives it daily of the light he was ordered TO GIVE IT. In the future, he will receive an account in writing from the cemetery, from Dumah FOR EACH BODY that he can show to his Master. He will turn that backbone into yeast TO BUILD THE BODY under the ground, to mend and wholly revive the body, AS IS PROPER FOR a body without a soul. Later, the Holy One, blessed be He, will send the soul to its place WITHIN THE BODY. THIS WILL BE AFTER IT COMES TO THE LAND OF YISRAEL.

156. אָמַר ר' יִצְחָק, בְּאוֹתָהּ שָׁעָה, מַה כְּתִיב, וַיֹּאמֶר אַבְרָהָם אֶל עַבְדּוֹ זְקַן בֵּיתוֹ הַמּוֹשֵׁל וְגו'. מַהוּ אֶל עַבְדּוֹ, אִי בְּחָכְמְתָא דָא נִסְתַּכֵּל, מַהוּ אֶל עַבְדּוֹ, אָמַר רַבִּי נְהוֹרַאי, לֹא נִסְתַּכֵּל, אֶלָּא בַּמֶּה שֶׁאָמַר עַבְדּוֹ, עַבְדּוֹ שֶׁל מָקוֹם. הַקָּרוֹב לַעֲבוֹדָתוֹ, וּמַאן אִיהוּ, זֶה מטטרון, כִּדְקָאָמְרָן, דְּאִיהוּ עָתִיד לְיַפּוֹת לַגּוּף בְּבָתֵּי קִבְרֵי.

156. Rabbi Yitzchak said, it is then written, "And Abraham said to the eldest servant of his house, that ruled..." (Beresheet 24:2). If we look at this from the aspect of wisdom, NAMELY AS IT CONCERNS THE RESURRECTION OF THE DEAD, what is THE MEANING OF THE WORDS, "his servant"? BECAUSE ABRAHAM IS THE SECRET OF THE SOUL "AND ABRAHAM SAID TO THE...SERVANT" REFERS TO THE SERVANT OF THE SOUL. HOW DO WE KNOW THAT THERE IS A SERVANT TO THE SOUL? Rabbi Nehorai responded, We need look only at the words "his servant" AND NOT CONNECT THEM TO ABRAHAM IN THE MEANING OF THE VERSE. THEN, THE MEANING IS the servant of Hashem, close to His worship. Who is he? He is Metatron, who will beatify the body in the grave, as we have said.

157. הֲדָא הוּא דִכְתִיב, וַיֹּאמֶר אַבְרָהָם אֶל עַבְדּוֹ, זֶה מטטרון, עַבְדּוֹ

CHAYEI SARAH

שֶׁל מָקוֹם. זָקֵן בֵּיתוֹ, שֶׁהוּא תְּחִלַּת בְּרִיּוֹתָיו, שֶׁל מָקוֹם. הַמּוֹשֵׁל בְּכָל אֲשֶׁר לוֹ, שֶׁנָּתַן לוֹ קוּדְשָׁא בְּרִיךְ הוּא, מֶמְשָׁלָה, עַל כָּל צִבְאוֹתָיו.

157. Thus the words, "And Abraham said to his eldest servant" refer to Metatron, the servant of Hashem. The phrase: "The eldest servant of his house" is the beginning of the creations of Hashem. "That ruled over all that he had" means that the Holy One, blessed be He, gave him power over all His hosts, NAMELY OVER THE UPPER ANGELS.

158. וְתָאנָא, אָמַר רָבִּי שִׁמְעוֹן אָמַר רָבִּי יוֹסֵי אָמַר רַב, כָּל צִבְאוֹתָיו שֶׁל אוֹתוֹ עֶבֶד, נוֹטְלִים אוֹר, וְנֶהֱנִין מִזִּיו הַנְּשָׁמָה, דְּתָאנָא אוֹר הַנְּשָׁמָה, לעה"ב, גָּדוֹל מֵאוֹר הַכִּסֵּא. וְהָא מֵהַכִּסֵּא נִטְלָה הַנְּשָׁמָה. אֶלָּא זֶה לְפִי הָרָאוּי לוֹ, וְזֶה לְפִי הָרָאוּי לוֹ. רַב נַחְמָן אָמַר גָּדוֹל מֵאוֹר הַכִּסֵּא מַמָּשׁ, דִּכְתִיב, דְּמוּת כְּמַרְאֵה אָדָם עָלָיו מִלְמַעְלָה מַאי עָלָיו עַל זָהֲרוֹ.

158. We learned that Rabbi Shimon quoted Rabbi Yosi who quoted Rav saying that all the hosts of the servant receive light and delight in the splendor of the soul, as the light of the soul in the World to Come is greater than the light of the throne, NAMELY THE THRONE OF GLORY. AND THE ANGELS RECEIVE THEIR LIGHT FROM THE THRONE, SO THE LIGHT OF THE SOUL IS GREATER THAN THAT OF THE THRONE. A DIFFICULT POINT IS THEN RAISED. It seems that the soul was taken from the throne, AND THE RECEIVER IS SMALLER THAN THE GIVER OF NECESSITY. THE EXPLANATION IS THAT each had according to what was appropriate for it. Rav Nachman added that it is actually greater than the light of the throne, as it is written: "The likeness as the appearance of a man above upon it" (Yechezkel 1:26), above it in splendor.

159. וּכְשֶׁהוּא הוֹלֵךְ לַעֲשׂוֹת שְׁלִיחוּתוֹ, כָּל צִבְאוֹתָיו וְהַמֶּרְכָּבָה שֶׁלוֹ נִזּוֹנִין מֵאוֹתוֹ הַזוֹהַר. הֲדָא הוּא שֶׁהַנְּשָׁמָה אוֹמֶרֶת לוֹ, שִׂים נָא יָדְךָ כְּלוֹמַר סִיַעְתְּךָ, תַּחַת יְרֵכִי, זֶהוּ אוֹר הַנִּשְׁפָּע מִן הַנְּשָׁמָה עֲלֵיהֶם.

159. When he goes to perform the errand OF THE HOLY ONE, BLESSED BE HE, all his hosts and his Chariot are nourished by that splendor OF THE

-93-

SOUL. And the soul says to him, "Put...your hand" – namely, your escort, NAMELY THE HOSTS OF METATRON-"under my thigh" (Beresheet 24:2). This is the light that flows from the soul.

160. אָמַר רַבִּי יְהוּדָה בְּרַבִּי שָׁלוֹם, כָּךְ קַבַּלְנוּ, בְּשָׁעָה שֶׁזֶּה הוֹלֵךְ בִּשְׁלִיחוּתוֹ שֶׁל מָקוֹם, קוּדְשָׁא בְּרִךְ הוּא, מֵנִיעַ כָּל צִבְאוֹתָיו שֶׁל מַעְלָה, בְּאוֹת אַחַת מִשְּׁמוֹ. אָמַר רַב הוּנָא, כָּךְ יְרֵכִ"י בְּגִימַטְרִיָּא רָ"ם. כְּלוֹמַר הַנְּשָׁמָה אוֹמֶרֶת, שִׂים נָא יָדְךָ, סִיעָתְךָ, תַּחַת מַעֲלָתוֹ שֶׁל רָם וְנִשָּׂא הַמּוֹשֵׁל עַל הַכֹּל. וּלְאַחַר שֶׁצִּוָּה סִיעַת עֶלְיוֹנִים, תַּחַת יָדוֹ, אֲנִי מַשְׁבִּיעֶךָ, שְׁבוּעָה גְדוֹלָה בּוֹ.

160. Rabbi Yehuda the son of Rabbi Shalom said that we have been taught that when he goes on an errand for the Holy One, blessed be He, He moves His upper hosts by one letter of His name, NAMELY BY THE LETTER YUD OF THE NAME YUD HEV VAV HEI. *HEI* IS THE SECRET OF IMA AND ABA, THE ROOT OF THE SOUL'S LIGHT. Rabbi Huna said, *Yerechi* ('my thigh') has the same numerical value as ram (lit. 'high'), which is what the soul says, that is, "Put...your hand," your escort, under the grade of the high and elevated, that rules over all. After the soul commanded the escort of high ones to be under Him, IT TOLD HIM, I make you swear a great oath.

161. אָמַר רַבִּי יִצְחָק, אֱלֹהֵי הַשָּׁמַיִם וֵאלֹהֵי הָאָרֶץ. הוֹאִיל וְאָמַר בָּהּ שֶׁהוּא הַכֹּל, לָמָּה נֶאֱמַר, אֱלֹהֵי הַשָּׁמַיִם, אָמַר רַבִּי יְהוּדָה, שֶׁהוּא אָדוֹן עַל הַכֹּל, בְּבַת אַחַת, וּבְרֶגַע אֶחָד הוּא מֵנִיעַ לַכֹּל, וְכֻלָּם כְּאַיִן נֶגְדּוֹ. רַבִּי יִצְחָק אוֹמֵר, עַל שְׁתַּיִם אוֹתִיּוֹת מִשְּׁמוֹ, לְהוֹרוֹת, שֶׁהוּא הַכֹּל וְאֵין אַחֵר בִּלְתּוֹ.

161. Rabbi Yitzchak said, It is written: "Elohim of the heaven, and Elohim of the earth" (Yechezkel 1:26). Since he already mentioned Hashem, NAMELY "I WILL MAKE YOU SWEAR BY HASHEM," why add "Elohim of the heaven, AND ELOHIM OF THE EARTH"? HE ASKS RABBI YEHUDA, WHO SAID THAT HE MOVES ALL HIS HOSTS BY ONE LETTER OF HIS NAME WHEN HE GOES. Rabbi Yehuda said, IT IS WRITTEN: "ELOHIM OF THE HEAVEN, AND ELOHIM OF THE EARTH" to show that He is Master over everything simultaneously. In one instant, He moves everything, and

everything is nothing compared to Him. THIS IS WHY HE MENTIONS HEAVEN
AND EARTH IN THE OATH, WHICH IS THE SECRET OF THE LETTER *YUD*,
WHICH INDICATES THAT THIS LIGHT GOVERNS ALL THE GRADES AND
EVREYTHING IS AS NAUGHT COMPARED TO IT. Rabbi Yitzchak said that by
two letters of His name HE MOVES HIS WHOLE HOSTS, WHEN METATRON
GOES TO DO HIS ERRAND. This is to show that He is all, and there is
nothing save Him.

162. וְאַשְׁבִּיעֲךָ בַּה' אֱלֹהֵי הַשָּׁמַיִם וֵאלֹהֵי הָאָרֶץ. אָמַר רַב הוּנָא, וְאִי
הֲוֵינָא עִמְּהוֹן, דְּמָארֵי מַתְנִיתָא, כַּד גְּלוּ רָזָא דְּנָא, לָא אִיפָּרַשְׁנָא מִנְּהוֹן
הָכִי, דְּהָא אֲנָא חָזֵי, עֲמִיקִין סַגִּיאִין בְּפוּמַיְיהוּ, דְּגָלוּ וְלָא אִתְחַזְיָין לְכָל
אֵינִשׁ. תָּא חֲזֵי, שְׁבוּעַת קָיָימָא דָא, אוֹמֵי לָהּ נִשְׁמָתָא, דִּכְתִיב אֲשֶׁר
לֹא תִקַּח אִשָּׁה לִבְנִי.

162. "And I will make you swear by Hashem, Elohim of the heaven..."
Rabbi Huna said, If he had been with those versed in the Baraita at the time
that they revealed the secret of this verse, he would not have left them
without knowing everything, for he saw great depth in their utterances.
They revealed much, but man does not understand what they revealed.
Come and behold: The soul causes to swear this oath of the covenant, as it is
written: "That you shall not take a wife to my son" (Beresheet 24:3).
ABRAHAM IS ALLUDING TO THE SOUL, AS HAS BEEN EXPLAINED.

163. אָמַר רָבִּי יִצְחָק, מֵהָכָא מַשְׁמַע, שֶׁהוֹאִיל וְאַתָּה הוֹלֵךְ בִּשְׁלִיחוּת
זֶה, לֹא תִקַּח אִשָּׁה לִבְנִי, כְּלוֹמַר שֶׁלֹא תִקַּח גּוּף לִבְנִי, לִיכָּנֵס בְּגוּף
אַחֵר, בְּגוּף זָר, בְּגוּף שֶׁאֵינוֹ רָאוּי לוֹ, אֶלָּא בְּהַהוּא מַמָּשׁ, שֶׁהוּא שֶׁלִּי,
בְּהַהוּא מַמָּשׁ, שֶׁיָצָאתִי מִמֶּנּוּ, הֲדָא הוּא דִכְתִיב כִּי אִם אֶל אַרְצִי וְאֶל
מוֹלַדְתִּי תֵּלֵךְ.

163. Rabbi Yitzchak said, from here, it is understood THAT THE SOUL SAID
TO METATRON, Because you are going on this mission TO RESURRECT THE
DEAD, "you shall not take a wife for my son." This means you shall not take
a body for my son, BECAUSE THE BODY IN RELATION TO THE SOUL IS
CALLED A WIFE. He cannot enter another body, an idolatrous body, a body
not worthy of him, but only the body which is actually my own, the very

one I came from. And this is what is meant by the verse: "But you shall go
to my country, and to my kindred" (Ibid. 4).

164. אָמַר ר׳ יוֹסֵי, מַהוּ וְלָקַחְתָּ אִשָּׁה לִבְנִי לְיִצְחָק. אָמַר רַבִּי יִצְחָק,
אוֹתוֹ הַגּוּף שֶׁנִּצְטַעֵר עִמִּי בְּאוֹתוֹ הָעוֹלָם, וְלֹא הָיָה לוֹ הֲנָאָה וְכִסּוּף בּוֹ,
מִפְּנֵי יִרְאַת קוֹנוֹ, אוֹתוֹ הַגּוּף מַמָּשׁ, תִּקַּח לְיִצְחָק עִמּוֹ בְּהַאי שִׂמְחַת
הַצַּדִּיקִים, לְיִצְחָק עִמּוֹ בְּשִׂמְחַת הַקּוּדְשָׁא בְּרִיךְ הוּא, לְיִצְחָק עִמּוֹ
דְּעַכְשָׁיו עֵת שְׂחוֹק בָּעוֹלָם, הה״ד אָז יִמָּלֵא שְׂחוֹק פִּינוּ וגו׳.

164. Rabbi Yosi said, What is meant by the verse: "And take a wife to my
son Isaac"? IF THIS REFERS TO THE ENCLOTHING OF THE SOUL, SHOULD
IT NOT HAVE SAID ABRAHAM? Rabbi Yitzchak replies: The very body that
suffered with me in that world and had no pleasure or content for fear of its
Possessor IS A REFERENCE TO THE LUZ BONE, WHICH DOES NOT
DELIGHT IN EATING AND DRINKING IN THIS WORLD. This very body shall
you take to laugh with, in that rejoicing of the righteous, to take delight in it
in the joy of the Holy One, blessed be He. Have pleasure with it, because it
is time for laughter AT THE RESURRECTION OF THE DEAD, as it is written:
"Then was our mouth filled with laughter" (Tehilim 126:2).

165. אָמַר רַבִּי יְהוּדָה בַּר יִצְחָק, ת״ש, אֵין מַלְאָךְ אֶחָד עוֹשֶׂה אֶלָּא
שְׁלִיחוּת אֶחָד וְלֹא ב׳ שְׁלִיחוּת בְּבַת אַחַת. וְתַנְיָא, אָמַר רַבִּי אַבָּא,
מַלְאָךְ אֶחָד, אֲשֶׁר קֶסֶת הַסּוֹפֵר בְּמָתְנָיו, עָתִיד לְהַרְשִׁים כָּל אֶחָד
וְאֶחָד, עַל מִצְחוֹ, וּלְאַחַר כֵּן, הַשַּׂר הַגָּדוֹל, הוֹלֵךְ לְתַקֵּן כָּל אֶחָד וְאֶחָד,
וּלְהַעֲמִידוֹ לְקַבֵּל נִשְׁמָתוֹ, הה״ד הוּא יִשְׁלַח מַלְאָכוֹ לְפָנֶיךָ וְלָקַחְתָּ
אִשָּׁה, מַאי לְפָנֶיךָ. לִפְנֵי שְׁלִיחוּתְךָ.

165. Rabbi Yehuda, the son of Rabbi Yitzchak, said, Come and listen: An
angel does only one errand, not two at the same time. THERE ARE,
HOWEVER, TWO ERRANDS TO PERFORM: TO RESURRECT THE BODY IN
THE GRAVE AND TO MAKE IT RISE TO THE LAND OF YISRAEL, WHERE
THE SOUL WILL BE ENCLOTHED IN IT. BUT ONE ANGEL DOES NOT
PERFORM TWO ERRANDS. Rabbi Aba said, There is one angel with an
inkstand at his waist. THIS IS GABRIEL. He will put a mark on the brow of
each, MEANING THAT HE WILL MEND THE BODY. Afterward, the great

minister METATRON will go and mend each one, preparing it to receive its soul. This is the meaning of the verse: "He shall send his angel before you, and you shall take a wife" (Beresheet 24:7). What is meant by "before you"? It indicates that THE HOLY ONE, BLESSED BE HE, WILL SEND AN ANGEL TO MEND THE BODY before your errand. THEN METATRON WILL BRING THE SOUL WITH WHICH MAN IS ENCLOTHED, AS NO ONE ANGEL DOES TWO ERRANDS.

166. רַבִּי אֱלִיעֶזֶר אֲזַל לְמֶחֱמֵי לְרַבָּן יוֹחָנָן בֶּן זַכַּאי רַבֵּיהּ, וְהַהוּא יוֹמָא רֵישׁ יַרְחָא הֲוָה, כַּד מָטָא גַּבֵּיהּ, אֲמַר לֵיהּ, בֵּירָא דִּלְסַרְיָין, וּמַלְיָין לֵיהּ, וְהוּא נָבִיעַ מִדִּידֵיהּ יַתִּיר, מַאי בָּעָא הָכָא.

166. Rabbi Eliezer went to see his Rabbi, Rabban Yochanan ben Zakai, on the first day of the month. When he arrived he told him, 'O Well for those who see, filled WITH DRAWN WATER, yet gushing more from its own source. What does it seek here?'

167. אֲמַר לֵיהּ חַיָּיב אָדָם לְהַקְבִּיל פְּנֵי רַבּוֹ. אֲמַר לֵיהּ, לָאו עַל כָּךְ אֲמָרִית. אֶלָּא אֲנָא חָמֵי בְּאַנְפָּךְ, דְּמִלָּה חַדְתָּא אִית גַּבָּךְ, מֵאִינוּן עֲמִיקִים, דְּאַתְּ עָתִיד לְמִתְבַּע.

167. He answers, It behooves a man to greet his Rabbi ON THE DAY OF A NEW MOON. He said to him, Not for that reason I said, 'WHAT DOES IT SEEK HERE?' I see in your face that there is a new deep secret about which you are going to ask. THEREFORE I ASKED, WHAT DOES SOMEONE AS GREAT AS YOU WANT WITH ME?

168. אֲמַר לוֹ, חָמֵינָא הַאי אוֹר הָרִאשׁוֹן, דְּמַטַלְנוֹי עֲשָׂרָה, וּבַעֲשָׂרָה נָטִיל, וּבְרָזָא דַּעֲשָׂרָה נָהִיג לְכֹלָּא, וּבְאַתְוָותָא דַּעֲשָׂרָה עָבֵיד עוֹבָדוֹי. וְתָאנָא, עֲשָׂרָה פְּתִקִין, עֲשָׂרָה מַפְתְּחָן דְּבֵי קַצְרֵי בִּידוֹי, וּפְתִקִין עֲשָׂרָה, נָטִיל בְּגִנְתָּא דְּעֵדֶן, לְאַתְקָנָא אַרְעָא, עַל גּוּפֵיהוֹן דְּצַדִּיקַיָּא.

168. He responded, I see that primordial light, THAT WAS IN USE AT THE TIME OF THE CREATION AND WAS THEN STORED FOR THE RIGHTEOUS IN THE FUTURE, travels by ten and conducts everything according to the secret of ten. We learned that there are ten writings, ten keys to the hospital in its hands. It takes these and ten notes in the Garden of Eden to mend the earth for the bodies of the righteous.

169. אָמַר לֵיהּ, אֱלִיעֶזֶר בְּרִי, חָמֵית הֲוֵית יַתִּיר מִמַּלְאָכָא קַדִּישָׁא, דְּעָלְמָא בַּעֲשָׂרָה אִתְבְּרֵי, בַּעֲשָׂרָה אִתְנְהֵיג, כָּרְסְיָיא קַדִּישָׁא, בַּעֲשָׂרָה, אוֹרַיְיתָא הוּא בַּעֲשָׂרָה, מַטְלָנוֹי בַּעֲשָׂרָה, עָלְמִין עִלָּאִין בַּעֲשָׂרָה, וְחַד עִלָּאָה עַל כֹּלָּא בְּרִיךְ הוּא.

169. He said, Eliezer my son, you have seen more than a holy angel, FOR THE LIGHT OF THE SOUL IS GREATER THAN THE LIGHT OF ANGELS. BECAUSE RABBI ELIEZER EXPLAINED THE SECRET OF THE TEN ONLY BY THE UPPER THREE COLUMNS – CHOCHMAH, BINAH AND DA'AT – RABBI YOCHANAN BEN ZAKAI IS GOING TO EXPLAIN THE SECRET OF THE TEN ALSO IN THE LOWER SEVEN SFIROT. HE SAYS: The world, MALCHUT, is created by ten, and it is conducted by ten. THIS IS YESOD THAT LEADS MALCHUT CALLED WORLD. The holy throne, NETZACH AND HOD CALLED THE LOWER THRONE, is according to ten. The Torah, THE SECRET OF TIFERET, is by ten. Its traveling, NAMELY GVURAH, is by ten. The supernal worlds, CHESED, WHICH IS SUPERIOR TO THE LOWER SEVEN, are by ten. And there is the supernal one above them all, blessed be He, NAMELY KETER, FROM WHICH EVERYTHING IS DRAWN, BOTH THE LIGHT OF CHASSADIM ALLUDED TO IN THE SECRET OF TEN, AND THE LIGHT OF CHOCHMAH.

170. וְאֵימָא לָךְ מִלָּה, דַּעְתֵּיהּ דְּמָארֵי דְּמַתְנִיתָא הֲוָה בְּהַאי, מַה כְּתִיב, וַיִּקַּח הָעֶבֶד עֲשָׂרָה גְמַלִּים מִגְּמַלֵּי אֲדֹנָיו וַיֵּלֶךְ. אָמַר לֵיהּ, רִבִּי, זְכֵינָא לְפְסוּקָא דָא, אֲבָל וְכָל טוּב אֲדֹנָיו בְּיָדוֹ מַהוּ. אָמַר לֵיהּ, הוּא שְׁמֵיהּ דְּמָארֵיהּ, דְּאָזֵיל גַּבֵּי, לְאַעֲלָא לֵיהּ, וּלְאַנְהָגָא לֵיהּ, אָמַר דָּא וַדַּאי הוּא, כִּי שְׁמִי בְּקִרְבּוֹ.

170. I will tell you something else. Those versed in the Mishnah put some thought into it, as it is written: "And the servant took ten camels" (Beresheet 42:10). RABBI ELIEZER said to him, Master, I know this verse, MEANING YOU DO NOT HAVE TO EXPLAIN IT TO ME, but what is the meaning of: "For all the goods of him master were in his hands" (Ibid.)? I DO NOT KNOW HOW TO EXPLAIN IT. HOW COULD IT BE THAT HE CARRIED ALL THE

PROPERTY OF ABRAHAM IN HIS HANDS? He replies: This is the name of his Master, NAMELY THE SHECHINAH CALLED NAME, that went with him to bring him TO THE DESIRABLE PLACE and to protect him, SO THAT NOTHING WOULD HAPPEN TO HIM. RABBI ELIEZER SAID, Assuredly this is THE SECRET OF THE VERSE: "For My name was in him" (Shemot 23:21).

171. תְּנַן, אָמַר רַבִּי אַבָּהוּ, תָּא חֲזֵי, מַאן דְּיָדַע שְׁמֵיהּ עַל בּוּרְיֵיהּ, יָדַע דְּהוּא וּשְׁמֵיהּ חַד הוּא, קוּדְשָׁא בְּרִיךְ הוּא וּשְׁמֵיהּ חַד, דִּכְתִיב ה' אֶחָד וְגו'. כְּלוֹמַר הַשֵּׁם וְהוּא אֶחָד.

171. Rabbi Abahu said, Come and behold: He who knows His name perfectly knows that He and his Name are one. The Holy One, blessed be He, and His Name, THE SHECHINAH, are one, as it is written: "Hashem shall be one, and his Name One" (Zecharyah 14:9). That is, the name, THE SHECHINAH, and He, ZEIR ANPIN, are one.

172. אָמַר רַבִּי אַבָּא, אִית לְאִסְתַּכְּלָא בְּפָרְשָׁתָא דָא, וַיַּבְרֵךְ הַגְּמַלִּים מִחוּץ לָעִיר אֶל בְּאֵר הַמָּיִם. אָמַר רַבִּי אַבָּא, מִחוּץ לָעִיר, דָּא הוּא בֵּי קִבְרֵי. אֶל בְּאֵר הַמַּיִם, דְּתַנְיָא, הַנְּקְדָּמִים בְּבָתֵּי קִבְרֵי אוֹתָם שֶׁנָּשְׂאוּ וְנָתְנוּ בַּתּוֹרָה, דְּהָא תְּנַן, כְּשֶׁנִּכְנָס אָדָם לַקֶּבֶר, מַה דְּשָׁאֲלוּ לֵיהּ תְּחִילָה, אִם קָבַע עִתִּים לַתּוֹרָה, דִּכְתִיב וְהָיָה אֱמוּנַת עִתֶּךָ וְגו'. וּכְשֶׁיֵּצֵא אֵינוּ דִין לַהֲקִימָם בַּתְּחִלָה.

172. Rabbi Aba said, We should look at the verse, "And he made his camels kneel down outside the city by a well of water" (Beresheet: 24:11). According to Rabbi Aba, outside the city means in the cemetery. "By a well of water" refers, as we learnt, that those who are the first TO BE REVIVED FROM THE DEAD in the cemetery, are those who dealt in Torah. As we have learned, when a man comes into his grave, he is first asked if he set appointed times to study Torah, as it is written: "And he shall be the faith of your times" (Yeshayah 33:6). Without question, he who responds yes, is revived first.

173. אָמַר רַבִּי אַבָּא, לְעֵת עֶרֶב, זֶהוּ יוֹם שִׁשִּׁי, שֶׁהוּא עֶרֶב הַשַּׁבָּת, שֶׁאָז הַזְּמַן לְקַיְּימָא מֵתַיָּיא, מַאי מַשְׁמַע, דִּתְנַן, שִׁיתָּא אַלְפֵי שְׁנִין הֲוֵי

20. About the resurrection of the dead

עָלְמָא וְהוּא אֶלֶף הַשִּׁשִּׁי, שֶׁהוּא סִיּוּם הַכֹּל, וְהַיְינוּ לְעֵת עֶרֶב, זְמַן סִיּוּם
הַכֹּל. לְעֵת צֵאת הַשּׁוֹאֲבוֹת, אֵלּוּ הֵם תַּלְמִידֵי חֲכָמִים, הַשּׁוֹאֲבִים
מֵימֵיהָ שֶׁל תּוֹרָה, שֶׁהוּא עֵת לָצֵאת וּלְהִתְנַעֵר מִן הֶעָפָר.

173. Rabbi Aba said that "at the time of evening" (Beresheet 24:11) refers
to Friday, Shabbat eve, the time of the resurrection of the dead. HE ASKS,
What is the meaning OF THESE THINGS? HE RESPONDS: We have learned
that the world exists for 6,000 years and that SHABBAT EVE is the 6th
millennium, the ending of all. Thus "at the time of evening" means the time
of ending for everything. The phrase: "At the time that the women go out to
draw water" refers to the scholars of the Torah, who draw the water of
Torah, the time to go out and shake off the dust, NAMELY THE TIME TO
RESURRECT.

174. וְאָמַר רָבִּי אַבָּא, עוֹד יֵשׁ לָדַעַת, דִּתְנַן, אוֹתָם הַמִּתְעַסְּקִים לָדַעַת
אֶת בּוֹרְאָם בָּעוֹה"ז, וְנִשְׁמָתָם בְּתַשְׁלוּמָה, לָעה"ב זָכוּ לָצֵאת מִשְּׁבוּעַת
הַנְּשָׁמָה, הוֹלֵךְ לָדַעַת מִי הוּא גוּפָה מַמָּשׁ, וּמַאי הוּא. הִנֵּה אָנֹכִי נִצָּב
עַל עֵין הַמַּיִם, אַף עַל גַּב שֶׁתַּלְמִיד חָכָם הוּא, הוֹלֵךְ אַחַר הַתַּשְׁלוּם,
דִּכְתִיב וְהָיָה הָעַלְמָה הַיּוֹצֵאת לִשְׁאוֹב וְאָמַרְתִּי אֵלֶיהָ הַשְׁקִינִי נָא מְעַט
מַיִם מִכַּדֵּךְ, אֱמוֹר לִי רֶמֶז יְדִיעָתוֹ מִמַּה שֶׁהִשְׂגַּתָּ.

174. Rabbi Aba added that there is more to know, as we have learned that
those occupied in knowing their Master in this world and their soul to
perfection in the World to Come, deserve to get out OF THE GRAVE by the
oath of the soul METATRON WAS MADE IT SWEAR. FOR METATRON comes
to know which is the soul's proper body, AS THE SOUL MADE HIM SWEAR,
and it is written: "Behold, I stand here by the well of water" (Beresheet
24:43). Although it is A BODY OF the scholar of the Torah, METATRON
GOES to look for perfection, as it is written: "And it shall come to pass, that
the maid who comes forth to draw, and I say to her, 'Give me, I pray you, a
little water from your pitcher'" (Ibid. 44), which means 'tell me by hint, the
knowledge of the name, from what you conceived'.

175. וְאָמְרָה אֵלַי גַּם אַתָּה שְׁתֵה, אַף אַתָּה עֶבֶד כָּמוֹנִי, וְלֹא נִתְחַלֵּף לִי
יְדִיעָתְךָ, בִּידִיעָתוֹ שֶׁל מָקוֹם בָּרוּךְ הוּא, וְצָרִיךְ אַתָּה לְהַשִּׂיג שֶׁאַתָּה

נִבְרָא כְּמוֹנִי.

175. "And she says to me, 'Both drink you'" (Beresheet 24:44). THIS MEANS THAT SHE LET HIM KNOW THREE THINGS: 1) You are a servant like me; 2) The knowledge of you does not compare with the knowledge of Hashem, blessed be He, AND 3) It behooves you to conceive that you are a creature like me AND, ALTHOUGH YOU ARE AN ANGEL, YOU ARE LIKE A CREATURE; NAMELY, THERE IS WANT IN YOU, AS THERE IS IN ME.

176. וְגַם לִגְמַלֶּיךָ אֶשְׁאָב, כְּלוֹמַר יְדִיעַת הַשָּׁגָתִי, שֶׁלֹּא הִשִּׂיגוּ סִיעָתְךָ וְיָדַעְתִּי כִּי מַעֲלָה יֵשׁ לִי עָלֶיךָ, וְהֵיאַךְ נִבְרָא אַתָּה מִזִּיו הַנָּתוּן אֶצְלָךְ. אִם הוּא אוֹמֵר סִימָן זֶה, יְהִי מָסוּר בְּיָדִי, עַל כָּל דְּבָרִים אֵלּוּ, וְאֵדַע שֶׁהִיא הָאִשָּׁה, הוּא הַגּוּף, מֵאוֹתָהּ הַנְּשָׁמָה הַשְּׁבוּעָה שֶׁהִשְׁבִּיעַנִי.

176. "I will draw water for your camels also" (Beresheet 24:19) INDICATES THAT IT ALSO DREW FORTH FOR HIS ATTENDANTS FROM WHAT IT PERCEIVED. THE WORDS "YOUR CAMELS" MEANS "YOUR RETINUE." IN OTHER WORDS, my understanding is that: 1) Your retinue was not aware, THEY ARE UNABLE TO CONCEIVE HIM; 2) "I know that I have an advantage over you" NAMELY FROM THE ASPECT OF BEING INCLUDED IN A POINT IN THIS WORLD, WHICH IS LACKING IN SUPERNAL ANGELS; AND 3) I know how you were created from the radiance that was placed with you. THAT IS, IT ALSO UNDERSTOOD THE SECRET OF HIS CREATION. If THE BODY mentions ALL THESE PERCEPTIONS, let this sign THAT WAS PRINTED ON ME be delivered to me. IF THE BODY SHALL SAY THESE THINGS AND NOT ONE SHALL BE MISSING, then I shall know she is the woman. She is the body from the same soul according to the oath it made me swear.

177. וַיְהִי הוּא טֶרֶם כִּלָּה לְדַבֵּר וְגו'. רִבִּי יִצְחָק אָמַר רִבִּי יְהוּדָה, בְּעוֹד שֶׁכָּל הָעִנְיָנִים, הוּא רוֹצֶה לְנַסּוֹת עַל הַגּוּף, מַאי כְּתִיב, וְהִנֵּה רִבְקָה יוֹצֵאת, זֶהוּ הַגּוּף קָדוֹשׁ, שֶׁנִּתְעַסֵּק בְּד"ת, וְכִתֵּת גּוּפוֹ לְהַשִּׂיג וְלָדַעַת אֶת קוֹנוֹ. אֲשֶׁר יָלְדָה לִבְתוּאֵל, אָמַר רַב יְהוּדָה, בִּתּוֹ שֶׁל אֵל. בֶּן מִלְכָּה, בֶּן מַלְכָּה שֶׁל עוֹלָם. אֵשֶׁת נָחוֹר אֲחִי אַבְרָהָם. חֶבְרַת הַשֵּׂכֶל, גּוּף שֶׁנִּדְבַּק בַּשֵּׂכֶל, וְהִיא אָח הַנְּשָׁמָה. וְכַדָּהּ עַל שִׁכְמָהּ, מַשָּׂא הַחָכְמָה עָלֶיהָ.

177. "And it came to pass, before he had done speaking" (Beresheet 24:15). According to Rabbi Yitzchak, Rabbi Yehuda said while he was thinking of how to try the body, it is written: "Behold, Rivkah came out," which is the holy body that is occupied in Torah. It pounds the body for knowledge of the conception of his Possessor, "who was born to Betuel" (Ibid.). Rav Yehuda said she was the daughter (Heb. *bat*) of El, the "son of Milkah" (Ibid.), who is a son to the king (Heb. *Malkah*) of the universe. "The wife of Nachor, Abraham's brother" alludes to the company of the mind, the body attached to the mind, and is the brother of the soul, and the phrase: "With her pitcher upon her shoulder" alludes to the weight of wisdom upon it.

178. וַיָּרָץ הָעֶבֶד לִקְרָאתָהּ, זֶה מטטרון. וַיֹּאמֶר הַגְמִיאִינִי נָא מְעַט מַיִם מִכַּדֵּךְ, אֱמוֹר לִי רֶמֶז חָכְמָתָא, בִּידִיעַת בּוֹרְאָךְ, מִמַּה שֶׁעָסַקְתְּ בְּעוֹלָם שֶׁיָּצָאת מִמֶּנּוּ. אָמַר רִבִּי אַבָּא, כִּדְפָּרְשִׁינָן, אַחַר כָּל זֶה מַה כְּתִיב, וָאָשִׂים הַנֶּזֶם עַל אַפָּהּ וְהַצְּמִידִים עַל יָדֶיהָ, אָמַר רִבִּי אַבָּא, אוֹתָם הָעֲצָמוֹת שֶׁנִּפְזְרוּ לְכָאן וּלְכָאן, הוּא צוֹמֵד אוֹתָם, וְשׁוֹקְלָם זֶה עַל זֶה, כְּמָה דְאַתְּ אָמֵר וְעַצְמוֹתֶיךָ יַחֲלִיץ.

178. "And the servant ran to meet her" (Beresheet 24:17) refers to Metatron. And said, "Let me, I pray you, drink a little water of your pitcher" give me a hint of the wisdom of the knowledge of your Maker that you dealt with in the world you left. Rabbi Aba said, We have explained that after that it is written: "And I put the ring upon her nose, and the bracelets upon her hands" (Ibid. 47). Rabbi Aba said that these are the bones that were scattered here and there. He puts them together and weighs them one upon the other, as is written: "And strengthen your bones" (Yeshayah 58:11).

179. אָמַר רִבִּי אַבָּא, בְּאוֹתָהּ שָׁעָה, אוֹתוֹ הַגּוּף עוֹמֵד בְּאֶרֶץ יִשְׂרָאֵל, וְשָׁם נִכְנָס בּוֹ נִשְׁמָתוֹ. אָמַר רִבִּי יוֹחָנָן, מִי מוֹלִיךְ הַגּוּף לְאֶרֶץ יִשְׂרָאֵל, אָמַר רִבִּי זֵירָא, קוּדְשָׁא בְּרִיךְ הוּא עוֹשֶׂה מְחִילוֹת תַּחַת הָאָרֶץ, וְהֵם מִתְגַּלְגְּלִים וְהוֹלְכִים לְאֶרֶץ יִשְׂרָאֵל, הֲדָא הוּא דִכְתִיב וְאֶרֶץ רְפָאִים תַּפִּיל.

179. Rabbi Aba said, At that time, the body stands in the land of Yisrael, where the soul enters it. Rabbi Yochanan asks, Who conducts the body to the land of Yisrael? Rabbi Zira said, The Holy One, blessed be He, digs caverns under the ground and they roll to the land of Yisrael. Hence it is written: "And the earth shall cast out the shades of the dead" (Yeshayah 26:19).

אָמַר רִבִּי יִצְחָק, גַּבְרִיאֵל מוֹלִיךְ אוֹתָם לְאֶרֶץ יִשְׂרָאֵל, מנ"ל, .180 דִּכְתִיב הֲתֵלְכִי עִם הָאִישׁ הַזֶּה, וּכְתִיב הָתָם וְהָאִישׁ גַּבְרִיאֵל. אָמַר רִבִּי יוֹסֵי, מַאי דִּכְתִיב, וּלְרִבְקָה אָח וּשְׁמוֹ לָבָן. אָמַר רַבִּי יִצְחָק, אֵין יצה"ר בָּטֵל מִן הָעוֹלָם אַף עַל פִּי שֶׁכֻּלּוֹ לֹא נִמְצָא קַצְתּוֹ נִמְצָא.

180. Rabbi Yitzchak said, Gabriel conducts them to the land of Yisrael. How do we know that? From the verse: "Will you go with this man?" (Beresheet 24:58). Elsewhere, it is written: "The man Gabriel" (Daniel 9:21). Rabbi Yosi asks, Why is it written: "And Rivkah had a brother and his name was Laban" (Ibid. 29)? Rabbi Yitzchak answered, The Evil Inclination does not pass away from the world, and though it is not entirely present, some of it is.

תָּא חֲזֵי בַּתְּחִלָּה כְּשֶׁהָיָה מוּטָל בעה"ז נִקְרָא לוֹט, לְעה"ב יִבָּטֵל .181 מִן הָעוֹלָם, אֲבָל לֹא כֻּלּוֹ וְנִקְרָא לָבָן, לֹא מְנֻוָּל כְּבָרִאשׁוֹנָה, אֶלָּא כְּמַאן דְּסָחֵי מִנְּוּוּלוֹ. לָבָן לְמַאי אִצְטְרִיךְ. אָמַר רַבִּי שִׁמְעוֹן, לְמֶעְבַּד פְּרִיָּה וּרְבִיָּה אִצְטְרִיךְ, דְּאָמַר רַבִּי שִׁמְעוֹן, אִם אֵין יֵצֶר הָרָע נִמְצָא, פְּרִיָּה וּרְבִיָּה אֵינוֹ מָצוּי.

181. Come and behold: When it was in this world, it was called Lot. In the World to Come, it will be partly canceled and called Laban, it not as corrupt as before, but as one who washed the filth off of himself. HE ASKS, Why is there need of Laban? NAMELY, WHY IS IT NEEDED? TO REMAIN IN THE WORLD Rabbi Shimon said, It is needed for being fruitful and multiply. If there is no Evil Inclination, nothing is fruitful or multiplies.

ת"ש, כֵּיוָן שֶׁהַגּוּף נִבְנָה וְעוֹמֵד בְּקִיּוּמוֹ, מַאי כְּתִיב וַיְשַׁלְּחוּ אֶת .182 רִבְקָה אֲחוֹתָם וגו'. מַאי וְאֶת מֵנִקְתָּהּ זֶה כֹּח הַתְּנוּעָה. רִבִּי יִצְחָק אָמַר זֶה כֹּח הַגּוּף.

182. Come and listen: Since the body was constructed and established, why is it then written, "And they sent away Rivkah, their sister, and her nurse..." (Beresheet 24:59). What does the phrase "and her nurse" imply? It is the power of movement. Rabbi Yitzchak further clarifies this by explaining that this is the power of the body.

183. רִבִּי אַבָּהוּ פָּתַח בְּהַאי קְרָא, אִתִּי מִלְּבָנוֹן כַּלָּה אִתִּי מִלְּבָנוֹן תָּבֹאִי וְגו', אָמַר רִבִּי אַבָּהוּ, כֵּיוָן שֶׁהַגּוּף נִבְנֶה עַל קִיּוּמוֹ, וּמְבִיאִין אוֹתוֹ, לְקַבֵּל נִשְׁמָתוֹ, לְאֶרֶץ יִשְׂרָאֵל, הַנְּשָׁמָה מַמְתֶּנֶת אֵלָיו, וְיוֹצֵאת לִקְרָאתוֹ, כְּמָה דְאַתְּ אָמַר וַיֵּצֵא יִצְחָק לָשׂוּחַ בַּשָּׂדֶה. הֲדָא הוּא דִכְתִיב אִתִּי מִלְּבָנוֹן כַּלָּה. זוֹ הִיא הַנְּשָׁמָה. תָּשׁוּרִי מֵרֹאשׁ אֲמָנָה, הַיְינוּ דִכְתִיב וַיִּשָּׂא עֵינָיו וַיַּרְא.

183. Rabbi Abahu opened with the verse, "Come with me from Lebanon, my bride, with me from Lebanon..." (Shir Hashirim 4:8). Rabbi Abahu said, Once the body was built and established, it is brought to the land of Yisrael to receive its soul. The soul awaits it there and comes out to greet it, as is written: "And Isaac went out to meditate in the field" (Beresheet 24:63). "Come with me from Lebanon, my bride" is the soul, and "Look from the top of Amana" (Ibid.) corresponds to: "And he lifted his eyes and saw" (Ibid.).

184. אָמַר ר' יְהוּדָה, אִם הִיא הַנְּשָׁמָה, תֵּינַח אַבְרָהָם כִּדְקָאֲמְרָן, אֲבָל יִצְחָק מַהוּ. אָמַר ר' אַבָּהוּ, הָא חַבְרַיָּיא אָמְרוּ, דְּעַכְשָׁיו אִתְקְרֵי יִצְחָק, עַל שׁוּם חֶדְוָותָא סַגִּיאָה דִּבְעָלְמָא.

184. Rabbi Yehuda said, If this is the soul, Abraham is satisfactory, as was said. What then is Isaac? Rabbi Abahu said, The friends said it is now called Isaac because of the increased joy in the world.

185. אָמַר ר' אַבָּהוּ, בַּתְּחִלָּה נִקְרֵאת הַנְּשָׁמָה אַבְרָהָם, וְהַגּוּף שָׂרָה עַכְשָׁיו נִקְרֵאת הַנְּשָׁמָה יִצְחָק וְהַגּוּף רִבְקָה. תְּנַן בְּמַתְנִיתִין, אָמַר ר' שִׁמְעוֹן, אַרְבָּעִים שָׁנָה קוֹדֶם קִיּוּם הַגּוּף, מַמְתֶּנֶת הַנְּשָׁמָה לַגּוּף בְּאֶרֶץ יִשְׂרָאֵל. בְּאֵיזֶה מָקוֹם, בִּמְקוֹם הַמִּקְדָּשׁ.

185. Rabbi Abahu said, First the soul was called Abraham and the body Sarah. Now the soul is called Isaac and the body Rivkah. Rabbi Shimon said, It was taught in the Mishnah that the soul awaited the body in the land of Yisrael forty years before the body existed. Where? At the Temple.

186. אָמַר ר' אַבָּהוּ, תָּא חֲזֵי, וַיִּקַּח אֶת רִבְקָה וַתְּהִי לוֹ לְאִשָּׁה וַיֶּאֱהָבֶהָ וַיִּנָּחֵם יִצְחָק אַחֲרֵי אִמּוֹ. אוֹהֵב לְאוֹתוֹ הַגּוּף, וּמִתְנַחֵם עִמּוֹ וְהוּא עֵת לִשְׂחוֹק וְהַחֶדְוָה בְּעוֹלָם.

186. Rabbi Abahu said, Look at the verse: "And took Rivkah, and she became his wife, and he loved her; and Isaac was comforted after his mother's death" (Beresheet 24:67). When he loves the body and is comforted by it, it is time for laughter and delight in the world.

187. אָמַר רִבִּי יְהוּדָה, הָא כָּל פָּרְשָׁתָא דָא אִתְבְּרִיר לָן, אֲבָל לָא יָכֵילְנָא לְמִנְדַּע מַהוּ, וַיּוֹסֶף אַבְרָהָם וַיִּקַּח אִשָּׁה וּשְׁמָהּ קְטוּרָה. וּלְשִׁקּוּלָא דְדַעְתָּא כָּל פָּרְשָׁתָא דָא לִיסְתּוּרֵי.

187. Rabbi Yehuda said, Now this whole portion of the scripture is made clear, but I do not know the meaning of the verse: "Then again Abraham took a wife, and her name was Kturah" (Beresheet 25:1). To a reasonable mind, this text is contradictory. IT CONTRADICTS THE EXPLANATION CONCERNING THE SOUL AND BODY AT THE TIME OF RESURRECTION.

188. כַּד אָתָא רַב דִּימֵי, אֲמַר הַאי פָּרְשָׁתָא דָא שְׁמַעְנָא, וְלָא אִדְכַּרְנָא, אֲמָרוּ, דְּעֶלָּאִין תַּקִּיפִין, לָא זְמִנוּהָ לְגַלָּאָה, וַאֲנַן מַאי נֵימָא. קָם רִבִּי יְהוּדָה וַאֲמַר, מִמְּתִיבָתָא דְּחַבְרָנָא, מָארֵי מַתְנִיתָא גַּלְיָא.

188. Rav Dimi arrived and said, I have heard an explanation for this portion, but I do not remember it. They said that the high and strong, NAMELY THE UPPER GRADES, did not present it for revelation. What have we to say? Rabbi Yehuda stood up and said that the portion is revealed in the Yeshivah of our friends, the sages of the Mishnah.

189. קָמוּ וַאֲזָלוּ, הוּא וְרִבִּי יֵיסָא וְרִבִּי חִיָּיא, אַשְׁכְּחוּהָ לְרִבִּי אֶלְעָזָר

בְּרִבִּי שִׁמְעוֹן, וַהֲוָה מְגַלֶּה רָזִין דִּתְפִילִין, עָאלוּ קַמֵּיהּ, וַאֲמָרוּ בְּמַאי אִתְעַסַּק מַר, אֲמַר לוֹן, טַעְמָא דִתְפִילִין אֲמִינָא, דְּהָא זַכָּאָה הוּא בַּר נָשׁ, דְּמַנַּח תְּפִילִין, וְיָדַע טַעְמָא דִידְהוּ.

189. They stood up and began walking, he, Rabbi Yesa, and Rabbi Chiya. They found Rabbi Elazar ben Rabbi Shimon, who was revealing the secret of Tfilin. They came before him and asks, Sir, what are you engaged in? He replies: I am recounting the reason for the Tfilin, for blessed is the man who dons Tfilin and knows the sense thereof.

190. אָמְרוּ אִי נִיחָא קַמֵּיהּ דְּמַר, לֵימָא לָן מִלָּה. אָמְרוּ, שְׁמַעְנָא מֵאָבוּךְ, דְּקוּדְשָׁא בְּרִיךְ הוּא, בִּרְחִימוּ סַגִּיאָה דַּהֲוָה לֵיהּ עִם יִשְׂרָאֵל, אֲמַר לוֹן לְמֶעְבַּד לֵיהּ בֵּי מַשְׁכְּנָא, כְּגַוְונָא דִּרְתִיכָא עִלָּאָה דִּלְעֵילָּא, וְיֵיתֵי דִיּוּרֵיהּ עִמְּהוֹן, הה"ד וְעָשׂוּ לִי מִקְדָּשׁ וְשָׁכַנְתִּי בְּתוֹכָם. וּשְׁמַעְנָא מֵאָבוּךְ דְּהָכָא סְתִים טַעְמָא דִתְפִילִין, בְּהַאי פְּסוּקָא.

190. They said, If it is well before you, Sir, may you tell us something. They said, We learned from your father that the Holy One, blessed be He, in His great love for the children of Yisrael, told them to build Him a tabernacle, reflecting the supernal high Chariot, so He might come and dwell among them. This is the meaning of: "And let them make Me a sanctuary: so that I may dwell among them" (Shemot 25:8). We learned from your father that the reason for the Tfilin was hidden in this verse.

191. אָמַר לוֹ תָּא חֲזֵי, כְּגַוְונָא עִלָּאָה, אִתְעֲבַד מִקְדָּשׁ בִּרְתִיכוֹי קַדִּישִׁין, וּבָתַר כֵּן, אַשְׁרֵי קוּדְשָׁא בְּרִיךְ הוּא דִיּוּרֵיהּ עִמְּהוֹן, כְּעִנְיָינָא דָּא, וּכְגַוְונָא דָּא, אִתְעָרוּ חַבְרַיָּיא מָארֵי מַתְנִיתָא בְּטַעְמָא דִתְפִילִין, לְמֶהֱוֵי הַהוּא גַּבְרָא דּוּגְמָא דִּרְתִיכֵי עִלָּאִין, רְתִיכָא תַּתָּאָה, רְתִיכָא עִלָּאָה, לְמֵיתֵי מַלְכוּתָא דִילֵיהּ, וְיִשְׁרֵי דִיּוּרֵיהּ עֲלֽוֵיהּ.

191. He said to them, Come and behold: The Temple was made to reflect the upper one in THE SHAPES OF its holy Chariots. And then the Holy One, blessed be He, caused His Shechinah to dwell among them. In this manner, those versed in the Mishnah discussed the reason for the Tfilin. Any man WHO WEARS TFILIN will be patterned after the upper Chariots: the lower Chariot and the upper Chariot so that His kingdom will come and the

Shechinah will dwell upon him.

192. וְתָנֵינָן, אִית בֵּיהּ, רָזִין עִלָּאִין, וְדוּגְמֵיהוֹן, וְאִית בֵּיהּ תְּלַת
רְתִיכִין, דּוּגְמַת עִלָּאִין קַדִּישִׁין, רָזִין דִּתְלַת אַתְוָותָא, דִּשְׁמָהָן קַדִּישֵׁי,
עִלָּאִין תְּלַת, רְתִיכִין, תְּלָתָא אַתְוָותָא, אַרְבַּע פָּרָשִׁיוֹת שַׁלִּיט עַל
אַרְבַּע, וְעַל כָּךְ, רָזָא דְשִׁי"ן דִּתְלַת כִּתְרִין, וְשִׁי"ן דְּאַרְבַּע כִּתְרִין,
תְּלָתָא מַלְכִין שַׁלִּיטִין בְּגוּפָא, תְּפִילִין עֲלוֹי קוּדְשָׁא בְּרִיךְ הוּא לְעֵילָּא,
אִלֵּין תְּפִלִּין דְּרֵישָׁא, תְּפִילִין דִּדְרוֹעָא אַרְבַּע פָּרָשִׁיָּין.

192. We learned that there are deep secrets in THE TFILIN and its patterns. There are three Chariots within them, like the high and holy ones, reflecting the secrets of the three letters of His Holy Name, *YUD-HEI-VAV*. For these three Chariots ARE the three letters *YUD-HEI-VAV*. The four sections govern the four LETTERS OF HIS HOLY NAME. This is therefore the secret of the Shin of three crowns and Shin of four crowns, WHICH MEANS the three kings ruling over the body, CORRESPONDING TO THE SHIN WITH THREE HEADS and the Tfilin upon the Holy One, blessed be He, above the head Tfilin and the hand Tfilin, AMOUNTING TO four sections, WHICH CORRESPOND TO THE SHIN WITH FOUR HEADS.

193. לִבָּא, רָכִיב דּוּגְמָא דִרְתִיכָא תַּתָּאָה, וְתַתָּאָה רָכִיב. עוֹד תָּנֵינָן,
דָּא רְכִיבָא דִּדְרוֹעָא לְתַתָּא. וְלִבָּא רָכִיב דּוּגְמָא דְּאִיהוּ לְתַתָּא,
וְאִתְמַסְרוֹן בִּידֵיהּ לְאַעֲלָאָה לוֹן כָּל חֵילֵי שְׁמַיָּא, כָּךְ לִבָּא הוּא רָכִיב
לְתַתָּא, וְאִתְמַסְרוּ בִּידוֹי כָּל אֶבְרֵי גוּפָא.

193. Similarly, the heart rides as if on the lower Chariot, THE SECRET OF THE NUKVA. And the lower one, THE NUKVA is mounted. We have also learned that this Chariot of the arm, THE NUKVA, is below, NAMELY THE SECRET OF THE HAND TFILIN, CALLED THE ARM. The heart rides as if beneath. It was given to it to bring in all the heavenly hosts. So the heart rides down below and all the limbs of the body are given to it.

194. וְעֵילָּא מִנֵּיהּ אַרְבַּע פָּרָשִׁיָּין עַל מוֹחָא דְּרֵישָׁא אִיהוּ, אֲבָל קוּדְשָׁא
בְּרִיךְ הוּא, שַׁלִּיטָא עִלָּאָה מַלְכָּא מִכֹּלָּא. וְרָזָא דְּחָכְמְתָא דָא, הוּא,

כְּגַוְונָא דְמַקְדְשָׁא דִכְתִיב, וַעֲשֵׂה כְּרוּב אֶחָד מִקָּצָה מִזֶּה וּכְרוּב אֶחָד
מִקָּצָה מִזֶּה, וַעֲלַיְיהוּ דִּיּוּרֵיהּ דְּמַלְכָּא, בְּאַרְבַּע אַתְוָון, תְּרֵין רְתִיכִין.

194. Above THE HEART are the four sections of the brain. The Holy One, blessed be He, is supreme ruler over them. He is King of all. And the secret of wisdom resembles the Temple, as it is written: "And make one Cherub on the one end, and the other Cherub on the other end" (Shemot 25:19). Above them is the King's Shechinah, within the four letters YUD HEV VAV HEI. *YUD-HEI* IS ON THE RIGHT CHERUB, AND *VAV-HEI* ON THE LEFT CHERUB. Within the two Chariots, THE UPPER CHARIOT IS ON THE RIGHT CHERUB AND THE LOWER CHARIOT IS ON THE LEFT CHERUB.

195. וּכְהַאי גַוְונָא, לִבָּא וּמוֹחָא, לִבָּא מִכָּאן, וּמוֹחָא מִכָּאן, וַעֲלַיְיהוּ
מְדוֹרֵיהּ דְּקוּדְשָׁא בְּרִיךְ הוּא, בְּאַרְבַּע פַּרְשִׁיָּין. אָמַר רִבִּי אֶלְעָזָר, מִכָּאן
וּלְהָלְאָה רָזֵי דִּכְתְרֵי אַתְוָותָא, וּפָרְשִׁיָּין בְּגוּפַיְיהוּ וּרְצוּעוֹתֵיהוֹן, הֲלָכָה
לְמשֶׁה מִסִּינַי, וּרְמִיזָא דִלְהוֹן אִתְגְּלֵי, וְטַעֲמָא דְכֹלָּא בִּתְלַת עֲשַׂר
מְכִילָן.

195. Similarly, the heart and the brain, THE HAND TFILIN AND THE HEAD TFILIN, the heart is on one side and the brain on the other side. Upon them is the King's Shechinah in four sections. Rabbi Elazar said, From now on, the secrets of the crowns of the letters, the sections in their bodies, NAMELY THEIR COMPARTMENTS, and the straps are an ancient tradition that Moses received in Sinai. They were already explained by allusion, NAMELY BY THE EXPLANATION BEFORE US, and the sense of all this is in the secret of the thirteen divine attributes OF MERCY.

196. אָמַר רִבִּי יְהוּדָה אִלְמָלֵא לָא אָתֵינָא, אֶלָּא בְּדִיל רָזָא דָא דַּיַּי.
אָמְרוּ לֵיהּ, זַכָּאָה חוּלָקָךְ לְעָלְמָא דְאָתֵי דְכָל רָז לָא אָנִיס לָךְ. אָמְרוּ
לֵיהּ אָתֵינָא קַמֵּיהּ דְּמַר, לְמִנְדַּע רָזָא דְהַאי פְּסוּקָא, וַיּוֹסֶף אַבְרָהָם וַיִּקַּח
אִשָּׁה וּשְׁמָהּ קְטוּרָה.

196. Rabbi Yehuda said, Even if we came only for this secret, it would have sufficed. They said to him, Happy is your lot in the World to Come, for no secret is withheld from you. They said to him, We came before you, Sir, to know the secret of the verse: "Then again Abraham took a wife, and her name was Kturah" (Beresheet 25:1).

197. אָמַר, פֵּירוּשָׁא דְּהַאי פְּסוּקָא, כְּמָה דְּגָלוֹ חַבְרָנָא, מָאבֵי מַתְנִיתִין, דְּכַד נִשְׁמָתָא יֵיתֵי בְּהַהוּא גּוּפָא קַדִּישָׁא דִּילָהּ, הָא מִילַיָּיא הֲווֹ, עַל חַיָּיבַיָּא, דִּיקוּמוּן וְיַכְשְׁרוּן עוֹבָדִין, וְיָהֵב לְהוּ מִזִיוָא יְקָרָא דִילֵיהּ, דְּיִנְדְּעוּן, וְיִתּוּבוּן, וְיִזְכּוּן זְכוּתָא שְׁלֵימָתָא.

197. He said, the explanation of this verse is revealed by the friends versed in the Mishnah. When the soul enters its holy body, these words, NAMELY "THEN AGAIN..." WILL BE SAID of the wicked, who will be resurrected and make better their deeds. And the soul will grant them its precious splendor, so they will know, repent and have full merit again.

198. וְכַד חָמָא שְׁלֹמֹה דָּא הֲוָה סַגֵּי וַאֲמַר וּבְכֵן רָאִיתִי רְשָׁעִים קְבוּרִים וָבָאוּ וּמִמְּקוֹם קָדוֹשׁ יְהַלֵּכוּ, שֶׁיָּבוֹאוּ וְיִחְיוּ, מִמְּקוֹם קָדוֹשׁ. וְתָנֵינָן, אָמַר רַבִּי אַבָּא אָמַר רַבִּי יוֹחָנָן, כְּתִיב הֲיַהֲפֹךְ כּוּשִׁי עוֹרוֹ וְנָמֵר חֲבַרְבֻּרֹתָיו, כָּךְ הָרְשָׁעִים, שֶׁלֹּא זָכוּ לָשׁוּב בָּעוֹלָם הַזֶּה, וּלְהַקְטִיר מַעֲשִׂים טוֹבִים, לְעוֹלָם לֹא יַקְטִירוּ בָּעוֹלָם הַבָּא. רְאֵה מַה כְּתִיב, וַיּוֹסֶף אַבְרָהָם וַיִּקַּח אִשָּׁה, וְשֶׁרוֹצֶה לַעֲשׂוֹת לָהֶם נְשָׁמָה לְגוּפָם, וּלְקָרְבָם בִּתְשׁוּבָה, כד"א וְאֶת הַנֶּפֶשׁ אֲשֶׁר עָשׂוּ בְחָרָן.

198. When Solomon saw this, he wondered very much, and said, "And so I saw the wicked buried, and come to their rest...gone from the holy place" (Kohelet 8:10), WHICH MEANS THAT THEY WILL COME AND LIVE AT THE HOLY PLACE, NAMELY THEY WILL RISE AT THE RESURRECTION OF THE DEAD. Rabbi Aba quoted Rabbi Yochanan, saying it is written: "Can the Kushite change his skin, or the leopard his spots?" (Yirmeyah 13:23), similarly the wicked who did not deserve to repent in this world and offer good deeds as sacrifices will never burn sacrifices in the World to Come. THOUGH THEY WILL RISE FROM THE DEAD, THEY WILL NOT BE ABLE TO DO GOOD DEEDS, BECAUSE THEY DID NOT LEAD MERITORIOUS LIVES. It is written: "Then again Abraham took a wife" and wanted to produce a soul for their bodies and bring them closer in repentance, as it is written: "And the souls that they had made in Charan" (Beresheet 12:5).

199. אָמַר רִבִּי אֶלְעָזָר, תָּא חֲזֵי, מַה כְּתִיב, וַתֵּלֶד לוֹ אֶת זִמְרָן וְאֶת
יָקְשָׁן, הַרְבֵּה מַעֲשִׂים רָעִים, עַד שֶׁנִּגְרָשִׁים מִן הָעוֹלָם, דִּכְתִיב וַיְשַׁלְּחֵם
מֵעַל יִצְחָק בְּנוֹ. וַעֲלֵיהֶם נֶאֱמַר וְרַבִּים מִישֵׁנֵי אַדְמַת עָפָר יָקִיצוּ וְגוֹ',
וְעַל הָאֲחֵרִים נֶאֱמַר וְהַמַּשְׂכִּילִים יַזְהִירוּ כְּזֹהַר הָרָקִיעַ וְגוֹ'.

199. Rabbi Elazar said, Look at the verse: "And she bore him Zimran, and Yokshan" (Beresheet 25:2). They did many evil deeds, until they were driven from the world, as it is written: "And sent them away from his son Isaac" (Ibid.). Of them it is written, "And many of those who sleep in the dust of the earth shall awake..." (Daniel 12:2). Of the others, it is written: "And they who are wise shall shine like the brightness of the firmament" (Ibid. 3).

200. אָמַר, רִבִּי יְהוּדָה הַאי מַשְׁמַע עַל פָּרָשָׁתָא, וּמַשְׁמַע דְּאוֹתוֹ זְמַן
נִקְרָא אַבְרָהָם וּבִמְקוֹמוֹ נִקְרֵאת יִצְחָק, כִּדְקָאַמְרָן, הה"ד וַיְהִי אַחֲרֵי
מוֹת אַבְרָהָם וַיְבָרֶךְ אֱלֹהִים אֶת יִצְחָק בְּנוֹ וַיֵּשֶׁב יִצְחָק עִם בְּאֵר לַחַי
רֹאִי. עִם יְדִיעַת הַחַי, שֶׁהוּא חַי הָעוֹלָמִים, לָדַעַת וּלְהַשִּׂיג, מַה שֶּׁלֹּא
הִשִּׂיג בָּעוֹלָם הַזֶּה הה"ד כִּי מָלְאָה הָאָרֶץ דֵּעָה אֶת ה'.

(עַד כָּאן מִדְרָשׁ הַנֶּעֱלָם)

200. Rabbi Yehuda said, This is the meaning of the text indicating that it was called Abraham at one time, and is now called Isaac in his place, as it is written: "And it came to pass after the death of Abraham, that Elohim blessed his son Isaac; and Isaac dwelt by Beer Lachai Roi (lit. 'the well of living and seeing')" (Beresheet 25:11). Through the knowledge of the living, the life of the world, he may know and conceive what he had not conceived in this world, as it is written: "For the earth shall be full of the knowledge of Hashem" (Yeshayah 11:9).

End of Midrash Hane'elam (homiletical interpretations on the obscure)

201. רִבִּי יִצְחָק פָּתַח וַאֲמַר, וְיָשׁב הֶעָפָר עַל הָאָרֶץ כְּשֶׁהָיָה וְהָרוּחַ
תָּשׁוּב אֶל הָאֱלֹהִים אֲשֶׁר נְתָנָהּ. תָּא חֲזֵי, כַּד בָּרָא קוּדְשָׁא בְּרִיךְ הוּא
לְאָדָם, נָטַל עַפְרֵיהּ מֵאֲתַר דְּמַקְדְּשָׁא, וּבָנָה גוּפֵיהּ מֵאַרְבַּע סִטְרִין

-110-

דְּעָלְמָא, דְּכֻלְּהוּ יָהֲבוּ לֵיהּ חֵילָא, לְבָתַר אֲתָרַק עֲלֵיהּ רוּחָא דְּחַיֵּי, כד"א וַיִּפַּח בְּאַפָּיו נִשְׁמַת חַיִּים וגו'. לְבָתַר קָם וְיָדַע דְּאִיהוּ מֵעֵילָּא וְתַתָּא, וּכְדֵין אִתְדַּבַּק וְיָדַע חָכְמָה עִלָּאָה.

201. Rabbi Yitzchak opened with the verse: "And the dust returns to the earth as it was: and the spirit returns to Elohim who gave it" (Kohelet 12:7). Come and behold: When the Holy One, blessed be He, created Adam, He took the dust from the place of the Temple and built his body from the four directions of the world, each of which gave him strength. Later, He poured the spirit of life upon him, as it is written: "And breathed into his nostrils the breath of life" (Beresheet 2:7). Then he stood up and knew that he comprised both high and low; he cleaved to Hashem and knew the supernal wisdom.

202. כְּגַוְונָא דָא, כָּל בַּר נָשׁ דְּעָלְמָא, אִיהוּ כָּלִיל מֵעֵילָּא וְתַתָּא, וְכָל אִינּוּן דְּיָדְעִין לְאִתְקַדְּשָׁא בְּהַאי עָלְמָא כְּדְקָא יָאוֹת, כַּד אוֹלִידוּ בַּר, מָשְׁכִין עֲלֵיהּ רוּחַ קַדִּישָׁא, מֵאֲתָר דְּכָל קַדִּישֵׁי נָפְקִין מִנֵּיהּ, וְאִלֵּין אִקְרוּן בְּנִין לְקוּדְשָׁא בְּרִיךְ הוּא, בְּגִין דְּגוּפָא אִתְעֲבֵיד בִּקְדוּשָׁה כִּדְקָא יָאוֹת, הָכֵי נָמֵי יָהֲבִין לֵיהּ רוּחָא מֵאֲתָר עִלָּאָה קַדִּישָׁא כִּדְקָא חֲזֵי, וְהָא אִתְּמַר.

202. Similarly, all people in the world are included from the upper and the lower. When all those who know how to properly sanctify themselves in this world beget a child, they draw on it a Holy Spirit from that place where all that is holy originates. These are called children to the Holy One, blessed be He, because their bodies were properly made in sanctity. He is also given a spirit from the holy supernal place, as he deserves. This has already been explained.

203. תָּא חֲזֵי, בְּשַׁעֲתָא דִּזְמִין בַּר נָשׁ, לְמֵיהַב חוּשְׁבַּן עוֹבָדוֹי, עַד לָא יִפּוֹק מֵעַלְמָא, הַהוּא יוֹמָא, יוֹמָא דְּחוּשְׁבַּן אִיהוּ, דְּגוּפָא וְנִשְׁמָתָא יָהֲבֵי חוּשְׁבְּנָא. לְבָתַר נִשְׁמָתָא אִתְפָּרְשָׁא מִינֵּיהּ, וְגוּפָא תָּב לְאַרְעָא, וְכֹלָּא תָּב לְאַתְרֵיהּ דְּאִתְנְסִיב מִתַּמָּן, וְהָא אוֹקִמוּהָ, עַד זִמְנָא דְּקוּדְשָׁא בְּרִיךְ הוּא זַמִּין לְאַחֲיָיא מֵתַיָּיא, כֹּלָּא גָּנִיז קַמֵּיהּ.

203. Come and behold: When man is called to account for his deeds before leaving this world, there will be a day of reckoning, a day when both the soul and body give reckoning. The soul then LEAVES THE BODY AND is separated from it, while the body, WHICH WAS CREATED FROM DUST, returns to dust, and all returns to the place from which it was taken. It has already been explained that everything will be stored before the Holy One, blessed be He, until the time when He resurrects the dead.

204. וְהַהוּא גוּפָא מַמָּשׁ, וְהַהִיא נִשְׁמָתָא מַמָּשׁ, זְמִין קוּדְשָׁא בְּרִיךְ הוּא לַאֲתָבָא לְעָלְמָא כְּמִלְקַדְמִין, וּלְחַדְתָּא אַנְפֵּי עָלְמָא, הֲדָא הוּא דִּכְתִיב יִחְיוּ מֵתֶיךָ נְבֵלָתִי יְקוּמוּן. וְהַהִיא נִשְׁמָתָא מַמָּשׁ, גְּנִיזָא קַמֵּי קוּדְשָׁא בְּרִיךְ הוּא, וְתָבַת לְאַתְרָה, כְּפוּם אָרְחָהָא. כְּדָבָר אַחֵר וְהָרוּחַ תָּשׁוּב אֶל הָאֱלֹהִים אֲשֶׁר נְתָנָהּ. וּלְזִמְנָא דְזַמִּין קוּדְשָׁא בְּרִיךְ הוּא לַאֲחָיָיא מֵתַיָיא זַמִּין אִיהוּ לְאַרְקָא טַלָּא מֵרֵישֵׁיהּ עֲלַיְיהוּ, וּבְהַהוּא טַלָּא יְקוּמוּן כֹּלָּא מֵעַפְרָא.

204. The Holy One, blessed be He, will return that very body and that very soul to the world as before, and renew the face of the world. This is according to the verse: "The dead men of your people shall live, my dead body shall arise" (Yeshayah 26:19). The same soul is stored before the Holy One, blessed be He, as it returns to its proper place AFTER THE DEATH OF THAT PERSON, according to its deeds, as it is written: "And the spirit returns to Elohim who gave it." At that time, He will revive the dead and pour dew from His head upon them. All the bodies will be resurrected from the dust by that dew.

205. הֲדָא הוּא דִּכְתִיב כִּי טַל אוֹרוֹת טַלֶּךָ. מַאי טַל אוֹרוֹת, אוֹרוֹת מַמָּשׁ, מֵאִינוּן נְהוֹרִין דִּלְעֵילָא, דִּבְהוֹן זַמִּין לַאֲרְקָא חַיִּין לְעָלְמָא, בְּגִין דְּאִילָנָא דְחַיֵּי יָרִיק חַיִּין דְּלָא פָּסְקִין לְעָלְמִין, דְּהָא הַשְׁתָּא פָּסְקִין, בְּגִין דְּהָא חִוְיָא בִּישָׁא שָׁלְטָא, וְאִתְכַּסֵּי סִיהֲרָא, וּבְגִין כָּךְ, כִּבְיָכוֹל פָּסְקִין מֵימוֹי, וְחַיִּין לָא שָׁלְטִין בְּעָלְמָא כִּדְקָא יָאוֹת.

205. It is written: "For your dew is as the dew on herbs (lit. 'of lights')" (Yeshayah 26:19). HE ASKS, What is the dew of lights? AND HE ANSWERS, These are real lights, the Lights of above, by which He will pour life upon the world, because the Tree of Life, ZEIR ANPIN, will then provide never-ending life. For now, there is an end to life, since WHEN the evil serpent has its way, the moon is covered, NAMELY THE UNION OF THE SUPERNAL SUN AND MOON, ZEIR ANPIN AND NUKVA, STOPS. For that reason, the water OF ZEIR ANPIN, THE SECRET OF THE TREE OF LIFE as it were, stops flowing. Therefore, life does not exist properly in the world.

206. וּבְהַהוּא זִמְנָא, הַהוּא יֵצֶר הָרָע, דְּאִיהוּ חִוְיָא בִּישָׁא, יִסְתַּלַּק מֵעַלְמָא, וְיַעֲבַר לֵיהּ קוּדְשָׁא בְּרִיךְ הוּא, כְּמָה דְאַתְּ אָמַר וְאֶת רוּחַ הַטֻּמְאָה אַעֲבִיר מִן הָאָרֶץ. וּלְבָתַר דְּאִיהוּ יִתְעֲבַר מֵעַלְמָא, סִיהֲרָא לָא אִתְכַּסְיָא, וְנַהֲרָא דְּנַגְיד, וְנָפִיק, לָא יִפְסְקוּן מַבּוּעוֹי, וּכְדֵין כְּתִיב וְהָיָה אוֹר הַלְּבָנָה כְּאוֹר הַחַמָּה וְאוֹר הַחַמָּה יִהְיֶה שִׁבְעָתַיִם כְּאוֹר שִׁבְעַת הַיָּמִים וְגו'.

206. At that time, the Evil Inclination, which is the wicked serpent, will be removed from the world, and the Holy One, blessed be He, will cause it to pass away, as written: "And I will cause...the unclean spirit to pass out of the land" (Zecharyah 13:2). After it passes from the world, the moon will no longer be covered and the sources of the river that flow out OF EDEN, WHICH IS ZEIR ANPIN, will never stop flowing. Then, it is written: "The light of the moon shall be as the light of the sun, and the light of the sun shall be sevenfold, as the light of seven days" (Yeshayah 30:26).

207. אָמַר ר' חִזְקִיָּה, אִי תֵימָא, דְּכָל גּוּפִין דְּעַלְמָא, יְקוּמוּן וְיִתְעָרוּן מֵעַפְרָא, אִינּוּן גּוּפֵי דְּאִתְנְטִיעוּ בְּנִשְׁמָתָא חֲדָא, מַה תְּהֵא מִנַּיְיהוּ. אָמַר רַבִּי יוֹסֵי, אִינּוּן גּוּפִין, דְּלָא זָכוּ וְלָא אַצְלָחוּ, הֲרֵי אִינּוּן כְּלָא הֲווֹ, כְּמָה דַּהֲווֹ עֵץ יָבֵשׁ בְּהַהִיא עַלְמָא, הָכִי נָמֵי בְּהַהוּא זִמְנָא, וְגוּפָא בַּתְרָאָה, דְּאִתְנְטַע וְאַצְלַח, וְנָטַל שָׁרְשׁוֹי, כְּדְקָא יָאוֹת, יְקוּם.

207. Rabbi Chizkiyah said, If you say that all the bodies in the world will rise to life and wake up from the dust, it behooves us to ask about the bodies that were planted with the same soul, MEANING THAT ONE SOUL INCARNATED WITHIN SEVERAL BODIES, ONE AFTER THE OTHER, AS IS KNOWN. What will become of them? WILL ALL OF THEM RISE AT THE REVIVAL OF THE DEAD, OR ONLY THE LAST ONE? Rabbi Yosi said, It is as if the bodies, which did not have merit THROUGH GOOD DEEDS and did not

succeed IN COMPLETING THE SOUL, never were. They are as a dried tree in that world, and so they will be at the time OF THE RESURRECTION OF THE DEAD. Only the last body that was planted and worthily received its SPIRITUAL roots will be revived AT THE RESURRECTION OF THE DEAD.

208. וַעֲלֵיהּ כְּתִיב וְהָיָה כְּעֵץ שָׁתוּל עַל מַיִם וְגו', וְהָיָה עָלֵהוּ רַעֲנָן וְגו'. דַּעֲבַד אִיבִּין, וְנָטַע שָׁרָשִׁין, וְאַצְלַח כִּדְקָא יָאוֹת. וְעַל הַהוּא גּוּפָא קַדְמָאָה, דְּלָא עֲבַד אִיבִּין, וְלָא נָטַע שָׁרָשִׁין, כְּתִיב וְהָיָה כְּעַרְעָר בָּעֲרָבָה וְלֹא יִרְאֶה כִּי יָבֹא טוֹב וְגו'. כִּי יָבֹא טוֹב, דָּא תְּחִיַית הַמֵּתִים.

208. Of this, it is written: "For he shall be like a tree planted by the waters... and its leaf shall be green" (Yirmeyah 17:8), because it bore fruit, NAMELY GOOD DEEDS, and struck roots properly ABOVE IN THE UPPER WORLD. EACH PRECEPT CORRESPONDS TO A SPIRITUAL ROOT THAT IS REVEALED ABOVE, AS IS KNOWN. Of the earlier body that did not bear fruit or strike roots, it is written: "For he shall be like the juniper tree in the desert, and shall not see when good comes" (Ibid. 6). "When good comes" refers to the resurrection of the dead.

209. וְיִתְנְהִיר הַהוּא נְהוֹרָא, דְּזַמִּין לְאַנְהָרָא לְהוּ לְצַדִּיקַיָּא, דַּהֲוָה גָּנִיז קַמֵּיהּ, מִיּוֹמָא דְּאִתְבְּרֵי עַלְמָא, דִּכְתִיב, וַיַּרְא אֱלֹהִים אֶת הָאוֹר כִּי טוֹב. וּכְדֵין, זַמִּין קוּדְשָׁא בְּרִיךְ הוּא לְאַחְיָיא מֵתַיָיא, וּכְתִיב וְזָרְחָה לָכֶם יִרְאֵי שְׁמִי שֶׁמֶשׁ צְדָקָה וְגו', וּכְדֵין יִתְגַּבַּר טוֹב בְּעַלְמָא, וְהַהוּא דְּאִתְקְרֵי רַע, יִתְעֲבַר מֵעַלְמָא, כִּדְאֲמָרָן. וּכְדֵין אִינוּן גּוּפִין קַדְמָאֵי, לֶהֱוֵי כְּלָא הֲוֵו.

209. And the Light that will illuminate the righteous will shine. It has been stored before Him since the day that the world was created, as written: "And Elohim saw the light, that it was good" (Beresheet 1:3). In the future, the Holy One, blessed be He, will revive the dead. It is written: "But to you who fear my name the sun of righteousness shall arise, etc." (Malachi 3:20), for then good will have the upper hand in the world, and that which is called evil will pass away from the world, as we said, then, the bodies that preceded the last one will be as if they never existed.

210. אֲמַר רִבִּי יִצְחָק זַמִּין קוּדְשָׁא בְּרִיךְ הוּא לְאַרְקָא עֲלַיְיהוּ, עַל אִינּוּן גּוּפִין, רוּחִין אָחֳרָנִין, וְאִי זָכָאן בְּהוֹן, יְקוּמוּן בְּעָלְמָא כִּדְקָא יָאוֹת, וְאִי לָאו, יְהוֹן קַטְמָא, תְּחוֹת רַגְלֵיהוֹן דְּצַדִּיקַיָּא, דִּכְתִיב וְרַבִּים מִיְּשֵׁנֵי אַדְמַת עָפָר יָקִיצוּ וְגוֹ'. וְכֹלָּא אִתָּקַם, וְאִתְעַתַּד קַמֵּי קוּדְשָׁא בְּרִיךְ הוּא, וְכֻלְּהוּ בְּמִנְיָינָא הֲווֹ, כְּד"א הַמּוֹצִיא בְמִסְפָּר צְבָאָם וְגוֹ'.

210. Rabbi Yitzchak said, The Holy One, blessed be He, will pour other spirits upon the bodies THAT CAME BEFORE THE LAST ONE. They will be properly revived in the world if they merit the spirits BY FOLLOWING THE RIGHT PATH. If they do not, they will be ashes under the feet of the righteous, as it is written: "And many of those who sleep in the dust of the earth shall awake, etc." (Daniel 12:2). Everything was established and prepared before the Holy One, blessed be He, and all were numbered for the time of resurrection, as it is written: "That brings out their host by number, etc." (Yeshayah 40:26).

211. תָּא חֲזֵי, הָא אִתְּמַר, כָּל אִינּוּן מֵתִין דִּבְאַרְעָא דְּיִשְׂרָאֵל, יְקוּמוּן בְּקַדְמֵיתָא, בְּגִין, דְּקוּדְשָׁא בְּרִיךְ הוּא יִתְעַר עֲלַיְיהוּ, וְיוֹקִים לוֹן, עֲלַיְיהוּ כְּתִיב יִחְיוּ מֵתֶיךָ, אִלֵּין אִינּוּן דִּי בְּאַרְעָא דְּיִשְׂרָאֵל. נְבֵלָתִי יְקוּמוּן, אִלֵּין אִינּוּן דִּבְגוֹ אַרְעָאן אָחֳרָנִין, דְּלָא כְּתִיב בְּהוֹ תְּחִיָּיה, אֶלָּא קִימָה. דְּהָא רוּחָא דְּחַיֵּי, לָא תַשְׁרֵי אֶלָּא בְּאַרְעָא קַדִּישָׁא דְּיִשְׂרָאֵל, וּבְגִין כָּךְ, כְּתִיב בְּהוֹ, יִחְיוּ מֵתֶיךָ, וְאִינּוּן דִּלְבַר, יִתְבְּרֵי גּוּפָא דִּלְהוֹן, וִיקוּמוּן גּוּפָא, בְּלָא רוּחָא, וּלְבָתַר יִתְגַּלְגְּלוּן תְּחוֹת עַפְרָא, עַד דְּיִמְטוּן לְא"י, וְתַמָּן יְקַבְּלוּן נִשְׁמָתָא, וְלָא בִּרְשׁוּ אָחֳרָא, בְּגִין דְּיִתְקַיְּימוּן בְּעָלְמָא כִּדְקָא חֲזֵי.

211. Come and behold: We have learned that all the dead in the land of Yisrael will be resurrected first, because the Holy One, blessed be He, will arouse them WITH A SPIRIT and revive them. Of them it is written: "The dead...shall live" (Yeshayah 26:19) This verse refers to those buried in the land of Yisrael. "My dead body shall arise" refers to those buried in other countries, for whom the term "restoration" is used in place of "resurrection." This is because the spirit of life dwells only in the Holy Land of Yisrael. Therefore, "The dead man of your people shall live" refers only

to those buried in the land Yisrael. The bodies of those outside THE LAND OF YISRAEL will be created, but they will be resurrected as a body with no spirit. Thereafter, they will roll under the soil of the land until they reach the land of Yisrael, where they will receive a soul. They will not receive this soul under any other authority, so they will be well established in the world.

212. רִבִּי אֶלְעָזָר וְרִבִּי יֵיסָא, הֲווֹ יַתְבֵי לֵילְיָא חַד, וְעָסְקֵי בְּאוֹרַיְיתָא. אֲמַר רִבִּי אֶלְעָזָר, תָּא חֲזֵי, בְּשַׁעֲתָא דְּקוּדְשָׁא בְּרִיךְ הוּא, זַמִּין לְאַחֲיָיא מֵתַיָּיא, כָּל אִינוּן נִשְׁמָתִין דְּיִתְעָרוּן קַמֵּיהּ, כֻּלְּהוּ קַיְימִין, דְּיוֹקְנִין דְּיוֹקְנִין קַמֵּיהּ, בְּהַהוּא דְּיוֹקְנָא מַמָּשׁ, דַּהֲווֹ בְּהַאי עַלְמָא, וְנָחִית לוֹן קוּדְשָׁא בְּרִיךְ הוּא, וְיִקְרֵי לוֹן בִּשְׁמָהָן, כְּמָה דְאַתְּ אָמֵר לְכֻלָּם בְּשֵׁם יִקְרָא. וְכָל נִשְׁמָתָא תֵּיעוֹל לְדוּכְתַּהּ, וִיקוּמוּן בְּקִיּוּמָא בְּעַלְמָא כִּדְקָא חֲזֵי, וּכְדֵין יְהֵא עַלְמָא שְׁלִים, וְעַל הַהוּא זִמְנָא כְּתִיב, וְחֶרְפַּת עַמּוֹ יָסִיר וְגו', מַאי וְחֶרְפַּת עַמּוֹ יָסִיר. דָּא יֵצֶר הָרַע, דְּאַחְשִׁיךְ אַנְפֵּי בְּרִיָּין, וְשַׁלִּיט בְּהוּ.

212. Rabbi Elazar and Rabbi Yesa were sitting one night, studying Torah. Rabbi Elazar said, Come and behold: In the future, when the Holy One, blessed be He, resurrects the dead, all the souls that will be aroused before Him will stand before Him in the very shape they had in this world. And the Holy One, blessed be He, will bring them down TO THEIR BODIES and call them by name, as written: "He calls them all by names" (Yeshayah 40:26). Each soul will enter its place IN THE BODY and be properly revived in the world. Then, the world will be perfected. Of that time it is written: "And the disgrace of his people shall He take away" (Yeshayah 25:8). What is "the disgrace of his people shall He take away"? It is the Evil Inclination THAT HE WILL REMOVE FROM THE WORLD, which darkens the faces of the people and rules over them.

213. אֲמַר רִבִּי יוֹסֵי, הָא חֲמֵינַן, כָּל זִמְנָא דְּבַר נָשׁ קָאִים בְּרוּחָא דָּא. לָאו אִיהוּ מְסָאָב, נָפְקָא נִשְׁמָתֵיהּ מִנֵּיהּ, אִיהוּ מְסָאָב. אֲמַר לֵיהּ וַדַּאי הָכֵי הוּא וְהָכֵי אִתְּמַר, דְּהָא הַהוּא יֵצֶר הָרַע, כַּד נָטִיל רוּחָא דְּבַר נָשׁ, סָאִיב לֵיהּ וְאִשְׁתָּאַר גּוּפָא מְסָאָב, וּשְׁאָר עַמִּין עכו"ם, כַּד אִינוּן בְּחַיֵּיהוֹן אִינוּן מְסָאֲבִין, דְּהָא מִסִּטְרָא מְסָאֲבָא אִית לוֹן נִשְׁמָתִין, וְכַד

אַתְרֵיק מִנֵּיה הַהוּא מְסָאֲבוּ, אִשְׁתְּאַר גּוּפָא בְּלָא מְסָאֲבוּ כְּלָל.

213. Rabbi Yosi said, We see that whenever the spirit is in a man, he is not defiled. Once his soul leaves him, he is defiled. HE WANTED TO KNOW THE MEANING OF THIS. He said to him, Assuredly this is so. We have also learned that when the Evil Inclination, WHICH IS THE ANGEL OF DEATH, takes the spirit of man, he becomes defiled and the body remains unclean. FOR WITH THE STRENGTH OF POLLUTION OF THE TREE OF KNOWLEDGE, THIS STRENGTH BEING THE ROOT OF ALL DEFILEMENT, IT TAKES AWAY MAN'S SOUL. THE REVERSE IS TRUE for the heathen nations. They are unclean while they live because their souls are drawn from the side of defilement. Once their bodies are emptied of that defilement, NAMELY WHEN THEY DIE AND THE SOUL LEAVES, the body stays without unholiness AND THEREFORE DOES NOT CAUSE DEFILEMENT. RABBI SHIMON SAID THAT THE CANOPIED GRAVES OF THE HEATHEN DO NOT DEFILE.

214. בְּגִין כָּךְ מַאן דְּאִתְדַּבַּק בְּאִתְּתָא דִּשְׁאָר עַמִּין עעכו"ם, אִסְתָּאַב אִיהוּ. וְהַהוּא בְּרָא דְּאִתְיְלֵיד לֵיהּ, יְקַבֵּל עֲלֵיהּ רוּחַ מְסָאֲבָא. וְאִי תֵימָא, הָא בְּסִטְרָא דַּאֲבוֹי דְּמִיִשְׂרָאֵל קָא אַתְיָא, אַמַּאי יְקַבֵּל עֲלֵיהּ רוּחַ מְסָאֲבָא. תָּא חֲזֵי, דְּהָא בְּקַדְמֵיתָא אִסְתָּאַב אֲבוֹי, בְּשַׁעְתָּא דְּאִתְדַּבַּק בְּהַהִיא אִתְּתָא, דְּאִיהִי מְסָאֲבָא, וְכֵיוָן דְּאַב אִיהוּ אִסְתָּאַב, בְּהַהִיא אִתְּתָא דְּאִיהִי מְסָאֲבָא, כָּל שֶׁכֵּן דְּאִיהוּ בְּרָא דְּאִתְיְלֵיד מִנָּהּ, יְקַבֵּל עֲלֵיהּ רוּחַ מְסָאֲבָא. וְלָא עוֹד, אֶלָּא דַּעֲבַר עַל אוֹרַיְיתָא דִּכְתִיב, כִּי לא תִשְׁתַּחֲוֶה לְאֵל אַחֵר כִּי ה' קַנָּא שְׁמוֹ, בְּגִין דְּקַנֵּי עַל הַאי בְּרִית קַדִּישָׁא.

214. For that reason, he who cleaves to a woman from the heathen nations is defiled, and the child that she bears him receives the spirit of defilement. You may ask, Is it not of Yisrael from the side of its father? If so, why should it receive the spirit of defilement? Come and behold: First its father was besmirched when he united with that tainted woman. All the more so, the child that she bears will receive the spirit of defilement upon it. Furthermore, he also transgressed the Torah, as it is written: "For you shall worship no other El; for Hashem whose name is jealous, is a jealous El" (Shemot 34:14), which means that He is zealous of the covenant, SO THAT IT WILL NOT BE TAINTED BY HEATHEN WOMEN.

21. "You shall not take a wife... of the daughters of the Canaanite"

A Synopsis

The rabbis discuss the dangers of a man marrying a woman of the heathen nations, and Abraham's desire that Isaac remain in the Central Column, where he would learn the ways of the Holy One.

The Relevance of this Passage

This pertains to the importance of our relationships in life, including, their effect on the spiritual state of things. Marriage is the union of two halves of one soul, and is considered an important tool for drawing the Light of the upper worlds [husband] into the lower world [wife]. All our actions in this material realm, including marital transactions, are a microcosm of the ebb-and-flow relationship endlessly playing out between the physical and metaphysical worlds. To secure a personal connection to the macrocosmic level of reality, thus ensuring its positive influence in our life, we must surround ourselves with those in whom the love of the Creator burns strongly, rather than those whose godlessness seeks to infect us with unbelief. Consciousness creates reality. People who are not conscious of the Creator create for themselves a Godless reality devoid of spiritual Light. Whether in business, social, or marital relationships, the Zohar helps prevent us from becoming entangled with negative partners, and to attract like-minded, virtuous people into our life.

215. אֲמַר רִבִּי אֶלְעָזָר, תָּא חֲזֵי, דְּהָא אִתְּמָר, דְּכֵיוָן דְּיָדַע אַבְרָהָם אָבִינוּ חָכְמְתָא, בָּעָא לְהִתְפְּרְשָׁא מִכָּל שְׁאָר עַמִּין, וְלָא לְאִתְדַּבְּקָא בְּהוֹ, וּבְגִין כָּךְ כְּתִיב, וְאַשְׁבִּיעֲךָ בַּה' אֱלֹקֵי הַשָּׁמַיִם וֵאלֹקֵי הָאָרֶץ אֲשֶׁר לֹא תִקַּח אִשָּׁה לִבְנִי מִבְּנוֹת הַכְּנַעֲנִי וְגוֹ', מִבְּנוֹת הַכְּנַעֲנִי וַדַּאי רָזָא אִיהוּ, כְּדָבָר אַחֵר וּבָעַל בַּת אֵל נֵכָר. אֲשֶׁר אָנֹכִי יוֹשֵׁב בְּקִרְבּוֹ, אָנֹכִי דַּיְיקָא, כְּתִיב הָכָא אֲשֶׁר אָנֹכִי, וּכְתִיב הָתָם אָנֹכִי עָשִׂיתִי אֶרֶץ. וְכָל דָּא, בְּגִין דְּלָא לְאִסְתָּאֲבָא בְּהוֹ.

215. Rabbi Elazar said, Come and behold: We have learned that because Abraham had wisdom, he wanted to be separated from and not cleave to all other nations. Therefore it is written: "And I will make you swear by Hashem, the Elohim of heaven, and the Elohim of the earth, that you shall

not take a wife to my son..." (Beresheet 24:3). The phrase "of the daughters of the Canaanite" (Ibid.) surely contains a secret, as it is written: "And has married the daughter of a strange El" (Malachi 2:11). In the phrase: "Among whom I dwell" (Beresheet 24:3), the "I" is exactly the same as that mentioned in "I have made the earth" (Yeshayah 45:12). THE "I" IN THE FIRST CASE REFERS TO THE SHECHINAH AS IT IN THE SECOND CASE, BECAUSE SHE WAS IN EXILE. HE MADE HIM SWEAR all that so to prevent him from being defiled by them.

216. תָּא חֲזֵי, הַאי מַאן דְּאָעֵיל הַאי בְּרִית קַדִּישָׁא, בְּהַהִיא אִתְּתָא דִּשְׁאָר עַמִּין עעכו״ם, גָּרֵים לְאִסְתָּאֲבָא אֲתַר אָחֳרָא, וְעַל דָּא כְּתִיב תַּחַת שָׁלֹשׁ רָגְזָה אֶרֶץ וְגוֹ׳. וְאַף עַל גַּב דְּאוֹמֵי לֵיהּ בְּהַאי בְּרִית, לָא אַבְטַח בֵּיהּ אַבְרָהָם, עַד דְּצַלֵּי צְלוֹתֵיהּ קַמֵּי קוּדְשָׁא בְּרִיךְ הוּא, וַאֲמַר ה׳ אֱלֹקֵי הַשָּׁמַיִם וְגוֹ׳ הוּא יִשְׁלַח מַלְאָכוֹ, וַדַּאי דָּא מַלְאַךְ הַבְּרִית, בְּגִין דְּיִתְנְטִיר הַאי בְּרִית, וְלָא יִתְחַלֵּל בֵּין אִינּוּן עַמִּין.

216. Come and behold: Whoever puts the holy covenant in a woman of a heathen nation causes another place to be defiled; NAMELY, HE BLEMISHES THE SUPERNAL COVENANT AND CAUSES IT TO GIVE PLENTY TO THE HANDMAID. Thus, it is written: "For three things the earth is disquieted..." (Mishlei 30:21). And though he made him swear by the covenant, Abraham did not yet trust him, but prayed before the Holy One, blessed be He, saying "Hashem, Elohim of the heaven... He shall send his angel before you" (Beresheet 24:7). His angel assuredly MEANS the angel of the covenant, whom He shall send so that the covenant will be kept and not defiled among the nations.

217. רַק אֶת בְּנִי לֹא תָשֵׁב שָׁמָּה. מ״ט, בְּגִין דְּיָדַע אַבְרָהָם, דְּהָא בְּכֻלְּהוּ, לָא הֲוָה מַאן דְּאִשְׁתְּמוֹדַע לֵיהּ לְקוּדְשָׁא בְּרִיךְ הוּא, בַּר אִיהוּ בִּלְחוֹדוֹי, וְלָא בָּעָא דְּלֶהֱווֹ מְדוֹרֵיהּ דְּיִצְחָק בֵּינַיְיהוּ, אֶלָּא דִּיהֵא מְדוֹרֵיהּ עִמֵּיהּ, וְיִצְחָק יוֹלִיף מִנֵּיהּ תָּדִיר אָרְחוֹי דְּקוּדְשָׁא בְּרִיךְ הוּא וְלָא יִסְטֵי לִימִינָא וְלִשְׂמָאלָא. וְעַל דָּא לָא בָּעָא אַבְרָהָם דְּלֶהֱוֵי מְדוֹרֵיהּ דְּיִצְחָק תַּמָּן.

217. He asks the meaning of the verse: "Only bring not my son back there"

(Beresheet 24:8). HE RESPONDS that Abraham alone – and no one else IN HIS FAMILY – recognized the Holy One, blessed be He. Abraham did not want Isaac to dwell among the heathen nations, but wanted him to remain with him, where he would learn the ways of the Holy One, blessed be He. Abraham did not want Isaac to turn right or left, BUT RATHER TO REMAIN IN THE CENTRAL COLUMN. For that reason Abraham did not want Isaac's dwelling place to be among the heathen nations.

218. אָמַר רִבִּי יֵיסָא, וַדַּאי זְכוּתֵיהּ דְּאַבְרָהָם, אֲעֵרַע קַמֵּיהּ דְּהַהוּא עַבְדָּא, דְּהַהוּא יוֹמָא נְפַק, וְהַהוּא יוֹמָא מָטָא לְעֵינָא דְמַיָּא, דִּכְתִיב וָאָבֹא הַיּוֹם אֶל הָעָיִן. וְהָא אוּקְמוּהָ.

218. Rabbi Yesa said, Assuredly the merit of Abraham was with the servant, for he arrived at the well that very day he went, as is written: "And I came this day to the well" (Beresheet 24:42). This has already been explained.

22. In Torah is the whole life

A Synopsis

Rabbi Elazar, here, emphasizes the importance of Torah study, saying that the Angel of Death has no power over those who are diligent in their study of the scriptures. Rabbi Yesa asks why, if this is so, Moses died. We learn that although Moses did indeed die, his death was not caused by the Angel of Death; instead, he cleaved directly to the Shechinah, the Divine presence of the Creator, and went on to eternal life. All those who seek and approach the Creator, we're told, are called 'living.' Because of their diligent study of Torah, no reckoning is demanded of them in the World to Come.

The Relevance of this Passage

People regularly experience some form of death. We die a little bit each day, whether financially, emotionally, spiritually, or physically. The death of the body, the loss of an individual's sanity, or the end of one's career – are all likewise executed by one Angel of Death. The intent of these verses is to help ease these transitions from death to rebirth, from the end of one phase in our life, into a new phase filled with continuity and Light.

219. רִבִּי אֶלְעָזָר פָּתַח וַאֲמַר, גַּל עֵינַי וְאַבִּיטָה נִפְלָאוֹת מִתּוֹרָתֶךָ. כַּמָּה אִינּוּן בְּנֵי נָשָׁא טִפְּשִׁין, דְּלָא יָדְעִין, וְלָא מִסְתַּכְּלִין, לְאִשְׁתַּדְּלָא בְּאוֹרַיְיתָא, בְּגִין דְּאוֹרַיְיתָא, כָּל חַיִּין וְכָל חֵירוּ, וְכָל טוּב, בְּעָלְמָא דֵין וּבְעָלְמָא דְאָתֵי. חַיִּין אִינּוּן בְּעָלְמָא דֵין, דְּיִזְכּוּן לְיוֹמִין שְׁלֵמִין, בְּהַאי עָלְמָא, כד"א אֶת מִסְפַּר יָמֶיךָ אֲמַלֵּא. וּלְיוֹמִין אֲרִיכִין בְּעָלְמָא דְאָתֵי. בְּגִין דְּאִינּוּן חַיִּין שְׁלֵימִין, אִינּוּן חַיִּין דְּחֵידוּ חַיֵּי בְּלָא עֲצִיבוּ, חַיִּין דְּאִינּוּן חַיִּין, חֵירוּ בְּעָלְמָא דֵין, חֵירוּ דְכֹלָּא, דְּכָל מַאן דְּאִשְׁתַּדַּל בְּאוֹרַיְיתָא, לָא יָכְלִין לְשַׁלְטָאָה עֲלוֹי כָּל עַמִּין דְּעָלְמָא.

219. Rabbi Elazar opened with the verse, "Open you my eyes, that I may behold wondrous things out of Your Torah" (Tehilim 119:17). How foolish men are, for they do not know, and do not seek to be occupied with, Torah. Torah is the whole life. All freedom and all goodness in this world and in the World to Come are contained within it. HE EXPLAINED THAT it is life in this world; namely, they may merit full days in this world, as it is written: "The number of your days I will fulfill" (Shemot 23:26). And one will merit

long days in the World to Come, for this whole life is a life of joy, life without sadness, life that is real life, freedom in this world, freedom from everything, because other nations cannot rule over anyone who is engaged in the study of Torah.

220. וְאִי תֵּימָא אִינּוּן בְּנֵי שְׁמַד. גְּזֵרָה הִיא מִלְעֵילָא, כְּגוֹן רַבִּי עֲקִיבָא וַחֲבְרוֹי, וְכָךְ סָלִיק בְּמַחֲשָׁבָה. חֵירוּ דְּמַלְאַךְ הַמָּוֶת, דְּלָא יָכִיל לְשַׁלְטָאָה עֲלוֹי, וְהָכֵי הוּא וַדַּאי, דְּאִי אָדָם הֲוָה אִתְדָּבַּק בְּאִילָנָא דְּחַיֵּי, דְּאִיהוּ אוֹרַיְיתָא, לָא גָּרֵים מוֹתָא לֵיהּ וּלְכָל עָלְמָא. וּבְגִין כָּךְ, כַּד יָהַב קוּדְשָׁא בְּרִיךְ הוּא אוֹרַיְיתָא לְיִשְׂרָאֵל, מַה כְּתִיב בָּהּ חָרוּת עַל הַלּוּחוֹת וְהָא אוֹקִמוּהָ. וְאִלְמָלֵא אִינּוּן לָא חָטוּ וְשָׁבְקוּ אִילָנָא דְּחַיֵּי, לָא גָּרְמוּ מוֹתָא לְעָלְמָא כְּמִלְּקַדְמִין. וְקוּדְשָׁא בְּרִיךְ הוּא אָמַר אֲנִי אָמַרְתִּי אֱלֹהִים אַתֶּם וּבְנֵי עֶלְיוֹן כֻּלְּכֶם. חַבַּלְתּוּן גַּרְמֵיכוֹן, אָכֵן כְּאָדָם תְּמוּתוּן וְגוֹ'. וְעַל דָּא, כָּל מַאן דְּאִשְׁתַּדַּל בְּאוֹרַיְיתָא, לָא יָכִיל לְשַׁלְטָאָה עֲלוֹי הַהוּא חִוְיָא בִּישָׁא, דְּאַחְשִׁיךְ עָלְמָא.

220. You may say that there were those who were persecuted, NAMELY THE MARTYRS WHO WERE EXECUTED FOR STUDYING TORAH WHEN SUCH STUDY WAS FORBIDDEN. HE ANSWERS THAT this is a decree from above, such as the one for Rabbi Akiva and his companions, WHO WERE KILLED FOR STUDYING TORAH, and so it came to THE SUPREME mind WHEN THE WORLD WAS CREATED. BUT USUALLY, STUDYING TORAH MEANS freedom from the Angel of Death, who cannot have sway over him. Assuredly this is so. If Adam had cleaved to the Tree of Life, which is Torah, death would not have been brought upon him and the whole world. BUT BECAUSE HE FORSOOK THE TREE OF LIFE, WHICH IS TORAH, AND ATE FROM THE TREE OF KNOWLEDGE, HE BROUGHT DEATH UPON HIMSELF AND THE WHOLE WORLD. It was "engraved upon the tablets" (Shemot 32:16) when the Holy One, blessed be He, gave Torah to Yisrael. This has already been explained. DO NOT PRONOUNCE IT "ENGRAVED" (HEB. *CHARUT*), BUT FREEDOM (HEB. *CHERUT*), BECAUSE THERE WAS FREEDOM FROM THE ANGEL OF DEATH. If it were not for THE CHILDREN OF YISRAEL committing the sin OF THE CALF and leaving the Tree of Life, WHICH IS TORAH, they would not have brought death back to the world. And the Holy One, blessed be He, said, "I had said, 'You are angels, all of you sons of the most High'" (Tehilim 82:6), NAMELY AT THE GIVING OF TORAH. You defiled yourself BY SINNING, "therefore, you shall die like a man" (Ibid. 7). Therefore, the evil serpent which darkened the world cannot have power over anyone occupied in the study of Torah.

221. אָמַר רַבִּי יֵיסָא, אִי הָכֵי, מֹשֶׁה אַמַּאי מִית, דְּאִי הָכֵי כֵּיוָן דְּלָא חָב לָא יְמוּת. אָמַר לֵיהּ, וַדַּאי מִית, אֲבָל לָא שָׁלְטָא בֵּיהּ קָאמְרִינָן, אֶלָּא לָא מִית עַל יְדוֹי, וְלָא אִסְתָּאַב בֵּיהּ, וְלָא מִית וַדַּאי, אֶלָּא אִתְדַּבַּק בִּשְׁכִינְתָּא, וְאָזִיל לְחַיֵּי עָלְמָא.

221. Rabbi Yesa said, If this is so, it should be true that he who does not sin will not die. If so, why then did Moses die? He said to him, Moses died, but THE ANGEL OF DEATH had no sway over him. He did not die by him, nor was he defiled by him. Therefore, it is considered that Moses did not really die, but rather that he cleaved to the Shechinah and has gone on to life eternal.

222. וְהַאי חַי אִקְרֵי, כְּמָה דְּאוֹקִימְנָא, דִּכְתִיב, וּבְנָיָהוּ בֶן יְהוֹיָדָע בֶּן אִישׁ חַי וְגוֹ'. וְעַל דָּא, כָּל מַאן דְּאִשְׁתַּדַּל בְּאוֹרַיְיתָא, חֵירוּ אִית לֵיהּ מִכֹּלָּא, בְּעָלְמָא דֵּין, מִשִּׁעְבּוּדָא דִּשְׁאָר עַמִּין עעכו"ם, חֵירוּ בְּעָלְמָא דְּאָתֵי, בְּגִין דְּלָא יִתְבְּעוּן מִנֵּיהּ דִּינָא בְּהַהוּא עָלְמָא כְּלָל.

222. As such, he is called "living", as we have explained in discussing the verse: "And Benaiah, son of Jehoida, the son of a valiant (lit. 'living') man" (II Shmuel 23:20). WHOEVER APPROACHES HASHEM IS CALLED LIVING. Thus, he who is occupied in studying Torah has freedom from everything, including freedom in this world from the enslavement of heathen nations and freedom in the World to Come, for no reckoning will be demanded from him in that world at all.

223. תָּא חֲזֵי, בְּאוֹרַיְיתָא כַּמָּה רָזִין עִלָּאִין סְתִימִין, אִית בָּהּ, בְּגִין כָּךְ כְּתִיב יְקָרָה הִיא מִפְּנִינִים. כַּמָּה גְּנִיזִין טְמִירִין אִית בָּהּ, וְעַל דָּא כַּד אִסְתַּכַּל דָּוִד, בְּרוּחָא דְּחַכְמְתָא, וְיָדַע כַּמָּה פְּלִיאָן נָפְקִין מֵאוֹרַיְיתָא, פָּתַח וְאָמַר, גַּל עֵינַי וְאַבִּיטָה נִפְלָאוֹת מִתּוֹרָתֶךָ.

223. Come and behold how many supernal mysteries exist in the Torah. For that reason, it is written: "She is more precious than pearls" (Mishlei 3:15). How many hidden treasures there are in it. For that reason, when David looked AT THE TORAH in the spirit of wisdom, he said, "Open you my eyes, that I may behold wondrous things out of Your Torah."

23. "Behold, Rivkah came out"

A Synopsis
The Zohar explains that although Rivkah was brought up in an evil town and an evil home, she was protected by her exceptional soul. Rivkah is preparing to marry Isaac. The Torah story shows that a connection existed between Isaac and Rivkah before they were married; this is indicated by her coming out at evening time. Here evening refers to the time of afternoon prayer, and we learn that Isaac was in fact performing his afternoon prayers. The phrase 'came out' also refers to Rivkah's liberation from the house of evil owing to the elevation of her soul.

The Relevance of this Passage
Man is born into this world with untamed desires and animal instincts. The will of a man's body is given dominion over his soul, so that man can work and strive toward spiritual transformation. The evil setting in which Rivkah was raised symbolizes the physical world and our self-indulgent desires. Each of us can 'come out' of our own 'house of evil' – that is, remove our own self-centered desires – through the energy of Rivkah's soul and the power of the Patriarch Isaac. All this can be gained through a meditative reading of this passage.

224. תָּא חֲזֵי, וַיְהִי הוּא טֶרֶם כִּלָּה לְדַבֵּר וְהִנֵּה רִבְקָה יוֹצֵאת. יוֹצֵאת, בָּאָה מִבָּעֵי לֵיהּ, מַאי יוֹצֵאת. דְּקוּדְשָׁא בְּרִיךְ הוּא אַפֵּיק לָהּ, מִכָּל אִינּוּן בְּנֵי מָתָא, דְּכֻלְּהוּ חַיָּיבִין, וְהִיא יוֹצֵאת מִכְּלָלָא דִלְהוֹן. וַתֵּרֶד הָעַיְנָה, כְּתִיב בְּה"א, רָזָא אִיהוּ, דְּאִעְרָעַת תַּמָּן בֵּירָא דְמִרְיָם, וּבְגִין כָּךְ, כְּתִיב הָעַיְנָה בְּה"א, וּסְלִיקוּ לָהּ מַיָּא.

224. Come and behold: "And it came to pass, before he had done speaking, that, behold, Rivkah came out" (Beresheet 24:15). HE ASKS, WHY IS IT WRITTEN "came out"? It should have been written 'came', AS IT IS WRITTEN: "RACHEL CAME WITH HER FATHER'S SHEEP" (BERESHEET 29:6). Why is it written "came out"? HE RESPONDED, IT INDICATES that the Holy One, blessed be He, brought her away from the people of the town who were all evil. She was separated from THE TOWNSPEOPLE BECAUSE SHE WAS RIGHTEOUS. The verse: "And she went down to the well (Heb. ha'eynah)" (Beresheet 24:16) is spelled with a *Hei*. This is a secret because Miriam's well, THE SECRET OF THE NUKVA OF ZEIR ANPIN SHINING BY

THE ILLUMINATION OF CHOCHMAH, chanced before her there. For that reason "to the well" is written with a *Hei*, WHICH ALLUDES TO THE NUKVA, THE SECRET OF THE LOWER HEI OF YUD HEV VAV HEI. ALSO THE WORD *HA'EYNAH* IS DERIVED FROM THE WORD FOR EYES (HEB. *EYNAYIM*), WHICH IS A NAME OF CHOCHMAH. And the water rose toward Rivkah.

225. דָּבָר אַחֵר, וְהִנֵּה רִבְקָה יוֹצֵאת, כְּמָה דִכְתִיב, יוֹצְאוֹת לִשְׁאוֹב מַיִם, אַמַּאי יוֹצְאוֹת, וְלֹא הוֹלְכוֹת, וְלֹא בָאוֹת. אֶלָּא בְּגִין דִּטְמִירִין הֲווֹ כָּל יוֹמָא, וּבְהַהִיא שַׁעְתָּא, נָפְקִין לְשָׁאֲבָא מַיָּא, וְסִימָנָא נָקִיט בִּידֵיהּ.

225. Another explanation is that in the verse: "And, behold, Rivkah came out," the words "came out" have a similar meaning to that in the verse "AND THE DAUGHTERS OF THE CITY come out to draw water" (Beresheet 24:13). Why is it written: "Come out", rather than 'go' or 'come'? This is an allusion to their proper conduct. They remained at home all day and came out at a specific time toward evening to draw water. Abraham's servant recognized her by this sign.

226. תָּא חֲזֵי, כַּד מָטָא עַבְדָּא לְחָרָן וְאַשְׁכַּח לָהּ לְרִבְקָה לְעֵת עֶרֶב, הֲוָה עִידָן צְלוֹתָא דְמִנְחָה. בְּהַהִיא שַׁעְתָּא, דְּמָטָא יִצְחָק לְצַלָּאָה צְלוֹתָא דְמִנְחָה, בְּהַהִיא שַׁעְתָּא מָטָא עַבְדָּא לְגַבָּהּ דְּרִבְקָה. וּבְהַהִיא שַׁעְתָּא, דְּמָטָא יִצְחָק, לִצְלוֹתָא דְמִנְחָה כְּמִלְּקַדְמִין, מָטָאת רִבְקָה לְגַבֵּיהּ. לְאִשְׁתַּכְּחָא כֹּלָּא בְּאַתְרֵיהּ דְּאִצְטְרִיךְ, כִּדְקָא יָאוֹת, וְכֹלָּא מָטָא בְּרָזָא דְחָכְמְתָא, וְעַל דָּא, אָתָא הַהוּא עַבְדָּא, לִבְאֵר הַמַּיִם, רָזָא דִּכְתִיב מַעְיַן גַּנִּים בְּאֵר מַיִם חַיִּים וְנוֹזְלִים מִן לְבָנוֹן. וְאוֹקִימְנָא, וְכֹלָּא רָזָא אִיהוּ.

226. Come and behold: When the servant reached Charan and found Rivkah "at the time of evening" (Beresheet 24:11), it was time for the afternoon prayer. At the exact time when Isaac said his afternoon prayer, the servant reached Rivkah. Rivkah came to him again at that time when he prayed Minchah. THIS IS IN ACCORDANCE WITH THE VERSE: "AND ISAAC WENT OUT TO MEDITATE IN THE FIELD AT THE EVENING TIME" (IBID. 63). This happened so that everything would be in its proper place, as indicated by the

supernal Wisdom. Therefore, the servant reached the well of water, which is the secret of the verse "a fountain of gardens, a well of living water, and streams from Lebanon" (Shir Hashirim 4:15). We established everything to pertain to that secret.

24. Prayer, cry, tears

A Synopsis

While walking to Tiberias, Rabbi Shimon and Rabbi Aba are approached by a Jew who has come to seek Rabbi Shimon's wisdom on the subject of prayer. As the great rabbi discourses on the threefold nature of prayer, the man asks why the prayers of the patriarchs, composed before the Temple existed, are still considered most important. He is told that these prayers are designed to unite Zeir Anpin [the upper world] with his fate, the Nukva [our lower world]. After this, all else is superfluous.

The Relevance of this Passage

Prayer is often misunderstood as an offering of thanks and praise to our Creator. Kabbalistically, an omnipotent Force of Creation has no need for thanks or praise. It is because of this misunderstanding that many prayers go unanswered. In truth, prayer creates a connection between the lower and upper worlds. Once the connection is established, the person 'praying' can draw from a wellspring of spiritual energy to remove unwanted traits and negative attributes from his own nature. It is our own negative qualities that prohibit us from attaining permanent fulfillment. By strengthening our connection to the upper worlds, reading this section endows our prayers with greater power.

227. רִבִּי שִׁמְעוֹן הֲוָה אָתֵי לִטְבֶרְיָה וַהֲוָה עִמֵּיה רִבִּי אַבָּא. אָמַר רִבִּי שִׁמְעוֹן לְרִבִּי אַבָּא, נֵזִיל, דְּהָא אֲנַן חָמֵינָן, דְּבַר נָשׁ חַד, יִמְטֵי הַשְׁתָּא לְגַבָּן וּמִלִּין חַדְתִּין בְּפוּמֵיה, וְאִינוּן מִלִּין דְּאוֹרַיְיתָא. אָמַר רִבִּי אַבָּא, הָא יְדַעְנָא, דִּבְכָל אֲתַר דְּמַר אָזִיל, קוּדְשָׁא בְּרִיךְ הוּא מְשַׁדַּר לֵיה מַלְאָכִין, טָסִין בְּגַדְפִין לְאִשְׁתַּעְשְׁעָא בֵּיה.

227. Rabbi Shimon was walking to Tiberias with Rabbi Aba. Rabbi Shimon said, Let us go, because a man is about to come to us with new words of Torah. Rabbi Aba said, I already know that, wherever my master goes, the Holy One, blessed be He, sends flying angels to give him pleasure.

228. עַד דַּהֲווֹ אָזְלֵי, סָלֵיק רִבִּי שִׁמְעוֹן עֵינוֹי, וְחָמָא בַּר נָשׁ, דַּהֲוָה רָהֵיט וְאָזֵיל. יָתְבוּ רִבִּי שִׁמְעוֹן וְרִבִּי אַבָּא. כַּד מָטָא גַּבַּיְיהוּ, אָמַר לֵיה רִבִּי שִׁמְעוֹן, מַאן אַנְתְּ. אָמַר לֵיה יוּדָאי אֲנָא, וּמִקַפּוֹטְקִיָא קָאָתֵינָא,

וַאֲנָא אָזֵילְנָא אַטִיטְרֵיהּ דְּבַר יוֹחָאי, דְּאִתְמַנּוּן חַבְרַיָּא בְּמִלִּין יְדִיעָן, וְשַׁדְּרוּנִי גַבֵּיהּ. אֲמַר לֵיהּ אֵימָא בְּרִי. אֲמַר לֵיהּ אַנְתְּ בַּר יוֹחָאי. אֲמַר לֵיהּ אֲנָא בַּר יוֹחָאי.

228. While they were traveling, Rabbi Shimon lifted up his eyes and saw a man who was running. They sat down TO WAIT FOR HIM. When he arrived, Rabbi Shimon asks him, Who are you? He responded, I am a Jew from the city of Cappadocia and I am going to the hiding place of the son of Yochai, THAT IS, TO HEAR HIDDEN MATTERS FROM HIM. The friends determined AND EXPLAINED certain things, and sent me to him TO KNOW WHETHER HE AGREES WITH THEM. Rabbi Shimon said to him, My son, talk. He asks, You are the son of Yochai? He told him, I am the son of Yochai.

229. אֲמַר לֵיהּ הָא אוֹקִימְנָא דְּלָא יַפְסִיק בַּר נָשׁ בִּצְלוֹתֵיהּ, בֵּינֵיהּ לְבֵין כּוֹתְלָא, כְּמָה דִּכְתִיב וַיַּסֵּב חִזְקִיָּהוּ פָּנָיו אֶל הַקִּיר וגו'. וּמַאן דְּצַלֵּי, אָסִיר לְמֶעְבַּר אַרְבַּע אַמּוֹת סָמִיךְ לֵיהּ, וְאוֹקִמוּהָ לְהָנֵי אַרְבַּע אַמּוֹת לְכָל סְטַר, בַּר לְקַמֵּיהּ. וְאוֹקִמוּהָ, דְּלָא יְצַלֵּי בַּר נָשׁ, אֲחוֹרֵי רַבֵּיהּ וכו' וְאִתְמַנּוּן בְּכָל הָנֵי מִילֵי.

229. The friends said that when a man prays nothing may come between him and the wall, as it is written: "Then Chizkiyahu turned his face toward the wall" (Yeshayah 38:2). When a man prays, no one may come within four cubits of him on every side. They said this means four cubits on every side except in front, AS IT IS FORBIDDEN TO COME BETWEEN HIM AND THE WALL. And they said that a man should not pray behind his Rabbi. They appointed me TO HEAR WHAT YOU HAVE TO SAY about these matters.

230. פָּתַח וַאֲמַר שִׁמְעָה תְפִלָּתִי ה' וְשַׁוְעָתִי הַאֲזִינָה אֶל דִּמְעָתִי אַל תֶּחֱרַשׁ. מַאי טַעְמָא שִׁמְעָה, וְלָא שְׁמַע, בַּאֲתַר חַד כְּתִיב שְׁמַע ה' וְחָנֵּנִי וגו', וּבַאֲתַר אָחֳרָא שִׁמְעָה. אֶלָּא, בְּכָל אֲתַר, לִזְמְנִין שְׁמַע לִדְכוּרָא, וּלְזִמְנִין שִׁמְעָה לְנוּקְבָא. שִׁמְעָה: כְּמָה דְאַתְּ אָמֵר שִׁמְעָה ה' צֶדֶק וגו'. שְׁמַע: כִּדְבָר אַחֵר שְׁמַע ה' וְחָנֵּנִי. שְׁמַע בְּנִי. הַסְכֵּת וּשְׁמַע.

230. THE JEW opened with the verse, "Hear my prayer, Hashem, and give ear to my cry; keep not silence at my tears" (Tehilim 39:13). HE ASKS,

Why is it written "hear" (Heb. *shim'ah*) and not 'sh'ma'? AND WHY is it written in one place: "Hear (Heb. *sh'ma*), Hashem, and be gracious to me" (Tehilim 30:11), and in another place, '*shim'ah*'? The reason is that it is written now *Shma* refering to the male, NAMELY TO ZEIR ANPIN, and now *Shim'ah* refering to the female, NAMELY TO THE NUKVA OF ZEIR ANPIN. For example, *shim'ah* is used in "Hear the right, Hashem" (Tehilim 17:1), WHERE THE RIGHT (HEB. *TZEDEK*) IS THE SECRET OF THE NUKVA OF ZEIR ANPIN. *Sh'ma* is used in "Hear (Heb. *sh'ma*) Hashem, and be gracious to me," AS HASHEM IS THE NAME OF ZEIR ANPIN. The masculine is also used in "Hear, Hashem" AS HASHEM IS THE NAME OF ZEIR ANPIN, "my son, hear (Heb. *sh'ma*) the instructions" (Mishlei 1:8) and "Take heed, and hearken (Heb. s*h'ma*)" (Devarim 27:9).

231. וְהָכָא שִׁמְעָה תְּפִלָּתִי ה', בְּגִין דְּהַאי דַרְגָּא, דִּמְקַבְּלָא כָּל צְלוֹתִין דְּעָלְמָא. וְהָא תָּנִינָן, דְּעַבְדָא מִנַּיְיהוּ עֲטָרָה, וְשַׁוֵּי לָהּ בְּרֵישָׁא דְּצַדִּיק חַי עוֹלָמִים, דִּכְתִיב בְּרָכוֹת לְרֹאשׁ צַדִּיק. וְעַל דָּא שִׁמְעָה תְּפִלָּתִי ה'.

231. "Hear (Heb. *shim'ah*) my prayer, Hashem" REFERS TO THE NUKVA, which is the grade that receives all the prayers in the world. We learned that THE NUKVA creates a diadem from the prayers and puts in on the head of the Righteous the life of the world. This is the meaning of the verse: "Blessings are upon the head of the just" (Mishlei 10:6). Hence SCRIPTURE SAYS: "Hear (Heb. *shim'ah*) my prayer, Hashem."

232. שִׁמְעָה תְּפִלָּתִי ה', דָּא צְלוֹתָא דִי בְּלַחַשׁ. וְשַׁוְעָתִי הַאֲזִינָה, דָּא צְלוֹתָא, דְּאָרֵים בַּר נָשׁ קָלֵיהּ בְּעַקְתֵּיהּ, כִּדְבָר אֶחָר וַתַּעַל שַׁוְעָתָם אֶל הָאֱלֹקִים. וּמַהוּ שַׁוְעָתָם, אֶלָּא דִּבְצְלוֹתֵיהּ, אָרֵים קָלֵיהּ, וְזָקִיף עֵינוֹי לְעֵילָא, כִּדְבָר אֶחָר וְשׁוֹעַ אֶל הָהָר. וּצְלוֹתָא דָּא מִתַּבַּר תַּרְעִין, וְדָפֵיק לוֹן לְאַעֲלָא צְלוֹתֵיהּ. אֶל דִּמְעָתִי אַל תֶּחֱרַשׁ, דָּא אָעֵיל קַמֵּי מַלְכָּא, וְלֵית תַּרְעָא דְּקָאֵים קַמֵּיהּ, וּלְעוֹלָם לָא אַהֲדָרוּ דִּמְעִין בְּרֵיקַנְיָא.

232. "Hear my prayer, Hashem" refers to the silent prayer, NAMELY THE AMIDAH, WHICH WE WHISPER. IN CONTRAST, "And give ear to my cry" is a prayer cried out loud. A man raises his voice AND CRIES TO HASHEM in his trouble, as it is written: "And their cry rose up to the Elohim" (Shemot 2:23). What is the cry MENTIONED IN THE VERSE? It is the cry heard when

one raises one's voice in prayer and lifts up one's eyes above, as it is written: "And a shouting to the mountains" (Yeshayah 22:5). This prayer breaks open all gates upon which he knocks to present his prayer BEFORE HASHEM. "Keep not silence at my tears," which enter before the King and cannot be stopped by any gate or turned away in vain.

233. תּוּ הָא כְּתִיב הָכָא תְּלַת דַּרְגִּין, תְּפִלָּה, שַׁוְעָה, דִּמְעָה, לָקֳבֵיל אִלֵּין תְּלַת אַחֲרָנִין: כִּי גֵר אָנֹכִי עִמָּךְ, לְבָתַר תּוֹשָׁב, לְבָתַר כְּכָל אֲבוֹתָי, עִקְּרָא דְעָלְמָא.

233. There are three grades of prayer. They are prayer, cry, and tears, AS IT IS WRITTEN: "HEAR MY PRAYER...GIVE EAR TO MY CRY...KEEP NOT SILENCE AT MY TEARS." These correspond to three other grades mentioned at the end of the verse: "For I am a stranger with you," then "a sojourner," and then "all my fathers" (Tehilim 39:13), who were the main founders of the world. A STRANGER CORRESPONDS TO A PRAYER, A SOJOURNER TO A CRY, AND ALL MY FATHERS TO A TEAR.

234. תָּא חֲזֵי, צְלוֹתָא דְּבַר נָשׁ מְעוֹמָד, בְּגִין דִּתְרֵי צְלוֹתָא נִינְהוּ: חַד מְיוּשָׁב, וְחַד מְעוֹמָד, וְאִינוּן חַד. לָקֳבֵיל תְּרֵין דַּרְגִּין: תְּפִלָּה שֶׁל יַד וּתְפִלָּה שֶׁל רֹאשׁ. לְגַבֵּי יוֹם וְלַיְלָה, וְכֹלָּא חַד. אוֹף הָכָא, תְּפִלָּה מְיוּשָׁב לְגַבֵּי תְּפִלָּה שֶׁל יַד, לְאַתְקִין לָהּ כְּמָה דְאַתְקִין לְכַלָּה, וְקַשִּׁיט לָהּ לַאֲעָלָא לְחוּפָּה, הָכִי נָמֵי מְקַשְּׁטִין לָהּ, בְּרָזָא דִרְתִיכָאָה וּמַשִּׁירְיָיהָא, יוֹצֵר מְשָׁרְתִים וַאֲשֶׁר מְשָׁרְתָיו, וְהָאוֹפַנִּים וְחַיּוֹת הַקֹּדֶשׁ וְכוּ'.

234. Come and behold: A man's prayer is done standing up, for a man can pray in two ways, sitting down or standing up, which two are one, corresponding to the two grades of prayers, the hand Tfilin and the head Tfilin, also known as day and night. THEY CORRESPOND TO THE GRADE OF ZEIR ANPIN, CALLED HEAD TFILIN OR DAY, AND TO THE GRADE OF THE NUKVA, CALLED THE HAND TFILIN OR NIGHT, AND THEY ARE ONE IN THEIR UNION. A prayer said sitting down, NAMELY THE PRAYERS OF "WHO HAS FORMED THE LIGHT" BEFORE THE AMIDAH, is for the sake of the hand Tfilin, NAMELY, FOR THE NUKVA, to fix her as one prepares a bride and adorns her for the Chupah (marriage canopy). Thus, THE NUKVA is decorated in the secret of the Chariots and the troops ALLUDED TO IN THE

WORDS: "Who formed ministering messengers, ministers who all do stand aloft" and "the Ofanim (wheels) and the holy living creatures." THESE ARE FOR THE ADORNMENT OF THE NUKVA.

235. וְעַל דָּא צְלוֹתָא מְיוּשָׁב כֵּיוָן דְּעָאֲלַת לְגַבֵּי מַלְכָּא עִלָּאָה, וְאִיהוּ אָתֵי לְקַבְּלָא לָהּ, כְּדֵין אֲנַן קַיְימִין קַמֵּי מַלְכָּא עִלָּאָה, דְּהָא כְּדֵין דְּכוּרָא אִתְחַבַּר בְּנוּקְבָא, וּבְגִין כָּךְ לָא יַפְסִיק בֵּין גְּאוּלָה לִתְפִלָּה.

235. After the prayer said sitting down, WHICH IS THE DECORATED NUKVA, enters the presence of the Supreme King, ZEIR ANPIN, NAMELY, DURING THE AMIDAH PRAYER, and he comes to receive her, we stand before the Supernal King, BECAUSE THEN ZEIR ANPIN IS UNITED WITH THE NUKVA. For this reason, it behooves us not to stop between "redemption" and the prayer, as the prayer sitting down and the prayer standing up should be joined.

236. וּבְגִין דְּבַר נָשׁ קָאִים קַמֵּי מַלְכָּא עִלָּאָה, נָטַל אַרְבַּע אַמּוֹת לִצְלוֹתֵיהּ, וְאוֹקְמוּהָ דְּבְשִׁיעוּרָא דְּסוּרְטָא דְּיוֹצֵר כֹּלָּא. וְכָל מַה דְּאָתֵי בְּסִטְרָא דִּדְכוּרָא, בָּעֵי לֵיהּ לְאִינִישׁ לְמֵיקַם בְּקִיּוּמֵיהּ וְאִזְדַּקַּף. כְּגַוְונָא דָּא, כַּד אִיהוּ כָּרַע, כָּרַע בְּבָרוּךְ, וְכַד אִיהוּ זָקִיף, זָקִיף בַּשֵּׁם, בְּגִין לְאַחֲזָאָה שְׁבָחָא דִּדְכוּרָא עַל נוּקְבָא.

236. When a man stands before the Supernal King, he needs four cubits for his prayer. This is the length of a rope in "who forms all." In all that pertains to the side of the male, it behooves a man to stand up. In the same way, whoever kneels, kneels when pronouncing 'blessed', WHICH IS THE SECRET OF THE NUKVA. Whoever stands up does so WHEN PRONOUNCING THE WORD 'Name,' WHICH IS THE SECRET OF THE MALE, to show the superiority of the male over the female.

237. וְתָא חֲזֵי, דְּהָא אוֹקִמוּהָ, לָא יְצַלֵּי בַּר נָשׁ אֲחוֹרֵי רַבֵּיהּ, וְאִתְּמַר, כְּמָה דִּכְתִיב, אֶת ה' אֱלֹקֶיךָ תִּירָא. אֶת לְאַכְלָלָא דְּבָעֵי לְמִדְחַל מֵרַבֵּיהּ כְּמוֹרָא דִּשְׁכִינְתָּא, וּדְחִילוּ דְּתַלְמִיד, רַבֵּיהּ אִיהוּ. בְּגִין כָּךְ, בְּשַׁעֲתָא דִּצְלוֹתָא, לָא יַשְׁוֵי הַהוּא מוֹרָא לְקַמֵּיהּ, אֶלָּא מוֹרָא דְּקוּדְשָׁא בְּרִיךְ הוּא בִּלְחוֹדוֹי, וְלָא מוֹרָא אַחֲרָא.

237. Come and behold: A man must not pray behind his Rabbi's back, as it is written: "You shall fear Hashem your Elohim" (Devarim 6:13). The particle *Et* before "Hashem" indicates that he should fear his Rabbi as much as he fears the Shechinah, and the disciple fears his Rabbi. But at the time of prayer, he should place before himself only the fear of the Holy One, blessed be He, and not any other fear.

238. וְתָא חֲזֵי, צְלוֹתָא דְמִנְחָה, אַתְקֵין לֵיהּ יִצְחָק. וַדַּאי כְּמָה דְּאַתְקֵין אַבְרָהָם צְלוֹתָא דְצַפְרָא, לָקֳבֵל הַהוּא דַּרְגָּא דְאִתְדַּבַּק בֵּיהּ. וְכֵן יִצְחָק, אַתְקֵין צְלוֹתָא דְמִנְחָה, לָקֳבֵל הַהוּא דַּרְגָּא דְאִתְדַּבַּק בֵּיהּ. וְע״ד צְלוֹתָא דְמִנְחָה, מִכִּי נָטֵי שִׁמְשָׁא לְנַחְתָּא בְּדַרְגּוֹי לִסְטַר מַעֲרָב.

238. Come and behold: Isaac composed the afternoon prayer, as Abraham composed the morning prayer in relation to the grade to which he cleaved, NAMELY THE GRADE OF CHESED AND THE RIGHT COLUMN. So Isaac composed the afternoon prayer in relation to the grade to which he cleaved, THE GRADE OF GVURAH AND THE LEFT COLUMN. Therefore, THE TIME OF the afternoon prayer service is when the sun sets down with its grades to the west; NAMELY, IMMEDIATELY AFTER MIDDAY.

239. דְּהָא עַד לָא נָטָה שִׁמְשָׁא לְצַד מַעֲרָב, אִקְרֵי יוֹם, מִצַּפְרָא עַד הַהוּא זִמְנָא, דִּכְתִיב חֶסֶד אֵל כָּל הַיּוֹם. וְאִי תֵימָא עַד חֲשֵׁכָה, תָּא חֲזֵי, דִּכְתִיב אוֹי נָא לָנוּ כִּי פָנָה הַיּוֹם כִּי יִנָּטוּ צִלְלֵי עָרֶב. כִּי פָנָה הַיּוֹם, לָקֳבֵל צְלוֹתָא דְצַפְרָא, דִּכְתִיב חֶסֶד אֵל כָּל הַיּוֹם, דְּהָא בְּדֵין, שִׁמְשָׁא אִיהוּ לִסְטַר מִזְרָח, כֵּיוָן דְּנָטָה שִׁמְשָׁא, וְנַחְתָּא לִסְטַר מַעֲרָב, הָא כְּדֵין אִיהוּ זְמַן צְלוֹתָא דְמִנְחָה, וּכְבָר פָּנָה הַיּוֹם, וְאָתֵי צִלְלֵי עָרֶב, וְאִתְעַר דִּינָא קַשְׁיָא בְּעָלְמָא.

239. As long as the sun does not set toward the west, it is day – that is, from morning till noon – as it is written: "The kindness of El endures for all time (lit. 'all the day')" (Tehilim 52:3). You may say that it is considered day until dark. But come and study the verse: "Woe to us, for the day declines, for the shadows of the evening are lengthened" (Yirmeyah 6:4). "For the day declines" refers to the morning service, as it is written: "The kindness (Lit. 'Chesed') of El endures for all the day," for then the sun is to the east. Once the sun sets and declines toward the west, it is time for the afternoon

prayer, because "the day declines, for the shadows of the evening are lengthened," and harsh Judgment is upon the world.

240. וּפָנָה הַיּוֹם, דְּאִיהוּ דַּרְגָּא דְּחֶסֶ"ד, וְנָטוּ צִלְלֵי עֶרֶב, דְּאִינּוּן דַּרְגָּא דְּדִינָא קַשְׁיָא, וּכְדֵין אִתְחָרַב בֵּי מַקְדְּשָׁא, וְאִתּוֹקַד הֵיכָלָא. וְעַ"ד תָּנֵינָן, דִּיהֵא בַּ"נ זָהִיר בִּצְלוֹתָא דְּמִנְחָה, דְּאִיהוּ זִמְנָא דְּדִינָא קַשְׁיָא, שַׁרְיָיא בְּעָלְמָא.

240. "The day declines" refers to the grade of Chesed, while "the shadows of the evening are lengthened" refers to the grades of the harsh Judgment. Then the Temple was destroyed and the Holy of Holies burned. Therefore, it behooves a man to be careful to attend the afternoon prayer service, because it is the time when harsh Judgment hovers about the world.

241. יַעֲקֹב אַתְקִין צְלוֹתָא דְּעַרְבִית, דְּהָא אִיהוּ אַתְקִין לָהּ, וְזָן לָהּ, בְּכָל מַה דְּאִצְטְרִיךְ, וַדַּאי, וָא"ו אַתְקִין לְהֵ"א, וְהֵ"א אִתְּזָנַת מִן וָא"ו, דְּלֵית לָהּ נְהוֹרָא מִגַּרְמָהּ כְּלָל.

241. Jacob composed the evening service, because he fixes THE NUKVA and nourishes her with whatever she needs. For the *Vav* OF YUD HEV VAV HEI, WHICH REPRESENTS TIFERET, corrects the *Hei* OF YUD HEV VAV HEI, WHICH IS THE NUKVA, and the Hei is nourished by the *Vav,* as THE NUKVA has nothing of herself. SHE RECEIVES EVERYTHING FROM TIFERET, WHICH IS THE *VAV* OF YUD HEV VAV HEI CALLED JACOB.

242. וּבְגִין כָּךְ, תְּפִלַּת עַרְבִית רְשׁוּת, דְּהָא אִתְכְּלִילַת בִּצְלוֹתָא דְּיוֹמָא, בְּגִין לְאִתְנַהֲרָא, וְהַשְׁתָּא לָאו זִמְנָא אִיהוּ. וְאוֹקִימְנָא לָהּ, דְּהָא לָא אִתְגַּלְיָא נְהוֹרָא דִּימָמָא, דְּיַנְהִיר לָהּ, וְאִיהִי שָׁלְטָא בַּחֲשׁוֹכָא, עַד זִמְנָא דְּפַלְגּוּת לֵילְיָא, דְּאִשְׁתַּעֲשַׁע קוּדְשָׁא בְּרִיךְ הוּא עִם צַדִּיקַיָּא, בְּגִנְתָא דְּעֵדֶן, וּכְדֵין אִיהוּ זִמְנָא לְאִשְׁתַּעְשְׁעָא בַּר נָשׁ בְּאוֹרַיְיתָא, כְּמָה דְּאִתְּמַר.

242. The evening service is optional for this reason, for only as a continuation of the afternoon service does it shine. But now AT NIGHT, there is no time for that. And we have explained that daylight does not shine upon

THE NUKVA, and she rules in the dark until midnight, when the Holy One, blessed be He, enjoys Himself with the righteous in the Garden of Eden. Then it is time for man to study Torah.

243. תָּא חֲזֵי, דָּוִד אָתָא, וַאֲמַר אִלֵּין תְּלַת זִמְנִין דְּצַלוֹתֵי, דִּכְתִיב עֶרֶב וָבֹקֶר וְצָהֳרַיִם, הָא תְּלָתָא, וְאִיהוּ לָא צַלֵי, אֶלָּא תְּרֵי מִנַּיְיהוּ, דִּכְתִיב אָשִׂיחָה וְאֶהֱמֶה, וְלָא יַתִּיר, דָּא לִצְלוֹתָא דְּצַפְרָא, וְדָא לִצְלוֹתָא דְּמִנְחָה, בְּגִין כָּךְ אָשִׂיחָה וְאֶהֱמֶה דַּיְיקָא, בְּצַפְרָא, דְּאִיהוּ שַׁעְתָּא דְּחֶסֶד, סַגִּי לֵיהּ בְּחֶסֶד בְּאָשִׂיחָה, וּבְמִנְחָה, דְּהוּא שַׁעְתָּא דְּדִינָא קַשְׁיָא, בָּעֵי הֲמָיָיה, וּבְגִין כָּךְ וְאֶהֱמֶה, וּלְבָתַר כַּד אִתְפְּלִיג לֵילְיָא, הֲוָה קָם בְּשִׁירִין וְתוּשְׁבְּחָן, כִּדְקָא יָאוֹת, דִּכְתִיב וּבַלַּיְלָה שִׁירֹה עִמִּי, וְהָא אִתְּמָר.

243. Come and behold: David came and said, There are three times for services, as it is written: "Evening, and morning, and at noon, I PRAY, AND CRY ALOUD, AND HE HEARS MY VOICE" (Tehilim 55:18). There are three times in all, but David prayed at only two of them, as is written: "I pray, and cry aloud" and no more. One is the morning service and the other the afternoon service. Therefore he said, "I pray, and cry aloud" because "I pray" suffices for the morning itself, the time of Chesed, but there is need for crying aloud during the afternoon, AS IT IS A TIME OF HARSH JUDGMENT. Therefore he added, "And cry aloud." BUT HE DID NOT PRAY AT THE EVENING SERVICE. At midnight, he would rise and sing chants and praises, as it is written: "And in the night His song shall be with me" (Tehilim 42:9). This has already been explained.

244. קָם ר' שִׁמְעוֹן וַאֲזָלוּ. אֲזַל הַהוּא בַּר נָשׁ בַּהֲדֵיהּ, עַד טְבֶרְיָה. עַד דַּהֲווֹ אָזְלֵי, אָמַר רִבִּי שִׁמְעוֹן, תָּא חֲזֵי, תְּפִלּוֹת כְּנֶגֶד תְּמִידִין, תִּקְנוּם רַבָּנָן דְּאַנְשֵׁי כְּנֶסֶת הַגְּדוֹלָה, בְּגִין דְּאַשְׁכְּחָן תְּרֵי, דִּכְתִיב אֶת הַכֶּבֶשׂ אֶחָד תַּעֲשֶׂה בַבֹּקֶר וְאֵת הַכֶּבֶשׂ הַשֵּׁנִי תַּעֲשֶׂה בֵּין הָעַרְבָּיִם. וְאִינוּן מִתְקָרְבִין בְּהַנֵּי תְּרֵי זִמְנֵי דְיוֹמָא, דְּאִינוּן זִמְנִין לִצְלוֹתָא.

244. Rabbi Shimon rose and they traveled with that man until Tiberias. While they were walking, Rabbi Shimon said, Come and behold that prayers correspond to the daily offerings. This was established by the sages of the

Great Assembly. There are two DAILY OFFERINGS, as it is written: "The one lamb shall you offer in the morning, and the other lamb shall you offer at evening" (Bemidbar 28:4), and they are offered at the same times each day, the times of prayer. THEY ESTABLISHED TWO ESSENTIAL PRAYERS, THE MORNING SERVICE AND THE AFTERNOON SERVICE. THE EVENING SERVICE IS OPTIONAL.

245. אָמַר הַהוּא גַּבְרָא הָא בְּקַדְמֵיתָא, אָבוֹת תְּקָנוּם לְהַנֵּי צְלוֹתֵי, וּמַה דְּאַתְקִינוּ אַבְרָהָם וְיִצְחָק, הוּא עִקְרָא, וּמַה דְּאַתְקִין יַעֲקֹב, דְּאִיהוּ שְׁבָחָא דַּאֲבָהָן, אַמַּאי אִיהוּ רְשׁוּת, וְלָא עִקְרָא כְּהַנֵּי.

245. The man said, But the patriarchs composed these prayers before THE MEN OF THE GREAT ASSEMBLY DID, AND THEY DID NOT ADJUST THEM TO CORRESPOND TO THE DAILY OFFERINGS. Why is what Abraham and Isaac established more important? And why is that what Jacob, who is chosen among the patriarchs, composed is considered optional and not as essential as those?

246. אָמַר רַבִּי שִׁמְעוֹן, הָא אִתְּמַר. אֲבָל תָּא חֲזֵי, הַנֵּי תְּרֵי זִמְנֵי, דִּתְרֵי צְלוֹתֵי לָאו אִינוּן, אֶלָּא לְחַבְּרָא לְיַעֲקֹב בְּעַדְבֵיהּ, כֵּיוָן דְּאִתְחַבָּרוּ דָּא בְּדָא, אֲנַן לָא צְרִיכִין יַתִּיר, דְּכֵיוָן דְּאִתְיְהִיבַת אִתְּתָא בֵּין תְּרֵין דְּרוֹעִין, וְאִתְחַבְּרַת בְּגוּפָא, לָא אִצְטְרִיךְ יַתִּיר, וְעַל דָּא אֲנַן בָּעֵינָן לְאִתְעָרָא תְּרֵין דְּרוֹעִין, בְּגִין דְּאִתְיְהִיבַת בֵּינַיְיהוּ, כֵּיוָן דְּאִיהִי בֵּינַיְיהוּ, גּוּפָא וְאִתְּתָא מִלַיְיהוּ בִּלְחִישׁוּ, דְּלָא לְאַדְכָּרָא.

246. Rabbi Shimon responded, this has already been explained, yet come and behold, the times for the morning and afternoon services are designed to unite Jacob, WHO IS ZEIR ANPIN, with his fate, THE NUKVA. Once they are united, we do not have to do anything else. AS THE NUKVA is put between the two arms – ABRAHAM AND ISAAC, WHICH CORRESPOND TO THE RIGHT AND LEFT COLUMNS – she is joined to the body, AS THE TORSO IS BUT THE INCLUSION OF THE TWO ARMS, and there is no more need to amend anything else. Thus, we should encourage the union of the two arms BY OBSERVING MORNING AND AFTERNOON PARYER SERVICES, because THE NUKVA was put between them. ONE NEEDS TO DRAW ILLUMINATION INTO THE NUKVA. After she is put between them, then the body, THE

CENTRAL COLUMN CALLED JACOB, and the Nukva whisper, so as not to
mention THE ASPECT OF JUDGMENT IN HER.

247. וּבְגִין כָּךְ, יַעֲקֹב מְשַׁמֵּשׁ בַּמָּרוֹם תָּנִינָן, מַאי בַּמָּרוֹם. כְּמָה דְאַתְּ
אָמֵר וְאַתָּה מָרוֹם לְעוֹלָם ה'. וְכֹלָּא אִיהוּ רָזָא לְיָדְעֵי מִדִין. אֲתוֹ רִבִּי
אַבָּא, וְהַהוּא יוּדָאי, וּנְשָׁקוּ יְדוֹי. אֲמַר רִבִּי אַבָּא, עַד יוֹמָא דֵין, לָא
קָאִימְנָא בְּמִלָּה דָא, בַּר הַשְׁתָּא. זַכָּאָה חוּלְקִי, דְּזָכֵינָא לְמִשְׁמַע לֵיהּ.

247. For that reason, THE WORDS ARE WHISPERED AND HER VOICE IS NOT
HEARD, and Jacob serves up high. We learned the meaning of "up high" is
as written in the verse: "And you, Hashem, are most high for evermore"
(Tehilim 92:9). All this is a secret known to those who understand Judgment
NAMELY FOR THOSE VERSED IN THE MYSTERIES OF THE TORAH. Rabbi
Aba and the Jew came and kissed the hands of Rabbi Shimon. Rabbi Aba
said, Until this day, I did not understand this matter. Only now do I
comprehend its meaning. Blessed is my fate, that I deserved to hear it.

25. "And Isaac brought her into his mother Sarah's tent"

A Synopsis

As Rabbi Yosi opens the discussion of this difficult verse, we learn that the images of Isaac and Rivkah were exactly the same as the images of Abraham and Sarah, in both physical and spiritual terms. The rabbis then reveal the hidden meaning in the stories of the patriarchs. They, we are told, all lived by the secret of Zeir Anpin, and thus each had four wives representing the Sfirot of Chochmah, Binah, Tiferet, and Malchut of the Nukva of Zeir Anpin. The entire physical world of the patriarchs was designed to mirror the structure and form of the spiritual dimension, thereby creating affinity and attachment to the Light of the Creator. Finally, we hear Rabbi Shimon's succinct explanation of the secret of holiness, and how all mysteries are really one secret, included within the secret of the Nukva of Zeir Anpin alone.

The Relevance of this Passage

Succeeding generations of mankind are not on the same spiritual level as the patriarchs. Nevertheless, we can still create affinity and attachment to their world and its superior spiritual structure, through the mystical words that bespeak their wonders, a privilege afforded to us through a thoughtful reading of this passage. This attachment invokes the Light of Creator, removing darkness and iniquity from our existence.

248. וַיְבִיאֶהָ יִצְחָק הָאֹהֱלָה שָׂרָה אִמּוֹ. אָמַר רַבִּי יוֹסֵי, הַאי קְרָא קַשְׁיָא, הָאֹהֱלָה, לְאֹהֶל שָׂרָה אִמּוֹ מִבָּעֵי לֵיהּ, מַאי הָאֹהֱלָה. דַּאֲהַדְּרַת תַּמָּן שְׁכִינְתָּא, בְּגִין דְּכָל זִמְנָא דְּשָׂרָה קַיְימָא בְּעָלְמָא, שְׁכִינְתָּא לָא אַעֲדֵי מִינָהּ, וּשְׁרַגָּא הֲוָה דְּלֵיקַת, מֵעֶרֶב שַׁבָּת לְעֶרֶב שַׁבָּת, וַהֲוָה נְהִיר כָּל אִינּוּן יוֹמֵי דְּשַׁבַּתָּא, בָּתַר דְּמִיתַת, כָּבְתָה הַהִיא שְׁרַגָּא, כֵּיוָן דְּאָתַת רִבְקָה, אַהֲדְּרַת שְׁכִינְתָּא, וּשְׁרַגָּא אַדְלֵיקַת. שָׂרָה אִמּוֹ: דְּדָמְיָא לְשָׂרָה בְּכָל עוֹבָדָהָא.

248. "And Isaac brought her into his mother Sarah's tent" (Beresheet 24:67). Rabbi Yosi said that this is a difficult verse. It is literally written: "...to the tent, Sarah his mother," but it should have been written 'Sarah's tent.' What is the meaning of "to the tent"? He says that the Shechinah returned, THAT IS CALLED TENT. THEREFORE IT SAYS 'HA'OHELAH (TO

THE TENT), WHICH IS THE SHECHINAH, for the Shechinah never left Sarah as long as she was in the world. And the candle burned in the tent all the days of the week, from Shabbat eve to Shabbat eve. After she died, the candle was extinguished. Since Rivkah came, the Shechinah returned and the candle burned again. "Sarah his mother" means that she resembled Sarah in everything she did.

249. רִבִּי יְהוּדָה אֲמַר כְּמָה דִּדְיוּקְנֵיהּ דְּיִצְחָק, הֲוָה כִּדְיוּקְנֵיהּ דְּאַבְרָהָם, וְכָל מַאן דְּחָמֵי לְיִצְחָק, אֲמַר דָּא אַבְרָהָם, וַדַּאי, אַבְרָהָם הוֹלִיד אֶת יִצְחָק, הָכֵי נָמֵי רִבְקָה, דְּיוּקְנָה מַמָּשׁ הֲוַת דְּיוּקְנָא דְּשָׂרָה, וּבְגִין כָּךְ שָׂרָה אִמּוֹ וַדַּאי.

249. Rabbi Yehuda said, "SARAH HIS MOTHER" MEANS THAT because the image of Isaac was the same as the image of Abraham, whoever saw Isaac said it was Abraham. Of course, they knew that Abraham begot Isaac, so the image of Rivkah was exactly the same as the image of Sarah. For that reason it is written, "Sarah his mother." THE IMAGES OF ISAAC AND RIVKAH WERE EXACTLY THE SAME AS THE IMAGES OF ABRAHAM AND SARAH. IT WAS APPARENT THAT ABRAHAM BEGAT ISAAC AND SARAH BORE RIVKAH.

250. אֲמַר רִבִּי אֶלְעָזָר, בְּכֹלָּא הָכֵי הוּא, אֲבָל תָּא חֲזֵי, רָזָא אִיהוּ, דְּאַף עַל גַּב דְּשָׂרָה מִיתַת, דְּיוּקְנָה לָא אַעֲדֵי מִן בֵּיתָא וְלָא אִתְחֲזֵי תַּמָּן, מִיּוֹמָא דְמִיתַת, עַד דְּאָתַת רִבְקָה, כֵּיוָן דְּעָאלַת רִבְקָה, אִתְחֲזִיאַת דְּיוּקְנָא דְּשָׂרָה, דִּכְתִיב וַיְבִיאֶהָ יִצְחָק הָאֹהֱלָה וְגו', מִיָּד שָׂרָה אִמּוֹ אִתְחֲזִיאַת תַּמָּן, וְלָא הֲוָה חָמֵי לָהּ בַּר יִצְחָק בִּלְחוֹדוֹי, כַּד אָעֵיל תַּמָּן, וְעַל דָּא וַיִּנָּחֵם יִצְחָק אַחֲרֵי אִמּוֹ. דְּאִמּוֹ אִתְחֲזִיאַת וְאִזְדַּמְּנָא בְּבֵיתָא, וְעַל דָּא לָא כְּתִיב אַחֲרֵי מִיתַת אִמּוֹ, אֶלָּא אַחֲרֵי אִמּוֹ.

250. Rabbi Elazar said, This EXPLANATION is exactly right, but come and behold this secret. Although Sarah died, her image did not leave the house. It remained unseen from the day she died until Rivkah came. Once Rivkah came, the image of Sarah was seen again, as it is written: "And Isaac brought her into his mother Sarah's tent", but it was seen only by Isaac when he entered the tent. Therefore, "Isaac was comforted after his mother" (Beresheet 24:67), because his mother was seen and chanced before him in the house. Therefore it is not written: 'After his mother's death', but rather "after his mother", BECAUSE SHE NEVER DIED FOR ISAAC.

251. רְבִּי שִׁמְעוֹן אָמַר, מַאי שְׁנָא דִכְתִיב בֵּיהּ בְּיִצְחָק, וַיִּקַּח אֶת רִבְקָה וַתְּהִי לוֹ לְאִשָּׁה וַיֶּאֱהָבֶהָ. כֵּיוָן דַּאֲמַר וַתְּהִי לוֹ לְאִשָּׁה, לָא יְדַעְנָא דְּהוּא רָחִים לָהּ, דְּהָא כָּל בְּנֵי עַלְמָא רַחֲמֵי לִנְשַׁיְיהוּ. מַאי שְׁנָא בְּיִצְחָק, דִּכְתִיב בֵּיהּ וַיֶּאֱהָבֶהָ.

251. Rabbi Shimon then discoursed on the difference in verse that is written of Isaac: "And took Rivkah, and she became his wife; and he loved her" (Beresheet 24:67). Because it is written that "she became his wife", we should assume that he loved her as all the inhabitants of the world love their wives. What was different here, that made it necessary to add, "And he loved her"?

252. אֶלָּא וַדַּאי אִתְעָרוּתָא דִרְחִימוּ דִּדְכוּרָא לְגַבֵּי אִתְּתָא, לָאו אִיהוּ אֶלָּא שְׂמָאלָא, דִּכְתִיב שְׂמֹאלוֹ תַּחַת לְרֹאשִׁי. וְחֹשֶׁךְ וְלַיְלָה כְּחַד אִינּוּן, וּשְׂמָאלָא אִתְעַר רְחִימוּ תָּדִיר, לְגַבֵּי נוּקְבָא, וְאָחִיד בָּהּ, וְעַל דָּא אַף עַל גַּב דְּאַבְרָהָם רָחִים לָהּ לְשָׂרָה, לָא כְתִיב בֵּיהּ וַיֶּאֱהָבֶהָ, אֶלָּא בְּיִצְחָק. וְאִי תֵימָא וַיֶּאֱהַב יַעֲקֹב אֶת רָחֵל, סִטְרָא דְיִצְחָק, דַּהֲוָה בֵּיהּ, קָעֲבִיד לֵיהּ.

252. HE ANSWERS, Assuredly the awakening of the love of the male for the female is from the Left COLUMN, as it is written: "His left hand is under my head" (Shir Hashirim 8:3). Darkness, THE LEFT COLUMN, and night, THE NUKVA, are as one, because the left always arouses love to the Nukva and holds on to her. Therefore, although Abraham loved Sarah, it is not written of him: "And he loved her", but only of Isaac, WHO IS THE LEFT COLUMN OF ZEIR ANPIN. If you say, however, that it is written: "And Jacob loved Rachel" (Beresheet 29:18); THOUGH HE IS NOT OF THE LEFT COLUMN, it is because that side of Isaac was included within him.

253. תָּא חֲזֵי, אַבְרָהָם כַּד חָמָא לְשָׂרָה, הֲוָה מְחַבֵּק לָהּ, וְלָא יַתִּיר, אֲבָל יִצְחָק דְּאִיהוּ בַּעֲלָה, אָחִיד בָּהּ, וְשַׁוֵּי דְרוֹעֵיהּ תְּחוֹת רֵישָׁהּ, דִּכְתִיב שְׂמֹאלוֹ תַּחַת לְרֹאשִׁי וִימִינוֹ תְּחַבְּקֵנִי. לְבָתַר אָתָא יַעֲקֹב, וְשִׁמֵּשׁ עַרְסָא,

וְאוֹלִיד תְּרֵיסַר שְׁבָטִין, כֹּלָּא כְּדְקָא יָאוֹת.

253. Come and behold: When Abraham, THE SECRET OF THE RIGHT COLUMN OF ZEIR ANPIN, saw Sarah, THE NUKVA OF ZEIR ANPIN, he only embraced her, AS IT IS WRITTEN: "AND HIS RIGHT HAND EMBRACES ME" (SHIR HASHIRIM 8:3). But Isaac, THE LEFT COLUMN OF ZEIR ANPIN, her husband, took her and put his arm under her head, as it is written: "His left hand is under my head" (Ibid.). When Jacob, THE CENTRAL COLUMN OF ZEIR ANPIN, arrived afterward, he performed his marital duty and begot twelve tribes. All is as it should be.

254. וְתָא חֲזֵי, אֲבָהָן כֻּלְּהוּ בְּרָזָא חֲדָא אַזְלוּ, וְכֻלְּהוּ שִׁמְּשׁוּ בְּאַרְבַּע נָשִׁין, כָּל חַד מִנַּיְיהוּ. אַבְרָהָם בְּאַרְבַּע: שָׂרָה, וְהָגָר, וּתְרֵי פְּלַגְשִׁים. דִּכְתִיב וְלִבְנֵי הַפִּלַגְשִׁים אֲשֶׁר לְאַבְרָהָם, פְּלַגְשִׁים תְּרֵי, הָא אַרְבַּע.

254. Come and behold: The patriarchs all lived by one secret, NAMELY THE SECRET OF ZEIR ANPIN. Therefore, they each had four wives REPRESENTING CHOCHMAH, BINAH, TIFERET AND MALCHUT OF THE NUKVA OF ZEIR ANPIN. Abraham also had four wives – Sarah, Hagar, and two concubines – as it is written: "But to the sons of the concubines, which Abraham had" (Beresheet 25:6). IT IS WRITTEN concubines, WHICH MEANS two, AND TOGETHER WITH SARAH AND HAGAR, there were four.

255. יִצְחָק בְּרָזָא דְאַרְבַּע, דִּסְטִירוּ דְרִבְקָה, דִּכְתִיב וַיִּקַּח אֶת רִבְקָה חַד, וַתְּהִי לוֹ לְאִשָּׁה תְּרֵי, וַיֶּאֱהָבֶהָ תְּלַת, וַיִּנָּחֵם יִצְחָק אַחֲרֵי אִמּוֹ הָא אַרְבַּע. לָקֳבֵל דָּא, הֲווֹ לְיַעֲקֹב, אַרְבַּע נָשִׁין. וְכֹלָּא בְּרָזָא חֲדָא.

255. Isaac also had four WIVES, all contained within Rivkah, as it is written: "And took Rivkah", which is one, "and she became his wife," which is two; "and he loved her," which is three "and Isaac was comforted after his mother," which is four. Correspondingly Jacob had four wives, and all of them, THE TWELVE WIVES, are one secret, NAMELY THE NUKVA OF ZEIR ANPIN ALONE, WHO CONTAINED ALL TWELVE ASPECTS.

256. רִבִּי חִיָּיא אָמַר, אַבְרָהָם וְיִצְחָק, שִׁמְּשׁוּ כָּל חַד בְּאִתְּתָא חֲדָא, בְּרָזָא דְקוּדְשָׁא. אַבְרָהָם בְּשָׂרָה, יִצְחָק בְּרִבְקָה, וְלָקֳבֵל תַּרְוַוייהוּ, הֲוֵי

אַרְבַּע נָשִׁין לְיַעֲקֹב, בִּתְרֵין חוּלָקִין. רִבִּי שִׁמְעוֹן אֲמַר סְלִיקוּ מִלִּין לְאַתְרַיְיהוּ. דְּהָא כֹּלָּא בְּרָזָא קַדִּישָׁא אִתְעֲבַד, וְכֹלָּא בְּרָזָא חֲדָא.

256. Rabbi Chiya said that Abraham and Isaac each performed their marital duties with one wife on the side of holiness, BECAUSE HAGAR AND THE CONCUBINES WERE NOT OF HOLINESS. Abraham did so with Sarah, and Isaac with Rivkah. In comparison, Jacob had four wives, two each REPRESENTING THE HOLY AND THE NOT HOLY. LEAH AND RACHEL REPRESENTED HOLINESS, BILHAH AND ZILPHAH REPRESENTED THE NOT HOLY THAT HE CHANGED TO HOLY. Rabbi Shimon said that these matters have reached their proper place IN HOLINESS. EVEN HAGAR AND THE CONCUBINES WERE PART OF THE SECRET OF HOLINESS, AS RABBI SHIMON EXPLAINS THAT THE TWELVE WOMEN WERE BUT TWELVE ASPECTS OF THE NUKVA. For everything is done in the secret of holiness, and all is one secret; NAMELY, ALL OF THEM ARE INCLUDED WITHIN THE SECRET OF THE NUKVA OF ZEIR ANPIN ALONE.

26. "Then again Abraham took a wife"

A Synopsis

Here we learn that Kturah, Abraham's wife, was really Hagar, who had atoned for her transgressions and had taken a new name reflecting this atonement. The rest of the discussion focuses on the meaning of Abraham's bequest to Isaac of "all that he had." We're told that the two patriarchs should be included one within the other, since they represent the Right and Left Columns in the secret of supernal faith, which is Binah.

The Relevance of this Passage

Man is endowed with three unique forces of intelligence – the *desire to receive*, the *desire to share*, and the *free will* to choose and manage between the two. *Desire to Share* is termed 'Right Column' by the Zohar. Abraham is the embodiment of Right Column and its particular sharing intelligence. *Desire to Receive* is termed 'Left Column', and 'Isaac' is the vessel that expresses its energy of receiving. The absence of either Column creates an extreme imbalance. Thus, sharing without receiving quickly depletes our resources. If we pour water from a glass to share with others without replenishment, the glass will soon be empty. And receiving without sharing is like casting a dehydrated man into the middle of the sea. Though he is in desperate need of water, the overabundance eventually drowns him. Reading this section has a stabilizing effect on our spirituality and on the decisions we make. Intuitively, our choices begin to strike a delicate balance between knowing when to share and when to receive.

257. וַיּוֹסֶף אַבְרָהָם וַיִּקַּח אִשָּׁה וּשְׁמָהּ קְטוּרָה. קְטוּרָה דָּא הִיא הָגָר. דְּהָא תָּנֵינָן, בָּתַר דְּאִתְפָּרְשָׁא הָגָר מִנֵּיהּ דְּאַבְרָהָם, וְטָעַת בָּתַר גְּלוּלֵי דַּאֲבוּהָ, לְבָתַר, אִתְקַשְׁרָא בְּעוֹבָדִין דְּכַשְׁרָן, וּבְגִין כָּךְ, אִשְׁתַּנֵּי שְׁמָהּ, וְאִקְרֵי קְטוּרָה, בְּעוֹבָדִין דְּכַשְׁרָן, וְשָׁדַר אַבְרָהָם, וּנְסָבָהּ לֵיהּ לְאִנְתּוּ. מִכָּאן דְּשִׁנּוּי שְׁמָא מְכַפֵּר חוֹבִין, וְעַל דָּא אִשְׁתַּנֵּי שְׁמָהּ.

257. "Then again Abraham took a wife, and her name was Kturah" (Beresheet 25:1). Kturah is Hagar, for we learned that after Hagar separated from Abraham and whored after her father's idols, she repented and was associated with good deeds. For that reason, her name was changed to Kturah, which alludes to her good deeds, FOR KTURAH MEANS CONNECTED. Then Abraham sent and took her for a wife. From this, it is

understood that changing a name atones for transgressions, because her name was changed TO KTURAH AFTER SHE ATONED FOR HER SINS.

258. וַיּוֹסֶף אַבְרָהָם, מַאי וַיּוֹסֶף, אִי תֵימָא דְּעַל שָׂרָה אִיהוּ דְּאוֹסִיף, לָאו הָכִי. אֶלָּא בְּיוֹמָהָא דְשָׂרָה, אִזְדַּוַּוג בַּהֲדָהּ זִמְנָא חֲדָא, וּלְבָתַר תָּרִיךְ לָהּ, עַל עִסְקֵי דְיִשְׁמָעֵאל, וּלְבָתַר וַיּוֹסֶף כְּמִלְּקַדְמִין, זִמְנָא אָחֳרָא, עַל מַה דְּנָסִיב לָהּ בְּקַדְמֵיתָא. וּכְפוּם דְּשַׁנֵּי עוֹבָדָהָא, הָכִי נָמֵי שַׁנֵּי שְׁמָהּ.

258. In the phrase: "Then again Abraham", what is meant by "again (lit. 'he added')"? If you say that Abraham took another wife in addition to Sarah, this is not so. Rather, in the days of Sarah he had already mated once with Hagar and then drove her away because of the deeds of Ishmael, WHO MOCKED ISAAC. The word "again" MEANS that he TOOK her again, a second time, because she atoned for her evil deeds. As a result, her name was changed AND SHE WAS CALLED KTURAH.

259. תָּא חֲזֵי, דְּאָמַר רַבִּי אֶלְעָזָר, וַיְבִאֶהָ יִצְחָק הָאֹהֱלָה שָׂרָה אִמּוֹ. דְּאִתְגַּלְיָיא דִּיּוֹקְנָא דְשָׂרָה, וְיִצְחָק אִתְנַחֵם, אַחֲרֵי דְּאִתְגַּלְיָא אִמּוֹ, וּדְיוֹקְנָהָא הֲוָה חָמֵי כָּל יוֹמָא. וְאַבְרָהָם אַף עַל גַּב דְּאִינְסִיב, לָא עָאל בְּהַהוּא בֵּיתָא, וְלָא עָיֵיל לָהּ לְהַאי אִתְּתָא תַּמָּן, בְּגִין דְּשִׁפְחָה לָא תִירַשׁ גְּבִרְתָּהּ. וּבְאֹהֶל דְּשָׂרָה, לָא אִתְחֲזֵי אִתְּתָא אָחֳרָא, אֶלָּא רִבְקָה.

259. Come and behold: Rabbi Elazar said about the verse: "And Isaac brought her into his mother Sarah's tent" (Beresheet 24:67) that the image of Sarah was revealed WITH RIVKAH'S ARRIVAL, and Isaac was comforted by the image of his mother, which he saw every day. Although Abraham married, he did not enter Sarah's house, nor did he allow that woman to enter, because a handmaid cannot be heir to her mistress. No other woman was seen in Sarah's tent except for Rivkah.

260. וְאַבְרָהָם אַף עַל גַּב דַּהֲוָה יָדַע דִּדְיוֹקְנָא דְשָׂרָה אִתְגַּלְיָיא תַּמָּן, שַׁבְקֵיהּ לְיִצְחָק הַהוּא אֹהֶל, לְמֶחֱמֵי דְיוֹקְנָא דְאִמֵּיהּ כָּל יוֹמָא. יִצְחָק, וְלָא אַבְרָהָם, הֲדָא הוּא דִכְתִיב וַיִּתֵּן אַבְרָהָם אֶת כָּל אֲשֶׁר לוֹ לְיִצְחָק. אֶת כָּל אֲשֶׁר לוֹ דַּיְיקָא, דָּא הַהוּא דְּיוֹקְנָא דְשָׂרָה בְּהַהוּא מַשְׁכְּנָא.

260. And although Abraham knew that Sarah's image was revealed there, he left the tent to Isaac, so he could see the image of his mother daily. Isaac, not Abraham, SAW HER IMAGE. This is the meaning of the verse: "And Abraham gave all that he had to Isaac" (Beresheet 25:5). "All that he had" alludes precisely to the image of Sarah that was inside the tent, FOR HE GAVE IT TO ISAAC TO LOOK AT HER.

261. דָּבָר אַחֵר, וַיִּתֵּן אַבְרָהָם אֶת כָּל אֲשֶׁר לוֹ לְיִצְחָק, רָזָא דִמְהֵימְנוּתָא עִלָּאָה, לְאִתְדַּבְּקָא, יִצְחָק בְּדַרְגָּא דְחוּלָקֵיהּ כְּדְקָא יָאוֹת. תָּא חֲזֵי, הָכָא אִתְכְּלִיל אֶשָׁא בְּמַיָא וַדַּאי, אֶשָׁא נָטִיל מַיָא, מַשְׁמַע וַיִּתֵּן אַבְרָהָם אֶת כָּל אֲשֶׁר לוֹ לְיִצְחָק, דָּא מַיָא דְאִתְכְּלִיל בְּאֶשָׁא, וּבְקַדְמֵיתָא, אִתְכְּלִיל כַּחֲדָא אֶשָׁא בְּמַיָא. אֵימָתַי, בְּשַׁעֲתָא דְּעָקַד לֵיהּ לְיִצְחָק, לְמֶעְבַּד בֵּיהּ דִּינָא, כְּדֵין אִתְכְּלִיל אֶשָׁא בְּמַיָא. וְהַשְׁתָּא אִתְכְּלִילוּ מַיָא בְּאֶשָׁא, לְמֶהֱוֵי כֹּלָא רָזָא דִמְהֵימְנוּתָא עִלָּאָה.

261. Another explanation of the verse: "And Abraham gave all that he had to Isaac," IS THAT HE GAVE HIM the secret of the supernal faith, WHICH IS BINAH, so that Isaac would be attached to his appropriate grade. IF HE HAD NOT GIVEN HIM THE SECRET OF BINAH, HE WOULD NOT HAVE BEEN ABLE TO CLEAVE TO THE LEFT COLUMN. Come and behold: Fire, WHICH IS LEFT, is here included within water, WHICH IS RIGHT. Assuredly fire took water, AS LEFT INCLUDED RIGHT WITHIN IT. This is understood from the verse: "And Abraham gave all that he had to Isaac." This is water included within fire, AS ABRAHAM, WHO IS THE SECRET OF WATER, GAVE HIS ASPECT TO ISAAC, THE SECRET OF FIRE. At first, fire was included within water. When was that? When Abraham bound Isaac to execute judgement upon him, NAMELY TO SACRIFICE HIM. Then, fire was included within water. Now, water is included within fire, so that all will be in the secret of the supernal faith, WHICH IS BINAH. FOR THE TWO COLUMNS – RIGHT AND LEFT – IN BINAH WERE INCLUDED WITHIN EACH OTHER, THEN THEY REACHED PERFECTION. THEREFORE, BOTH ABRAHAM AND ISAAC, WHO ARE DRAWN FROM THE TWO COLUMNS IN BINAH, SHOULD ALSO BE INCLUDED WITHIN ONE ANOTHER. FIRST, THE LEFT WAS INCLUDED WITHIN THE RIGHT AT THE TIME OF SACRIFICE. AND NOW, WHEN ABRAHAM GAVE ALL HE HAD TO ISAAC, THE RIGHT WAS INCLUDED WITHIN THE LEFT.

27. "But to the sons of the concubines...Abraham gave gifts"

A Synopsis

This very brief passage discusses questions relating to the concubines of Abraham. Rabbi Chiya maintains that the term does not allude to Kturah, one of Abraham's wives, but there is no unanimous agreement. In section 26 of the Zohar, we're told that Abraham gave "all that he had" to his son Isaac. Here it is said that Abraham now "gave gifts" to the "sons of the concubines." It is speculated that these sons then went on to become great sorcerers and mystics living "in the east."

The Relevance of this Passage

This seemingly simple section of Zohar sheds light on the origins of spiritual disciplines found in the Far East. The Zohar tells us that Abraham gave everything he had to his son Isaac. Thereafter, the Patriarch gave gifts to the sons of his concubines and sent them to live "in the east." Clearly, the Zohar is not referring to material items, for if Abraham gave away all his physical possessions to his son Isaac, there would be nothing left to give to the sons of his concubines. A candle flame provides an analogy: One candle can share its flame and light with countless others, without ever diminishing itself. The Zohar is referring to the light of wisdom when speaking of Abraham's possessions and gifts. The term "all that he had" pertains to the complete wisdom of Kabbalah, also known as the Three Column System. These Three Columns are the pillars of all spiritual wisdom. The "gifts" given to the sons of the concubines refer to other spiritual teachings that offered their own unique pathway to the Light of the Creator, described accordingly as One and Two Column spiritual systems. The sons of the concubines, we're told, were sent by Abraham to live "in the east" where, to this day, there exist spiritual doctrines that exemplify the Two Column system – such as the Ying/Yang principle of Taoist cosmology. A connection can be made between the name Abraham – or Abraham – and the Eastern religious concept of Brahman, which refers to the absolute reality or Self, as explained in the Hindu Upanishads. The words of wisdom portrayed in this passage strengthen our bond to the original seed of spiritual wisdom – Kabbalah – and its Three Column System of *desire to share, desire to receive*, and *free will* to choose and balance between the two. The wisdom to use our free will in a spiritually correct manner is instilled within us.

262. וְלִבְנֵי הַפִּילַגְשִׁים אֲשֶׁר לְאַבְרָהָם נָתַן אַבְרָהָם מַתָּנוֹת. מַאי

מַתְּנוֹת. אִלֵּין סִטְרֵי דַרְגִּין תַּתָּאִין, דְּאִינוּן שְׁמָהָן דְּסִטְרֵי רוּחַ מְסָאֲבָא, בְּגִין לְאַשְׁלָמָא דַרְגִּין, וְאִסְתַּלַּק יִצְחָק עַל כֹּלָּא, בִּמְהֵימְנוּתָא עִלָּאָה כַּדְקָא חָזֵי.

262. "But to the sons of the concubines, which Abraham had, Abraham gave gifts" (Beresheet 25:6). HE ASKS, What are these gifts? AND HE ANSWERS, These are all kinds of lower UNBALANCED grades OF UNHOLINESS, names of all sorts of impure spirits. HE GAVE THEM to perfect the grades, SO THAT THEY WOULD PURIFY THEM AND PERFECT THE GRADES OF HOLINESS. And Isaac was elevated above them all in the proper supernal faith, WHICH IS BINAH.

263. בְּנֵי הַפִּילַגְשִׁים אִלֵּין הֲווֹ בְּנֵי קְטוּרָה, פִּלֶגֶשׁ בְּקַדְמֵיתָא, וּפִלֶגֶשׁ הַשְׁתָּא. ר' חִיָּיא אָמַר, פִּילַגְשִׁים מַמָּשׁ. וַיְשַׁלְּחֵם מֵעַל יִצְחָק בְּנוֹ, דְּלָא לְשַׁלְּטָאָה לְגַבֵּיהּ דְּיִצְחָק. בְּעוֹדֶנּוּ חַי, בְּעוֹד דַּהֲוָה אַבְרָהָם חַי וְקַיָּים בְּעַלְמָא, דְּלָא יְקַטְרְגוּן לֵיהּ לְבָתַר, וּבְגִין דְּיִתְתַּקַּן יִצְחָק בְּסִטַר דִּינָא קַשְׁיָא עִלָּאָה, לְאִתְתַּקְּפָא עַל כֻּלְּהוּ, וְכֻלְּהוּ אִתְכַּפְיָין קַמֵּיהּ. קֵדְמָה אֶל אֶרֶץ קֶדֶם, בְּגִין דְּתַמָּן אִינוּן סִטְרֵי חֲרָשֵׁי מְסָאֲבֵי.

263. "The sons of the concubines" are the children of Kturah, WHO IS CALLED CONCUBINES because she was a concubine before ABRAHAM SENT HER AWAY and was a concubine now THAT HE TOOK HER BACK AGAIN. Rabbi Chiya said that this alludes to actual concubines AND IN NO WAY DOES IT ALLUDE TO KTURAH. "And sent them away from his son, Isaac" (Ibid.), so that they would not have control over Isaac "while he yet lived," while Abraham was alive and well in this world. This way, they would not quarrel with him later, and Isaac would be strengthened and subjugate everyone before him. "Eastward, to the east country" (Ibid.), because one finds there all kinds of witchcraft.

264. תָּא חֲזֵי, כְּתִיב וַתֵּרֶב חָכְמַת שְׁלֹמֹה מֵחָכְמַת כָּל בְּנֵי קֶדֶם. אִלֵּין אִינוּן דַּהֲווֹ מִבְּנֵי בְּנֵי פִּילַגְשִׁים דְּאַבְרָהָם, וְהָא אוֹקִימְנָא, דְּהָא בְּאִינוּן הָרֵרֵי קֶדֶם, אִינוּן דְּאוֹלְפִין חֲרָשִׁין לִבְנֵי נָשָׁא, וּמֵהַהִיא אֶרֶץ קֶדֶם, נָפְקוּ: לָבָן, וּבְעוֹר, וּבִלְעָם בְּנוֹ, וְכֻלְּהוּ חֲרָשֵׁי, וְהָא אוּקְמוּהָ.

264. Come and behold: It is written, "And Solomon's wisdom excelled the wisdom of all the children of the east country" (I Melachim 5:10). These are the sons of the concubines of Abraham. It was said that those who teach sorcery to men are found in these east mountains. And from the east country came Laban, Beor, his son Bilaam and all the sorcerers, as has already been explained.

28. "Who gave Jacob for a spoil"

A Synopsis

Here the rabbis discuss the above verse and its various, intricate meanings, which relate both to the time of the Exile and the time of the Resurrection, when The Creator will rebuild the Temple. We learn that these stories are all really metaphors for the spiritual work of unification, which is always here and now.

The Relevance of this Passage

The Torah and Zohar are not books of recorded history or mystical fables of antiquity. Rather, both are links to the upper world which connect man to the fountainhead and primal source of spiritual Light. Each passage offers a particular blend of energy that can be put to use in the present moment. Here, the spiritual influence to hasten the final Redemption, quicken the Resurrection, and accelerate the process of rebuilding the Temple, is summoned forth through the letters forming these verses. All three happenings will occur both individually and globally. Thus, every individual has his own "rock" in the Temple, which becomes manifest through personal acts of spiritual elevation.

265. רִבִּי חִזְקִיָּה פָּתַח וַאֲמַר, מִי נָתַן לִמְשִׁיסָּה יַעֲקֹב וְיִשְׂרָאֵל לְבוֹזְזִים הֲלֹא ה' וגו'. תָּא חֲזֵי, מִזִּמְנָא דְּאִתְחָרַב בֵּי מַקְדְּשָׁא, בִּרְכָאן לָא שַׁרְיָין בְּעָלְמָא, וְאִתְמְנָעוּ, כִּבְיָכוֹל, אִתְמְנָעוּ מֵעֵילָּא וְתַתָּא, וְכָל אִינוּן שְׁאָר דַּרְגִּין, תַּתָּאִין מִתְתַּקְפֵי וְאָזְלֵי וְשָׁלְטֵי עֲלַיְיהוּ דְּיִשְׂרָאֵל, בְּגִין דְּאִינוּן גָּרְמוּ בְּחוֹבַיְיהוּ.

265. Rabbi Chizkiyah opened with the verse, "Who gave Jacob for a spoil, and Yisrael to the robbers? Did not Hashem..." (Yeshayah 42:24). Come and behold: From the time the Temple was destroyed, no blessings hovered about the world. They stopped, as if detained above IN THE UPPER WORLDS and below IN THE LOWER WORLDS. All these lower grades were strengthened and ruled over Yisrael, because Yisrael had brought it about by their transgression. THIS ABSENCE OF BLESSINGS IN THE UPPER WORLDS OCCURRED BECAUSE THE LOWER BEINGS WERE NOT WORTHY OF RECEIVING THEM, AND ALL THE ABUNDANCE THAT THEY SHOULD HAVE GIVEN TO THE LOWER WORLDS WAS WITHHELD, FOR THERE WAS NO ONE TO GIVE TO.

266. הַאי קְרָא לָא אִתְיַישְׁבָן מִלֵּיה, דִּכְתִיב מִי נָתַן לִמְשִׁיסָה יַעֲקֹב כֵּיוָן דַּאֲמַר מִי נָתַן לִמְשִׁיסָה יַעֲקֹב וְיִשְׂרָאֵל, מַהוּ חָטָאנוּ לוֹ, חָטְאוּ לוֹ מִבָּעֵי לֵיה, וְאִי אֲמַר חָטָאנוּ לוֹ, מַאי וְלֹא אָבוּ, וְלֹא אָבִינוּ מִבָּעֵי לֵיה.

266. This verse contains a contradiction. It is written: "Who gave Jacob for a spoil, AND YISRAEL TO THE ROBBERS? DID NOT HASHEM, HE AGAINST WHOM WE HAVE SINNED." After it said, "Who gave Jacob for a spoil, and Yisrael", why does it continue with "we have sinned"? It should have said, 'They sinned'; NAMELY, IT SHOULD HAVE USED THE THIRD PERSON AND NOT SPOKEN AS IF THEY WERE TALKING FOR THEMSELVES. Since it said, "We have sinned," NAMELY THEY REFER TO THEMSELVES, why does it continue with, "They would not walk" IN WHICH HE USES THE THIRD PERSON AGAIN, instead of saying, 'We would not walk', AS IF THEY WERE SPEAKING FOR THEMSELVES.

267. אֶלָּא, בְּשַׁעְתָּא דְּאִתְחֲרַב מַקְדְּשָׁא, וְאִתּוֹקַד הֵיכָלָא, וְעַמָּא אִתְגְּלֵי, בָּעְיָא שְׁכִינְתָּא לְאִתְעַקְּרָא מְדּוּכְתָּהּ, וּלְמֵיהַךְ עִמְּהוֹן בְּגָלוּתָא, אָמְרָה אֵיהַךְ בְּקַדְמֵיתָא לְמֶחֱמֵי בֵּיתָאי וְהֵיכָלָאי, וְאֶפְקוֹד עַל דּוּכְתֵּי דְּכַהֲנֵי וְלֵיוָאֵי, דַּהֲווֹ פָּלְחִין בְּבֵיתָאי.

267. HE ANSWERS THAT when the Temple was destroyed, the Holy of Holies burned and the people were exiled. The Shechinah wanted to move from Her place and go into exile with them. THE SHECHINAH said, I will first go and see my house and palace and visit the places of the priests and the Levites, who worshipped in my house.

268. אָמַר רְבִּי אֶלְעָזָר, בְּהַהִיא שַׁעְתָּא, אִסְתַּכְּלַת כְּנֶסֶת יִשְׂרָאֵל לְעֵילָּא, וְחָמַאת דְּבַעֲלָהּ אִסְתַּלַּק מִנָּהּ לְעֵילָּא לְעֵילָּא, נָחֲתַת לְתַתָּא, עָאלַת בְּבֵיתָא, וְאִסְתַּכְּלַת בְּכָל אִינּוּן דּוּכְתֵּי, וְאִשְׁתְּמַע קָלָא, לְעֵילָּא לְעֵילָּא, וְאִשְׁתְּמַע קָלָא לְתַתָּא, הֲדָא הוּא דִּכְתִיב קוֹל בְּרָמָה נִשְׁמָע נְהִי בְּכִי תַמְרוּרִים רָחֵל מְבַכָּה עַל בָּנֶיהָ וְגוֹ', וְאוֹקִמוּהָ.

268. Rabbi Elazar said that at the time the Congregation of Yisrael, THE SHECHINAH, looked up and saw that Her husband, ZEIR ANPIN, had left Her and ascended up high, She went down, entered the Temple, and looked

at places. SHE WEPT and the sound was heard up above IN HEAVEN and below ON EARTH. This is the meaning of the verse: "A voice was heard up high, lamentation, and bitter weeping; Rachel weeping for her children" (Yirmeyah 31:14). This has been explained.

269. כֵּיוָן דְּעָאלַת בְּגָלוּתָא, אִסְתַּכְּלַת בְּעַמָּא, וְחָמַאת דְּדָחֲקֵי לוֹן, וְרָמְסֵי לוֹן בְּגָלוּתָא, בֵּין רַגְלַיְיהוּ דִּשְׁאָר עַמִּין, כְּדֵין אָמְרַת מִי נָתַן לִמְשִׁסָּה יַעֲקֹב וגו'. וְאִינּוּן אָמְרִין, הֲלֹא ה' זוֹ חָטָאנוּ לוֹ. וְהִיא אָמְרַת וְלֹא אָבוּ בִדְרָכָיו הָלוֹךְ וְלֹא שָׁמְעוּ בְּתוֹרָתוֹ.

269. When She went into exile, She looked at the people and saw how they were pushed and trampled under the feet of other nations in exile. Then She said, "Who gave Jacob for a spoil..." And YISRAEL responded, "Did not Hashem, He against whom we have sinned." IN THIS IT IS UNDERSTOOD THAT HE SPEAKS FOR HIMSELF. The Shechinah asks, "And in whose ways they would not walk, and to whose Torah they were not obedient?" (Yeshayah 42:24) THUS, THE QUESTION OF WHY IT IS WRITTEN IN THE THIRD PERSON IS AGAIN SETTLED.

270. וּבְשַׁעֲתָא דְּזַמִּין קוּדְשָׁא בְּרִיךְ הוּא, לְמִפְקַד עַל עַמֵיהּ, כְּנֶסֶת יִשְׂרָאֵל תֵּיתוּב מִן גָּלוּתָא בְּקַדְמֵיתָא, תְּהַךְ לְבֵיתָא, בְּגִין דְּבֵית הַמִּקְדָּשׁ יִתְבְּנֵי בְּקַדְמֵיתָא, וְיֵימָא לָהּ קוּדְשָׁא בְּרִיךְ הוּא, קוּמִי מֵעַפְרָא. הִיא תָּבַת וְאָמְרָה, לְאָן אֲתַר אֵיהַךְ, בֵּיתָאי חָרַב, הֵיכְלִי אִתּוֹקַד בְּנוּרָא. עַד דְּקוּדְשָׁא בְּרִיךְ הוּא, יִבְנֵי בֵּי מַקְדְּשָׁא בְּקַדְמֵיתָא, וְיַתְקִין הֵיכָלָא, וְיִבְנֵי קַרְתָּא דִּירוּשְׁלֵם, וּלְבָתַר יוֹקִים לָהּ מֵעַפְרָא. הֲדָא הוּא דִכְתִּיב, בּוֹנֵה יְרוּשָׁלַיִם ה' וגו'. בּוֹנֵה יְרוּשָׁלַיִם בְּקַדְמֵיתָא, וּלְבָתַר נִדְחֵי יִשְׂרָאֵל יְכַנֵּס, וְיֵימָא לָהּ הִתְנַעֲרִי מֵעָפָר קוּמִי שְׁבִי יְרוּשָׁלַיִם וגו'. וְיִתְכַּנֵּשׁ גָּלוּתְהוֹן דְּיִשְׂרָאֵל. הֲדָא הוּא דִכְתִּיב בּוֹנֵה יְרוּשָׁלַיִם ה' בְּקַדְמֵיתָא, וּלְבָתַר נִדְחֵי יִשְׂרָאֵל יְכַנֵּס. וּכְדֵין הָרוֹפֵא לִשְׁבוּרֵי לֵב וּמְחַבֵּשׁ לְעַצְּבוֹתָם, דָּא תְּחִיַּית הַמֵּתִים. וּכְתִיב וְאֶת רוּחִי אֶתֵּן בְּקִרְבְּכֶם וְעָשִׂיתִי אֶת אֲשֶׁר בְּחֻקַּי תֵּלֵכוּ וגו'.

270. When the Holy One, blessed be He, visits His people, the

Congregation of Yisrael, TO TAKE THEM OUT OF EXILE, THE SHECHINAH will return first and go to the Temple, because the Temple will be built before THE GATHERING OF THE EXILES, WHERE THE DWELLING OF THE SHECHINAH RESTS. THEREFORE, THE SHECHINAH IS ALSO ANXIOUS TO GET OUT OF EXILE. And the Holy One, blessed be He, said to Her, "Rise from the dust." But the Shechinah responded, Whither do I go? My house is destroyed and my palace is burned. This will continue until the Holy One, blessed be He, will first rebuild the Temple, fix the palace, and establish the city of Jerusalem. Only then does He raise THE SHECHINAH from the dust, as it is written: "Hashem builds Jerusalem" (Tehilim 147:2). Then "He gathers together the outcasts of Yisrael" (Ibid.) and tells Her, "Shake yourself from the dust; arise, and sit down, O Jerusalem" (Yeshayah 42:2). Then He gathers the exiles of Yisrael. Thus it first says: "Hashem builds Jerusalem" and then "He gathers together the outcasts of Yisrael." Then: "He heals the brokenhearted, and binds up their wounds" (Tehilim 147:3), which refers to the resurrection of the dead. And it is written: "And I will put my spirit within you, and cause you to follow my statutes, and you shall keep my judgments, and do them" (Yechezkel 36:27).

בָּרוּךְ ה׳ לְעוֹלָם אָמֵן וְאָמֵן:

Blessed is Hashem for ever. Amen, amen.

TOLDOT

Names of the articles

1. "And these are the generations of Isaac"

A Synopsis

Rabbi Chiya leads us to an understanding of the relationship between The Creator and the Torah. We learn how the world is maintained by Torah study, and why it is man's supreme duty to continue this study. Rabbi Yitzchak and Rabbi Yehuda explain the significance of the forms of blessing from Abraham to Isaac to Jacob, in whom all that has come before is manifested. We learn that true servants of The Creator are not only those from Yisrael, but anyone anywhere who studies the Torah.

The Relevance of this Passage

"The study of Torah" does not refer to a cerebral, academic approach to thousands of words on parchment. Through the eyes of the Kabbalists, the Torah is understood as the medium through which the energy of The Creator is expressed in our physical dimension of existence. The sinewy parchment, the coal black ink, and the primordial letters are all intricate components of a divine communication instrument serving one express purpose: to help willing students uproot all their character flaws, in order to attain similarity of nature and thus, closeness to the Light of The Creator. That said, Abraham, Isaac, and Jacob signify the Right, Left, and Central Column forces – that is, the *desire to share*, the *desire to receive,* and the *free will* to choose between and balance the two.

Jacob also corresponds to the Sfirah of Yesod, the gateway through which all the Light of the supernal realms enters our world. Essentially, the purpose of this passage is to ignite the primordial Light of the Torah. As we meditate upon the words, the emitted Light refines our imperfections. The strength of the Patriarchs, and especially The Central Column Force of Jacob, enhances our ability to resist and triumph over our reactive, self-indulgent drives. Finally, the Light accumulated through our interaction with the Zohar shines universally, helping to awaken the world to the internal truths of the Torah and all that the Light of The Creator can offer us.

1. וְאֵלֶּה תּוֹלְדוֹת יִצְחָק וְגוֹ'. פָּתַח ר' חִיָּיא וַאֲמַר מִי יְמַלֵּל גְּבוּרוֹת יי'
יַשְׁמִיעַ כָּל תְּהִלָּתוֹ, תָּא חֲזֵי, בָּעָא קוּדְשָׁא בְּרִיךְ הוּא וְסָלֵיק בִּרְעוּתָא
קַמֵּיהּ לְמִבְרֵי עָלְמָא, הֲוָה מִסְתַּכֵּל בְּאוֹרַיְיתָא, וּבָרָא לֵיהּ, וּבְכָל עוֹבָדָא
וְעוֹבָדָא דִּבְרָא קוּדְשָׁא בְּרִיךְ הוּא בְּעָלְמָא, הֲוָה מִסְתַּכֵּל בְּאוֹרַיְיתָא,

1. "And these are the generations of Isaac"

וּבְרָא לֵיהּ, הֲדָא הוּא דִכְתִיב, וָאֶהְיֶה אֶצְלוֹ אָמוֹן וָאֶהְיֶה שַׁעֲשׁוּעִים יוֹם אַל תִּקְרֵי אָמוֹן, אֶלָּא אוּמָן.

1. "And these are the generations of Isaac..." (Beresheet 25:19). Rabbi Chiya opened the discussion with the verse: "Who can utter the mighty acts of Hashem? Who can declare all His praise?" (Tehilim 106:2). Come and behold: when the Holy One, blessed be He, wished to create the world, He did so according to the Torah. And every act that the Holy One, blessed be He, used to create the world was done according to the Torah. This is the meaning of: "then I was by him, as a nursling: and I was daily his delight" (Mishlei 8:30). Do not pronounce it as "a nursling," (Heb. *amon*) but rather 'a craftsman' (Heb. *oman*), BECAUSE IT WAS A TOOL FOR HIS CRAFT.

2. כַּד בָּעָא לְמִבְרֵי אָדָם אָמְרָה תּוֹרָה קַמֵּיהּ, אִי בַּר נָשׁ יִתְבְּרֵי, וּלְבָתַר יֶחֱטֵי, וְאַנְתְּ תֵּידוֹן לֵיהּ, אַמַּאי יְהוֹן עוֹבָדֵי יְדָךְ לְמַגָּנָא, דְּהָא לָא יֵיכוֹל לְמִסְבַּל דִּינָךְ, אָמַר לָהּ קוּדְשָׁא בְּרִיךְ הוּא, הָא אַתְקֵינַת תְּשׁוּבָה, עַד לָא בָרָאתִי עַלְמָא, אָמַר קוּדְשָׁא בְּרִיךְ הוּא לְעַלְמָא, בְּשַׁעֲתָא דַּעֲבַד לֵיהּ, וּבְרָא לְאָדָם, אָמַר לוֹ עַלְמָא עַלְמָא, אַנְתְּ וְנִימוּסָךְ, לָא קַיְימִין אֶלָּא עַל אוֹרַיְיתָא. וּבְגִין כָּךְ בָּרָאתִי לֵיהּ לְאָדָם בָּךְ, בְּגִין דְּיִתְעַסַּק בָּהּ. וְאִי לָאו, הָא אֲנָא אַהֲדַר לָךְ, לְתֹהוּ וָבֹהוּ וְכֹלָּא בְּגִינֵיהּ דְּאָדָם קַיְימָא, הה"ד אָנֹכִי עָשִׂיתִי אֶרֶץ וְאָדָם עָלֶיהָ בָרָאתִי. וְאוֹרַיְיתָא קַיְימָא וּמַכְרְזָא קַמַּיְיהוּ דִּבְנֵי נָשָׁא, בְּגִין דְּיִתְעַסְּקוּ וְיִשְׁתַּדְּלוּ בָּהּ וְלֵית מָאן דְּיַרְכִין אוּדְנֵיהּ.

2. When He wanted to create man, the Torah said to him: 'If man is created, he will sin, and you will punish him. Would not Your handwork then be in vain? After all, he will not be able to endure the punishment.' The Holy One, blessed be He, replied: 'I created repentance before I created the world. IF HE WILL SIN, HE WILL BE ABLE TO REPENT AND BE FORGIVEN.' When the Holy One, blessed be He, created the world and created Adam, He said to it: 'World, world, you and your nature are based solely upon the Torah, and for that reason I created man in you, to be occupied with the study of the Torah. And if he does not STUDY THE TORAH, I will return you to chaos. Everything is for man.' This is the meaning of the verse: "I have made the earth, and created man upon it" (Yeshayah 45:12). The Torah

proclaims to men to be occupied with and endeavor in the study of the Torah, but no one lends an ear.

3. תָּא חֲזֵי כָּל מַאן דְּאִשְׁתַּדַּל בְּאוֹרַיְיתָא אִיהוּ קַיַּים עַלְמָא, וְקַיַּים כָּל עוֹבָדָא וְעוֹבָדָא עַל תִּקּוּנֵיהּ כְּדְקָא יָאוֹת, וְלֵית לָךְ כָּל שַׁיְיפָא וְשַׁיְיפָא דְּקַיְימָא בֵּיהּ בְּבַר נָשׁ, דְּלָא הֲוֵי לָקֳבְלֵיהּ בְּרִיָּה בְּעָלְמָא. דְּהָא כְּמָה דְּבַר נָשׁ אִיהוּ מִתְפַּלַּג שַׁיְיפִין, וְכֻלְּהוּ קַיְימִין דַּרְגִּין עַל דַּרְגִּין מִתְתַּקְנִין אַלֵּין עַל אַלֵּין וְכֻלְּהוּ חַד גּוּפָא, הָכֵי נָמֵי עַלְמָא, כָּל אִינּוּן בְּרִיָּין כֻּלְּהוּ שַׁיְיפִין שַׁיְיפִין, וְקַיְימִין אַלֵּין עַל אַלֵּין, וְכַד מִתְתַּקְּנָן כֻּלְּהוּ, הָא גּוּפָא מַמָּשׁ. וְכֹלָּא כְּגַוְונָא דְּאוֹרַיְיתָא, דְּהָא אוֹרַיְיתָא כֹּלָּא, שַׁיְיפִין וּפִרְקִין, וְקַיְימִין אַלֵּין עַל אַלֵּין, וְכַד מִתְתַּקְּנָן כֻּלְּהוּ, אִתְעֲבִידוּ חַד גּוּפָא. כֵּיוָן דְּאִסְתַּכַּל דָּוִד בְּעוֹבָדָא דָּא, פָּתַח וַאֲמַר מָה רַבּוּ מַעֲשֶׂיךָ יְיָ' כֻּלָּם בְּחָכְמָה עָשִׂיתָ מָלְאָה הָאָרֶץ קִנְיָנֶךָ.

3. Come and behold: whoever studies the Torah sustains the world and properly sustains every act in the world. There is no part within man that does not have a counterpart creature in the world. Just as the body of man is composed of levels of parts that act together to form a unified body, so is the world. All the creatures in the world are hierarchical parts that act on and react with each other, so they will actually be as one body. Everything, WHETHER IT BE MAN OR THE WORLD, resembles the Torah, because the Torah is made of different parts and sections that support each other. When they are all correct, they will become as one body. When David looked at this work, he said: "Hashem, how manifold are your works! In wisdom You have made them all: the earth is full of Your creatures" (Tehilim 104:24).

4. בְּאוֹרַיְיתָא אִינּוּן כָּל רָזִין עִלָּאִין חֲתִימִין, דְּלָא יָכְלִין לְאִתְדַּבְּקָא, בְּאוֹרַיְיתָא כָּל אִינּוּן מִלִּין עִלָּאִין, דְּאִתְגַּלְיָין וְלָא אִתְגַּלְיָין, בְּאוֹרַיְיתָא אִינּוּן כָּל מִלִּין דִּלְעֵילָּא וּלְתַתָּא, כָּל מִלִּין דְּעָלְמָא דֵין, וְכָל מִלִּין דְּעָלְמָא דְּאָתֵי בְּאוֹרַיְיתָא אִינּוּן, וְלֵית מַאן דְּיַשְׁגַּח וְיָדַע לוֹן, וּבְגִין כָּךְ כְּתִיב, מִי יְמַלֵּל גְּבוּרוֹת יְיָ' יַשְׁמִיעַ כָּל תְּהִלָּתוֹ.

4. The Torah contains supernal, sealed mysteries, that man cannot grasp; it

contains all supernal matters – those revealed and those not revealed. BECAUSE OF THEIR DEPTH, THEY ARE REVEALED TO THE SCHOLAR, BUT DISAPPEAR IMMEDIATELY ONLY TO BE REVEALED IN THE NEXT INSTANT AND DISAPPEAR AGAIN. AND SO IT CONTINUES FOR THOSE WHO STUDY THEM. The Torah contains all the matters above IN THE SUPERNAL WORLDS and below. Everything in this world and everything in the World to Come is in the Torah, but there is no one to observe and understand them. Thus, it is written, "Who can utter the mighty acts of Hashem? Who can declare all His praise?" (Tehilim 106:2).

5. תָּא חֲזֵי אָתָא שְׁלֹמֹה וּבָעָא לְמֵיקַם עַל מִלּוֹי דְּאוֹרַיְיתָא, וְעַל דְּקְדּוּקֵי אוֹרַיְיתָא, וְלָא יָכִיל, אֲמַר אָמַרְתִּי אֶחְכָּמָה וְהִיא רְחוֹקָה מִמֶּנִּי. דָּוִד אֲמַר, גַּל עֵינַי וְאַבִּיטָה נִפְלָאוֹת מִתּוֹרָתֶךְ. תָּא חֲזֵי כְּתִיב בִּשְׁלֹמֹה וַיְדַבֵּר שְׁלֹשֶׁת אֲלָפִים מָשָׁל וַיְהִי שִׁירוֹ חֲמִשָּׁה וָאָלֶף. וְהָא אוֹקְמוּהָ. דַּחֲמִשָּׁה וָאֶלֶף טְעָמִים, הֲווֹ בְּכָל מָשָׁל וּמָשָׁל דַּהֲוָה אֲמַר. וּמַה שְׁלֹמֹה, דְּאִיהוּ בָּשָׂר וָדָם, כָּךְ הֲווֹ בְּמִלּוֹי. מִלִּין דְּאוֹרַיְיתָא דְּקָאֲמַר קוּדְשָׁא בְּרִיךְ הוּא, עַל אַחַת כַּמָּה וְכַמָּה, דְּבְכָל מִלָּה וּמִלָּה, אִית בָּהּ כַּמָּה מְשָׁלִים, כַּמָּה שִׁירִין, כַּמָּה תּוּשְׁבְּחָן, כַּמָּה רָזִין עִלָּאִין, כַּמָּה חָכְמָאן, וְעַל דָּא כְּתִיב מִי יְמַלֵּל גְּבוּרוֹת יְיָ'.

5. Come and behold: when Solomon unsuccessfully tried to understand the words and subtleties of the Torah, he said: "I said, 'I will be wise'; but it was far from me" (Kohelet 7:23). David said: "Open my eyes that I may behold wondrous things out of Your Torah" (Tehilim 119:18). Come and behold: it is written of Solomon that he "spoke 3,000 proverbs, and his poems were a 1,005" (I Melachim 5:12). This is because there were 5,000 interpretations of each proverb he told. If this is true of the words of Solomon, who was flesh and blood, how many proverbs, chants, praises, mysteries, and wise thoughts are contained in the words of the Torah, as spoken by the Holy One, blessed be He? Therefore, it is written: "Who can utter the mighty acts of Hashem."

6. תָּא חֲזֵי, מַה כְּתִיב לְעֵילָא, וְאֵלֶּה תּוֹלְדוֹת יִשְׁמָעֵאל, דְּאִינוּן תְּרֵיסַר נְשִׂיאִין, לְבָתַר אֲמַר וְאֵלֶּה תּוֹלְדוֹת יִצְחָק, ס״ד, דְּכֵיוָן דִּכְתִיב בֵּיהּ בְּיִשְׁמָעֵאל דְּאוֹלִיד תְּרֵיסַר נְשִׂיאִין, וְיִצְחָק אוֹלִיד תְּרֵין בְּנִין, דְּדָא

אִסְתַּלַּק, וְדָא לָא אִסְתַּלַּק, עַל דָּא כְּתִיב מִי יְמַלֵּל גְּבוּרוֹת יְיָ', דָּא
יִצְחָק, וְיִצְחָק אַפֵּיק לֵיה לְיַעֲקֹב, דַּהֲוָה אִיהוּ בִּלְחוֹדוֹי, יַתִּיר מִכֻּלְּהוּ,
דְּאוֹלִיד תְּרֵיסַר שְׁבָטִין, קִיּוּמָא דִּלְעֵילָּא וְתַתָּא, אֲבָל יִצְחָק לְעֵילָּא
בִּקְדוּשָׁה עִלָּאָה וְיִשְׁמָעֵאל לְתַתָּא, וְעַל דָּא כְּתִיב, מִי יְמַלֵּל גְּבוּרוֹת יְיָ'
יַשְׁמִיעַ כָּל תְּהִלָּתוֹ, דָּא יַעֲקֹב כַּד אִתְדְּבַּק שִׁמְשָׁא בְּסִיהֲרָא, כַּמָּה
כֹּכְבַיָּא נְהִירִין מִנַּיְיהוּ.

6. Come and behold: it is written, "Now these are the generations of Ishmael" (Beresheet 25:12), and they are twelve princes. Then it is written: "And these are the generations of Isaac" (Ibid. 19). Is it possible that because it is written that Ishmael sired twelve princes and Isaac sired two, he (Ishmael) is more RIGHTEOUS THAN ISAAC? It is therefore written: "Who can utter the mighty (Heb. *gvurot*) acts of Hashem." This refers to Isaac – AS ISAAC IS GVURAH OF ZEIR ANPIN – for Isaac sired Jacob, who alone is more important than all of them, for he fathered the twelve tribes, and sustained the upper and the lower, while Isaac supported the higher in supernal holiness and Ishmael only below. Therefore the verse, "Who can utter the mighty acts of Hashem," REFERS TO ISAAC, AS EXPLAINED ABOVE. The words, "declare all His praises," refers to Jacob, BECAUSE JACOB, REPRESENTING EXISTENCE BOTH ABOVE AND BELOW, CONTAINS ALL HIS PRAISES. When the sun, ZEIR ANPIN, connects with the moon, NUKVA, many stars shine from them. THEY ARE THE TWELVE TRIBES OF YAH, LIKENED TO THE STARS IN JOSEPH'S DREAM.

7. וְאֵלֶּה תוֹלְדוֹת יִצְחָק בֶּן אַבְרָהָם. אָמַר רִבִּי יוֹסֵי, מַאי שְׁנָא דְּעַד
הָכָא, לָא כְּתִיב בֶּן אַבְרָהָם, וְהַשְׁתָּא אָמַר, אֶלָּא אַף עַל גַּב דִּכְתִיב
וַיְבָרֶךְ אֱלֹהִים אֶת יִצְחָק בְּנוֹ, הַשְׁתָּא דְּמִית אַבְרָהָם, דְּיוֹקְנֵיהּ הֲוָה בֵּיהּ,
וְאִשְׁתָּאַר בֵּיהּ בְּיִצְחָק, דְּכָל מַאן דְּחָמֵי לְיִצְחָק, הֲוָה אָמַר דָּא אַבְרָהָם
וַדַּאי, וַהֲוָה סָהִיד וַאֲמַר אַבְרָהָם הוֹלִיד אֶת יִצְחָק.

7. "And these are the generations of Isaac, Abraham's son." Rabbi Yosi asks: What has changed? It did not say, "Abraham's son" previously. For although it is written, "Elohim blessed his son Isaac," (Beresheet 25:11) Abraham is now dead; THAT IS, HE BLESSED AND RAISED THE LEVEL OF ISAAC, WHICH IS GVURAH, AFTER THE DEATH OF ABRAHAM. THUS, the

image of Abraham was upon Isaac and stayed with him – WHICH MEANS
THAT THE QUALITY OF ABRAHAM, WHICH IS CHESED, REMAINED WITHIN
ISAAC – so that whoever saw Isaac said: "...this is surely Abraham," and
pronounced that Abraham begat Isaac – WHO WAS INCLUDED IN AND
CLOTHED WITH THE QUALITY OF ABRAHAM, WHICH IS CHESED.
THEREFORE, THE SCRIPTURE HERE SPECIFICALLY READS, "ABRAHAM'S
SON," AS WELL AS, "ABRAHAM BEGOT ISAAC."

8. ר' יִצְחָק קָם לֵילְיָא חַד לְמִלְעֵי בְּאוֹרַיְיתָא, וְר' יְהוּדָה קָם בְּקִסְרוֹי,
בְּהַהִיא שַׁעֲתָא. אָמַר ר' יְהוּדָה, אֵיקוּם וְאֵיזִיל לְגַבֵּי רַבִּי יִצְחָק, וְאֶלְעֵי
בְּאוֹרַיְיתָא וְנִתְחַבַּר כַּחֲדָא אֲזַל עִמֵּיה חִזְקִיָּה בְּרֵיה, דַּהֲוָה רַבְיָא, כַּד
קָרִיב אַבָּבָא, שָׁמַע לֵיה לְרַבִּי יִצְחָק, דַּהֲוָה אָמַר, וַיְהִי אַחֲרֵי מוֹת
אַבְרָהָם וַיְבָרֶךְ אֱלֹקִים אֶת יִצְחָק בְּנוֹ וַיֵּשֶׁב יִצְחָק עִם בְּאֵר לַחַי רוֹאִי,
הַאי קְרָא, לָאו רֵישֵׁיה סֵיפֵיה וְלָאו סֵיפֵיה רֵישֵׁיה, מַאי שְׁנָא דְקוּדְשָׁא
בְּרִיךְ הוּא אִצְטְרִיךְ לְבָרְכָא לֵיה לְיִצְחָק, בְּגִין דְּאַבְרָהָם לָא בֵּרְכֵיה.
מַאי טַעֲמָא, מִשּׁוּם דְּלָא יִתְבָּרֵךְ עֵשָׂו, וְע"ד סְלִיקוּ אִינּוּן בִּרְכָאן
לְקוּדְשָׁא בְּרִיךְ הוּא, וְאוֹקְמוּהָ. וַיֵּשֶׁב יִצְחָק עִם בְּאֵר לַחַי רֹאִי, מַאי לַחַי
רֹאִי, אֶלָּא דְּאִתְחַבַּר בָּה בִּשְׁכִינְתָּא, בֵּירָא דְמַלְאָךְ קַיָּימָא אִתְחֲזֵי עֲלָה,
כְּתַרְגּוּמוֹ וּבְגִין כָּךְ בֵּרְכֵיה.

8. Rabbi Yitzchak rose one night to study Torah, while Rabbi Yehuda, who
was in the city of Caesarea, also rose at the same hour TO STUDY TORAH.
Rabbi Yehuda said: I will walk to Rabbi Yitzchak and study Torah together
with him. He went with his son, Hezekiah, who was then a boy. When he
approached the door, he heard Rabbi Yitzchak say, "And it came to pass
after the death of Abraham, that Elohim blessed his son Isaac; and Isaac
dwelt by Be'er Lachai Ro'i" (Beresheet 25:11). HE THEN ASKS A
DIFFICULT QUESTION: In this verse, the beginning does not fit the end and
the end does not fit the beginning; IT BEGINS WITH THE DEATH OF
ABRAHAM AND ENDS WITH THE BLESSING OF ISAAC, AND THERE IS NO
CONNECTION BETWEEN THESE EVENTS. HE THEN POSED ANOTHER
DIFFICULT QUESTION: Why this change? Why should the Holy One,
blessed be He, bless Isaac AND NOT ABRAHAM? HE ANSWERS: Since
Abraham did not bless Isaac, HASHEM BLESSED HIM AFTER HE DIED.
THIS IS THE CONNECTION BETWEEN THE BEGINNING AND END OF THE

VERSE: "AND IT CAME TO PASS..." HE ASKS: Why did Abraham not bless him? AND HE REPLIED: So that Esau, HIS SON, would not be blessed with him – THAT IS, SO THAT ESAU WOULD NOT DRAW DOWN THE ILLUMINATION OF THE LEFT AS IS HIS UNHOLY WONT. Therefore these blessings passed to the Holy One, blessed be He, AND THE HOLY ONE, BLESSED BE HE, BLESSED ISAAC. Of the verse, "and Isaac dwelt at Be'er Lachai Ro'i," HE ASKS: What is the meaning of "Lachai Ro'I," AND ANSWERS that he was united with the Shechinah, as the Aramaic translation reads, "the well where the angel of the covenant was seen." THIS IS THE WELL, NAMELY, THE SHECHINAH, UPON WHICH THE ANGEL OF THE COVENANT, YESOD, WAS SEEN. Therefore He blessed him. BY THIS WE MAY UNDERSTAND THE CONNECTION OF THE THREE PARTS OF THIS VERSE: "AND IT CAME TO PASS AFTER THE DEATH OF ABRAHAM," WHO DID NOT BLESS ISAAC, "THAT ELOHIM BLESSED HIS SON ISAAC." WHY DID HE BLESS HIM? BECAUSE "ISAAC DWELT AT BE'ER LACHAI RO'I," FOR HE JOINED THE SHECHINAH.

9. אַדְהָכֵי, בָּטַשׁ ר' יְהוּדָה אַבָּבָא, וְעָאל, וְאִתְחַבְּרוּ אֲמַר ר' יִצְחָק, הַשְׁתָּא זִוּוּגָא דִּשְׁכִינְתָּא בַּהֲדָן. אֲמַר רִבִּי יְהוּדָה, הַאי בְּאֵר לַחַי רוֹאִי דְּקָאֲמַרְתְּ שַׁפִּיר, אֲבָל בְּמִלָּה אִשְׁתְּמַע. פְּתַח וַאֲמַר מַעְיַן גַּנִּים בְּאֵר מַיִם חַיִּים וְנוֹזְלִים מִן לְבָנוֹן, הַאי קְרָא אִתְּמַר אֲבָל הָא אוּקְמוּהַ, מַעְיַן גַּנִּים דָּא אַבְרָהָם בְּאֵר מַיִם חַיִּים דָּא יִצְחָק, וְנוֹזְלִים מִן לְבָנוֹן דָּא יַעֲקֹב. בְּאֵר מַיִם חַיִּים דָּא יִצְחָק, הַיְינוּ דִּכְתִיב וַיֵּשֶׁב יִצְחָק עִם בְּאֵר לַחַי רֹאִי. וּמַאי בְּאֵר, דָּא שְׁכִינְתָּא, לַחַי דָּא חֵי הָעוֹלָמִים, צַדִּיק חֵי הָעוֹלָמִים וְלֵית לְאַפְרָשָׁא לוֹן, חַי הוּא בִּתְרֵי עָלְמִין, חַי לְעֵילָּא, דְּאִיהוּ עַלְמָא עִלָּאָה, חַי לְגַבֵּי עַלְמָא תַּתָּאָה, וְעַלְמָא תַּתָּאָה בְּגִינֵיהּ קַיְימָא וְנָהֲרָא.

9. In the meantime, Rabbi Yehuda knocked on the door, entered, and joined him. Rabbi Yitzchak said: Now the Shechinah is with us. Rabbi Yehuda said that this explanation concerning "Be'er Lachai Ro'i" is good, but there is more to be understood from the words. ONE SHOULD UNDERSTAND YOUR INTERPRETATION FROM THE WORDS THEMSELVES. He began with the verse: "a fountain of gardens, a well of living waters, and streams from Lebanon" (Shir Hashirim 4:15). This verse was already explained: "a fountain of gardens" is Abraham; "a well of living waters" is Isaac; and "streams from the Lebanon" is Jacob. HE EXPLAINED THAT "a well of

living waters" is Isaac, as it is written: "and Isaac dwelt at Be'er Lachai Ro'i" (lit. 'a well of living and seeing'). What is 'a well'? It is the Shechinah, while 'living' is he who is the Life of the Worlds, namely, the Righteous – YESOD who is the Life of the Worlds – and they are not to be separated. He lives in both worlds – he lives above, in the higher world, NAMELY BINAH, and he lives in the lower world, WHICH IS MALCHUT. The lower world lives and shines from his strength.

10. תָּא חֲזֵי, סִיהֲרָא לָא אִתְנְהֵירַת, אֶלָּא כַּד חַזְיָא לֵיהּ לְשִׁמְשָׁא, וְכֵיוָן דְּחַזְיָא לֵיהּ, אִתְנְהֵיר. וְע"ד הַאי בְּאֵר לַחַי רוֹאִי וַדַּאי, וּכְדֵין אִתְנָהֲרָא, וְקַיְימָא בְּמַיָּין חַיִּין, לַחַי רֹאִי, בְּגִין לְאִתְמַלְיָא וּלְאִתְנַהֲרָא מֵהַאי חַי.

10. Come and behold: the moon, NUKVA, shines only when she sees the sun, ZEIR ANPIN. When she sees him, she shines. Therefore this is called 'Be'er Lachai Ro'i,' for assuredly then she shines and stands filled with living water, "Lachai Ro'i," 'living and seeing', so as to be filled and illuminated by that which lives, YESOD OF ZEIR ANPIN, AS MENTIONED.

11. תָּא חֲזֵי, כְּתִיב וּבְנָיָהוּ בֶּן יְהוֹיָדָע בֶּן אִישׁ חַי דַּהֲוָה צַדִּיק, וְנָהֵיר לְדָרֵיהּ, כְּמָה דְּחַי דִּלְעֵילָּא, נָהֵיר לְעָלְמָא, וּבְכָל זִמְנָא, הַאי בְּאֵר, לַחַי אִסְתַּכַּל וְחָמֵי, בְּגִין לְאִתְנַהֲרָא, כִּדְקָאֲמָרָן. וַיֵּשֶׁב יִצְחָק עִם בְּאֵר לַחַי רֹאִי. הַיְינוּ דִּכְתִיב בְּקַחְתּוֹ אֶת רִבְקָה, וְיָתֵיב בַּהֲדָהּ, וְאִתְאֲחִיד עִמָּהּ, חֹשֶׁךְ בַּלַּיְלָה, דִּכְתִיב שְׂמֹאלוֹ תַּחַת לְרֹאשִׁי. וְתָא חֲזֵי, יִצְחָק בְּקִרְיַת אַרְבַּע הֲוָה בָּתַר דְּמִית אַבְרָהָם, מַהוּ וַיֵּשֶׁב יִצְחָק עִם בְּאֵר לַחַי רוֹאִי, דְּאִזְדַּוּוֹג בֵּיהּ, וְאָחִיד בֵּיהּ בְּהַהוּא בֵּירָא, לְאִתְעָרָא רְחִימוּתָא כִּדְקָאֲמָרָן.

11. Come and behold: it is written, "And Benaiah the son of Jehoida, the son of a valiant (lit. 'living') man" (II Shmuel 23:20). This means that he was righteous and illuminated his generation as the living one above, YESOD OF ZEIR ANPIN, illuminates the world, NUKVA. Thus, the well, WHICH IS NUKVA, constantly looks to the living one, WHO IS YESOD, in order to be illuminated. "And Isaac dwelt by Be'er Lachai Ro'i." It is written, "When he took Rivkah," FOR THE WELL IS THE SECRET OF RIVKAH, NAMELY THE NUKVA OF ZEIR ANPIN, and as he united with her, IT REPRESENTED the

joining of darkness and night, as it is written: "his left hand is under my head" (Shir Hashirim 2:6) Come and behold: Isaac was in Kiryat Arba after Abraham died. HE ASKS: What about the verse that reads, "And Isaac dwelt by Be'er Lachai Ro'i?" THE RESPONSE IS THAT THIS DOES NOT NECESSARILY INDICATE HIS ABODE, BUT RATHER THE NAME OF THE NUKVA with which he joined and was united in that well, to stir up love, as we said.

12. פְּתַח רִבִּי יִצְחָק וַאֲמַר, וְזָרַח הַשֶּׁמֶשׁ וּבָא הַשֶּׁמֶשׁ וְאֶל מְקוֹמוֹ שׁוֹאֵף זוֹרֵחַ הוּא שָׁם. וְזָרַח הַשֶּׁמֶשׁ, דָּא שִׁמְשָׁא, דְּנָהֵיר לְסִיהֲרָא, דְּכַד אִתְחֲזֵי בַּהֲדָהּ, כְּדֵין נָהֲרָא, וְאִתְנְהֵיר וְזָרַח, מֵאֲתַר עִלָּאָה, דְּקַיְימָא עֲלֵיהּ, מִתַּמָּן זָרַח תָּדִיר. וּבָא הַשֶּׁמֶשׁ, לְאִזְדַּוְּוגָא בַּהֲדָהּ דְּסִיהֲרָא. הוֹלֵךְ אֶל דָּרוֹם, דְּאִיהוּ יְמִינָא, וְשַׁוֵּי תּוּקְפֵיהּ בֵּיהּ, וּבְגִין דְּתוּקְפֵּיהּ בֵּיהּ, כָּל חֵילָא דְּגוּפָא בִּימִינָא הוּא, וּבֵיהּ תַּלְיָא. וּלְבָתַר סוֹבֵב אֶל צָפוֹן, נָהֵיר לְסִטְרָא דָּא, וְנָהֵיר לְסִטְרָא דָּא. סוֹבֵב סוֹבֵב הוֹלֵךְ הָרוּחַ, בְּקַדְמֵיתָא כְּתִיב שֶׁמֶשׁ, וְהַשְׁתָּא רוּחַ. אֶלָּא כֹּלָּא חַד, וְרָזָא חֲדָא, וְכָל דָּא, בְּגִין דְּסִיהֲרָא אִתְנָהֲרָא מִנֵּיהּ, וְיִתְחַבְּרוּן תַּרְוַויְיהוּ.

12. Rabbi Yitzchak began the discussion with the verse: "The sun also rises and the sun goes down and hastens to its place where it rises again" (Kohelet 1:5). "The sun also rises," refers to the sun, ZEIR ANPIN, which shines on the moon, THE NUKVA. For when the sun is seen by her, she shines, AND THE SUN illuminates and shines from the supreme place that is above it, WHICH IS BINAH, from where IT RECEIVES HIS ILLUMINATION, AND it always rises. "And the sun goes down," means that when it comes to mate with the moon, NUKVA, it "goes towards the south" (Ibid. 6), which is the Right COLUMN OF ZEIR ANPIN, and there reposes its strength. THIS MEANS THAT ITS MAIN ILLUMINATION IS IN THE RIGHT, WHICH IS CHASSADIM, because its strength is in the right. As a result, all the strength of a man's body is in the right side, from which stems the strength of the body. Later IT READS, "and veers to the north," and shines upon this side, NAMELY, THE SOUTH, and shines upon that side, NAMELY, THE NORTH. "Round and round goes the wind" (Ibid.). HE ASKS: Why is it first written, "sun," and now IT IS CALLED "wind." HE RESPONDED THAT all is one secret, BECAUSE ZEIR ANPIN IS THE INNER MEANING OF THE LIGHT OF THE WIND, AND IS CALLED 'SUN'. And all this happens – "ROUND AND

ROUND GOES THE WIND" – so that the moon will illuminate by its light and the two will join.

13. תָּא חֲזֵי, כַּד אֲתָא אַבְרָהָם לְעַלְמָא חֲבֵיק לַהּ לְסִיהֲרָא וְקָרֵיב לַהּ, כֵּיוָן דַּאֲתָא יִצְחָק אָחֵיד בַּהּ, וְאַתְקֵיף בַּהּ כְּדְקָא יָאוֹת, וּמְשִׁיךְ לָהּ בִּרְחִימוּ, כְּמָה דְּאִתְּמַר, דִּכְתִיב שְׂמֹאלוֹ תַּחַת לְרֹאשׁ. כֵּיוָן דַּאֲתָא יַעֲקֹב, כְּדֵין אִתְחַבַּר שִׁמְשָׁא בְּסִיהֲרָא, וְאִתְנְהֵיר, וְאִשְׁתַּכַּח יַעֲקֹב שְׁלִים בְּכָל סִטְרִין, וְסִיהֲרָא אִתְנְהֵירַת, וְאִתְתַּקְנַת בִּתְרֵיסַר שִׁבְטִין.

13. Come and behold: when Abraham came into the world, he embraced the moon and brought her near. When Isaac came, he took her and held her and drew her lovingly, as it is written: "his left hand is under my head" (Shir Hashirim 2:6). When Jacob came, he united the sun, ZEIR ANPIN, with the moon, THE NUKVA, and THE NUKVA shone. So Jacob became whole in every aspect, and the moon shone, and was perfected by the twelve tribes.

14. פָּתַח רִבִּי יְהוּדָה וְאָמַר הִנֵּה בָּרְכוּ אֶת יְיָ' כָּל עַבְדֵי יְיָ', וְגוֹ'. הַאי קְרָא אוּקְמוּהָ, אֲבָל תָּא חֲזֵי, הִנֵּה בָּרְכוּ אֶת יְיָ', וּמַאן אִינוּן, דְּיִתְחֲזוּן לְבָרְכָא לֵיהּ לְקוּדְשָׁא בְּרִיךְ הוּא, כָּל עַבְדֵי יְיָ', בְּגִין דְּכָל בַּר נָשׁ בְּעַלְמָא מִיִּשְׂרָאֵל, אַף עַל גַּב דְּכֹלָּא יִתְחֲזוּן לְבָרְכָא לֵיהּ לְקוּדְשָׁא בְּרִיךְ הוּא, בִּרְכָתָא דִּבְגִינַיְיהוּ יִתְבָּרְכוּן עִלָּאִין וְתַתָּאִין מַאן הִיא, הַהִיא דְּבָרְכִין לֵיהּ עַבְדֵי יְיָ', וְלָא כֻּלְּהוּ. וּמַאן אִינוּן דְּבִרְכָתְהוֹן בִּרְכָתָא, הָעוֹמְדִים בְּבֵית יְיָ' בַּלֵּילוֹת, אִלֵּין אִינוּן דְּקַיְימוּ בְּפַלְגוּת לֵילְיָא, וְאִתְעָרֵי לְמִקְרֵי בְּאוֹרַיְיתָא, אִלֵּין קַיְימֵי בְּבֵית יְיָ' בַּלֵּילוֹת, דְּהָא כְּדֵין קוּדְשָׁא בְּרִיךְ הוּא אָתֵי לְאִשְׁתַּעְשְׁעָא עִם צַדִּיקַיָּא בְּגִנְתָּא דְּעֵדֶן. וַאֲנַן קַיְימֵי הָכָא לְאִתְעָרָא בְּמִלֵּי דְאוֹרַיְיתָא, נֵימָא בְּמִלֵּי דְיִצְחָק, דַּאֲנַן בֵּיהּ.

14. Rabbi Yehuda opened the discussion with the verse: "Behold, bless Hashem, all you servants of Hashem..." (Tehilim 134:1). This verse was explained, yet come and behold: it is written, "Behold, bless Hashem." Who are those worthy of blessing the Holy One, blessed be He? THE SCRIPTURE SAYS, "all you servants of Hashem." Although anyone from Yisrael is worthy of blessing the Holy One, blessed be He, NEVERTHELESS, who

gives the blessings for the sake of the supernal and lower beings? THE SCRIPTURE SAYS, "all you servants of Hashem," yet not everyone. Whose blessing is considered a blessing? THE SCRIPTURE SAYS, THOSE "who stand by night in the house of Hashem" (Ibid.); those who wake up at midnight to study Torah. These are those "who stand by night in the house of Hashem." ACCORDING TO THE SCRIPTURE, THEY MUST BE BOTH THE SERVANTS OF HASHEM AND ALSO RISE AT MIDNIGHT. For then the Holy One, blessed be He, comes to delight with the righteous in the Garden of Eden. And we are here awakened by the words of the Torah. Let us discuss Isaac, for we are on his level.

2. "And Isaac was forty years old"

A Synopsis

We learn that Rivkah, because she was "like the lily among thorns," countervails the harsh judgments of Abraham and Isaac. Next, Rabbi Yitzchak teaches the inner meaning of the marriage of Isaac to Rivkah: how she represents his opposite, and how their union provides the balance that sweetens the world.

The Relevance of this Passage

"Thorns" signify the severe judgments that appear in our world. The "lily" represents the tenderness and beauty of life. Isaac [thorns] and Rivkah [the lily] are the vessels through which these spiritual forces are established. The key to any fulfilling relationship lies in a delicate balance between both qualities. A husband and wife bring their own particular attributes to a marriage. By harnessing the forces of Isaac and Rivkah, we create greater balance in all our human interactions, and particularly in our marital ties.

15. פָּתַח רַבִּי יִצְחָק וַאֲמַר. וַיְהִי יִצְחָק בֶּן אַרְבָּעִים שָׁנָה בְּקַחְתּוֹ אֶת רִבְקָה וגו' בֶּן אַרְבָּעִים שָׁנָה, אַמַּאי אָתָא לְמִמְנֵי הָכָא, דַּהֲוָה בֶּן אַרְבָּעִים שָׁנָה, כַּד נָסִיב לָה לְרִבְקָה, אֶלָּא וַדַּאי, הָא אִתְכְּלִיל יִצְחָק בְּצָפוֹן וְדָרוֹם, בְּאֶשָׁא וּמַיָּא, וּכְדֵין, הֲוָה יִצְחָק בֶּן אַרְבָּעִים שָׁנָה בְּקַחְתּוֹ אֶת רִבְקָה. כְּמַרְאֵה הַקֶּשֶׁת, יָרוֹק חִוָּור סוּמָק. בַּת שָׁלֹש שָׁנִים אָחִיד בָּהּ כַּד אָחִיד בָּהּ בְּרִבְקָה, וְכַד אוֹלִיד, אוֹלִיד בֶּן שִׁשִׁים, לְאוֹלָדָא כְּדְקָא יָאוֹת, בְּגִין דְּיִפּוֹק יַעֲקֹב שְׁלֵם, מִבֶּן שִׁשִׁים שָׁנָה כְּדְקָא יָאוֹת, וְכֻלְּהוּ אָחִיד לְהוּ יַעֲקֹב לְבָתַר, וְאִתְעֲבֵיד גְּבַר שְׁלִים.

15. THE SCRIPTURE READS: "and Isaac was forty years old when he took Rivkah for a wife" (Beresheet 25:20). Why is Yitzchak's age given here? Why does it say he was forty years old when he married Rivkah? HE BEGAN HIS ANSWER BY SAYING THAT Isaac was included within north and south, which are fire and water, and was then forty years old when he took Rivkah. Further, the text, "As the appearance of the bow" (Yechezkel 1:28), means THAT RIVKAH HAD "THE APPEARANCE OF THE RAINBOW," WHICH IS green, white, and red, WHICH ARE CHESED, GVURAH AND TIFERET OF NUKVA. She (the Nukva) was three years old when he seized it, when he

took Rivkah, THAT IS, MARRIED HER. And he sired a son when he was sixty, WHICH WAS AFTER ATTAINING THE SIX SFIROT – CHESED TO YESOD – so that he would properly sire Jacob who, as the issue of a man of sixty years, held on to all THE SIX SFIROT and became a whole man.

16. בַּת בְּתוּאֵל הָאֲרַמִּי מִפַּדַּן אֲרָם אֲחוֹת לָבָן הָאֲרַמִּי, מַאי אִכְפַּת לָן כּוּלֵי הַאי, דְּהָא כְּבָר אִתְּמַר וּבְתוּאֵל יָלַד אֶת רִבְקָה וגו', וְהַשְׁתָּא אֲמַר בַּת בְּתוּאֵל הָאֲרַמִּי, וּלְבָתַר מִפַּדַּן אֲרָם, וּלְבָתַר אֲחוֹת לָבָן הָאֲרַמִּי, אֶלָּא אוּקְמוּהָ, דַּהֲוַת בֵּין רְשָׁעִים וְאִיהִי לָא עַבְדַת כְּעוֹבָדַיְיהוּ, דַּהֲוַת בַּת בְּתוּאֵל וּמִפַּדַּן אֲרָם, וַאֲחוֹת לָבָן, וְכֻלְּהוּ חַיָּיבִין לְאַבְאָשָׁא, וְהִיא סָלְקָא עוֹבָדִין דְּכַשְׁרָן, וְלָא עַבְדַת כְּעוֹבָדַיְיהוּ.

16. Why are we told: "The daughter of Betu'el the Arammian of Paddan-aram, the sister to Laban the Arammian?" Why should we care to know all this – it had already been written, "And Betu'el sired Rivkah" (Beresheet 22:23), and now she is described as "of Paddan-aram, the sister to Laban the Arammian." HE ANSWERS THAT IT IS to teach us that ALTHOUGH she was born among the misled, she did not follow their ways. Therefore it is written that she was the daughter of Betu'el, of Paddan-aram, and the sister of Laban, who were all wicked and evil doers; but she did good deeds and did not behave as they did.

17. הַשְׁתָּא אִית לְאִסְתַּכְּלָא, אִי רִבְקָה הֲוַת בַּת עֶשְׂרִין שְׁנִין, אוֹ יַתִּיר, אוֹ בַּת שְׁלֹש עֶשְׂרֵה, כְּדֵין הוּא שְׁבָחָא דִילָהּ, דְּלָא עַבְדַת כְּעוֹבָדַיְיהוּ, אֲבָל עַד כְּעָן בַּת שָׁלֹש שָׁנִים הֲוַת, מַאי שְׁבָחָא דִילָהּ. אָמַר רִבִּי יְהוּדָה בַּת שָׁלֹש שָׁנִים הֲוַת, וַעֲבִידַת לְעָבְדָּא כָּל הַהוּא עוֹבָדָא.

17. Now we should study this further. If Rivkah was twenty years old, or at least thirteen, it would be considered praiseworthy that she did not do as they did. But since she was only three years old, how can she be praised for her actions? Rabbi Yehuda replied that although she was only three years old, she can be judged by how she behaved toward the servant. THIS MUST MEAN THAT SHE HAD THE WISDOM OF A TWENTY YEAR OLD, AND THEREFORE SHE MAY BE PRAISED FOR NOT LEARNING FROM WHAT THEY DID.

18. אֲמַר רְבִּי יִצְחָק, אַף עַל גַּב דְּכוּלֵי הַאי עָבְדַת, לָא יְדַעְנָא עוֹבָדְהָא אִי אִינּוּן כְּשַׁרְאָן, אוֹ לָאו. אֶלָּא, תָּא חֲזֵי, כְּתִיב כְּשׁוֹשַׁנָּה בֵּין הַחוֹחִים כֵּן רַעְיָתִי בֵּין הַבָּנוֹת. כְּשׁוֹשַׁנָּה: דָּא כְּנֶסֶת יִשְׂרָאֵל, דְּאִיהִי בֵּין אוֹכְלוּסָהָא, כְּוַרְדָּא בֵּין כּוּבִין וְרָזָא דְמִלָּה, יִצְחָק אָתֵי מִסְּטְרָא דְאַבְרָהָם דְּאִיהוּ חֶסֶד עִלָּאָה, וַעֲבֵיד חֶסֶד עִם כָּל בִּרְיָין, וְאַף עַל גַּב דְּאִיהוּ דִינָא קַשְׁיָא. וְרִבְקָה אָתַת מִסִּטְרָא דְדִינָא קַשְׁיָא, וְאִסְתַּלְּקַת מִבֵּינַיְיהוּ, וְאִתְחַבְּרַת בְּיִצְחָק, דְּהָא רִבְקָה מִסִּטְרָא דְדִינָא קַשְׁיָא אַתְיָא, וְאַף עַל גַּב דְּאִיהִי מִסְּטְרָא דְדִינָא רַפְיָא הֲוַת, וְחוּטָא דְחֶסֶד תָּלֵי בָּהּ, וְיִצְחָק דִינָא קַשְׁיָא, וְאִיהִי רַפְיָא, כְּשׁוֹשַׁנָּה בֵּין הַחוֹחִים הֲוּוֹ. וְאִי לָאו דְּאִיהִי רַפְיָא, לָא יָכִיל עָלְמָא לְמִסְבַּל דִּינָא קַשְׁיָא דְיִצְחָק. כְּגַוְונָא דָא, קוּדְשָׁא בְּרִיךְ הוּא מְזַוֵּוג זִוּוּגִין בְּעַלְמָא, חַד תַּקִּיף וְחַד רַפְיָא, בְּגִין לְאִתְתַּקָּנָא כֹּלָּא, וְיִתְבַּסֵּם עָלְמָא.

18. Rabbi Yitzchak said: Though she acted WISELY TOWARD THE SERVANT, I do not yet know if her behavior was right or not. Come and behold: it is written, "Like the lily among thorns, so is my love among the daughters" (Shir Hashirim 2:2). The lily is the congregation of Yisrael, NAMELY, THE NUKVA OF ZEIR ANPIN, which is among the legions as a lily among the thorns. The hidden meaning is that Isaac came from the side of Abraham, supernal Chesed, who is kind to all creatures. And although he represented Severe Judgment, HE NEVERTHELESS DRAWS CHESED FROM ABRAHAM. Rivkah also came from the side of Harsh Judgment OF BETU'EL AND LABAN. Although she was herself of Weak Judgment, IN THE SECRET OF THE REDNESS OF THE LILY, and a thread of Chesed was attached to her, IN THE SECRET OF THE WHITENESS OF THE LILY, nevertheless she came from Severe Judgment. Thus, because Isaac was severe in his judgment and Rivkah was softer in her Judgment, she was as a lily among the thorns. AND IF THE NUKVA were not of Weak Judgment, the world would not have been able to bear the Harsh Judgment of Isaac. In this manner, the Holy One, blessed be He, joins couples in the world – the severe with the weak. THUS ISAAC WAS OF SEVERE JUDGMENT AND RIVKAH OF SOFT JUDGMENT, so as to balance everything. THEY WOULD BE ABLE TO RECEIVE THE ILLUMINATION OF CHOCHMAH, and the world would be sweetened.

3. "And Isaac entreated..."

A Synopsis
We are instructed in the prayer and spiritual actions practiced by
Isaac in order for the child Jacob to be born. We see also how The
Creator responded to Yitzchak's entreaties. This discussion
enlightens us about the structure of prayer, and of how the prayers
of the righteous allow the prayers of less good men to be heard.
Next, the puzzling fact that Isaac loved Esau more than Ya'akov is
explained in terms of its spiritual significance: the son of Abraham
represents Left Column Energy, which expresses judgment. Esau,
we're told, denotes this same negative force, which is an indication
that Isaac has not yet learned to modify and balance the severity of
his own judgment.

The Relevance of this Passage
This powerful passage influences many areas of life, including the
miracle of childbirth.
Though our own prayers might not have wings to ascend to the
highest worlds, we can still contact the Upper Realms through the
updraft created by the prayers of the righteous. Finally, the text
points out that our tendency is to welcome and embrace people
into our lives whose nature is similar to our own. In contrast, we're
quick to pass judgment and distance ourselves from those who
differ from us. This negative predisposition is weakened and
abated so that we can live according to the principle, "Love thy
neighbor as thyself."

19. פָּתַח רִבִּי יְהוּדָה אֲבַתְרֵיה וְאָמַר, וַיֶּעְתַּר יִצְחָק לַיְיָ' לְנֹכַח אִשְׁתּוֹ.
מַהוּ וַיֶּעְתַּר, דְּקָרֵיב לֵיה קָרְבָּנָא, וְצַלֵּי עֲלָה. וּמַה קָרְבָּנָא קָרֵיב. עוֹלָה
קָרֵיב, דִּכְתִיב וַיֵּעָתֶר לוֹ יְיָ', כְּתִיב הָכָא וַיֵּעָתֶר לוֹ יְיָ', וּכְתִיב הָתָם
וַיֵּעָתֶר אֱלֹהִים לָאָרֶץ וְגוֹ', מַה לְהַלָּן קָרְבָּן, אַף כָּאן קָרְבָּן. כְּתִיב וַיֶּעְתַּר
יִצְחָק, וּכְתִיב וַיֵּעָתֶר לוֹ, דְּנָפַק אֶשָּׁא מִלְּעֵילָא, לְקַבְלָא אֶשָּׁא דִלְתַתָּא.

19. Rabbi Yehuda continued with the verse: "And Isaac entreated Hashem
for his wife" (Beresheet 25:21). HE ASKS: What is the meaning of
"entreated?" AND HE REPLIED that he offered a sacrifice and prayed for
her. What offering did he sacrifice? A burnt offering. IT IS UNDERSTOOD
THAT "ENTREATED" INDICATES THAT HE SACRIFICED by studying the
verses "and Hashem was entreated of him" (Ibid.), and "So Hashem was

-169-

entreated for the land" (II Shmuel 24:25). There it means that a sacrifice has been offered, SO here too it means, a sacrifice has been offered. It is written: "And Isaac entreated," "and Hashem was entreated." IF "ENTREATED" INDICATE A SACRIFICE, WHAT IS THE MEANING OF, "AND HASHEM WAS ENTREATED"? HE REPLIED THAT THIS TOO REFERS TO AN OFFERING, a celestial fire that came to meet the lower fire. FOR TWO FIRES ARE NEEDED TO CONSUME THE OFFERING, THE FIRE OF A HOLY MAN AND THE FIRE OF A LAYMAN. THEREFORE "ISAAC ENTREATED," WHICH REFERS TO THE LOWER FIRE, AND "HASHEM WAS ENTREATED," WHICH CORRESPONDS TO THE UPPER FIRE.

20. דָּבָר אַחֵר וַיֶּעְתַּר יִצְחָק, דְּצַלֵּי צְלוֹתֵיה, וְחָתַר חֲתִירָה לְעֵילָא, לְגַבֵּי מַזָּלָא עַל בְּנִין, דְּהָא בְּהַהוּא אֲתַר תַּלְיָין בְּנִין, דִּכְתִיב וַתִּתְפַּלֵּל עַל ה', וּכְדֵין וַיֵּעָתֶר לוֹ יי', אַל תִּקְרֵי וַיֵּעָתֶר לוֹ, אֶלָּא וַיֵּחָתֶר לוֹ, חֲתִירָה חָתַר לֵיה קוּדְשָׁא בְּרִיךְ הוּא, וְקַבֵּיל לֵיה, וּכְדֵין וַתַּהַר רִבְקָה אִשְׁתּוֹ.

20. Another explanation for, "And Isaac entreated," is that by his prayer he hollowed out a passage that reached above to Mazal that bestows children. It is upon that place – IN MAZAL, WHICH IS THE DIKNA OF ARICH ANPIN – that giving birth to children depends, as it is written, "and she prayed to (lit. 'above') Hashem" (I Shmuel 1:10), WHICH IS ZEIR ANPIN. "...ABOVE HASHEM..." REFERS TO DIKNA OF ARICH ANPIN, WHICH ENCIRCLES ZEIR ANPIN, CALLED 'MAZAL'. Then, "Hashem was entreated of him." Do not pronounce it "entreated" (Heb. vaye'ater), but "hollowed out" (Heb. vayechater). For the Holy One, blessed be He, cleared the way and accepted the prayer. Then, "Rivkah his wife conceived."

21. תָּא חֲזֵי, עֶשְׂרִין שְׁנִין, אִשְׁתְּהֵי יִצְחָק עִם אִתְּתֵיה, וְלָא אוֹלִידַת, עַד דְּצַלֵּי צְלוֹתֵיה בְּגִין דְּקוּדְשָׁא בְּרִיךְ הוּא אִתְרְעֵי בִּצְלוֹתְהוֹן דְּצַדִּיקַיָא, בְּשַׁעְתָּא דְּבָעָאן קַמֵּיה צְלוֹתְהוֹן, עַל מַה דְּאִצְטְרִיכוּ, מַאי טַעְמָא, בְּגִין דְּיִתְרַבֵּי וְיִתּוֹסַף רְבוּת קוּדְשָׁא, לְכָל מַאן דְּאִצְטְרִיךְ בִּצְלוֹתְהוֹן דְּצַדִּיקַיָּא.

21. Come and behold: Isaac was with his wife for twenty years, but she did not give birth until he had said his prayer This is because the Holy One, blessed be He, desires the prayer of the righteous, when they ask Him in

prayer for their needs. Why? Because the anointing oil will be increased by the prayer of the righteous for all those in need of it. FOR THE RIGHTEOUS IN THEIR PRAYER OPEN THE SUPERNAL CHANNEL, AND THEN EVEN THE PRAYERS OF THE UNWORTHY ARE ANSWERED.

22. תָּא חֲזֵי, אַבְרָהָם לָא צַלֵּי קַמֵּי קוּדְשָׁא בְּרִיךְ הוּא, דְּיִתֵּן לֵיהּ בְּנִין, אַף עַל גַּב דְּשָׂרָה עֲקָרָה הֲוַת. וְאִי תֵימָא, הָא כְּתִיב, הֵן לִי לֹא נָתַתָּ זַרַע, הַהוּא לָאו בְּגִין צְלוֹתָא הֲוָה אֶלָּא כְּמַאן דְּמִשְׁתָּעֵי קַמֵּי מָרֵיהּ. אֲבָל יִצְחָק, צַלֵּי עַל אִתְּתֵיהּ, בְּגִין דְּהָא אִיהוּ הֲוָה יָדַע, דְּלָאו אִיהוּ עָקָר, אֶלָּא אִתְּתֵיהּ, דְּיִצְחָק הֲוָה יָדַע בְּרָזָא דְחָכְמְתָא, דְּיַעֲקֹב זַמִּין לְמֵיפַּק מִנֵּיהּ, בִּתְרֵיסַר שִׁבְטִין, אֲבָל לָא יָדַע, אִי בְּהַאי אִתְּתָא, אִי בְּאָחֳרָא, וְעַל דָּא לְנֹכַח אִשְׁתּוֹ, וְלָא לְנֹכַח רִבְקָה.

22. Come and behold: Abraham did not pray before the Holy One, blessed be He, so that He would give him sons, even though Sarah was barren. And although it may be said that he prayed, saying, "Behold, to me You gave no seed," (Beresheet 15:3) it is not a prayer, but simply a statement to his Master. But Isaac prayed for his wife because he knew that his wife, and not he, was sterile. And although Isaac knew by the inner meaning of wisdom that Jacob was bound to come from him and produce the twelve tribes, he did not know whether this would be from this wife or from another. Therefore the scripture reads, "for his wife" (Beresheet 25:21), and not specifically "for Rivkah."

23. אָמַר הַהוּא רַבְיָא, בְּרֵיהּ דְּרִבִּי יְהוּדָה, אִי הָכֵי אַמַּאי לָא רָחִים לֵיהּ יִצְחָק לְיַעֲקֹב, כָּל כָּךְ כְּמוֹ לְעֵשָׂו, הוֹאִיל וַהֲוָה יָדַע דְּזַמִּין אִיהוּ לְקַיְּימָא מִנֵּיהּ תְּרֵיסַר שִׁבְטִין. אָמַר לוֹ שַׁפִּיר קָאֲמַרְתְּ, אֶלָּא כָּל זִינָא רָחִים לֵיהּ לְזִינֵיהּ, וְאִתְמְשִׁיךְ וְאָזֵיל זִינָא בָּתַר זִינֵיהּ.

23. Rabbi Yehuda's son asks: Why then did not Isaac love Jacob as he loved Esau, if he knew that he would sire the twelve tribes? He replied: Well said. HE LOVED ESAU BETTER BECAUSE everyone loves and is attracted to his own kind.

24. תָּא חֲזֵי, עֵשָׂו נָפַק סוּמָק, כְּמָה דִכְתִיב וַיֵּצֵא הָרִאשׁוֹן אַדְמוֹנִי כֻּלּוֹ

וגו', וְאִיהוּ זִינָא דְּיִצְחָק, דְּאִיהוּ דִּינָא קַשְׁיָא דִּלְעֵילָא, וּנְפַק מִנֵּיהּ עֵשָׂו,
דִּינָא קַשְׁיָא לְתַתָּא, דְּדַמְיָא לְזִינֵיהּ, וְכָל זִינָא אָזִיל לְזִינֵיהּ, וְעַל דָּא
רָחִים לֵיהּ לְעֵשָׂו יַתִּיר מִיַּעֲקֹב, כְּמָה דִּכְתִיב וַיֶּאֱהַב יִצְחָק אֶת עֵשָׂו כִּי
צַיִד בְּפִיו. כְּתִיב הָכָא כִּי צַיִד בְּפִיו, וּכְתִיב הָתָם עַל כֵּן יֵאָמַר כְּנִמְרֹד
גִּבּוֹר צַיִד לִפְנֵי יְיָ'.

24. Come and behold: Esau was born all red, as it is written, "And the first came out red all over" (Beresheet 25:25). Thus, he is the same as Isaac, who is of Harsh Judgment above, IN HOLINESS, and Esau, who issued from him, is the Harsh Judgment below. ESAU'S HEAD WAS IN THE HOLY SYSTEM, BUT HIS BODY WAS NOT. THEREFORE, he resembled Isaac. And because each is drawn to his own kind, Isaac loved Esau more than Jacob, as it is written, "And Isaac loved Esau, he relished his venison" (Ibid. 28), WHICH MEANS THAT HIS HEAD IS IN THE HOLY SYSTEM. Here it is written, "For he relished his venison," which is similar to, "wherefore it is said, 'like Nimrod the mighty hunter before Hashem'" (Beresheet 10:9). IN BOTH PLACES, HUNTING REFERS TO HARSH JUDGMENT, AND THE SCRIPTURES TELL US THAT HE LOVED HIM BECAUSE THEY WERE BOTH OF SEVERE JUDGMENT.

4. "And the children struggled together within her" (A)

A Synopsis

Here we explore the relationship of Jacob to Esau. We are shown Esau's identification with the serpent, and the necessity of Jacob to deal with this evil in order transform Holy Yisrael into the chosen part and portion of The Creator. Jacob's battles with Esau are a metaphor denoting the establishment of a spiritual system that expresses the paradigm of good versus evil in human existence. We see more clearly how the naming of Jacob signifies his special role, and his difference from Abraham and Isaac. The importance of the struggle of Jacob with Esau for the future is also explained, along with the methods used in this ongoing battle with evil.

The Relevance of this Passage

Jacob and Esau were born together in the womb of Rivkah. On a macrocosmic level, Jacob represents the forces of good, Esau, the forces of evil, and the womb of Rivkah symbolizes our physical world. On the micro-level, this dynamic represents the positive and negative aspects of our own nature. This portion of Zohar gives us power over our dark side, so that we can overcome our internal demons.

25. אָמַר רָבִּי יִצְחָק, כְּתִיב וַיִּתְרֹצֲצוּ הַבָּנִים בְּקִרְבָּהּ וַתֹּאמֶר אִם כֵּן לָמָּה זֶה אָנֹכִי וַתֵּלֶךְ לִדְרֹשׁ אֶת יי', לְאָן אֲתַר אָזְלַת. לְבֵי מִדְרָשָׁא דְּשֵׁם וְעֵבֶר. וַיִּתְרֹצֲצוּ הַבָּנִים בְּקִרְבָּהּ, דְּתַמָּן הֲוָה הַהוּא רָשָׁע דְּעֵשָׂו אֲגַח קְרָבָא בֵּיהּ בְּיַעֲקֹב. וַיִּתְרֹצֲצוּ: אִתְבָּרוּ כְּמָה דְּאַמְרִינָן, רָצַץ אֶת מוֹחוֹ. אִתְבָּרוּ דָּא עִם דָּא, וְאִתְפְּלְגוּ. תָּא חֲזֵי, דָּא סִטְרָא דְּרוֹכֵב נָחָשׁ, וְדָא סִטְרָא דְּרוֹכֵב עַל כָּרְסְיָא שְׁלֵימָתָא קַדִּישָׁא, בְּסִטְרָא דְּשִׁמְשָׁא, לְשַׂמְשָׁא בְּסִיהֲרָא.

25. Rabbi Yitzchak said: It is written, "And the children struggled together within her; and she said, 'if it be so, why am I thus?' And she went to inquire of Hashem" (Beresheet 25:22). Where did she go? To the academy of Shem and Ever. "...the children struggled together within her," because the wicked Esau was warring against Jacob there. The term 'struggle' (Heb. *vayitrotzatzu*) is similar to the expression 'to break' (Heb. *ratzatz*) one's head, for they struggled and were divided. Come and behold: ESAU was of the side of he who rides the serpent, SAMAEL, while JACOB was of the side

who rides the perfect Holy Throne, of the side of the sun, ZEIR ANPIN, that is united with the moon, THE NUKVA.

26. וְתָא חֲזֵי, בְּגִין דְּאִתְמְשַׁךְ עֵשָׂו אֲבַתְרֵיהּ דְּהַהוּא נָחָשׁ, אָזִיל עִמֵּיהּ יַעֲקֹב בַּעֲקִימָא, כְּנָחָשׁ, דְּאִיהוּ חַכִּים, וְאִיהוּ אָזִיל בַּעֲקִימוּ, כִּדְּבַר אַחֵר וְהַנָּחָשׁ הָיָה עָרוּם וְגו', חַכִּים. וְעוֹבָדוֹי דְּיַעֲקֹב לְגַבֵּיהּ, הֲווֹ לֵיהּ כְּנָחָשׁ, וְהָכֵי אִצְטְרִיךְ לֵיהּ, בְּגִין לְאַמְשָׁכָא לֵיהּ לְעֵשָׂו, בַּתְרֵיהּ דְּהַהוּא נָחָשׁ, וְיִתְפְּרַשׁ מִנֵּיהּ, וְלָא יְהֵא לֵיהּ חוּלָקָא עִמֵּיהּ בְּעָלְמָא דֵין וּבְעָלְמָא דְּאָתֵי. וְתָנֵינָן, בָּא לְהָרְגָךְ, אַקְדִּים אַנְתְּ וְקַטְלֵיהּ. כְּתִיב, בַּבֶּטֶן עָקַב אֶת אָחִיו דְּאַשְׁרֵי לֵיהּ לְתַתָּא, בְּהַהוּא עָקֵב, הה"ד וְיָדוֹ אוֹחֶזֶת בַּעֲקֵב עֵשָׂו, דְּשַׁוֵּי יְדוֹי עַל הַהוּא עָקֵב, לְאִכְפְּיָא לֵיהּ.

26. Come and behold: since Esau followed on the serpent, Jacob dealt with him slyly, as the serpent was cunning and had crooked ways. As it is written, "the serpent was craftier" (Beresheet 3:1), which means that he was cunning AND SLY. What Jacob did with Esau was serpent-like. This was as it ought to have been; by making Esau go after that serpent, so that he would be separated from Jacob, and thus share nothing with him in this world or in the World to Come. Thus we learn, "he who comes to kill you, hasten to kill him first." It is written: "in the womb he took his brother by the (Hoshea 12:4), which means that he lowered him down by the heel, THAT IS, SEPARATED HIM FROM HOLINESS AND LOWERED HIM INTO THE SIDE OF DEFILEMENT CALLED 'HEEL', WHICH WAS AT THE END OF HOLINESS. This is the meaning of, "and his hand took hold of Esau's heel" (Beresheet 25:26), for he put his hands on the heel to subjugate him TO HOLINESS.

27. דָּבָר אַחֵר וְיָדוֹ אוֹחֶזֶת, דְּלָא יָכִיל לְמֵיפַק מִנֵּיהּ מִכֹּל וָכֹל, אֶלָּא וְיָדוֹ אוֹחֶזֶת בַּעֲקֵב עֵשָׂו, דָּא סִיהֲרָא, דְּאִתְכַּסְיָא נְהוֹרָא, בְּגִין עָקֵב דְּעֵשָׂו, וְעַל דָּא אִצְטְרִיךְ לֵיהּ, לְמֵיהַךְ עִמֵּיהּ בְּחָכְמְתָא, בְּגִין לְדַחֲיָיא לֵיהּ לְתַתָּא, וְיִתְדַּבַּק בַּאֲתְרֵיהּ.

27. Another explanation of the verse, "and his hand took hold..." is that Jacob could not be separated from him entirely, so his hand held the heel of

Esau. His hand is the moon, WHICH IS THE NUKVA, CALLED THE 'HAND OF TIFERET', WHICH IS JACOB, whose light was darkened because he held Esau's heel. Therefore, Jacob needed to be clever with him, to push him down, so he would cleave to his place IN THE OTHER SIDE AND BE COMPLETELY SEVERED FROM HOLINESS.

28. וַיִּקְרָא שְׁמוֹ יַעֲקֹב. קוּדְשָׁא בְּרִיךְ הוּא קָרֵי לֵיהּ יַעֲקֹב וַדַּאי. תָּא חֲזֵי, כְּתִיב הָכִי קָרָא שְׁמוֹ יַעֲקֹב, נִקְרָא שְׁמוֹ לָא כְּתִיב, אֶלָּא קָרָא שְׁמוֹ, וַיַּעְקְבֵנִי, וַדַּאי חָמָא לֵיהּ קוּדְשָׁא בְּרִיךְ הוּא, דְּהָא הַהוּא חִוְיָא קַדְמָאָה, אִיהוּ חַכִּים לְאַבְאָשָׁא, כֵּיוָן דַּאֲתָא יַעֲקֹב, אָמַר הָא וַדַּאי חַכִּים לְקַבְלֵיהּ, וּבְגִין כָּךְ קָרָא לֵיהּ יַעֲקֹב.

28. "And he called his name Jacob," MEANS THAT the Holy One, blessed be He, assuredly called him 'Jacob'. Come and behold: it is written, "and he called his name 'Jacob'" (Beresheet 27:36), and not, 'and his name was called Jacob'. But "Did he not rightly call him "Jacob?' for he has supplanted me (Heb. *ya'akveni*)?" (Ibid.) THIS REFERS TO THE HOLY ONE, BLESSED BE HE, WHO CALLED HIM 'JACOB'. Surely the Holy One, blessed be He, saw that the primordial serpent was wise in an evil way. When Jacob came, THE HOLY ONE, BLESSED BE HE, said that he must be wiser than the serpent. Therefore He called him 'Jacob', WHO BECAME KNOWN FOR HIS WISDOM. HE KNEW HOW TO DECEIVE THE SERPENT AND TO SEPARATE HIM FROM ALL THINGS HOLY.

29. הָא אוּקִימְנָא בְּכָל אֲתַר, וַיִּקְרָא סְתָם, הַאי הוּא דַּרְגָּא בַּתְרָאָה, כְּמָה דִּכְתִיב, וַיִּקְרָא אֶל מֹשֶׁה וְגוֹ'. וְהָכָא וַיִּקְרָא שְׁמוֹ יַעֲקֹב, בְּכָל אֲתַר, שְׁמֵיהּ לָא אִקְרֵי עַל יְדָא דְּבַר נָשׁ, בַּאֲתַר אָחֳרָא מַה כְּתִיב, וַיִּקְרָא לוֹ אֵל אֱלֹהֵי יִשְׂרָאֵל קוּדְשָׁא בְּרִיךְ הוּא קָרָא לֵיהּ לְיַעֲקֹב אֵל. אָמַר לוֹ אֲנָא אֱלָהָא בְּעֶלָּאֵי, וְאַנְתְּ אֱלָהָא בְּתַתָּאֵי.

29. We have already explained that wherever it is written, "He called," WITHOUT ALLUDING TO WHO CALLED, it is the lower grade, THE NUKVA, as it is written: "And ...called Moses" (Vayikra 1:1). IT IS THE NUKVA, WHO CALLED TO MOSES. And here it is written, "and he called his name

'Jacob'" (Beresheet 25:26). HERE, TOO, IT IS THE NUKVA OF ZEIR ANPIN
WHO CALLED HIS NAME 'JACOB'. For no man even named Jacob, as it is
written elsewhere, "And called it (lit. 'him') El the Elohim Yisrael"
(Beresheet 33:20). This is the Holy One, blessed be He, who called Jacob
'El'. He said to him: 'I am El among the upper, and you are El among the
lower.' THIS IS TO SHOW THAT HE WAS NOT NAMED BY FLESH AND
BLOOD, BUT BY THE HOLY ONE, BLESSED BE HE.

30. וְתָא חֲזֵי, יַעֲקֹב הֲוָה יָדַע, דְּעֵשָׂו הֲוָה לֵיהּ לְאִתְדַּבְּקָא, בְּהַהוּא חִוְיָא
עֲקִימָא, וְעַל דָּא, בְּכָל עוֹבָדוֹי, אִתְמַשַּׁךְ עֲלֵיהּ, כְּחִוְיָא עֲקִימָא אָחֳרָא,
בְּחָכְמְתָא בַּעֲקִימוּ, וְהָכֵי אִצְטְרִיךְ. וְאַתְיָיא דָא, כִּי הָא דַּאֲמַר רִבִּי
שִׁמְעוֹן, מַאי דִכְתִיב, וַיִּבְרָא אֱלֹהִים אֶת הַתַּנִּינִם הַגְּדוֹלִים, דָא יַעֲקֹב
וְעֵשָׂו. וְאֶת כָּל נֶפֶשׁ הַחַיָּה הָרוֹמֶשֶׂת, אִלֵּין שְׁאַר דַּרְגִּין דְּבֵינַיְיהוּ, וַדַּאי
אִתְעֲבֵיד יַעֲקֹב חַכִּים, לְקִבְלֵיהּ דְּהַהוּא חִוְיָא אָחֳרָא, וְהָכֵי אִצְטְרִיךְ.

30. Come and behold: Jacob knew that Esau had to cleave to the tortuous
serpent. As a result, in all that Esau did, he acted as slyly and crookedly, just
like another tortuous serpent. This is as it ought to be. This agrees with the
words of Rabbi Shimon, "And Elohim created the great crocodiles," which
refer to Jacob and Esau, "and every living creature that moves" (Beresheet
1:21), refers to the levels between them. FOR JACOB AND ESAU ARE
CALLED 'CROCODILES', THAT IS, 'SERPENTS', AS HAS BEEN EXPLAINED.
ESAU WAS THE TORTUOUS SERPENT, AND JACOB DREW AGAINST
HIMSELF A KIND OF TORTUOUS SERPENT. By necessity, Jacob needed to
behave wisely TO STAND against the other serpent. This is as it must be.

31. וּבְגִין כָּךְ, בְּכָל יַרְחָא וְיַרְחָא, חַד שָׂעִיר, בְּגִין לְאַמְשָׁכָא לֵיהּ
לְאַתְרֵיהּ וְיִתְפְּרַשׁ מִן סִיהֲרָא, וְכֵן בְּיוֹמֵי דְכִפּוּרֵי, לְאַקְרָבָא הַהוּא
שָׂעִיר, וְדָא בְּחָכְמָה, לְשַׁלְטָאָה עֲלֵיהּ, וְלָא יָכִיל לְאַבְאָשָׁא, דִּכְתִיב,
וְנָשָׂא הַשָּׂעִיר עָלָיו אֶת כָּל עֲוֹנֹתָם אֶל אֶרֶץ גְּזֵרָה, וְאוֹקִמוּהָ דְּדָא עֵשָׂו,
דְּאִיהוּ שָׂעִיר, וְכֹלָּא בְּחָכְמָה וּבְרַמָּאוּת לְגַבֵּיהּ. מַאי טַעְמָא, מִשּׁוּם
דִּכְתִיב, וְעִם עִקֵּשׁ תִּתְפַּתָּל, בְּגִין דְּאִיהוּ חִוְיָא בִּישָׁא, עָקִים, רוּחָא
חַכִּים לְאַבְאָשָׁא, אַסְטֵי לְעֵילָא, וְאַסְטֵי לְתַתָּא.

31. For that reason, one he goat is sacrificed monthly, to draw the serpent to his place so that he will be separated from the moon, THE NUKVA OF ZEIR ANPIN, WHOSE LIGHT WAS COVERED BY ESAU'S HEEL. In addition, a he goat should be sacrificed on Yom Kippur. This is done with wisdom, so as to control the serpent, so that he can not do evil. This is the meaning of the verse: "and the goat (Heb. *sa'ir*) shall bear upon it all their iniquities…" (Vayikra 16:22). This refers to Esau, who is hairy (Heb. *sa'ir*). All of this was done wisely and cleverly. Why? Because it is written: "and with the perverse you will show yourself subtle" (Tehilim 18:27). This is the evil serpent, the tortuous spirit, wise in wickedness, who accuses above and incites below.

32. וּבְגִין כָּךְ, יִשְׂרָאֵל מְקַדְּמִין, וְחַכְּמִין לֵיהּ בְּחָכְמָה, בַּעֲקִימוּ, בְּגִין דְּלָא יָכִיל לְאַבְאָשָׁא, וּלְשַׁלְטָאָה. וְעַל דָּא, יַעֲקֹב דְּאִיהוּ בְּרָזָא דִּמְהֵימְנוּתָא, כָּל עוֹבָדוֹי לְגַבֵּי דְעֵשָׂו, בְּגִין דְּלָא יָהַב דּוּכְתָּא לֵיהּ, לְהַהוּא חִוְיָא, לְסָאֲבָא מַקְדְּשָׁא וְלָא יַקְרִיב לְגַבֵּיהּ וְלָא יִשְׁלוֹט בְּעָלְמָא, וְעַל דָּא, לָא אִצְטְרִיךְ לֵיהּ לְאַבְרָהָם, לְאִתְנַהֲגָא בְּעוּקְמָא, וְלָא לְיִצְחָק, בְּגִין דְּעֵשָׂו, דְּאִיהוּ סִטְרָא דְּהַהוּא חִוְיָא, עַד לָא אָתָא לְעָלְמָא. אֲבָל יַעֲקֹב, דְּאִיהוּ מָארֵיהּ דְּבֵיתָא, אִיבָּעֵי לֵיהּ, לְקַיְּימָא לְקָבְלֵיהּ דְּהַהוּא חִוְיָא, דְּלָא יְהֵיב לֵיהּ שָׁלְטָנוּתָא כְּלָל, לְסָאֲבָא בֵּי מַקְדְּשָׁא דְיַעֲקֹב, וְעַל דָּא, אִצְטְרִיךְ לְיַעֲקֹב, יַתִּיר מִכָּל בְּנֵי עָלְמָא, וּבְגִין כָּךְ, יִשְׂרָאֵל קַדִּישִׁין, אִתְבְּרִירוּ חוּלָק עַדְבֵיהּ דְּקוּדְשָׁא בְּרִיךְ הוּא, דִּכְתִיב, כִּי חֵלֶק יְיָ' עַמּוֹ יַעֲקֹב חֶבֶל נַחֲלָתוֹ.

32. For this reason, Yisrael hasten to treat him with sly wisdom, so he will not be able to cause evil and rule. Therefore Jacob, who is imbued with the true Faith, treated Esau in all that he did so that there would be no place for that serpent to defile the Temple, or approach it and thereby rule the world. Thus, Abraham did not need to behave slyly, and neither did Isaac. For Esau, who was on the side of the serpent, had not yet come into the world. But Jacob, the landlord, THE HUSBAND OF THE SHECHINAH, had to stand against that serpent to prevent him from ruling and defiling the Temple of Jacob, THE NUKVA. Therefore, Jacob had to FIGHT HIM more CLEVERLY than the rest of the people in the world. Hence, BECAUSE JACOB FOUGHT

WITH HIM SLYLY AND BOUGHT HIS BIRTHRIGHT AND BLESSINGS FROM HIM, Holy Yisrael were chosen to be the part and portion of the Holy One, blessed be He, as it is written, "For Hashem's portion is His people; Jacob is the lot of His inheritance" (Devarim 32:9).

5. The feast of the righteous in the future to come

A Synopsis
Here the Rabbis discuss the shape of things to come – the time when The Creator will raise the dead. The discussion first centers on the physical nature of this event, then explores the question of the soul's place in heaven, along with its movement into a new body no longer made of dust. The feast that The Creator will prepare for His people is described in all its many levels of meaning, from mundane food and drink, to the meal of supernal splendor. This meal, we're told, includes no physical food or drink, and is the kind of meal that was eaten by Moses during his forty days and forty nights with The Creator. We learn, too, about who will partake of each kind of meal and what comprises the meals. The passage concludes with an inspiring vision of the future, which is described as begetting laughter and joy in the world.

The Relevance of this Passage
As usual, the wisdom of the Zohar pertains to both cosmic and personal realms. The supernal feast of joy that awaits us in the future can be tasted today through a reflective reading of this passage. Moreover, our interaction with these holy verses helps hasten the universal redemption.

מִדְרָשׁ הַנֶּעֱלָם

33. וְאֵלֶּה תּוֹלְדוֹת יִצְחָק בֶּן אַבְרָהָם אַבְרָהָם הוֹלִיד אֶת יִצְחָק. רַבִּי יִצְחָק פָּתַח, הַדּוּדָאִים נָתְנוּ רֵיחַ וְגוֹ'. ת"ר, לֶעָתִיד לָבֹא, הַקּוּדְשָׁא בְּרִיךְ הוּא מְחַיֶּה אֶת הַמֵּתִים, וִינַעֵר אוֹתָם מֵעַפְרָם, שֶׁלֹּא יִהְיוּ בִּנְיַן עָפָר, כְּמוֹת שֶׁהָיוּ בַּתְּחִלָּה, שֶׁנִּבְרְאוּ מֵעָפָר מַמָּשׁ, דָּבָר שֶׁאֵינוֹ מִתְקַיֵּים, הה"ד וַיִּיצֶר ה' אֱלֹקִים אֶת הָאָדָם עָפָר מִן הָאֲדָמָה.

Midrash Hane'elam (Homiletical interpretations on the obscure)

33. "And these are the generations of Isaac, Abraham's son: Abraham begot Isaac" (Beresheet 25:19). Rabbi Yitzchak began the discussion with the verse: "The mandrakes give a fragrance..." (Shir Hashirim 7:14). The sages taught that in the future, the Holy One, blessed be He, will raise the dead

and shake the dust off them. As a result, they will no longer be made of dust, as they were when first created from dust, which does not endure, as it is written, "And Hashem Elohim formed man of the dust of the ground" (Beresheet 2:7).

34. וּבְאוֹתָהּ שָׁעָה יִתְנַעֲרוּ מֵעָפָר, מֵאוֹתוֹ הַבִּנְיָן, וְיַעַמְדוּ בְּבִנְיָן מְקוּיָים, לִהְיוֹת לָהֶם קִיּוּמָא, הה"ד הִתְנַעֲרִי מֵעָפָר קוּמִי שְׁבִי יְרוּשָׁלַם, יִתְקַיְּימוּ בְּקִיּוּמָא. וְיַעֲלוּ מִתַּחַת לָאָרֶץ, וִיקַבְּלוּ נִשְׁמָתָם בְּאֶרֶץ יִשְׂרָאֵל. בְּאוֹתָהּ שָׁעָה, יַצִּיף קוּדְשָׁא בְּרִיךְ הוּא, כָּל מִינֵי רֵיחִין שֶׁבַּגַּ"ע עֲלֵיהֶם, הה"ד הַדּוּדָאִים נָתְנוּ רֵיחַ.

34. The instant they shake the dust from their bodily frames, they will have enduring frames, as it is written: "Shake yourself from the dust; arise, and sit down, Jerusalem" (Yeshayah 52:2). They will endure and rise from beneath the ground to receive their souls in the land of Yisrael. At that time, the Holy One, blessed be He, will pour upon them all the kinds of fragrances that are in the Garden of Eden, as it is written, "The mandrakes give a fragrance."

35. אָמַר רְבִּי יִצְחָק, אַל תִּקְרֵי הַדּוּדָאִים, אֶלָּא הַדּוֹדִים, זֶהוּ הַגּוּף וְהַנְּשָׁמָה, שֶׁהֵם דּוֹדִים וְרֵעִים זֶה עִם זֶה. רַב נַחְמָן אָמַר, דּוּדָאִים מַמָּשׁ, מַה הַדּוּדָאִים מוֹלִידִים אַהֲבָה בָּעוֹלָם, אַף הֵם מוֹלִידִים אַהֲבָה בָּעוֹלָם. וּמַאי נָתְנוּ רֵיחַ, כִּשְׁרוֹן מַעֲשֵׂיהֶם, לָדַעַת וּלְהַכִּיר לְבוֹרְאָם.

35. Rabbi Yitzchak said: Do not pronounce it *dudaim* ('mandrakes'), but rather *dodim* ('lovers'). They are the body and the soul, who are lovers and friends to each other. Rav Nachman said: They are real mandrakes. As the mandrakes bring love into the world, so they create love in the world. And they give off a fragrance, which is how they know and recognize their Creator.

36. וְעַל פִּתְחֵינוּ: אֵלּוּ פִּתְחֵי שָׁמַיִם, שֶׁהֵם פְּתוּחִים לְהוֹרִיד נִשְׁמוֹת לִפְגָרִים. כָּל מְגָדִים: אֵלּוּ הַנְּשָׁמוֹת. חֲדָשִׁים גַּם יְשָׁנִים: אוֹתָם שֶׁיָּצְאוּ נִשְׁמָתָם מֵהַיּוֹם כַּמָּה שָׁנִים, וְאוֹתָם שֶׁיָּצְאוּ נִשְׁמָתָם מִיָּמִים מוּעָטִים,

וְזָכוּ בְּכִשְׁרוֹן מַעֲשֵׂיהֶם, לְהִכָּנֵס בָּעוֹלָם הַבָּא, כֻּלָּם עֲתִידִים לֵירֵד בְּבַת אַחַת, לְהִכָּנֵס בַּגּוּפוֹת הַמּוּכָנִים לָהֶם.

36. The verse: "And at our gates…" (Shir Hashirim 7:14) refers to the gates of heaven, which are open to brings down souls for cadavers. "…all manner of choice fruits…" refers to the souls; "new and old" refers to those whose souls left them years ago and those whose souls left them only a few days ago. They merited, by their skillful deeds, to enter the World to Come. All of them are destined to descend simultaneously to enter the bodies that are prepared for them.

37. אָמַר רַבִּי אַחָא בַּר יַעֲקֹב, בַּת קוֹל יוֹצֵאת וְאוֹמֶרֶת, חֲדָשִׁים גַּם יְשָׁנִים דּוֹדִי צָפַנְתִּי לָךְ. צָפַנְתִּי אוֹתָם, בְּאוֹתָם הָעוֹלָמוֹת. לָךְ: בִּשְׁבִילָךְ, בִּשְׁבִיל שֶׁאַתָּה גּוּף קָדוֹשׁ וְנָקִי. דָּבָר אַחֵר הַדּוּדָאִים, אֵלּוּ מַלְאֲכֵי שָׁלוֹם. נָתְנוּ רֵיחַ, אֵלּוּ הַנְּשָׁמוֹת, שֶׁהֵם רֵיחַ הָעוֹלָם. נָתְנוּ: שָׁבְקוּ, כְּדָבָר אַחֵר וְלֹא נָתַן סִיחוֹן אֶת יִשְׂרָאֵל.

37. Rabbi Acha bar Jacob, said that a divine voice resounded, saying: "new and old, which I have laid up for you, O my beloved" (Shir Hashirim 7:14). "I have laid up for you" – in these same worlds. "…for you…" means because of you, because you are a holy and clean body. Another explanation is that these mandrakes are the Angels of Peace. "…give a fragrance…" refers to souls, the fragrance of the world; "give" means to allow, as it is written: "and Sichon would not allow Yisrael" (Bemidbar 21:23).

38. דְּתָאנָא אָמַר רַבִּי יְהוּדָה, שָׁלֹשׁ כִּתּוֹת שֶׁל מַלְאֲכֵי הַשָּׁרֵת, הוֹלְכִים בְּכָל חֹדֶשׁ וּבְכָל שַׁבָּת, לְלַוּוֹת לַנְּשָׁמָה עַד מָקוֹם מַעֲלָתָהּ. וּבְמַאן נוֹקִים עַל פְּתָחֵינוּ כָּל מְגָדִים. אָמַר רַבִּי יְהוּדָה, אֵלּוּ הֵן הַגּוּפוֹת, שֶׁהֵם עוֹמְדִים בְּפִתְחֵי קְבָרוֹת לְקַבֵּל נִשְׁמָתָן. וְדוֹמֶ"ה נוֹתֵן פִּתְקָא דְּחֻשְׁבָּנָא, וְהוּא מַכְרִיז וְאוֹמֵר, רִבּוֹנוֹ שֶׁל עוֹלָם, חֲדָשִׁים גַּם יְשָׁנִים, אוֹתָם שֶׁנִּקְבְּרוּ מִכַּמָּה יָמִים, וְאוֹתָם שֶׁנִּקְבְּרוּ מִזְּמַן מוּעָט, כֻּלָּם צָפַנְתִּי לָךְ, לְמֵיפַק לְהוּ בְּחוּשְׁבָּנָא.

38. Rabbi Yehuda said that three classes of ministering angels appear at the beginning of every month and on every Shabbat to escort the soul to its place of ascension. What does the verse, "And at our gates are all manner of choice fruits," refer to? Rabbi Yehuda said: These are bodies standing at the openings of the graves to receive their souls. And Dumah offers a note of reckoning, and proclaims: Master of the Universe, "old and new," those who were buried long ago, and those buried not so long ago, all these "I have laid up for you," to take them into account.

39. אָמַר רַב יְהוּדָה אָמַר רַב, עָתִיד הַקּוּדְשָׁא בְּרִיךְ הוּא, לִשְׂמוֹחַ בְּאוֹתוֹ זְמַן, עִם הַצַּדִּיקִים, לְהַשְׁרוֹת שְׁכִינָתוֹ עִמָּהֶם, וְהַכֹּל יִשְׂמְחוּ בְּאוֹתָהּ שִׂמְחָה, הה"ד יִשְׂמַח ה' בְּמַעֲשָׂיו. אָמַר רַבִּי יְהוּדָה, עֲתִידִים הַצַּדִּיקִים בְּאוֹתוֹ זְמַן, לִבְרֹא עוֹלָמוֹת, וּלְהַחֲיוֹת מֵתִים. אָמַר לֵיה רַבִּי יוֹסֵי, וְהָתְנַן אֵין כָּל חָדָשׁ תַּחַת הַשָּׁמֶשׁ. אָמַר לוֹ רַבִּי יְהוּדָה, ת"ש, בְּעוֹד שֶׁהָרְשָׁעִים בָּעוֹלָם, וְיִרְבּוּ, כָּל הָעוֹלָם אֵינוֹ בְּקִיּוּם, וּכְשֶׁהַצַּדִּיקִים בָּעוֹלָם, אֲזַי הָעוֹלָם מִתְקַיֵּים. וַעֲתִידִים לְהַחֲיוֹת מֵתִים, כִּדְקָאֲמָרָן, עוֹד יֵשְׁבוּ זְקֵנִים וּזְקֵנוֹת בִּרְחוֹבוֹת יְרוּשָׁלַם וְאִישׁ מִשְׁעַנְתּוֹ בְּיָדוֹ מֵרוֹב יָמִים, כִּדְכְתִיב לְעֵיל.

39. In the name of the Rav, Rabbi Yehuda said that in the future, the Holy One, blessed be He, will rejoice with the righteous, and will let His Shechinah dwell among them. Everybody will rejoice in that joy, as it is written: "let Hashem rejoice in His works" (Tehilim 104:31). Rabbi Yehuda said that at that time the righteous will create worlds and raise the dead. Rabbi Yosi said to him: We have learned that "there is nothing new under the sun" (Kohelet 1:9). Rabbi Yehuda responded: Come and hearken. While the wicked are in the world and multiply, the whole world does not endure, but when the Righteous are in the world, it does endure. And in the future they will raise the dead, as it is written: "Old men and old women shall yet again dwell in the streets of Jerusalem, and every man with his staff in his hand for very age" (Zecharyah 8:4).

40. בְּאוֹתוֹ זְמַן, יַשִׂיגוּ הַצַּדִּיקִים דַּעַת שְׁלֵמָה, דְּאָמַר רַבִּי יוֹסֵי, בְּיוֹמָא דִּיְיֶחֱדֵי קוּדְשָׁא בְּרִיךְ הוּא בְּעוֹבָדוֹי, זְמִינִין אִינוּן צַדִּיקַיָּא, לְמִנְדַּע לֵיה בְּלִבְּהוֹן, וּכְדֵין יִסְגֵּי סֻכְלְתָנוּ בְּלִבְּהוֹן, כְּאִילוּ חָזוּ לֵיה בְּעֵינָא, הֲדָא

הוּא דִּכְתִיב, וְאָמַר בַּיּוֹם הַהוּא הִנֵּה אֱלֹהֵינוּ זֶה וְגוֹ'. וְשִׂמְחַת הַנְּשָׁמָה בַּגּוּף, יֶתֶר מִכּוּלָּם, עַל שֶׁיִּהְיוּ שְׁנֵיהֶם קַיָּימִים, וְיֵדְעוּ וְיַשִׂיגוּ אֶת בּוֹרְאָם, וְיֵהֱנוּ מִזִּיו הַשְּׁכִינָה, וְזֶהוּ הַטּוֹב הַגָּנוּז לַצַּדִּיקִים לֶעָתִיד לָבֹא. הַהַ"ד, וְאֵלֶּה תּוֹלְדֹת יִצְחָק בֶּן אַבְרָהָם, אֵלּוּ הֵם תּוֹלְדוֹת הַשִּׂמְחָה, וְהַשְּׂחוֹק, שֶׁיְּהֵא בָּעוֹלָם בְּאוֹתוֹ זְמַן. בֶּן אַבְרָהָם, הִיא הַנְּשָׁמָה הַזּוֹכָה לְכָךְ, וְלִהְיוֹת שְׁלֵימָה בְּמַעֲלָתָהּ. אַבְרָהָם הוֹלִיד אֶת יִצְחָק, הַנְּשָׁמָה מוֹלִידָה הַשִּׂמְחָה וְהַשְּׂחוֹק הַזֶּה בָּעוֹלָם.

40. At that time, the Righteous will attain complete knowledge, for as Rabbi Yosi said: When "Hashem rejoices in His works," then the Righteous are destined to grasp the Holy One, blessed be He, in their hearts. And wisdom will abound in their hearts, as if they are seeing Him with their eyes. This is the meaning of the verse: "And it shall be said on that day, this is our Elohim" (Yeshayah 25:9). And for their existence together, the soul shall delight in the body more than anything, and that they shall have knowledge and perception of their Master, and shall have the enjoyment of the splendor of the Shechinah. This is the goodness hidden for the Righteous in the future to come. Thus, "And these are the generations of Isaac, Abraham's son," refers to the generations of gladness and laughter that will exist at that time. Abraham's son is the soul worthy of it and is perfect in its ascent; "Abraham begot Isaac," means that the soul sires joy and laughter in the world.

41. אָמַר רָבִּי יְהוּדָה לְרַבִּי חִיָּיא, הָא דְּתָנִינָן דְּעָתִיד הַקוּדְשָׁא בְּרִיךְ הוּא לַעֲשׂוֹת סְעוּדָה לַצַּדִּיקִים לֶעָתִיד לָבֹא, מַאי הִיא. אָמַר לֵיהּ, עַד לָא אָזְלֵית קַמֵּי אִינוּן מַלְאָכִין קַדִּישִׁין, מָארֵי מַתְנִיתִין, הָכֵי שָׁמִיעַ לִי, כֵּיוָן דִּשְׁמַעֲית הָא דְּאָמַר רַבִּי אֶלְעָזָר, אִתְיַשְּׁבָא בְּלִבָּאי, דְּאָמַר רַבִּי אֶלְעָזָר, סְעוּדַת הַצַּדִּיקִים לֶעָתִיד לָבֹא, כְּהַאי דִּכְתִיב וַיֶּחֱזוּ אֶת הָאֱלֹהִים וַיֹּאכְלוּ וַיִּשְׁתּוּ. וְדָא הוּא דְּתָנַן נִיזוֹנִין. וַאֲמַר רָבִּי אֶלְעָזָר בַּאֲתַר חַד תָּנִינָן נֶהֱנִין, וּבַאֲתַר אַחֲרָא תָּנִינָן נִיזוֹנִין, מַאי בֵּין הַאי לְהַאי. אֶלָּא הָכֵי אָמַר אַבּוֹי, הַצַּדִּיקִים שֶׁלֹּא זָכוּ כָּל כָּךְ, נֶהֱנִין מֵאוֹתוֹ זִיו, שֶׁלֹּא יַשִׂיגוּ כָּל כָּךְ, אֲבָל הַצַּדִּיקִים שֶׁזָּכוּ, נִזוֹנִין, עַד שֶׁיַּשִׂיגוּ הַשָּׂגָה שְׁלֵמָה. וְאֵין אֲכִילָה וּשְׁתִיָּה אֶלָּא זוֹ, וְזוֹ הִיא הַסְּעוּדָה וְהָאֲכִילָה. וּמְנָא

לָן הָא, מִמּשֶׁה, דִּכְתִיב וַיְהִי שָׁם עִם ה' אַרְבָּעִים יוֹם וְאַרְבָּעִים לַיְלָה
לֶחֶם לֹא אָכַל וּמַיִם לֹא שָׁתָה. מ"ט לֶחֶם לֹא אָכַל, וּמַיִם לֹא שָׁתָה.
מִפְּנֵי שֶׁהָיָה נִזּוֹן מִסְּעוּדָה אַחֶרֶת, מֵאוֹתוֹ זִיו שֶׁל מַעְלָה, וּכְהַאי גַּוְונָא
סְעוּדָתָן שֶׁל צַדִּיקִים לֶעָתִיד לָבֹא.

41. Rabbi Yehuda said to Rabbi Chiya: We have learned that the Holy One, blessed be He, will prepare a feast for the righteous in the future. What is this feast? He replied: Before you went before these holy angels, the sages of the Mishnah, I heard what Rabbi Elazar said. It set my heart at peace. For Rabbi Elazar said that the feast of the Righteous in the future is as it is written: "and they beheld the Elohim, and did eat and drink" (Shemot 24:11). Here it is written, "eat," but Rabbi Elazar noted that in one place it is explained as, "enjoy" and in another, "eat." What is the difference? He responded: Woe to the Righteous who do not have as much merit; they enjoy the splendor, though they do not understand everything. However, the Righteous who merit the divine splendor eat until they grasp it fully. Food and drink refers to this feast and eating alone. From whom do we know this? From Moses, as it is written: "he did neither eat bread, nor drink water" (Shemot 34:28). Why so? Because he ate another meal, which is the supernal splendor. The meal of the Righteous in the future will be in that manner.

42. אָמַר רִבִּי יְהוּדָה סְעוּדַת הַצַּדִּיקִים לֶעָתִיד לָבֹא, לִשְׂמוֹחַ בְּשִׂמְחָתוֹ, הה"ד יִשְׁמְעוּ עֲנָוִים וְיִשְׂמָחוּ. רַב הוּנָא אָמַר מֵהָכָא, וְיִשְׂמְחוּ כָל חוֹסֵי בָךְ לְעוֹלָם יְרַנֵּנוּ. אָמַר רִבִּי יִצְחָק, הַאי וְהַאי אִיתָא לֶעָתִיד לָבֹא. וְתָאנָא אָמַר רִבִּי יוֹסֵי, יַיִן הַמְשׁוּמָר בַּעֲנָבָיו, מִשֵּׁשֶׁת יְמֵי בְרֵאשִׁית, אֵלּוּ דְּבָרִים עַתִּיקִים, שֶׁלֹּא נִגְלוּ לְאָדָם, מִיּוֹם שֶׁנִּבְרָא הָעוֹלָם, וַעֲתִידִים לְהִגָּלוֹת לַצַּדִּיקִים לֶעָתִיד לָבֹא, וְזוֹ הִיא הַשְׁתִיָּה וַאֲכִילָה, וַדַּאי דָא הִיא.

42. Rabbi Yehuda said that the feast of the Righteous in the future is to partake of His joy, according to the verse: "the humble shall hear of it, and be glad" (Tehilim 34:3). Rav Huna said that it is understood from the verse: "But let all those that put their trust in You rejoice: let them ever shout for joy" (Tehilim 5:12). Rabbi Yitzchak said: Both will occur in the future. We were taught by Rabbi Yosi that cellared wine with its grapes, from the six days of Creation, contains the ancient matters that were not revealed to man from the day the world was created. These are destined to be revealed to the Righteous in the future; this is assuredly their food and drink.

43. אָמַר רבִּי יְהוּדָה בְּרַבִּי שָׁלוֹם, א"כ מַהוּ לִוְיָתָן, וּמֵהוּ הַשׁוֹר, דִּכְתִיב, כִּי בוּל הָרִים יִשְׂאוּ לוֹ. אָמַר רבִּי יוֹסֵי, וְהָא כְּתִיב בָּעֵת הַהִיא יִפְקוֹד ה' בְּחַרְבּוֹ הַקָּשָׁה וְהַגְּדוֹלָה וְהַחֲזָקָה עַל לִוְיָתָן נָחָשׁ בָּרִיחַ וְעַל לִוְיָתָן נָחָשׁ עֲקַלָּתוֹן וְהָרַג אֶת הַתַּנִּין אֲשֶׁר בַּיָּם. הָא הָכָא תְּלָתָא, אֶלָּא רֶמֶז הוּא, דְּקָא רָמַז עַל מַלְכְּוָותָא. אָמַר רבִּי תַּנְחוּם לֵית לְמֵימַר, עַל מַה דְּאָמְרוּ רַבָּנָן, וַדַּאי כָּךְ הִיא.

43. In the name of Rabbi Shalom, Rabbi Yehuda said that if that is true, what about the Livyatan and the bull, as it is written: "Surely the mountains bring him forth food" (Iyov 40:20). Rabbi Yosi said that it is also written: "On that day, Hashem with His sore and great and strong sword will punish Livyatan the flying serpent, and the Livyatan that crooked serpent; and He will slay the crocodile that is in the sea" (Yeshayah 27:1). This was said thrice, to hint at the kingdom. Rabbi Tanchum added that there is nothing to reveal in addition to what the wise men said. This is assuredly so.

44. אָמַר רבִּי יִצְחָק, אֲנָא הֲוֵינָא קַמֵּיה דְּרבִּי יְהוֹשֻׁעַ, וְשָׁאִילְנָא הַאי מִלָּה, אֲמַרְנָא הַאי סְעוּדָתָא דְּצַדִּיקַיָּא לֶעָתִיד לָבֹא, אִי כָּךְ הוּא, לָא אִתְיַישְׁבָא בְּלִבַּאי, דְּהָא אָמַר רבִּי אֶלְעָזָר, סְעוּדַת הַצַּדִּיקִים לֶעָתִיד לָבֹא, כְּהַאי גַוְונָא דִּכְתִיב, וַיֶּחֱזוּ אֶת הָאֱלֹהִים וַיֹּאכְלוּ וַיִּשְׁתּוּ. אָמַר רבִּי יְהוֹשֻׁעַ שַׁפִּיר קָאָמַר רבִּי אֶלְעָזָר, וְכָךְ הוּא.

44. Rabbi Yitzchak said: I was present before Rabbi Yehoshua and asked him about this. I said that this feast of the Righteous that will be held in the future WAS SAID TO CONSIST OF THE LIVYATAN AND THE WILD BULL. If this is so, there is a contradiction, because Rabbi Elazar said that the feast of the Righteous in the future will be as it is written in the verse: "and they beheld the Elohim, and did eat and drink." Rabbi Yehoshua said that Rabbi Elazar was correct.

45. עוֹד אָמַר רִבִּי יְהוֹשֻׁעַ, הַאי מְהֵימְנוּתָא, דַּאֲמָרוּ רַבָּנָן לְרוּבָּא דְעָלְמָא, דִּזְמִינִין אִינוּן בְּהַאי סְעוּדָתָא דְלִוְיָתָן וְהַהוּא תּוֹרָא, וּלְמִשְׁתֵּי חַמְרָא טַב, דְּאִתְנַטָּר מִכַּד אִתְבְּרֵי עָלְמָא, קְרָא אַשְׁכָּחוּ וְדָרְשׁוּ, דִּכְתִיב וַאֲכַלְתֶּם לַחְמְכֶם לָשׂוֹבַע, דְּאָמַר רִבִּי זֵירָא, כָּל מִינֵי פִּתּוּי, פָּתָה הַקּוּדְשָׁא בְּרִיךְ הוּא לְיִשְׂרָאֵל, לְהַחֲזִירָם לְמוּטָב, וְדָא הוּא יַתִּיר מִכֻּלְּהוֹן, דַּאֲמַר לְהוֹ וַאֲכַלְתֶּם לַחְמְכֶם לָשׂוֹבַע. וּבַקְלָלוֹת, וַאֲכַלְתֶּם וְלֹא תִשְׂבָּעוּ, וְדָא קַשְׁיָא לְהוֹ מִכֻּלְּהוּ. מ"ט, דִּכְתִיב מִי יִתֵּן מוּתֵנוּ בְיַד ה' בְּאֶרֶץ מִצְרַיִם וְגוֹ'. אָמַר רִבִּי זֵירָא, מְלַמֵּד, דְּמִשּׁוּם הָאֲכִילָה מָסְרוּ נַפְשָׁם לָמוּת בְּיָדָם. כֵּיוָן שֶׁרָאָה הַקּוּדְשָׁא בְּרִיךְ הוּא תַּאֲוָתָם, אָמַר לָהֶם, אִם תִּשְׁמְעוּ לְקוֹל הַמִּצְוֹת, וַאֲכַלְתֶּם לָשׂוֹבַע כְּדֵי לְהָנִיחַ דַּעְתָּם. כה"ג, חָמוּ רַבָּנָן דְּגָלוּתָא אִתְמַשַּׁךְ, אִסְתַּכְּמוּ עַל קְרָאֵי דְאוֹרַיְיתָא, וַאֲמָרוּ דִּזְמִינִין לְמֵיכַל וּלְמֶחְדֵי בִּסְעוּדָתָא רַבָּה, דְּזַמִּין קוּדְשָׁא בְּרִיךְ הוּא לְמֶעְבַּד לְהוֹ, וְע"ד רוּבָּא דְעָלְמָא סָבְלוּ גָלוּתָא בְּגִין הַהִיא סְעוּדָתָא.

45. Rabbi Yehoshua further stated the belief that the sages communicated to most of the people: that they are invited to this meal of the Livyatan and the wild bull, where they will drink of the good CELLARED wine preserved from the time of the Creation. They came upon this verse: "and you shall eat your bread to the full" (Vayikra 26:5), and interpreted it thus. Rabbi Zira said: The Holy One, blessed be He, used all kinds of enticements to encourage the children of Yisrael to return to the good path. The greatest of them all was when He said to them, "and you shall eat your bread to the full," or among the curses, the worst is: "and you shall eat, and not be satisfied" (Ibid. 26). Why so? Because it is written: "Would we had died by the hand of Hashem in the land of Egypt" (Shemot 16:3). Rabbi Zira said: This teaches us that for the sake of eating, sacrificed their lives to die by their hands. When the Holy One, blessed be He, noticed their lust, He said to them: "If you will hearken to keep the commandments, you shall eat your bread to the full', in order to appease their minds. In this manner, the wise men saw that the exile would continue. They relied on the verses in the Torah, and said that they would eat and be merry at the great feast that the Holy One, blessed be He, will hold for them. Therefore, most of the people in the world suffer this exile for the sake of that feast.

46. אָמַר רַבִּי יוֹחָנָן, לֵית לָן לִסְתּוֹר מְהֵימְנוּתָא דְּכֹלָּא, אֶלָּא לְקַיְימָא לֵיהּ, דְּהָא אוֹרַיְיתָא אַסְהֵידַת עֲלוֹי, דְּהָא אֲנַן יָדְעִין מְהֵימְנוּתָא דְּצַדִּיקַיָּא, וְכִסּוּפָא דִּלְהוֹן מַאי הִיא, דִּכְתִיב נָגִילָה וְנִשְׂמְחָה בָּךְ, וְלֹא בַּאֲכִילָה. נַזְכִּירָה דּוֹדֶיךָ מִיַּיִן. וְהַהִיא סְעוּדָתָא דִּזְמִינִין בָּהּ, יְהֵא לָן חוּלָק לְמֶהֱוֵי מִנָּהּ, וְזוֹ הִיא הַשִּׂמְחָה וְהַשְׂחוֹק. וְאֵלֶּה תּוֹלְדוֹת יִצְחָק, שֶׁיִּצְחֲקוּ הַצַּדִּיקִים לֶעָתִיד לָבוֹא, אַבְרָהָם הוֹלִיד אֶת יִצְחָק, זְכוּת הַנְּשָׁמָה, מוֹלִיד הַשְׂחוֹק הַזֶּה, וְהַשִּׂמְחָה בָּעוֹלָם.

46. Rabbi Yochanan said that we should not contradict this belief, but support the idea THAT THE FEAST CONSISTS OF EATING AND DRINKING, because the Torah bears witness to it IN THE VERSE: "AND YOU SHALL EAT YOUR BREAD TO THE FULL" (VAYIKRA 26:5). We already know the Faith of the Righteous and their desire from the verses: "we will be glad and rejoice in You" (Shir Hashirim 1:4), and not in eating, and "we will praise you love more than wine" (Vayikra 26:5), WHICH ALLUDES TO THE WINE OF THE TORAH. That feast, that they – MOST OF THE PEOPLE IN THE WORLD – are destined for, FOR EATING AND DRINKING, we will partake of it too. This is the part of joy and laughter. "And these are the generations of Isaac (lit. 'will laugh')," for the righteous will laugh in the future. "Abraham begot Isaac," as it is the virtue of the soul that begets that laughter and joy in the world.

6. The combining of the attribute of Mercy with Judgment

A Synopsis

The discussion continues to explore the uniting of Jacob and Rivkah. It evolves toward a more complete understanding, explaining the more subtle meanings that arise from this combination of Malchut (an aspect of judgment) and Binah (an aspect of mercy). The Rabbis also discuss the role of the Evil Inclination, explaining how this, too, derives from The Creator. They describe how evil is placed in the human heart, discuss its formidably enduring nature, and explain its role in reproduction. The creation of the Evil Inclination actually denotes the Creation of the *Desire to Receive*.

This *Desire to Receive* is a vital and necessary component in man, for without it, The Creator cannot share His infinite beneficence. There must be a willing recipient in order for sharing to take place. The angel Satan, however, manipulates this vital *desire to receive* into a *desire to receive for the self alone*. This additional aspect of receiving in a selfish manner is the "root of all evil." Man's spiritual work is to negate the Satan's influence and to express our *desire to receive* through sharing.

The Relevance of this Passage

A story is told of an arrogant tycoon who tosses a few gold coins to a poverty-stricken man in the streets. The poor man is of high principles and refuses the condescending handout. The tycoon is taken aback and insists that the pauper accept his gift. The poor man refuses. Initially, the tycoon was indifferent to the plight of the poor man. His charity was more an act of haughty self-regard, but now the tycoon is overcome with guilt and embarrassment. He pleads with the poor man to accept the gift. Seeing how much distress and anxiety his refusal is causing the wealthy man, the poor man decides to accept the gold coins so that his benefactor will feel better about himself. Kabbalistically, the poor man's receiving has taken the form of sharing.

A reading of this section helps us transform our selfish desires into actions that embody the principle of *receiving for the sake of sharing*.

47. וַיְהִי יִצְחָק בֶּן אַרְבָּעִים שָׁנָה. רִבִּי בּוֹ בְּשֵׁם רִבִּי יוֹסֵי, פְּתַח וְאָמַר, יִשָּׁקֵנִי מִנְּשִׁיקוֹת פִּיהוּ וגו', בְּכַמָּה מַעֲלוֹת נִבְרָא הָעוֹלָם, דִּתְנִינָן אָמַר

רִבִּי אַחָא בַּר יַעֲקֹב כָּל מַה שֶׁבָּרָא קוּדְשָׁא בְּרִיךְ הוּא בְּעוֹלְמוֹת שֶׁלּוֹ,
חוּץ מִמֶּנּוּ, הָיוּ בְּשׁוּתָּף. וּמִי אָמַר רִבִּי אַחָא הָכֵי, חַס וְשָׁלוֹם, דְּהָא
בְּמִלָּה דָא יִסְגֵּי פְלוּגְתָּא בְּעַלְמָא, דְּאִי תֵימָא הָכֵי, הַמַּלְאָכִים שֶׁהֵם
נִבְרָאִים רוּחַ הַקֹּדֶשׁ מַמָּשׁ, יֹאמַר שֶׁיֵּשׁ שׁוּתָּף בָּהֶם, הָא כָּל אַפַּיָּיא
דִּדְהוֹן וְדִידָן שַׁוְיָין.

47. "And Isaac was forty years old." Rabbi Bo began in the name of Rabbi Yosi with the verse: "Let him kiss me with the kisses of his mouth…" (Shir Hashirim 1:2). With how many GOOD qualities was the world created? We have learned that Rabbi Acha bar Jacob said that everything the Holy One, blessed be He, created in His worlds, outside of Himself, was in collaboration – THAT IS, THE COMBINING OF MALCHUT, AN ASPECT OF JUDGMENT, WITH BINAH, AN ASPECT OF MERCY. IT IS FROM THESE PARTNERSHIPS THAT MANY QUALITIES ARE FOUND IN THE WORLD. ONE THOUGHT THIS PARTNERSHIP OF GOOD AND EVIL APPLIES TO CREATURES, SO HE RAISED A QUESTION. Rabbi Acha asks: Is that so? Heaven forbid, for this will add dissension in the world, FOR EVERYBODY WHO HEARS HIM WILL DISAGREE. For if you say that it means that the angels, created as the Holy Spirit itself, have a blend OF GOOD AND EVIL in them, then their faces and ours are the same – THAT IS, ANGELS AND MEN ARE EQUAL.

48. אָמַר רִבִּי אַבָּא, בְּמִלָּה דָא יִסְגֵּי פְלוּגְתָּא בְּעַלְמָא, דְּהָא תְּנַן
בְּמַתְנִיתִין דִּידָן, דְּכָל דַּעֲבַד קוּדְשָׁא בְּרִיךְ הוּא, עֲבַד כְּגוֹן גּוּפָא
וְנִשְׁמָתָא, וְאִי תֵימָא דְּהָא לֵית גּוּפָא לַמַּלְאָכִים, כָּךְ הוּא, אֲבָל לֵית
אִינוּן יָכְלִין לְמֶעְבַּד עֲבִידְתָּא, עַד שֶׁיִּשְׁתַּתֵּף בְּהוֹ הַהִיא נִשְׁמָתָא
קַדִּישָׁא, דְּהִיא סִיּוּעָא דִּלְעֵילָּא, וּבְהַאי גַּוְונֵי כָּל מַאי דַּעֲבֵיד אִצְטְרִיךְ
לְהַהִיא סִיּוּעָא דִּלְעֵילָּא מִנֵּיהּ.

48. Rabbi Aba said THAT IT IS TRUE, and through this, dissension will increase in the world. For we learned in the Mishnah that all that the Holy One, blessed be He, did, He made as body and soul. THE HOLY ONE, BLESSED BE HE, JOINED TOGETHER THE BODY FROM MALCHUT AND THE SOUL FROM BINAH. THIS IS THE SECRET OF JOINING JUDGMENT WITH MERCY. One may argue that the angels have no bodies and cannot perform actions until the Holy Soul, THE LIGHT OF BINAH, joins them which is help from above.

49. אָמַר רַבִּי יוֹסֵי, בְּהַהִיא שַׁעְתָּא דְּזַמִּין קוּדְשָׁא בְּרִיךְ הוּא לְאַחֲיָא מֵתַיָּא, וְהָא סוֹפָא כָּל עֲקַתִּין, בְּאַרְבָּעִים לֶהֱוֵי. וּגְזַר קַיָּים, אַרְבָּעִים יַכֶּנּוּ לֹא יוֹסִיף. סוֹף הֲלִיכָתָם שֶׁל יִשְׂרָאֵל בַּמִּדְבָּר, בִּשְׁנַת הָאַרְבָּעִים. אַרְבָּעִים שָׁנָה, קוֹדֶם תְּחִיַּית הַגּוּף, מַמְתֶּנֶת לוֹ הַנְּשָׁמָה בְּאֶרֶץ יִשְׂרָאֵל. בִּשְׁנַת הָאַרְבָּעִים יְקוּמוּן הַגּוּפוֹת מֵעַפְרָא. בְּאַרְבָּעִים נִכְלָא הַגֶּשֶׁם, הה״ד וַיְהִי הַגֶּשֶׁם עַל הָאָרֶץ אַרְבָּעִים יוֹם, וּכְתִיב וַיְהִי מִקֵּץ אַרְבָּעִים יוֹם וַיִּפְתַּח נֹחַ. זְמַן גְּאוּלָתָם שֶׁל יִשְׂרָאֵל, בִּשְׁנַת הָאַרְבָּעִים הוּא. וּבַחֲמִשִּׁים אָתָא יְשׁוּב עָלְמָא, דְּהִיא הַיּוֹבֵל. הַחְזָרַת הַנְּשָׁמָה לַגּוּף, בִּשְׁנַת הָאַרְבָּעִים, שֶׁהַמְתִּינָה לוֹ בְּאֶרֶץ יִשְׂרָאֵל, הֲדָא הוּא דִכְתִיב וַיְהִי יִצְחָק בֶּן אַרְבָּעִים שָׁנָה, שֶׁהַמְתִּין לַגּוּף. בְּקַחְתּוֹ אֶת רִבְקָה, בְּהַכְנָסָתָהּ בַּגּוּף הַמְזוּמָּן לוֹ. בְּאוֹתָהּ שָׁעָה, בְּהַכְנָסָתָהּ בּוֹ, אֵין תַּאֲוָתָם וְכִסּוּפָם, אֶלָּא לֵיהָנוֹת מִזִּיו הַשְּׁכִינָה, וְלִיזּוֹן מִזִּיוָהּ, הה״ד יִשָּׁקֵנִי מִנְּשִׁיקוֹת פִּיהוּ. אָמַר רַבִּי אַבָּא, יְשַׁקֵּנִי יְפַרְנְסֵנִי, שֶׁאֵין פַּרְנָסָתָן אֶלָּא לֵיהָנוֹת וְלִיזּוֹן מִזִּיוָהּ שֶׁל מַעֲלָה. אָמַר רַבִּי יוֹסֵי סוֹפֵיהּ דִּקְרָא מוֹכַח דִּכְתִיב כִּי טוֹבִים דּוֹדֶיךָ מִיָּיִן.

49. Rabbi Yosi said that the instant the Holy One blessed be He, resurrects the dead, all troubles will end, on the fortieth year FOLLOWING THE GATHERING OF THE EXILES. It has been resolved by law "Forty stripes he may give him, and not exceed" (Devarim 25:3). The journey of Yisrael in the desert WAS COMPLETED in the fortieth year. Forty years before the body is resurrected, the soul awaits it in the land of Yisrael. IT APPEARS THEN that in the fortieth year OF THE WAITING OF THE SOUL IN THE LAND OF YISRAEL, the bodies will rise from the dust. After forty days the rain stopped, this is the meaning of the verses "And the rain was upon the earth forty days and forty nights" (Beresheet 7:12), and "it came to pass at the end of forty days, that Noah opened" (Beresheet 8:6). Also, the time of the Redemption of Yisrael is during the fortieth year. During the fiftieth year the world, which is Jubilee, will be populated. The return of the soul to the body occurs after forty years of waiting in the land of Yisrael. This is the

meaning of, "and Isaac was forty years old." That is, he was waiting for the body. "When he took Rivkah," who was put in the body prepared for him. Their passion and longing at that moment was for the splendor of the Shechinah only and to nourish of Her splendor. This is the meaning of the verse, "Let him kiss me with the kisses of his mouth." Rabbi Aba said: "Let him kiss me" means let him nourish me. Their sole nourishment is the enjoyment and sustenance of the supernal splendor. Rabbi Yosi said that this is proven by the end of the verse, which reads: "for your love is better than wine" (Shir Hashirim 1:2).

50. בַּת בְּתוּאֵל בַּת בִּתוֹ שֶׁל אֵל. רַב הוּנָא אָמַר, לֹא כָךְ הוּא, וַאֲנָא הֲוֵית בְּכַרְכֵּי הַיָּם, וְשָׁמַעְנָא דַּהֲווֹ קָרָאן לְהַהוּא גַּרְמָא דְשִׁדְרָה, הַהוּא דְּאִשְׁתָּאַר בְּקִבְרָא מִכָּל גּוּפָא, בְּתוּאֵל רַמָּאָה, שָׁאֵלִית עֲלֵיה, אָמְרוּ דְּהוּא כְּרֵישָׁא דְחִוְיָא, דְּאִיהוּ רַמָּאָה, וְהַהוּא גַּרְמָא הוּא רַמָּאָה, מִכָּל שְׁאָר גַּרְמֵי.

50. "The daughter of Betu'el" means the daughter (Heb. *bat*) of El. Rav Huna disagreed with this. He said that BETU'EL is not ONE OF MALCHUT'S NAMES. I have been to distant lands, and heard there that this is the name of the bone of the spine. Of all the bones this one remains in the grave, AND DOES NOT ROT. It is called 'Betu'el the deceitful', THAT IS, THE 'SCOUNDREL'. I asked about it, ABOUT ITS NATURE, and they said that its shape resembles a head of a serpent, which is deceitful. And that more than any other bone in the body, this bone is deceitful.

51. דְּתָאנָא אָמַר רַבִּי שִׁמְעוֹן, הַהוּא גַּרְמָא, לָמָּה אִשְׁתָּאַר בְּקִיּוּמָא, יַתִּיר מִכָּל שְׁאָר גַּרְמֵי. מִשּׁוּם דְּאִיהוּ רַמָּאָה, וְלֵית סָבִיל טַעֲמָא דִמְזוֹנָא דִּבְנֵי נָשָׁא כִּשְׁאָר גַּרְמֵי, וּבְגִינֵי כָךְ הוּא תַּקִּיף מִכָּל גַּרְמֵי, וְהוּא לֶיהֱוֵי עִקְּרָא, דְּגוּפָא אִתְבְּנֵי מִנֵּיה. הֲדָא הוּא דִכְתִיב בַּת בְּתוּאֵל הָאֲרַמִּי.

51. For we have learned that Rabbi Shimon asks: Why does this bone endure longer than the other bones? This is because it is deceitful and does not bear the taste of human food like the other bones. For that reason, it is stronger than all the other bones. And at the resurrection of the dead, the body will be built on this root. This is the meaning of the verse, "the daughter of Betu'el the Arammian."

52. וְתָאנָא אָמַר רַבִּי שִׁמְעוֹן, הוּא רַמַּאי, וּמֵעוֹלָם רַמַּאי, וְשָׁכֵּן יֵצֶר הָרָע, דְּאִיהוּ רַמַּאי. הֲדָא הוּא דִכְתִיב בַּת בְּתוּאֵל הָאֲרַמִּי גַּרְמָא רַמָּאָה, מִפַּדַּן אֲרָם, מְצַמֵּד רַמָּאִין, כְּדִתְנַן פַּדָּנָא דְּתוֹרָא שְׁהוּא צֶמֶד. אֲחוֹת לָבָן, אֲחוֹת יֵצֶר הָרָע הָאֲרַמִי, כְּדִתְנַן, בְּתְחִלָּה שֶׁהָיָה מְנֻוָּל בְּחַטָּאוֹת בָּזֶה הָעוֹלָם, נִקְרָא לוֹט. לֶעָתִיד לָבֹא, שְׁלֹא יְהֵא מְנֻוָּל כְּדִבְקַדְמֵיתָא, כְּמַאן דְּסָחֵי וּמִטְבִּיל מִסֻּאָבוּתֵיה, קַרְאַן לֵיה לָבָן. עַל כָּל פָּנִים אֵין יֵצֶר הָרָע בָּטֵל מִן הָעוֹלָם.

52. We learned that Rabbi Shimon said: It, THE BONE OF THE SPINE, is deceitful, and IT CAME from a deceitful world, NAMELY, FROM PADDAN-ARAM. Also, deceitful is the Evil Inclination, WHICH IS THE HEAD OF THE SERPENT, WHICH IS THE EVIL INCLINATION, THE ANGEL OF DEATH. This is the meaning of the verse: "the daughter of Betu'el the Arammian," who is the deceitful bone of the spine. The words, "of Paddan-Aram," WHICH MEANS THAT HE CAME FROM A DECEITFUL (HEB. RAMAI) WORLD, represent two deceivers, as we have learned that *Paddana* means a 'couple'. The two deceivers are "the sister of Laban," NAMELY, the sister of the deceitful Evil Inclination. At first, when it was corrupted by sins in this world, it was called 'Lot'. In the future, when it will no longer be as corrupted, IT WILL BE as someone who has washed and was cleansed of his impurities, and it will be called 'Laban' (lit. 'white'). Nevertheless, the Evil Inclination is not eliminated from the world.

53. ת״ש, דְּהָכֵי אֲנַן אוּקִימְנָא בְּמַתְנִיתָא. שְׁתֵּי בְּנוֹת לוֹט, שֶׁהֵן שְׁתֵּי כֹּחוֹת הַגּוּף, הַמְעוֹרְרוֹת לַיֵּצֶר הָרָע, עַכְשָׁיו שְׁאֵינוֹ מְנֻוָּל כ״כ, וְנִטְבַּל מִלִּכְלוּכוֹ, נִקְרָא לָבָן, וְאוֹתָן שְׁתֵּי בָּנוֹת אֵינָן בְּטֵלוֹת מַמָּשׁ, הה״ד וּלְלָבָן שְׁתֵּי בָנוֹת. אָמַר רַבִּי יוֹסֵי כָּךְ הוּא, תַּמָּן כְּתִיב בְּכִירָה וּצְעִירָה, וְהָכָא כְּתִיב גְּדוֹלָה וּקְטַנָּה.

53. Come and hearken: we learned from the Mishnah that the two daughters of Lot symbolize the two forces of the body that arouse the Evil Inclination. Because it has bathed and is no longer so impure, it is called 'Laban'. And the two daughters are not completely negated, as it is written, "And Laban had two daughters" (Beresheet 29:16). Rabbi Yosi asks: Why are they there

referred to as the firstborn and the younger, and here the elder and the younger?

‏54. אָמַר רִבִּי יוֹסֵי, אֲבָל אֵינָן בְּכֹחַ לַעֲשׂוֹת רָע, וּלְהִתְעוֹרֵר לֵיצֶ״ר כְּמִתְּחִלָּה, מַשְׁמַע דִּכְתִיב שֵׁם הַגְּדוֹלָה לֵאָה, שֶׁלֵּאָה מִכֹּחָה וּמֵרִשְׁעָתָה, וְשֵׁם הַקְּטַנָּה רָחֵל, שֶׁאֵין בָּהּ כֹּחַ הַמִּתְעוֹרֵר, כְּמָה דְאַתְּ אָמַר וּכְרָחֵל לִפְנֵי גוֹזְזֶיהָ נֶאֱלָמָה. אָמַר רַב הוּנָא, זֶה יֵצֶ״ר, וּשְׁתֵּי בְנוֹתָיו, מִתְחַלְּפוֹת מִכְּמוֹת שֶׁהָיוּ בָרִאשׁוֹנָה. בַּתְּחִלָּה לוֹט, מְקוּלָל מְנֻוָּל, עַכְשָׁיו לָבָן, מְלֻבָּן, שֶׁאֵינוֹ מְקוּלָל וּמְנֻוָּל בְּנִיווּלוֹ כְּבָרִאשׁוֹנָה. בַּתְּחִלָּה שְׁתֵּי בְנוֹתָיו חֲזָקוֹת, כָּל אַחַת וְאַחַת בְּכֹחָהּ, וְעַכְשָׁיו שֵׁם הַגְּדוֹלָה לֵאָה: לֵאָה בְּלֹא כֹחַ, לֵאָה בְּלֹא חִזּוּק. לֵאָה מִמַּעֲשֶׂיהָ הָרִאשׁוֹנִים. וְשֵׁם הַקְּטַנָּה רָחֵל, כִּדְקָאָמְרָן, וְלֹא כְּמוֹ שֶׁהָיוּ בָרִאשׁוֹנָה.

54. Rabbi Yosi said that they no longer have the power to do evil or arouse the Evil Inclination. This is understood from the verse, "the name of the elder (lit. 'bigger') was Leah" (Beresheet 29:16), for she was weary (Heb. *leah*) from her wickedness and evil, while Rachel, "the younger (lit. 'smaller')," did not have the power to incite. As it is written, "and as a sheep (lit. 'Rachel') before her shearers is dumb" (Yeshayah 53:7). Rav Huna said: This is the Evil Inclination. Its two daughters are different than they were at first. First it was Lot, cursed and corrupted; now it is Laban (lit. 'white'), who has been cleansed, not as cursed and corrupted as it was before. First its two daughters were strong; each had her individual strength. Now the name of the elder was Leah – weary ('Leah') without power; weary without strength; Leah, fatigued from her former deeds. And the name of the younger was Rachel, as we have said, not as they were at first.

‏55. אָמַר רִבִּי אַחָא בַּר יַעֲקֹב, תָּא חֲזֵי, מַה כְּתִיב, וַיֶּעְתַּר יִצְחָק לַה׳ לְנֹכַח אִשְׁתּוֹ כִּי עֲקָרָה הִיא. אָמַר רִבִּי אַחָא מִפְּנֵי מָה הִיא עֲקָרָה, מִפְּנֵי שֶׁיֵּצֶר הָרַע אֵינוֹ נִמְצָא בְּכֹחוֹ בָּעוֹלָם, וְעַל כָּךְ אֵין נִמְצָא פְּרִיָּה וּרְבִיָּה, זוּלָתִי בַּתְּפִלָּה, מַה כְּתִיב, וַיֵּעָתֶר לוֹ ה׳, וַתַּהַר רִבְקָה אִשְׁתּוֹ. כֵּיוָן שֶׁמִּתְעוֹרֵר יֵצֶר הָרַע, נִמְצָא פְּרִיָּה וּרְבִיָּה.

55. Rabbi Acha bar Jacob, said: Come and behold. It is written, "And Isaac entreated Hashem for his wife, because she was barren" (Beresheet 25:21). Rabbi Acha asks: Why is she barren? Because the Evil Inclination does not have its full strength in the world, the only fruition and multiplying comes through prayer. It is then written: "and Hashem was entreated by him, and Rivkah his wife conceived." Once the Evil Inclination is aroused, there is procreation!

56. אָמַר רִבִּי יוֹסֵי, אִם כֵּן מַה הֶפְרֵשׁ בֵּין הָעוֹלָם הַזֶּה, לְאוֹתוֹ הַזְּמַן, וְעוֹד דְּהָא קְרָא קָאֲמַר, דְּקוּדְשָׁא בְּרִיךְ הוּא עָבֵיד. אָמַר רִבִּי אַחָא, כָּךְ הוּא, דְּקוּדְשָׁא בְּרִיךְ הוּא אַתְעַר לֵיהּ לְהַהוּא עִנְיָינָא, דְּצָרִיךְ לְזִוּוּגָא, וְלָא לְכָל שַׁעֲתָא, דְּיֶהֱא תָּדִיר עִם בַּר נָשׁ כְּמוֹ כְּעַן, דְּאִיהוּ אִשְׁתַּכַּח תָּדִיר, וְחָטָאן בֵּיהּ בְּנֵי נָשָׁא, אֶלָּא לְהַהוּא זִוּוּגָא בִּלְחוֹדוֹי, וְאִתְעֲרוּתָא הַהִיא, אִתְעֲרוּתָא דְּקוּדְשָׁא בְּרִיךְ הוּא לֶיהֱוֵי, הֲדָא הוּא דִכְתִיב וַהֲסִירוֹתִי אֶת לֵב הָאֶבֶן מִבְּשַׂרְכֶם וְנָתַתִּי לָכֶם לֵב בָּשָׂר. מַהוּ לֵב בָּשָׂר. אָמַר רִבִּי יְהוּדָה, לֵב לְהוֹצִיא בָּשָׂר, וְלֹא לְדָבָר אַחֵר.

56. Rabbi Yosi asks: What then is the difference between this world and the world at that time; WILL THERE BE EVIL INCLINATION TOO? The scripture also says, "AND HASHEM WAS ENTREATED BY HIM, AND RIVKAH HIS WIFE CONCEIVED," WHICH MEANS that the Holy One, blessed be He, does it Himself, AND AWAKENS THE EVIL INCLINATION AT THAT TIME, WHICH IS ALSO PUZZLING. Rabbi Acha said: It is so. The Holy One, blessed be He, arouses THE EVIL INCLINATION for the specific purpose of mating, but not all the time, so that the Evil Inclination may be with men always, and they sin because of it. But it is aroused only for mating, and the arousal OF THE EVIL INCLINATION AT THE TIME OF UNION will be caused by the Holy One, blessed be He. This is the meaning of the verse: "and I will take away the stony heart out of your flesh, and I will give you a heart of flesh" (Yechezkel 36:26). What is a heart of flesh? Rabbi Yehuda replies: It is a heart that would issue flesh and nothing else, AS, FOR EXAMPLE, A HEART THAT WOULD ONLY BEGET CHILDREN. THEREFORE IT IS WRITTEN, "AND I WILL GIVE YOU," FOR THE HOLY ONE, BLESSED BE HE, WILL HIMSELF AROUSE THE EVIL INCLINATION AT THE TIME OF MATING.

57. רִבִּי יִצְחָק בְּרִבִּי יוֹסֵי, הֲוָה אָתֵי מִקַּפּוֹטְקְיָא לְלוֹד, פָּגַע בֵּיהּ רִבִּי

יְהוּדָה, אָמַר לוֹ רִבִּי יִצְחָק, תֹּאמַר דַּחֲבֵירָנָא חַכִּימֵי מַתְנִיתָא, אִתְעָרוּ לְהַאי עִנְיָינָא, דְּיֵצֶר הָרָע יִתְנְשֵׁי מִן עַלְמָא, בַּר הַהִיא שַׁעֲתָא לְזִיווּגָא. א״ל, חַיֶּיךָ הָכֵי אִצְטְרִיךְ יֵצֶר הָרָע לְעוֹלָם, כְּמִטְרָא לְעוֹלָם, דְּאִלְמָלֵא יֵצֶר הָרָע, חֶדְוָותָא דִּשְׁמַעְתָא לָא לֶיהֱוֵי, אֲבָל לָא מְנֻוָּולָה כְּקַדְמֵיתָא, לְמֶחֱטֵי בֵּיה, הֲה״ד לֹא יָרֵעוּ וְלֹא יַשְׁחִיתוּ בְּכָל הַר קָדְשִׁי וגו'. אָמַר רִבִּי שִׁמְעוֹן, הוּא לִבָּא, דִּמְדוֹרֵיהּ דְּיֵצֶר הָרָע בֵּיהּ. רִבִּי אֱלִיעֶזֶר אוֹמֵר, לִבָּא טָבָא, בִּנְיָינָא דְּגוּפָא וְנִשְׁמָתָא, וּבְגִין כָּךְ כְּתִיב וְאָהַבְתָּ אֶת ה' אֱלֹהֶיךָ בְּכָל לְבָבְךָ דְּהוּא עִקָּרָא דְּכֹלָּא.

57. Rabbi Yitzchak, the son of Rabbi Yosi, traveled from Cappadocia to Lod, where he met Rabbi Yehuda. Rabbi Yitzchak asks him: Why are the companions, the sages of the Mishnah, not aroused in this matter of removing the Evil Inclination from the world, except at the time of mating? He replied: Upon your life! The world needs the Evil Inclination as much as it needs rain, because without the Evil Inclination there would not be the joy of study in the world. But it also would not be as corrupted as it was before, which caused sinning. This is the meaning of the verse: "They shall not hurt or destroy in all My holy mountain" (Yeshayah 11:9). Rabbi Shimon said: "MY HOLY MOUNTAIN" is the heart," the dwelling place of the Evil Inclination. Rabbi Eliezer said: A good heart is the foundation of the body and soul. For that reason, it is written: "And you shall love Hashem your Elohim with all your heart" (Devarim 6:5), for the heart is the essence of all!

7. "And the children struggled together within her" (B)

A Synopsis
The story of Esau and Jacob is illuminated using an analogy with man's body and internal organs. The "children struggling together within her" refers to the brain and heart. Their struggle for primacy between these two is metaphorically expressed in Esau's selling his birthright to Jacob in exchange for porridge, which signifies the world. We also learn that the heart and liver are the most important organs. Next, the Rabbis more deeply explore the nature of life after the Resurrection, identifying the elements of our prior existence that will still be present after the Final Redemption

The Relevance of this Passage
Man is inclined to sacrifice long-term fulfillment and well-being for immediate ego gratification. This is the true significance of Esau selling his birthright to his brother. We settle for bowls of porridge every day, blinded by the moment, carrying only for our self-interest at the expense of our loved ones. Moreover, we delude ourselves with the belief that our selfish actions are really for the sake of our families. This delusion is fabricated by the dark side of our nature. This passage removes the veils of illusion, giving us the strength and foresight not to sell our souls when temptation for self-indulgence arises.

58. כַּד אֲתָא רַב כַּהֲנָא אֲמַר, הָכֵי אָמְרִין מִשְׁמֵיהוֹן דְּמָארֵי מַתְנִיתָא, תְּרֵי בִּנְיָינִין דְּגוּפָא אִינוּן, כַּבְדָא וְלִבָּא, דַּאֲמַר רִבִּי שִׁמְעוֹן אָמַר רִבִּי יְהוּדָה, כַּבְדָא וְלִבָּא, אִינוּן מְנַהֲגֵי גוּפָא בְּכָל סִטְרֵי אֶבְרוֹי, מְנַהֲגָא דְרֵישָׁא מוֹחָא, אֲבָל דְּגוּפָא אִינוּן תְּרֵין, וְקַדְמָאָה הוּא כַּבְדָא, תִּנְיָינָא לִבָּא. וְהַיְינוּ דִּכְתִיב בְּפָרְשָׁתָא, וַיִּתְרוֹצְצוּ הַבָּנִים בְּקִרְבָּה אִלֵּין תְּרֵין בִּנְיָינֵי דְגוּפָא.

58. When Rav Kahana arrived, he said that this was said in the name of those versed in the Mishnah. The body is built upon the liver and the heart. As Rabbi Yehuda said, the heart and the liver are the leaders of the various organs of the body. The leaders of the head is the brain, but there are two leaders in the body. The first is the liver and the second is the heart. This is the meaning of the verse: "And the children struggled together within her." These are the two foundations of the body: THE BRAIN AND THE HEART.

59. מַאי טַעְמָא וַיִּתְרוֹצְצוּ. מִשּׁוּם דְּלִבָּא אִתְנְשֵׁי מִנֵּיהּ יֵצֶר הָרָע. וַיִּתְרוֹצְצוּ וַיִּשְׁלָיוּ מִבָּעֵי לֵיהּ. אֶלָּא אָמַר רַב הוּנָא, וַיִּתְרוֹצְצוּ וַיִּשָּׁבְרוּ, כְּלוֹמַר, נִשְׁבַּר כֹּחָם וְחֵילָם. אָמַר רַבִּי יְהוּדָה, הַגּוּף מַהוּ אוֹמֵר, אִם כֵּן לָמָּה זֶה אָנֹכִי, וְלָמָּה נִבְרֵאתִי. מִיָּד וַתֵּלֶךְ לִדְרֹשׁ אֶת ה'.

59. HE ASKS: Why did THE HEART AND THE LIVER struggle? AND HE REPLIED: Because the Evil Inclination was abolished from the heart. HE THEN WONDERED WHY, IF THE EVIL INCLINATION WAS ABOLISHED, IT IS WRITTEN, "struggled." It should have been written, 'And they were at peace'. Rav Huna explained that "struggled" means that the strength and vigor OF THE HEART AND LIVER, THE LEADERS OF THE BODY, were broken, BECAUSE THE EVIL INCLINATION WAS REMOVED. Rabbi Yehuda asks: What does the body say then? The body asks: 'If it be so, why am I thus?' and 'Why was I created?' Immediately, "she went to inquire of Hashem" (Beresheet 25:22).

60. וַיֹּאמֶר ה' לָהּ שְׁנֵי גוֹיִם בְּבִטְנֵךְ וּשְׁנֵי לְאֻמִּים וְגוֹ'. אֵלּוּ הַשְּׁנֵי גֵאִים, הַכָּבֵד וְהַלֵּב. רַבִּי יוֹסֵי אָמַר, הַמֹּחַ וְהַלֵּב. רַבִּי יְהוּדָה אָמַר, הַמֹּחַ אֵין בִּכְלָל זֶה, מַשְׁמַע דִּכְתִיב בְּבִטְנֵךְ, וְהַמֹּחַ אֵין בַּבֶּטֶן אֶלָּא בָּרֹאשׁ. וּשְׁנֵי לְאֻמִּים מִמֵּעַיִךְ וְגוֹ', וְרַב יַעֲבֹד צָעִיר, זֶהוּ הַכָּבֵד, שֶׁהוּא רַב וְגָדוֹל, וְהוּא מְשַׁמֵּשׁ לִפְנֵי הַלֵּב, דְּאָמַר רַבִּי יְהוּדָה, הַכָּבֵד קוֹלֵט הַדָּם, וּמְשַׁמֵּשׁ בּוֹ לִפְנֵי הַלֵּב.

60. "And Hashem said to her, 'Two nations are in your womb, and two peoples...'" (Beresheet 25:23). These are the two proud ones, the liver and the heart. Rabbi Yosi said that these are the brain and the heart, but Rabbi Yehuda said: The brain is not included in this, for it is written, "in your womb (lit. 'belly')," and the brain is not in the belly, but in the head. "And two peoples...from your bowels...and the elder (lit. 'great') shall serve the younger." This is the liver, which is great and big, and which serves the heart, as Rabbi Yehuda said: The liver receives the blood, and serves it to the heart!

61. וַיֵּצֵא הָרִאשׁוֹן אַדְמוֹנִי. אָמַר רַב כַּהֲנָא, הַכָּבֵד הוּא הָרִאשׁוֹן וְהוּא אַדְמוֹנִי, לָמָּה הוּא אַדְמוֹנִי, עַל שֶׁבּוֹלֵעַ אֶת הַדָּם תְּחִלָּה. רַבִּי אֱלִיעֶזֶר

אוֹמֵר, לָמָּה נִקְרָא שְׁמוֹ רִאשׁוֹן, עַל שֶׁהוּא רִאשׁוֹן, לִבְלוֹעַ הַדָּם, מִכָּל
הַמַּאֲכָל, וְהוּא רִאשׁוֹן לַדָּם אֲבָל לֹא לַיְצִירָה. וּבְמַאן נוֹקִים וְרַב יַעֲבוֹד
צָעִיר, עַל שֶׁהוּא רַב וְגָדוֹל בְּשִׁעוּרוֹ מִן הַלֵּב, וְהוּא עוֹבֵד לַלֵּב. אָמַר
רַבִּי אַבָּא, לָמָּה אֲתָא פַּרְשְׁתָּא דָא, אֶלָּא לְאַחֲזָאָה לִבְנֵי עָלְמָא, דְּאַף
עַל גַּב דְּהַהִיא שְׁלִימוּתָא לֶיהֱוֵי בְּאַרְעָא, אָרְחֵיהּ וְטִבְעֵיהּ דְּעָלְמָא לָא
אִשְׁתַּנֵּי. רַבִּי יֵיסָא אֲמַר בֹּא וּרְאֵה הַכָּבֵד הוּא הַצָּד צַיִד וְהוּא צַיִד בְּפִיו,
וְהַלֵּב הוּא הַחוֹשֵׁב, וְהוּא יוֹשֵׁב אֹהָלִים הה"ד וַיָּזֶד יַעֲקֹב נָזִיד, חוֹשֵׁב
מַחֲשָׁבוֹת, נוֹשֵׂא וְנוֹתֵן בַּתּוֹרָה.

61. "And the first came out red" (Beresheet 25:21). Rav Kahana explained that the liver is the first and is red. Why is it red? Because it is first to swallow the blood. Rabbi Eliezer asks: Why is it called 'first'? Because it is the first to swallow the blood from all the food; the first in blood but not in creation. And why is it that "the great shall serve the younger?" Because despite its being greater and bigger in size than the heart, it serves the heart. Rabbi Aba then asks: What is the purpose of this text if not to teach the people in the world that though there will be perfection upon earth, the path and nature of the world will not change? Rabbi Yisa said: Come and behold. The liver hunts and has venison in its mouth, while the heart contemplates and is "dwelling in tents" (Ibid. 27). As it is written, "And Jacob cooked pottage" (Ibid. 29), while thinking deep thoughts and occupying himself with the Torah.

62. וַיָּזֶד יַעֲקֹב נָזִיד. רַבִּי בָּא בְּשֵׁם רַבִּי אֲחָא אָמַר, לְעוֹלָם טִבְעוֹ שֶׁל
עוֹלָם אֵינוֹ מִשְׁתַּנֶּה, בֹּא וּרְאֵה, מַה כְּתִיב, וַיָּזֶד יַעֲקֹב נָזִיד, כְּדָבָר אַחֵר
אֲשֶׁר זָדוּ עֲלֵיהֶם, וְתַרְגּוּמוֹ דַּחֲשִׁיבוּ. כְּלוֹמַר, הַלֵּב חוֹשֵׁב וּמְהַרְהֵר
בַּתּוֹרָה, בִּידִיעַת בּוֹרְאוֹ, מַה כְּתִיב, וַיָּבֹא עֵשָׂו מִן הַשָּׂדֶה וְהוּא עָיֵף.
הַכָּבֵד שֶׁדֶּרֶךְ טִבְעוֹ, לָצֵאת וְלָצוּד צַיִד בְּפִיו לִבְלוֹעַ, וְאֵינוֹ מוֹצֵא, נִקְרָא
עָיֵף, וְהוּא אוֹמֵר לַלֵּב, עַד שֶׁאַתָּה מְהַרְהֵר בִּדְבָרִים אֵלּוּ בְּד"ת, הַרְהֵר
בַּאֲכִילָה וּבִשְׁתִיָּה, לְקַיֵּים גּוּפְךָ, הה"ד, וַיֹּאמֶר עֵשָׂו אֶל יַעֲקֹב הַלְעִיטֵנִי
נָא מִן הָאָדֹם הָאָדֹם הַזֶּה, כִּי כֵן דַּרְכִּי לִבְלוֹעַ הַדָּם, וּלְשַׁגֵּר לִשְׁאָר
הָאֵבָרִים, כִּי עָיֵף אָנֹכִי, בְּלֹא אֲכִילָה וּשְׁתִיָּה. וְהַלֵּב אוֹמֵר, תֵּן לִי

הָרִאשׁוֹן וְהַמּוּבְחָר מִכָּל מַה שֶׁתִּבְלַע, תֵּן לִי בְּכוֹרָתְךָ, הֲדָא הוּא דִּכְתִיב מִכְרָה כַיּוֹם אֶת בְּכוֹרָתְךָ לִי, קוֹנְמִיתָא דְּתָאִיבָא, עַד שֶׁהַלֵּב מְהַרְהֵר וְחוֹשֵׁב בַּמַּאֲכָל, בּוֹלֵעַ הַכָּבֵד, דְּאִלְמָלֵי הַהוּא כִּסּוּפָא וְהִרְהוּרָא דְּלִבָּא בַּמַּאֲכָל, לֹא יוּכְלוּ הַכָּבֵד, וְהָאֵבָרִים לִבְלוֹעַ דְּאָמַר רִבִּי יוֹסֵי, כֵּן דֶּרֶךְ הָעֲבָדִים, שֶׁאֵינָם אוֹכְלִים עַד שֶׁהָאָדוֹן אוֹכֵל.

62. "And Jacob cooked pottage." In the name of Rabbi Acha, Rabbi Bo said that the nature of the world never changes. Come and behold: it is written, "And Jacob cooked pottage (Heb. *nazid*)," as in the verse "they dealt (Heb. *zadu*)" (Shemot 18:11), which was translated into Aramaic as "they thought." It means that the heart thinks of and contemplates Torah, which represents the knowledge of its Creator. Thus, it is written: "and Esau came from the field, and he was faint" (Beresheet 25:29). It is the nature of the liver to go out hunting and swallow with its mouth. If it does not find any prey, it becomes tired and says to the heart: 'Before you think of the words of Torah, think of eating and drinking to nourish your body.' This is the meaning of the verse, "and Esau said to Jacob 'Give me to swallow, I pray you, of that red pottage,'" for it is my way to swallow the blood and transmit it to the other parts; "for I am faint," without food and drink. And the heart replies: 'Give me the first and choicest of whatever you swallow, give me your birthright,' this is the meaning of "Sell me this day your birthright" (Ibid. 31). That is, swear by your desire. As the heart contemplates food, the liver swallows. If it were not for the heart, longing and thinking about food, the liver and other organs would not be able to swallow. As Rabbi Yosi said: This is the way of slaves, who do not to eat before their master.

63. אָמַר רִבִּי יוֹסֵי, כְּתִיב לְאַחַר כֵּן, וְיַעֲקֹב נָתַן לְעֵשָׂו לֶחֶם וּנְזִיד עֲדָשִׁים, מַהוּ עֲדָשִׁים, סְגַלְגַּלִּין כְּגַלְגַּלְתָּא, וְגַלְגַּלָּא סָבֵיב בְּעָלְמָא, כְּלוֹמַר, דְּלָא אִתְנְשֵׁי מֵאָרְחֵיה. כָּךְ הוּא בַּר נָשׁ, בְּהַהוּא זִמְנָא אַף עַל גַּב דְּכָל הַהוּא טִיבוּ, וִיקָר וּשְׁלֵימוּתָא לֶיהֱוֵי, אָרְחֵיה דְּעָלְמָא לְמֵיכַל וּלְמִשְׁתֵּי לָא יִתְנְשֵׁי.

63. Rabbi Yosi said: It is later written, "Then Jacob gave Esau bread and pottage of lentils" (Beresheet 25:34). What are these lentils? HE ANSWERS:

They are round as a circle, and as the circle which revolves around the world does not deviate from its path, so man in that time will never deviate from his. Although there will yet be all that is good and precious and perfect, with all that, the worldly habit of eating and drinking will not change.

64. מַתְנִיתִין, תְּנָן אַרְבַּע רוּחוֹת הָעוֹלָם מְנַשְׁבָן, וְעָתִיד קוּדְשָׁא בְּרִיךְ הוּא לְהִתְעוֹרֵר רוּחַ אֶחָד, לְקַיֵּם הַגּוּף, שֶׁיְּהֵא כָּלוּל מִד' רוּחוֹת, הה"ד מֵאַרְבַּע רוּחוֹת בֹּאִי הָרוּחַ, בְּאַרְבַּע לָא כְתִיב, אֶלָּא מֵאַרְבַּע רוּחוֹת הָעוֹלָם, שֶׁיְּהֵא כָּלוּל מֵאַרְבַּעְתָּם. וְתָאנָא, אוֹתוֹ הָרוּחַ, הוּא רוּחַ הַמּוֹלִיד, הוּא הָרוּחַ הָאוֹכֵל וְשׁוֹתֶה וְאֵין בֵּין הָעוֹלָם הַזֶּה לִימוֹת הַמָּשִׁיחַ, אֶלָּא שֶׁעְבּוּד מַלְכִיּוֹת בִּלְבָד, וְאֵין בֵּין עוֹלָם הַזֶּה, לִתְחִיַּית הַמֵּתִים, אֶלָּא נְקִיּוּת וְהַשָּׂגַת יְדִיעָה. רַב נַחְמָן אָמַר וַאֲרִיכוּת יָמִים.

64. We learned in the Mishnah that four winds blow in the world, and the Holy One, blessed be He, will raise one spirit to establish the body to include four spirits, as it is written: "Come from the four winds, O breath" (or: spirit) (Yechezkel 37:9). It is not written, 'in the four,' but, "from the four winds," for it will be composed of the four of them. We learned that this spirit (or: wind) is the wind that procreates, the wind that eats and drinks. And there is no difference between this world and the days of Messiah's coming, save the delivery from servitude to the empires alone, and there is no difference between this world and the resurrection of the dead, save cleanliness and the attainment of knowledge. Rav Nachman added longevity.

8. The gathering of the exiles and the resurrection of the dead

A Synopsis

The Rabbis, here, discuss the timing of the Resurrection after the coming of Messiah. Using Torah verses, they demonstrate that it is possible to tell the difference between the timing of the Resurrection of the righteous from that of the good. We're told that the evil people of our world will not experience Resurrection. Rabbi Elazar expresses his sorrow at the thought that the vast majority of mankind will have to wait longer than the righteous – although those who repent during their lives help advance the time of their own Resurrection.

The Relevance of this Passage

Evolving a consciousness of repentance is the first step in hastening our own redemption and eventual Resurrection after the arrival of the Messiah. The Light of this passage stimulates feelings of repentance and helps hasten the arrival of the Messiah, and thus, Resurrection for the entire world.

65. אָמַר רַב יוֹסֵף וְכִי יְמוֹת הַמָּשִׁיחַ וּתְחִיַּית הַמֵּתִים לַאו חַד הוּא. אָמַר לוֹ לֹא, דִּתְנַן, בֵּית הַמִּקְדָּשׁ, קוֹדֶם לְקִבּוּץ גָּלִיּוֹת, קִבּוּץ גָּלִיּוֹת, קוֹדֶם לִתְחִיַּית הַמֵּתִים, וּתְחִיַּית הַמֵּתִים הוּא אַחֲרוֹן שֶׁבְּכֻלָּם. מנ"ל דִּכְתִיב בּוֹנֵה יְרוּשָׁלַיִם ה' נִדְחֵי יִשְׂרָאֵל יְכַנֵּס הָרוֹפֵא לִשְׁבוּרֵי לֵב וּמְחַבֵּשׁ לְעַצְּבוֹתָם. זוֹ הִיא תְּחִיַּית הַמֵּתִים, שֶׁהִיא הָרְפוּאָה לִשְׁבוּרֵי לֵב, עַל מֵתֵיהֶם. בּוֹנֶה יְרוּשָׁלַם תְּחִלָּה, וְאַחֲרָיו נִדְחֵי יִשְׂרָאֵל יְכַנֵּס, וְהָרוֹפֵא לִשְׁבוּרֵי לֵב אַחֲרוֹן עַל הַכֹּל.

65. Rav Yosef asks if the days of Messiah's coming and the resurrection of the dead are the same. He responded: No, as we have learned that the building of the Temple precedes the gathering of the exiles, which precedes the resurrection of the dead. The resurrection of the dead is the last act of all. We know this from the verse, "Hashem builds Jerusalem: He gathers together the outcasts of Yisrael. He heals the broken-hearted, and binds up their wounds" (Tehilim 147:2-3). This refers to the resurrection of the dead, which is the healing of the brokenhearted and their dead. First He builds Jerusalem; then He gathers the outcasts of Yisrael; last of all, He heals the brokenhearted.

‫66. תְּנַן, מ' שָׁנָה קוֹדֶם הַקִּבּוּץ גָּלִיּוֹת, לִתְחִיַּית הַמֵּתִים, כִּדְאַמְרִינָן‬
‫וַיְהִי יִצְחָק בֶּן אַרְבָּעִים שָׁנָה. הַאי מ' שָׁנָה, מַאי עֲבִידְתַּיְיהוּ. אָמַר רַב‬
‫כַּהֲנָא אָמַר רָבִּי בְּרוֹקָא, מִקִּבּוּץ גָּלִיּוֹת עַד תְּחִיַּת הַמֵּתִים, כַּמָּה צָרוֹת,‬
‫כַּמָּה מִלְחָמוֹת יִתְעוֹרְרוּ עַל יִשְׂרָאֵל, וְאַשְׁרֵי הַנִּמְלָט מֵהֶם, דִּכְתִיב בָּעֵת‬
‫הַהִיא יִמָּלֵט עַמְּךָ כָּל הַנִּמְצָא כָּתוּב בַּסֵּפֶר. רָבִּי יְהוּדָה אָמַר מֵהָכָא,‬
‫יִתְבָּרְרוּ וְיִתְלַבְּנוּ וְיִצָּרְפוּ רַבִּים. רָבִּי יִצְחָק אָמַר מֵהָכָא, וּצְרַפְתִּים‬
‫כִּצְרוֹף אֶת הַכֶּסֶף וּבְחַנְתִּים כִּבְחוֹן אֶת הַזָּהָב. וּבְאוֹתָם הַיָּמִים, יִהְיוּ‬
‫יָמִים, אֲשֶׁר יֹאמְרוּ אֵין לִי בָהֶם חֵפֶץ, וּמִשָּׁעָה שֶׁיַּעַבְרוּ הַצָּרוֹת עַד‬
‫תְּחִיַּית הַמֵּתִים מ' שָׁנָה.‬

66. We have learned that the gathering of the exiles preceded the raising of the dead by forty years, as it is written: "And Isaac was forty years old." What is to be made of these forty years? According to Rav Kahana, Rabbi Broka said: How many troubles, how many wars waged against the children of Yisrael will there be from the gathering of the exiles until the resurrection of the dead. He who escapes them is happy, as it is written, "and at that time your people shall be delivered, every one who shall be found written in the book" (Daniel 12:1). Rabbi Yehuda said that this teaches us, "Many shall purify themselves, and make themselves white, and be tried" (Ibid. 10). Rabbi Yitzchak added, "and will refine them as silver is refined, and will try them as gold is tried" (Zecharyah. 13:9). During these very days, there will be days when people will say, "I have no pleasure in them" (Kohelet 12:1). And from the time the troubles disappear until the resurrection of the dead there will be forty years.

‫67. רַב הוּנָא אָמַר תָּא חֲזֵי כִּי אַרְבָּעִים שָׁנָה הָלְכוּ בְנֵי יִשְׂרָאֵל בַּמִּדְבָּר‬
‫וְגו' אֲשֶׁר לֹא שָׁמְעוּ בְּקוֹל ה', כְּהַאי גַוְונָא הָכָא. אָמַר רָבִּי יוֹסֵף, כָּל‬
‫אִלֵּין חַד מִלָּה אָמְרוּ, וּלְסוֹף מ' שָׁנָה, שֶׁהַצָּרוֹת יַעַבְרוּ, וְהָרְשָׁעִים יִכְלוּ,‬
‫יִחְיוּ הַמֵּתִים שׁוֹכְנֵי עָפָר, מ"ט, מִשּׁוּם דִּכְתִיב לֹא תָקוּם פַּעֲמַיִם צָרָה,‬
‫וְדַי לָהֶם בַּמֶּה שֶׁעָבְרוּ. וּמִזְּמַן תְּחִיַּית הַמֵּתִים, יִתְיַישֵׁב עָלְמָא בְּיִשׁוּבוֹ,‬
‫הה"ד בַּיּוֹם הַהוּא יִהְיֶה ה' אֶחָד וּשְׁמוֹ אֶחָד.‬

67. Rav Huna said: Come and behold. "For the children of Yisrael walked forty years in the wilderness...because they obeyed not the voice of Hashem" (Yehoshua 5:6). In this verse, it is the same. Rabbi Yosef said: Everything that was said is the same, but for one thing. At the end of forty years, when the troubles pass away and the wicked are exterminated, the dead, the dwellers of the dust, shall live. Why? Because it is written: "affliction shall not rise up the second time" (Nechemyah 1:9). They had their fill with what they had. After the resurrection of the dead, the world will be settled, as it is written, "on that day Hashem shall be One and His Name One" (Zecharyah 14:9).

68. ר' אֶלְעָזָר בֶּן עֲרָךְ, הֲוָה יָתִיב, וַהֲוָה קָא מִצְטַעֵר בְּנַפְשׁוֹי טְפֵי, עָאל לְקַמֵּיהּ רִבִּי יְהוֹשֻׁעַ, א"ל, חֵיזוּ נְהִירוּ דְּבוֹצִינָא דְּעָלְמָא לָמָּה חֲשׁוֹכָן, אֲמַר לֵיהּ, חֵיזוּ וּדְחִילוּ סַגִּי עָאל בִּי, דְּהָא אֲנָא חָמֵי מַה דְּאִתְעָרוּ חַבְרָנָא, מָארֵי מַתְנִיתָא, דְּשַׁרְאַת עֲלַיְיהוּ רוּחַ קַדִּישִׁין, וְהַהוּא דְּאִתְעָרוּ, דִּבְשְׁתִיתָאֵי יְהֵא פּוּרְקָנָא שַׁפִּיר, אֲבָל אֲנָא חָמֵי אוֹרְכָא יְתֵירָא, עַל אִינּוּן דַּיְירֵי עַפְרָא, דְּבְאֶלֶף שְׁתִיתָאֵי לִזְמַן אַרְבַּע מֵאוֹת וּתְמַנְיָא שְׁנִין מִנֵּיהּ, יְהוֹן קַיְימִין כָּל דַּיְירֵי עַפְרָא בְּקִיּוּמֵיהוֹן, וּבְגִינֵי כָּךְ אִתְעָרוּ חֲבֵירָנָא, עַל פְּסוּקָא דִּקְרָא לוֹן בְּנֵי חֵת, ח"ת, דְּיִתְעָרוּן לְח"ת שָׁנָה, וְהַיְינוּ דִּכְתִיב בִּשְׁנַת הַיּוֹבֵל הַזֹּאת תָּשׁוּבוּ אִישׁ אֶל אֲחֻזָּתוֹ, כְּשֶׁיִּשְׁתַּלֵּם הַזֹא"ת, שֶׁהוּא חֲמֵשֶׁת אֲלָפִים וְאַרְבַּע מֵאוֹת וּתְמַנְיָא, תָּשׁוּבוּ אִישׁ אֶל אֲחֻזָּתוֹ, אֶל נִשְׁמָתוֹ, שֶׁהִיא אֲחוּזָתוֹ וְנַחֲלָתוֹ.

68. Rabbi Elazar was sitting and was exceedingly sad. Rabbi Yehoshua came before him and asks why the appearance of the candlelight of the world had become dark. He said: Great fear entered me, for I see how the companions versed in the Mishnah have responded on whom the spirit of saints dwells. They said that redemption will be in the sixth millennium. This was well said, but I see a longer time for the dwellers of the dust, who shall wait until the four hundred and eighth year of the sixth millennium, when they will rise. For this reason, the companions were stimulated by the verse that referred to THE DWELLERS OF DUST as the children of Chet, for Chet alludes to their rising after four hundred and eight (Heb. *Chet Tav*) years. As it is written, "In the year of this Jubilee you shall return every man to his possession" (Vayikra 25:13), when this (Heb. *hazot*) shall be finished. The numerical value of Hazot is 5,408, AS THE *HEI* OF *HAZOT* ALLUDES TO

THE *Hei* (= 5) THOUSANDS; AND *ZOT* IS 408 IN NUMERICAL VALUE. Then, "you shall return every man to his possession," means that THE BODY will return to its soul, which is its possession and lot.

69. אָמַר רָבִּי יְהוֹשֻׁעַ לֹא תִּקְשֵׁי לָךְ הַאי, דְּהָא תָּנִינָן ג׳ כִּתּוֹת הֵן, שֶׁל צַדִּיקִים גְּמוּרִים, וְשֶׁל רְשָׁעִים גְּמוּרִים, וְשֶׁל בֵּינוֹנִים, צַדִּיקִים גְּמוּרִים יְקוּמוּן בְּקִימָה שֶׁל מֵתֵי אֶרֶץ יִשְׂרָאֵל, מֵהַיּוֹם כַּמָּה שָׁנִים, שֶׁהֵם קוֹדְמִים בַּתְּחִלָּה, בִּשְׁנַת הָאַרְבָּעִים שֶׁל קִבּוּץ גָּלֻיּוֹת, וְהָאַחֲרוֹנִים כֻּלָּם, לִזְמַן אַרְבַּע מֵאוֹת וּשְׁמֹנֶה שָׁנָה, לָאֶלֶף הַשִּׁשִּׁי, כְּדְקָאֲמָרָן. מָאן יִזְכֶּה לְהַאי אָרְכָּא, מָאן יִתְקַיֵּים בְּקִיּוּם דָּתֵיה בֵּין הַאי זִמְנָא, וְעַל דָּא אִצְטַעֵירְנָא בְּנַפְשָׁאי.

69. Rabbi Yehoshua said: This LENGTH OF TIME should not be difficult for you, as we have learned that there are three classes: the Completely Righteous, the Completely Wicked, and the Average. The completely righteous will rise with the resurrection of the dead of the land of Yisrael a few years earlier THAN THE FOUR HUNDRED AND EIGHTH YEAR, namely, at the fortieth year after the gathering of the exiles. In the end, everybody will rise at the four hundred and eighth year of the sixth millennium. Who will merit this length of time? He who will keep the precepts at that time. For that reason, I am sad.

70. אָמַר לֵיה, רִבִּי, הָא תָּנִינָן, יְהִי אוֹר, יְהִי רָ"ז. חָזַר וְאָמַר, בִּתְשׁוּבָה יִתְקַדֵּם כֹּלָּא. אָמַר רִבִּי יְהוֹשֻׁעַ, אִי לָאו דַּאֲמַרְתְּ הָכֵי, אַחְסִימְנָא פּוּמִין, לִמְצַפֵּי פּוּרְקָנָא כָּל יוֹמָא, דִּכְתִיב חֹסֶן יְשׁוּעוֹת, מַהוּ יְשׁוּעוֹת, אֵלּוּ הַמְצַפִּים יְשׁוּעוֹת בְּכָל יוֹם.

70. He said to him: Rabbi, we have studied the verse, "Let there be light," (Beresheet 1:2) which means let there be secret, BECAUSE LIGHT IS THE SECRET OF REDEMPTION. AND THE NUMERICAL VALUE OF *Or* ('LIGHT') IS *Raz* ('SECRET'). THUS, THE VERSE, "LET THERE BE LIGHT," HINTS THAT THE TIME OF REDEMPTION WILL BE A SECRET UNKNOWN TO ALL MEN. RABBI ELAZAR BEN ARACH HINTED THAT HE DISAGREED WITH THIS LONG PERIOD. Again, he said that through repentance everyone will RISE FROM THE DEAD early. Rabbi Yehoshua said: Unless you said so, we

would not have left an opening for those waiting daily for redemption, as it is written, "a store of salvation" (Yeshayah 33:6). What is this "salvation"? It alludes to those who seek salvation daily. IF REDEMPTION IS TIED TO A SPECIFIC TIME, HOW CAN IT BE EXPECTED DAILY? THIS ASSUREDLY DEPENDS UPON REPENTANCE. WHEN THEY REPENT, THEY WILL BE REDEEMED. AND FORTY YEARS AFTER REDEMPTION THE RESURRECTION OF THE DEAD WILL COME, AS WAS SAID.

71. מַאי הוּא דַעְתּוֹי דְּרִבִּי אֶלְעָזָר. הַיְינוּ דִכְתִיב, וְרַבִּים מִיּשֵׁנֵי אַדְמַת עָפָר יָקִיצוּ, מַשְׁמַע דִּכְתִיב מִיּשֵׁנֵי, אֵלּוּ הֵם הַצַּדִּיקִים, הַנִּקְדָּמִים בְּחַיֵּיהֶם קוֹדֶם זֶה. וְכַמָּה שָׁנִים הֵם נִקְדָּמִים, רִבִּי יְהוּדָה אוֹמֵר מָאתַיִם וְעֶשֶׂר שָׁנִים. רִבִּי יִצְחָק אוֹמֵר, רד"י שָׁנָה, דִּכְתִיב וְיֵר"ד מִיַּעֲקֹב וְגוֹ'. יר"ד שָׁנָה, נִקְדָּמִים הַצַּדִּיקִים, לִשְׁאָר כָּל אָדָם. רַב נַחְמָן אָמַר, לְפִי הַשִּׁיעוּר שֶׁנִּבְלָה בֶּעָפָר. אָמַר לוֹ רִבִּי יוֹסֵי, אִם כֵּן הַרְבֵּה תְחִיּוֹת הָווּ, אֶלָּא כָּל הַתְּחִיּוֹת יִהְיוּ בְּאוֹתוֹ הַזְּמַן וְהַאי דְּאִתְּמַר בְּחֶזְוֹן וֶאֱמֶת הַדָּבָר וְצָבָא גָדוֹל.

71. HE ASKS HIM: What is the opinion of Rabbi Elazar, WHO SAID THAT IT DEPENDED ON REPENTANCE? HOW DID HE KNOW THIS? HE ANSWERS: From the verse, "And many of those who sleep in the dust of the earth shall awake" (Daniel 12:2). It is understood by, "those who sleep," THAT ONLY SOME WILL RISE; these are the Righteous WHO REPENTED while they were alive, who will rise early. FOR THROUGH REPENTANCE, THEY SHALL RISE A FEW YEARS EARLY. HE ASKS: By how many years do they precede other people? Rabbi Yehuda replied: By two hundred and ten years. Rabbi Yitzchak said: *Resh Dalet Yud* ('210') years, as it is written, "Out of Jacob shall come (Heb. *Yerd, Yud Resh Dalet*) a ruler" (Bemidbar 24:19). This indicates that the Righteous precede other men by two hundred and ten years. Rav Nachman said: Precedence depends on how much the body is worn in the dust, THAT IS, THE SOONER THE BODY WEARS OUT IN THE DUST, THE SOONER IT RISES. Rabbi Yosi said to him: If this be true, then there are many resurrections, FOR EACH BODY HAS ITS OWN RESURRECTION ACCORDING TO ITS WEARING OUT IN THE DUST. HE ANSWERS: All revivals will occur at the same time, as was said in the vision: "and the word was true, and for a long period ahead" (Daniel 10:1).

72. וַיְהִי רָעָב בָּאָרֶץ מִלְּבַד הָרָעָב הָרִאשׁוֹן אֲשֶׁר הָיָה בִּימֵי אַבְרָהָם. רַבִּי אַבָּהוּ פָּתַח וַאֲמַר, עַד שֶׁהַמֶּלֶךְ בִּמְסִבּוֹ נִרְדִּי נָתַן רֵיחוֹ. דִּתְנִינָן אַרְבַּע תְּקוּפוֹת, וְאַרְבַּע זְמַנִּים מְשׁוּנִים זוֹ מִזּוֹ, יַעַבְרוּ הַצַּדִּיקִים לֶעָתִיד לָבֹא. הָאֶחָד, אוֹתוֹ זְמַן יִשְׂגָּא הַחָכְמָה בָּעוֹלָם, וְיַשִּׂיגוּ הַשָּׂגָה, מַה שֶׁלֹּא הִשִּׂיגוּ בָּזֶה הָעוֹלָם, דִּתְנִינָן, אָמַר רַבִּי פִּנְחָס, הַשָּׂגַת הַצַּדִּיקִים לֶעָתִיד לָבֹא, יוֹתֵר מִמַּלְאֲכֵי הַשָּׁרֵת דִּכְתִיב כַּמַּיִם לַיָּם מְכַסִּים הַשֵּׁנִי תִּתְעַסְקוּן:

(עד כאן מדרש הנעלם)

72. "And there was a famine in the land, beside the first famine that was in the days of Abraham" (Beresheet 26:1). Rabbi Abahu opened the discussion with the verse: "While the king was reclining at his board, my spike nard sent forth its fragrance" (Shir Hashirim 1:12). We learned that the righteous will pass through four eras and four times, each different from the other. During the first, knowledge will increase in the world, and the righteous will conceive what they have not conceived in this world. As we have learned from Rabbi Pinchas, in the future, the perception of the righteous will be greater than that of the ministering angels, as it is written, "as the waters cover the sea" (Yeshayah 11:9). During the second time, you shall be occupied.

(End of Midrash Hane'elam)

9. "And the boys grew...for he relished his venison"

A Synopsis

The discussion moves to a more profound understanding of the metaphor of Esau as a hunter. Even in the womb, Jacob was drawn to The Creator, while Esau was drawn to idolatry. As a cunning hunter, Esau stole the minds of men and led them astray so that they would rebel against The Creator. As the Rabbis probe the issue of why Isaac did not know these things about his son, we discover that the Shechinah wanted only Jacob to be blessed with the spirit of The Creator, which is precisely what transpired.

The Relevance of this Passage

The verses pertaining to Esau's coercing men into idolatry, function as a kind of spiritual homeopathy. Just as the cure for a deadly snake bite resides within the venom of the snake, the remedy for strengthening our consciousness against temptations of the material world resides within the verses that speak these matters. We also draw the Light of the Shechinah into our lives through the merit of Jacob.

73. וַיִּגְדְּלוּ הַנְּעָרִים. סִטְרָא דְאַבְרָהָם גָּרִים לוֹן לְאִתְגַּדְּלָא, וּזְכוּתֵיהּ סַיְּיע לוֹן, הוּא הֲוָה מְחַנֵּךְ לוֹן בְּמִצְוֹת, דִּכְתִיב, כִּי יְדַעְתִּיו לְמַעַן אֲשֶׁר יְצַוֶּה אֶת בָּנָיו וגו', לְאַסְגָּאָה יַעֲקֹב וְעֵשָׂו. וַיִּגְדְּלוּ הַנְּעָרִים וַיְהִי עֵשָׂו אִישׁ יוֹדֵעַ צַיִד וגו'. אָמַר רִבִּי אֶלְעָזָר, כָּל חַד וְחַד, אִתְפְּרַשׁ לְאָרְחֵיהּ דָּא לְסִטְרָא דִמְהֵימְנוּתָא, וְדָא לְסִטְרָא דַּעֲבוֹדָה זָרָה.

73. "And the boys grew..." (Beresheet 25:27). This refers to the side of Abraham, THE RIGHT SIDE, WHICH IS CHASSADIM AND which caused them to grow. His merit supported them, for he was teaching them the precepts, as it is written: "For I know him, that he will command (Et) his children" (Beresheet 18:19). THE PARTICLE ET means that Jacob and Esau are included AMONG HIS SONS. Therefore, the explanation of, "And the boys grew," IS THAT THEY GREW IN HOLINESS, ONLY AFTERWARDS ESAU BECAME CORRUPTED. Rabbi Elazar disagreed. HE BELIEVES THAT each went his own way – one toward s faith, and the other towards idolatry.

74. וְכֵן הֲוָה בִּמְעוֹי דְרִבְקָה, דְּתַמָּן כָּל חַד אָזִיל לְסִטְרֵיהּ, דְּכַד אִיהִי

אִשְׁתַּדְּלַת בְּעוֹבָדִין דְּכַשְׁרָן, אוֹ עֲבָרַת סְמִיךְ לַאֲתָר טָב, לְמֶעְבַּד פְּקוּדֵי
דְּאוֹרַיְיתָא, הֲוָה יַעֲקֹב חָדֵי, וְדָחִיק לְנָפְקָא, וְכַד הֲוַות אָזְלָא, סְמִיךְ
לַאֲתָר ע"ז, הַהוּא רָשָׁע בָּטַשׁ לְנָפְקָא, וְאוֹקִמוּהָ. וּבְגִין כָּךְ, כַּד
אִתְבְּרִיאוּ וּנְפָקוּ לְעָלְמָא, כָּל חַד אִתְפְּרַשׁ, וְאָזִיל וְאִתְמְשַׁךְ בְּדוּכְתֵּיהּ.
דְּאִתְחֲזֵי לֵיהּ, וְעַל דָּא, וַיִּגְדְּלוּ הַנְּעָרִים וַיְהִי עֵשָׂו אִישׁ יוֹדֵעַ צַיִד וְגוֹ'.

74. So it was. While still in Rivkah's womb, each went toward his own side. When she was performing good deeds or passing near a place that is favorable to the precepts of Torah, Jacob was glad and struggled to come out. And when she walked past a place of idolatry, the wicked one struggled to come out. This has already been explained. For that reason, when they were born into the world, each was drawn to the place he deserved. Therefore it is written, "And the boys grew: and Esau was a cunning hunter..." WHICH MEANS THAT HE LED PEOPLE ASTRAY TO REBEL AGAINST HASHEM.

75. וַיֶּאֱהַב יִצְחָק אֶת עֵשָׂו כִּי צַיִד בְּפִיו, הָא אוֹקִמוּהָ, דִּכְתִיב, אִישׁ
יוֹדֵעַ צַיִד אִישׁ שָׂדֶה. וּכְתִיב הָתָם, הוּא הָיָה גִּבּוֹר צַיִד אִישׁ שָׂדֶה,
לְקַפְּחָא לוֹן לִבְנֵי נָשָׁא, וּלְקַטְלָא לוֹן, וְאִיהוּ אָמַר דַּעֲבֵיד צְלוֹתָא, וְצַיֵּיד
לֵיהּ בְּפוּמֵיהּ. אִישׁ שָׂדֶה, בְּגִין דְּחוּלָק עַדְבֵיהּ, לָאו אִיהִי בְּיִשׁוּבָא,
אֶלָּא בַּאֲתָר חָרוּב, בְּמַדְבְּרָא, בְּחַקְלָא, וְעַל דָּא אִישׁ שָׂדֶה.

75. "And Isaac loved Esau, for he relished his venison" (Beresheet 24:28). This verse has been explained. Here, it is written: "a cunning hunter, a man of the field," while elsewhere it is written, "he was a mighty hunter" (Beresheet 10:9). THERE IT MEANS THAT HE DELUDED MEN AND LED THEM ASTRAY TO REBEL AGAINST HASHEM; HERE, IT MEANS THE SAME. THUS, "a man of the field" is one who robbed and murdered people. And ESAU said HE WENT TO THE FIELD to pray, AS IT IS WRITTEN OF ISAAC: "AND ISAAC WENT OUT TO MEDITATE IN THE FIELD" (BERESHEET 24:63). He hunted AND CHEATED ISAAC through his mouth, AS IT IS WRITTEN, "HE RELISHED HIS VENISON (LIT. THERE WAS VENISON IN HIS MOUTH)." HE WAS CALLED "a man of the field," because his lot was not in a populated place, but in a desolate place, in the open wilderness, in the field. Thus, he was called "a man of the field."

76. וְאִי תֵימָא, הֵיךְ לָא יָדַע יִצְחָק, כָּל עוֹבָדוֹי בִּישִׁין דְּעֵשָׂו, וְהָא שְׁכִינְתָּא הֲוַת עִמֵּיהּ, דְּאִי לָא שַׁרְיָא עִמֵּיהּ שְׁכִינְתָּא, הֵיךְ יָכִיל לְבָרְכָא לֵיהּ לְיַעֲקֹב, בְּשַׁעְתָּא דְּבָרְכֵיהּ. אֶלָּא וַדַּאי, שְׁכִינְתָּא הֲוַת דַּיְּירָא עִמֵּיהּ בְּבֵיתָא, וְדַיְּירָא עִמֵּיהּ תָּדִיר, אֲבָל לָא אוֹדְעָא לֵיהּ, בְּגִין דְּיִתְבָּרֵךְ יַעֲקֹב בְּלָא דַעְתֵּיהּ, אֶלָּא בְּדַעְתֵּיהּ דְּקוּדְשָׁא בְּרִיךְ הוּא, וְהָכֵי אִצְטְרִיךְ, דִּבְהַהִיא שַׁעְתָּא דְּעָאל יַעֲקֹב קַמֵּי אֲבוּהִי, עָאלַת עִמֵּיהּ שְׁכִינְתָּא, וּכְדֵין חָמָא בְּדַעְתּוֹי יִצְחָק, דְּאִתְחֲזֵי לְבָרְכָא, וְיִתְבָּרֵיךְ מִדַּעְתָּא דִשְׁכִינְתָּא.

76. You may ask why Isaac did not know of all the wicked deeds of Esau, as the Shechinah was with him AND HE SHOULD HAVE KNOWN IT THROUGH THE HOLY SPIRIT. For without the Shechinah, how could he have blessed Jacob when he did? Assuredly, the Shechinah dwelt in his house and was with him always. But the Shechinah did not inform him of that, because Jacob was to be blessed only with the knowledge of the Holy One, blessed be He. And so it had to be. For when Jacob came before his father, the Shechinah came with him, and then Isaac saw in his mind that Jacob was worthy of being blessed and that he would be blessed by the approval of the Shechinah.

10. "And Jacob cooked a pottage…"

A Synopsis

Rabbi Shimon discourses on the character of Jacob, and the fact that Esau despised his birthright. The Torah tells us that Isaac bestowed numerous blessings upon his son Jacob, all the while thinking it was Esau. Although Isaac did not know Esau's evil side, this was in order to preserve the purity of his blessing of Jacob. However, Jacob did know about Esau, and he dealt with his brother in a manner that enabled him to avoid defilement. The discussion also describes the exact manner in which Jacob embodied judgment, mercy, and subtlety.

The Relevance of this Passage

Despite his highly spiritual nature, Jacob was cunning enough to receive his father's blessing – for he was fully aware of the enemy he confronted in his brother Esau. The dark side of our nature is cunning and sly, endlessly deceiving us into making wrong choices. We must be as cunning and clever as our Evil Inclination. If we remain passive and complacent, our negative traits will control us. Summoning the shrewdness of Jacob through the spiritual influences of this passage, imbues us with artful and deft intellectual power to outwit the Other Side.

77. תָּא חֲזֵי זִמְנָא חָדָא, הֲוָה יָתִיב רַבִּי שִׁמְעוֹן, וּשְׁאָר חַבְרַיָּיא, עָאל קַמֵּיה רַבִּי אֶלְעָזָר בְּרֵיה, אָמְרוּ לֵיה לְר' שִׁמְעוֹן, מִלְתָא רַבְתָא בְּעֵינָן לְמִבְעֵי קַמָּךְ, בְּעִנְיָינָא דְיַעֲקֹב וְעֵשָׂו, אֵיךְ לָא בָּעָא יַעֲקֹב, לְמֵיהַב לְעֵשָׂו, תַּבְשִׁיל דִּטְלוֹפְחִין, עַד דְּזַבִּין לֵיה בְּכֵירוּתָא דִּילֵיה, וְעוֹד דְּאָמַר עֵשָׂו לְיִצְחָק אֲבוּהִי, וַיַּעְקְבֵנִי זֶה פַעֲמָיִם.

77. Come and behold: Rabbi Shimon was sitting with the other friends, when his son, Rabbi Elazar, appeared. The friend said to Rabbi Shimon: We have an important question to ask you concerning Jacob and Esau. Why was Jacob unwilling to give Esau a pottage of lentils unless he sold him his birthright? In addition, Esau said to Isaac, his father, "for he has supplanted me these two times" (Beresheet 27:36). HOW CAN JACOB DECEIVE ESAU?

78. אָמַר לוֹן, בַּהֲדֵין שַׁעְתָּא, אַתּוּן חַיָּיבִים לְקַבְּלָא מַלְקוֹת, דְּהָאֱמְנָתוּן

לְפִתְגָמֵי דְעֵשָׂו, וְשַׁקַרְתּוּן לְפִתְגָמֵי דְיַעֲקֹב, דְהָא קְרָא אַסְהַד עֲלֵיהּ, וְיַעֲקֹב אִישׁ תָּם, וְתוּ כְּתִיב תִּתֵּן אֱמֶת לְיַעֲקֹב. אֶלָּא, כָּךְ הוּא עִנְיָינֵיהּ דְיַעֲקֹב עִם עֵשָׂו, בְּגִין דְעֵשָׂו הֲוָה סָנֵי לִבְכֵירוּתָא בְּקַדְמֵיתָא, וַהֲוָה בָּעֵי מִנֵּיהּ דְיַעֲקֹב, דְלִסְבָּהּ לֵיהּ אֲפִילוּ בְּלָא כֶסֶף, הה"ד וַיֹּאכַל וַיֵּשְׁתְּ וַיָּקָם וַיֵּלַךְ וַיִּבֶז עֵשָׂו אֶת הַבְּכוֹרָה.

78. He responded: Now you deserve a whipping, because you believed Esau and lied about Ya'akov's words. The scripture bears witness that "Jacob was a plain man" (Beresheet 25:27), WHICH MEANS THAT HE CAN NOT CHEAT. Also, it is written: "You will show truth to Jacob" (Michah 7:20). This was the situation concerning Jacob and Esau. Even before, Esau detested his birthright, and he asked Jacob to take the birthright without payment! Thus, it is as written: "and he did eat and drink, and rose up, and went his way: thus Esau despised the birthright" (Beresheet 25:34).

79. וַיָּזֶד יַעֲקֹב נָזִיד וַיָּבֹא עֵשָׂו מִן הַשָּׂדֶה וְהוּא עָיֵף. אָמַר רִבִּי אֶלְעָזָר, וַיָּזֶד יַעֲקֹב, הָא אוּקְמוּהָ דְהָא בְּגִין אֲבֵלוּתָא דְאַבְרָהָם הֲוָה, אֲבָל וַיָּזֶד יִצְחָק נָזִיד מִבָּעֵי לֵיהּ, אֶלָּא וַיָּזֶד יַעֲקֹב נָזִיד, דְאִיהוּ הֲוָה יָדַע עִקָּרָא דִילֵיהּ, בְּהַהוּא סִטְרָא דְאִתְדַּבַּק בֵּיהּ, וּבְגִין כָּךְ עֲבַד תַּבְשִׁילִין סוּמְקִין, עֲדָשִׁים, תַּבְשִׁיל סוּמְקָא, דְתַבְשִׁילָא דָא, מִתְבַּר חֵילָא וְתוּקְפָּא דְדָמָא סוּמְקָא בְּגִין לְתַבְרָא תּוּקְפֵּיהּ וְחֵילֵיהּ, וּבְגִין כָּךְ, עֲבַד לֵיהּ בְּחָכְמְתָא, כְּהַהוּא גְוָונָא סוּמְקָא.

79. Of the verse, "And Jacob cooked a pottage: and Esau came from the field, and he was faint," Rabbi Elazar explained that, "And Jacob cooked," refers to the mourning for Abraham, WHO HAD DIED ON THAT DAY. AND JACOB COOKED ROUND LENTILS, WHICH HAVE NO MOUTH. THIS ALLUDES TO THE MOURNERS, WHO ARE WITHOUT A MOUTH. HE ASKS: But should not it have been written, 'And Isaac cooked a pottage,' SINCE HE, AND NOT JACOB, WAS THE MOURNER? HE ANSWERS: "Jacob cooked a pottage," because Jacob knew the origin of Esau and the side he cleaved to. Therefore, he cooked red dishes, namely, red lentils, for this dish breaks the power and might of the red blood, AND CAN BREAK THE POWER AND MIGHT OF ESAU, WHO IS THE SECRET OF THE RED BLOOD, AS IT IS

WRITTEN: "AND THE FIRST CAME OUT RED" (BERESHEET 25:25).

80. וְעַל הַהוּא תַּבְשִׁילָא, אִזְדַּבַּן לֵיהּ לְעַבְדָּא, וְזַבִּין בְּכֵירוּתֵיהּ לְיַעֲקֹב וּבְהַהִיא שַׁעֲתָא יָדַע יַעֲקֹב, דִּבְגִין שָׂעִיר חַד, דְּיַקְרִיבוּן יִשְׂרָאֵל לְגַבֵּי דַרְגָּא דִּילֵיהּ, יִתְהַפֵּךְ לְעַבְדָּא לִבְנוֹי, וְלָא יְקַטְרֵג לוֹן, וּבְכֹלָּא אֲזַל יַעֲקֹב לְגַבֵּי דְעֵשָׂו בְּחָכְמְתָא, בְּגִין הַהוּא דַרְגָּא חַכִּים דְּעֵשָׂו, וְלָא יָכִיל לְשַׁלְטָאָה, וְאִתְכַּפְיָא וְלָא אִסְתָּאַב בֵּיתֵיהּ וְאִיהוּ יָגִין עֲלֵיהּ.

80. For that dish, by selling Jacob his birthright, Esau became a slave. Instantly, Jacob knew that for the one goat that the children of Yisrael sacrificed on Yom Kippur to his level – NAMELY, "TO AZAZEL INTO THE WILDERNESS," (VAYIKRA 16:10) THE SECRET OF THE SAMAEL, THE MINISTER OF ESAU – he becomes a slave to his descendants and will not accuse them. And because of the level of wisdom of Esau, Jacob dealt wisely with Esau everywhere, so that Esau was unable to rule and was submissive. Jacob was not defiled by him, but ruled over him.

81. וַיֹּאמֶר עֵשָׂו אֶל יַעֲקֹב הַלְעִיטֵנִי נָא מִן הָאָדֹם הָאָדֹם הַזֶּה, אַמַּאי כְּתִיב תְּרֵי זִמְנֵי הָאָדֹם, אֶלָּא, בְּגִין דְּכֹל מַה דְּאִית בֵּיהּ אָדֹם, כִּדְבָר אַחֵר וַיֵּצֵא הָרִאשׁוֹן אַדְמוֹנִי. וְתַבְשִׁילוֹ אָדֹם, דִּכְתִיב מִן הָאָדֹם הָאָדֹם הַזֶּה, וְאַרְעָא דִּילֵיהּ אֲדוּמָה, דִּכְתִיב אַרְצָה שֵׂעִיר שְׂדֵה אֱדוֹם, וְגוּבְרִין דִּילֵיהּ אֲדוּמִין, דִּכְתִיב הוּא עֵשָׂו אֲבִי אֱדוֹם, וּמַאן דְּזַמִּין לְאִתְפָּרְעָא מִנֵּיהּ אָדֹם, דִּכְתִיב דּוֹדִי צַח וְאָדֹם, וּלְבוּשֵׁיהּ אָדֹם, דִּכְתִיב מַדּוּעַ אָדֹם לִלְבוּשֶׁךָ, וּכְתִיב מִי זֶה בָּא מֵאֱדוֹם.

81. We do not accept this paragraph, for it does not belong in the discussion.

82. אָמַר רַבִּי יְהוּדָה, וְכֵן בְּלָבָן אִתְחֲזֵי הָכִי, בְּגִין דְּהָא אִיהוּ חָרָשָׁא הֲוָה, כְּמָה דִּכְתִיב נִחַשְׁתִּי וַיְבָרֲכֵנִי יְיָ' בִּגְלָלֶךָ, וְאַף עַל גַּב דְּיַעֲקֹב אִקְרֵי גְּבַר שָׁלִים, בְּגִין כָּךְ הֲוָה שָׁלִים, עִם מַאן דְּאִצְטְרִיךְ לֵיהּ לְמֵיהַךְ עִמֵּיהּ בְּרַחֲמֵי הֲוָה אָזִיל, וְעִם מַאן דְּאִצְטְרִיךְ לְמֵיהַךְ עִמֵּיהּ בְּדִינָא קַשְׁיָא, וּבַעֲקִימוּ, הֲוָה אָזִיל, בְּגִין דִּתְרֵי חוּלָקֵי הֲווֹ בֵּיהּ, וַעֲלֵיהּ כְּתִיב עִם חָסִיד

תִּתְחַסָּד, וְעִם עִקֵּשׁ תִּתְפַּתָּל. עִם חָסִיד בְּסִטְרָא דְּחֶסֶ״ד, וְעִם עִקֵּשׁ בְּסִטְרָא דְּדִינָא קַשְׁיָא, כֹּלָּא כִּדְקָא יָאוֹת.

82. Rabbi Yehuda said that this should have been true of Laban as well, because he was also a sorcerer, as it is written: "I have learned by signs that Hashem has blessed me for your sake" (Beresheet 30:27). THEREFORE JACOB WAS DECEITFUL TOWARD HIM. And although Jacob was a plain and whole man, he was merciful with whomever he had to be merciful with. He was strict in judgment and deceitful when necessary. For he consisted of two parts, CHESED AND JUDGMENT, FOR JACOB IS THE SECRET OF THE CENTRAL COLUMN, WHICH COMPRISES THE TWO COLUMNS, CHESED AND GVURAH. It is written of him: "With the merciful you will show yourself merciful; ...and with the perverse you will show yourself subtle" (Tehilim 18:26), which means that with the merciful HE DEALT on the side of Chesed, and with the perverse on the side of Strict Judgment, all as it ought to be.

11. "And there was a famine in the land..."

A Synopsis

The Rabbis discuss The Creator's testing of the righteous, and His treatment of the wicked. There is a delay in executing judgment against the wicked in order to give them time to repent. The Creator, we're told, tests the righteous in order to help them lift up their heads. The discussion shows how this applies to Adam, Abraham, Noah, and Isaac; then Rabbi Shimon expounds on the need for an understanding of the relationship between soul, body, and the Shechinah. We learn that it is only when the soul is reunited with Shechinah that is truly worthy.

The Relevance of this Passage

A child learns to walk by falling down and standing up again. Measured against a lifetime of walking, this period of continual stumbling is relatively short. Similarly, the hardships and afflictions in our lives are learning opportunities. They are sent to us to help us learn to walk in the ways of The Creator. When we understand our afflictions in this way, their duration is brief compared to a lifetime of spiritual fulfillment. Conversely, when life appears strangely calm and placid, The Creator may be delaying judgments against us for self-centered behavior. We should be wary of our connection to the Light during these moments and begin to reflect with humility and repentance.

83. וַיְהִי רָעָב בָּאָרֶץ מִלְּבַד הָרָעָב הָרִאשׁוֹן וְגוֹ'. ר' יְהוּדָה פְּתַח וְאֲמַר, יי' צַדִּיק יִבְחָן וְרָשָׁע וְאוֹהֵב חָמָס שָׂנְאָה נַפְשׁוֹ. כַּמָּה עוֹבָדוֹי דְּקוּדְשָׁא בְּרִיךְ הוּא מִתְתַּקְּנָן, וְכָל מַה דְּאִיהוּ עָבֵיד, כֹּלָּא עַל דִּינָא וּקְשׁוֹט, כְּמָה דִּכְתִיב הַצּוּר תָּמִים פָּעֳלוֹ כִּי כָל דְּרָכָיו מִשְׁפָּט אֵל אֱמוּנָה וְאֵין עָוֶל צַדִּיק וְיָשָׁר הוּא.

83. "And there was a famine in the land..." (Beresheet 26:1). Rabbi Yehuda opened the discussion with the verse: "Hashem tries the righteous: but the wicked and him who loves violence His soul hates" (Tehilim 11:5). How orderly and right are the deeds of the Holy One, blessed be He, and all He does is according to justice and truth, as it is written, "He is the Rock, His work is perfect..." (Devarim 32:4).

84. תָּא חֲזֵי, לָא דָן קוּדְשָׁא בְּרִיךְ הוּא לְאָדָם קַדְמָאָה, עַד דְּפַקִּיד לֵיהּ

לְתוֹעַלְתֵּיהּ, דְּלָא יִסְטֵי לִבֵּיהּ וּרְעוּתֵיהּ לְאָרַח אָחֳרָא, בְּגִין דְּלָא יִסְתָּאַב, וְאִיהוּ לָא אִסְתַּמַּר, וַעֲבַר עַל פִּקּוּדֵי דְמָארֵיהּ, וּלְבָתַר כֵּן דָּן לֵיהּ דִּינָא.

84. Come and behold: the Holy One, blessed be He, did not judge Adam before He commanded him for his own good not to let his heart and will stray in another direction – THAT IS, NOT TO EAT FROM THE TREE OF KNOWLEDGE – so that he would not be defiled. But he was not careful, and transgressed the precepts of his Master BY EATING FROM THE TREE OF KNOWLEDGE. Then the Holy One, blessed be He, judged him.

85. וְעִם כָּל דָּא, לָא דָן לֵיהּ, כְּדְקָא חָזֵי לֵיהּ, וְאוֹרִיךְ עִמֵּיהּ רוּגְזֵיהּ, וְאִתְקַיַּים יוֹמָא חַד, דְּאִיהוּ אֶלֶף שְׁנִין, בַּר אִינּוּן שִׁבְעִים שָׁנִים, דִּמְסַר לֵיהּ לְדָוִד מַלְכָּא, דְּלָא הֲוָה לֵיהּ מִגַּרְמֵיהּ כְּלוּם.

85. Even then, the Holy One, blessed be He, did not judge him as harshly as he deserved, THAT IS, ACCORDING TO THE VERSE: "FOR ON THE DAY THAT YOU EAT OF IT YOU SHALL SURELY DIE" (BERESHEET 2:17). He refrained from wrath and let him be among the living for one day, THAT IS, THE DAY OF THE HOLY ONE, BLESSED BE HE, which is one thousand years, AS IT IS WRITTEN: "FOR A THOUSAND YEARS IN YOUR SIGHT ARE BUT LIKE YESTERDAY WHEN IT IS PAST" (TEHILIM 90:4), minus the seventy years that he gave to king David, who had no life of his own. THEREFORE HE LIVED 930 YEARS, NAMELY, ONE THOUSAND YEARS MINUS SEVENTY.

86. כְּגַוְונָא דָא, לָא דָן לֵיהּ לְבַר נָשׁ, כְּעוֹבָדוֹי בִּישִׁין דְּאִיהוּ עָבֵיד תָּדִיר, דְּאִי הָכֵי, לָא יָכִיל עַלְמָא לְאִתְקַיְּימָא, אֶלָּא קוּדְשָׁא בְּרִיךְ הוּא, אָרִיךְ רוּגְזֵיהּ עִם צַדִּיקַיָּא, וְעִם רְשִׁיעַיָּא, יַתִּיר מִצַּדִּיקַיָּא, עִם רְשִׁיעַיָּא, בְּגִין דִּיתוּבוּן בִּתְיוּבְתָּא שְׁלֵימָתָא, דְּיִתְקַיְּימוּן בְּהַאי עַלְמָא, וּבְעַלְמָא דְאָתֵי, כְּמָה דִכְתִיב חַי אָנִי נְאֻם יְיָ' וְגוֹ' אִם אֶחְפֹּץ וְגוֹ' כִּי אִם בְּשׁוּב רָשָׁע מִדַּרְכּוֹ וְחָיָה. וְחָיָה בְּעַלְמָא דֵין, וְחָיָה בְּעַלְמָא דְאָתֵי, וְעַל דָּא אוֹרִיךְ רוּגְזֵיהּ לוֹן תָּדִיר. אוֹ בְּגִין דְּיִפּוֹק מִנְּהוֹן גִּזְעָא טָבָא בְּעַלְמָא,

כְּמָה דְּאַפֵּיק אַבְרָהָם מִתֶּרַח, דְּאִיהוּ גִּזְעָא טָבָא, וְשָׁרְשָׁא וְחוּלָקָא טָבָא לְעַלְמָא.

86. Similarly, THE HOLY ONE, BLESSED BE HE, does not judge man according to his evil deeds, which he continually does, for if He did so, the world would not have survived. But the Holy One, blessed be He, refrains from wrath with the Righteous and the wicked. With the wicked, HE IS EVEN more FORBEARING than with the righteous, so that they may repent completely and exist in this world and in the World to Come. As it is written: "'As I live,' says Adonai Elohim. 'I have no pleasure in the death of the wicked; but that the wicked turn from his way and live'" (Yechezkel 33:11), WHICH MEANS to live in this world and in the World to Come. For that reason, He is always forbearing. Another reason is that good stock may issue from them, as Abraham was begotten of Terah, who issued good stock and good origin and portion in the world.

87. אֲבָל קוּדְשָׁא בְּרִיךְ הוּא מְדַקְדֵּק עִם צַדִּיקַיָּא תָּדִיר, בְּכָל עוֹבָדִין דְּאִינּוּן עָבְדִין בְּגִין דְּיָדַע דְּלָא יִסְטוּן לְיָמִינָא וּשְׂמָאלָא, וּבְגִין כָּךְ אַבְחִין לוֹן, לָאו בְּגִינֵיה, דְּהָא אִיהוּ יָדַע יִצְרָא וְתוּקְפָא דִּמְהֵימְנוּתָא דִּלְהוֹן, אֶלָּא בְּגִין לַאֲרָמָא רֵישֵׁיהוֹן בְּגִינַיְיהוּ.

87. But the Holy One, blessed be He, is always strict with the Righteous in every deed they do. Because He knows they will not turn away, neither to the right nor the left, He constantly tests them. Not for His own sake DOES THE HOLY ONE, BLESSED BE HE, TEST THEM, as He knows their desire and the firmness of their faith and has no need of trying them. He tries them only to lift up their heads, to give them confidence as they earn their merits through these EXPERIENCES.

88. כְּגַוְונָא דָּא, עֲבַד לֵיהּ לְאַבְרָהָם, דִּכְתִיב וְהָאֱלֹהִים נִסָּה אֶת אַבְרָהָם, מַאי נִסָּה, הֲרָמַת נֵס, כְּמָה דְּאַתְּ אָמֵר הָרִימוּ נֵס, שְׂאוּ נֵס, אָרֵים דִּגְלָא דִּילֵיהּ בְּכָל עָלְמָא, וְאַף עַל גַּב דְּהָא אִתְּמַר, בְּגִין דָּא קוּדְשָׁא בְּרִיךְ הוּא אָרֵים דִּגְלָא דְּאַבְרָהָם, בְּעֵינַיְיהוּ דְּכֹלָּא, הֲדָא הוּא דִּכְתִיב נִסָּה אֶת אַבְרָהָם, אוּף הָכֵי קוּדְשָׁא בְּרִיךְ הוּא, בְּגִין לַאֲרָמָא

דְּגְלָא דְצַדִּיקַיָא, אִיהוּ בָּחִין לוֹן, לְאַרְמָא רֵישַׁיְיהוּ בְּכָל עַלְמָא.

88. THE HOLY ONE, BLESSED BE HE, behaved similarly toward Abraham, as it is written: "that the Elohim did test Abraham" (Beresheet 22:1). What is meant by "test (Heb. *nisah*)?" It means the raising of the banner (Heb. *nes*), as it is written: "lift up a standard" (Yeshayah 62:10), and "set up the standard" (Yirmeyah 4:6). He raised his standard over the whole world. And for this, FOR THE TEST AT THE SACRIFICE, the Holy One, blessed be He, raised the banner of Abraham before everybody's eyes, as it is written: "did test Abraham." Thus the Holy One, blessed be He, in order to lift the standard of the righteous, tries them, so they will lift up their heads throughout the world.

89. צַדִּיק יִבְחָן, מַאי טַעְמָא, אָמַר רִבִּי שִׁמְעוֹן בְּגִין דְּקוּדְשָׁא בְּרִיךְ הוּא, כַּד אִתְרְעֵי בְּהוֹ בְּצַדִּיקַיָא, מַה כְּתִיב, וַיְיָ' חָפֵץ דַּכְּאוֹ הֶחֱלִי. וְאוֹקְמוּהָ. אֲבָל בְּגִין דִּרְעוּתָא דְּקוּדְשָׁא בְּרִיךְ הוּא, לָא אִתְרְעֵי, אֶלָּא בְּנִשְׁמָתָא, אֲבָל בְּגוּפָא לָא, דְּהָא נִשְׁמָתָא, אִיהִי דַּמְיָא לְנִשְׁמָתָא דִּלְעֵילָּא, וְגוּפָא לָאו אִיהוּ חֲזֵי לְאִתְאַחֲדָא לְעֵילָּא, וְאַף עַל גַּב דִּדְיוּקְנָא דְּגוּפָא בְּרָזָא עִלָּאָה אִיהוּ.

89. "…tries the Righteous…" (Tehilim 11:5): What is the reason thereof? According to Rabbi Shimon, it is because the Holy One, blessed be He, wishes for the Righteous. As it is written, "But it pleased Hashem to crush him by disease" (Yeshayah 53:10). This has already been explained. The Holy One, blessed be He, wishes for the soul and not the body, because the soul resembles the supernal soul, NAMELY, THE SHECHINAH, and the body is not worthy of being united WITH THE SHECHINAH above. Thus, although the shape of the body is in the image of the supernal secret, THAT IS, ALTHOUGH THE BODY IS DRAWN FROM THE SHECHINAH, NAMELY MALCHUT, NEVERTHELESS IT IS NOT WORTHY OF BEING UNITED WITH HER.

90. וְתָא חֲזֵי, בְּזִמְנָא דְּקוּדְשָׁא בְּרִיךְ הוּא אִתְרְעֵי בְּנִשְׁמָתֵיהּ דְּבַר נָשׁ, לְאִתְנַהֲרָא בָּהּ, מָחֵי לְגוּפָא, בְּגִין דְּתִשְׁלוֹט נִשְׁמָתָא, דְּהָא בְּעוֹד

דְּנִשְׁמָתָא עִם גּוּפָא, נִשְׁמָתָא לָא יָכְלָא לְשַׁלְטָאָה, דְּכַד אִתְרַע גּוּפָא, נִשְׁמָתָא שָׁלְטָא. צַדִּיק יִבְחָן, מַאי צַדִּיק יִבְחָן, כִּדְבַר אֶחָר אֶבֶן בֹּחַן, הָכֵי נָמֵי צַדִּיק יִבְחָן, אַתְקֵיף לֵיהּ, כְּהַאי אֶבֶן בֹּחַן, דְּהִיא פִּנַּת יְקָרַת, הָכֵי נָמֵי צַדִּיק יִבְחָן.

90. Come and behold: when the Holy One, blessed be He, wishes to illuminate the soul of a man, He crushes the body so that the soul will govern. As long as the soul is with the body, THEY ARE EQUAL, AND the soul can not rule. After the body is crushed, the soul becomes powerful. What is the meaning of the verse: "...tries the righteous..." (Tehilim 11:5)? It is as is written: "...a tried stone..." (Yeshayah 28:16); in the same way He "tries the righteous," which means that He strengthens him by this "tried stone," which is a precious cornerstone. So does He try the righteous!

91. וְרָשָׁע וְאוֹהֵב חָמָס שָׂנְאָה נַפְשׁוֹ, מַאי שָׂנְאָה נַפְשׁוֹ, ס"ד דְּקוּדְשָׁא בְּרִיךְ הוּא הֲוֵי דְּנַפְשׁוֹ שָׂנְאָה לְהַהוּא רָשָׁע. אֶלָּא, הַהוּא דַּרְגָּא דְּכָל נִשְׁמָתִין תַּלְיָין בֵּיהּ, שָׂנְאָה נַפְשׁוֹ דְּהַהוּא רָשָׁע, דְּלָא בָּעְיָא לָהּ כְּלָל, לָא בָּעְיָא לָהּ לָא בְּעָלְמָא דֵּין וְלָא בְּעָלְמָא דְּאָתֵי, וּבְגִין כָּךְ כְּתִיב, וְרָשָׁע וְאוֹהֵב חָמָס שָׂנְאָה נַפְשׁוֹ, וַדַּאי. דָּבָר אֶחָר שָׂנְאָה נַפְשׁוֹ, כִּדְבַר אֶחָר נִשְׁבַּע אֲדֹנָי יֱהוֹה בְּנַפְשׁוֹ, וּבְגִין כָּךְ צַדִּיק יִבְחָן.

91. "but the wicked and him who loves violence his soul hates" (Tehilim 11:5). What is the meaning of "his soul (lit. *Nefesh*) hates"? COULD IT POSSIBLY BE THAT IT ALLUDES TO THE HOLY ONE, BLESSED BE HE, WHOSE NEFESH HATES THE WICKED? FOR THE WORD *NEFESH* IS NOT APPROPRIATE FOR THE HOLY ONE, BLESSED BE HE. The explanation is that the very level upon which all souls depend, MALCHUT, hates the Nefesh of that wicked man. For it does not want it [this soul] TO CLEAVE TO IT in this world or in the World to Come. For that reason, it is written, "but the wicked and him who loves violence his soul hates." Another explanation of, "His soul hates," is as it is written: "Adonai Elohim has sworn by His Nefesh" (Amos 6:8), WHICH MEANS THAT THE WORD *NEFESH* IS USED IN RELATION TO HASHEM. IF SO, THEN THE EXPLANATION IS SIMPLY THAT THE SOUL OF HASHEM HATES THE WICKED AND HIM WHO LOVES VIOLENCE. For that reason He "tries the righteous," for He loves him.

‏92. תָּא חֲזֵי, כַּד בָּרָא קוּדְשָׁא בְּרִיךְ הוּא לְאָדָם, פַּקֵּיד לֵיהּ, לְאוֹטָבָא לֵיהּ, יָהַב לֵיהּ חָכְמְתָא אִסְתַּלָּק בְּדַרְגּוֹי לְעֵילָא, כַּד נָחַת לְתַתָּא, חָמָא תֵּיאוּבְתָּא דְּיֵצֶר הָרַע, וְאִתְדַּבַּק בֵּיהּ, וְאַנְשֵׁי כָּל מַה דְּאִסְתַּלָּק, בִּיקָרָא עִלָּאָה דְּמָרֵיהּ.

92. Come and behold: when the Holy One, blessed be He, created Adam, He commanded him NOT TO EAT OF THE TREE OF KNOWLEDGE, in order to benefit him. He gave him wisdom, so he would ascend through the grades TO THE HOLY ONE, BLESSED BE HE. When he descended, he saw the desires of the Evil Inclination and clung to it, thereby forgetting all that he beheld of the Supernal Glory of his Master.

‏93. אֲתָא נֹחַ, בְּקַדְמֵיתָא כְּתִיב נֹחַ אִישׁ צַדִּיק תָּמִים הָיָה, וּלְבָתַר נָחַת לְתַתָּא, וְחָמָא חַמְרָא תַּקִּיף, דְּלָא צָלֵיל, מֵחַד יוֹמָא, וְאַשְׁתֵּי מִנֵּיהּ, וְאִשְׁתַּכַּר וְאִתְגַּלֵּי, כְּמָה דִּכְתִיב, וַיֵּשְׁתְּ מִן הַיַּיִן וַיִּשְׁכָּר וַיִּתְגַּל בְּתוֹךְ אָהֳלֹה.

93. Of Noah, it is first written: "Noah was a just man and perfect" (Beresheet 6:9). Then he descended and saw strong wine that was one day old and not clear, AS IT WAS FULL OF DREGS. He drank from it, became drunk, and was uncovered, as it is written: "and he drank of the wine, and was drunk; and he was uncovered within his tent" (Beresheet 9:21).

‏94. אֲתָא אַבְרָהָם, אִסְתַּלָּק בְּחָכְמְתָא, וְאִסְתַּכַּל בִּיקָרָא דְּמָארֵיהּ, לְבָתַר וַיְהִי רָעָב בָּאָרֶץ וַיֵּרֶד אַבְרָם מִצְרַיְמָה לָגוּר שָׁם כִּי כָבֵד הָרָעָב בָּאָרֶץ וְגוֹ', לְבָתַר מַה כְּתִיב, וַיַּעַל אַבְרָם מִמִּצְרַיִם הוּא וְאִשְׁתּוֹ וְכָל אֲשֶׁר לוֹ וְלוֹט עִמּוֹ הַנֶּגְבָּה, וְאִסְתַּלָּק לְדַרְגֵּיהּ קַדְמָאָה, דַּהֲוָה בֵּיהּ בְּקַדְמֵיתָא, וְעָאל בִּשְׁלָם, וּנְפַק בִּשְׁלָם.

94. Then Abraham was elevated with wisdom and beheld the glory of his Master. Subsequently, it is written, "And there was famine in the land: and Abram went down to Egypt" (Beresheet 12:10), and "And Abram went up out of Egypt..." (Beresheet 13:1) and was elevated to the grade he had at the beginning. He came in peace and went in peace.

95. אֲתָא יִצְחָק, מַה כְּתִיב, וַיְהִי רָעָב בָּאָרֶץ, מִלְּבַד הָרָעָב הָרִאשׁוֹן
וגו'. וַאֲזַל יִצְחָק וְאִסְתַּלַּק מִתַּמָּן לְבָתַר בִּשְׁלָם, וְכֻלְּהוּ צַדִּיקַיָּיא, כֻּלְּהוּ
בָּחִין לוֹן קוּדְשָׁא בְּרִיךְ הוּא, בְּגִין לְאַרְמָא רֵישַׁיְיהוּ, בְּעַלְמָא דֵּין
וּבְעַלְמָא דְּאָתֵי.

95. And then Isaac, of whom it is written: "And there was a famine in the land..." (Beresheet 26:1). And Isaac went TO GERAR. From there, he later ascended peacefully. And so all the Righteous are tested by the Holy One, blessed be He, to raise their heads in this world and in the World to Come.

12. "And he said, 'She is my sister'"

A Synopsis

Here the discussion explains why Abraham and Isaac replied as above when they were asked about their wives. This episode is linked to the Shechinah, the Divine Presence of Creator in the physical realm. The dual meaning of the word *sister* is revealed as an allusion to the patriarchs own connection to the Shechinah, which is the source of human happiness and protection. The Rabbis further discuss the nature and whereabouts of the dwelling place of the Shechinah, which resides both in their wives and in the Holy Land.

The Relevance of this Passage

The Shechinah can only dwell within us, offering protection and fulfillment, when we are in an appreciative and joyful state of mind. The moment a person feels depressed, negative, or victimized, the Shechinah departs. A positive state of mind and appreciation is summoned forth in this passage, thus drawing the Shechinah into our lives. This Light also serves to enrich our marital relationships.

96. וַיִּשְׁאֲלוּ אַנְשֵׁי הַמָּקוֹם לְאִשְׁתּוֹ וַיֹּאמֶר אֲחוֹתִי הִיא, כְּמָה דַּאֲמַר אַבְרָהָם, בְּגִין דִּשְׁכִינְתָּא הֲוָה עֲמֵיהּ, וְעִם אִתְּתֵיהּ, וּבְגִין שְׁכִינְתָּא קָאֲמַר, דִּכְתִיב אֱמוֹר לַחָכְמָה אֲחוֹתִי אָתְּ, וְעַל דָּא אִתְתַּקַּף, וַאֲמַר אֲחוֹתִי הִיא. תּוּ, אַבְרָהָם וְיִצְחָק, הָכֵי אִתְחֲזֵי, דְּוַדַּאי בְּגִין קְרָא דִּכְתִיב אֲחוֹתִי רַעְיָתִי יוֹנָתִי תַמָּתִי, וּבְגִין כָּךְ וַדַּאי, אִתְחֲזֵי לוֹן לוֹמַר, אֲחוֹתִי הִיא, וְעַ"ד אִתְתַּקָּפוּ צַדִּיקַיָּיא בֵּיהּ בְּקוּדְשָׁא בְּרִיךְ הוּא.

96. "And the men of the place asked him of his wife; and he said, 'She is my sister'" (Beresheet 26:7), that is, just like Abraham said, "SHE IS MY SISTER," REFERRING TO THE SHECHINAH. For the Shechinah was with Isaac and his wife, and he said of the Shechinah, "SHE IS MY SISTER," as it is written, "Say to wisdom: 'you are my sister'" (Mishlei 7:4). Thus, he was strengthened BY THE SHECHINAH and said, "She is my sister." Abraham and Isaac deserved TO SAY OF THE SHECHINAH, "SHE IS MY SISTER." This is assuredly so because of the verse IN WHICH ZEIR ANPIN SAID TO THE SHECHINAH, "My sister, my love, my dove, my undefiled" (Shir Hashirim 5:2). ABRAHAM AND ISAAC WERE A CHARIOT TO ZEIR ANPIN

and were therefore worthy, LIKE ZEIR ANPIN, of saying ABOUT THE SHECHINAH, "She is my sister." Thus, the Righteous were strengthened by the Holy One, blessed be He, THAT IS, THEY BECAME A CHARIOT TO HIM.

97. וַיְהִי כִּי אָרְכוּ לוֹ שָׁם הַיָּמִים וגו'. אֶת רִבְקָה אִשְׁתּוֹ דַּיְיקָא, דָּא שְׁכִינְתָּא, דַּהֲוַת עִמָּה דְּרִבְקָה. דָּבָר אַחֵר, וְכִי ס"ד דְּיִצְחָק הֲוָה מְשַׁמֵּשׁ עַרְסֵיהּ בִּימָמָא, דְּהָא תָּנֵינָן יִשְׂרָאֵל קַדִּישִׁין אִינוּן, וְלָא מְשַׁמְּשֵׁי עַרְסַיְיהוּ בִּימָמָא, וְיִצְחָק דַּהֲוָה קַדִּישׁ הֲוָה מְשַׁמֵּשׁ עַרְסֵיהּ בִּימָמָא.

97. "And it came to pass, when he had been there a long time...with Rivkah his wife" (Beresheet 26:8): IT IS SAID "with (Heb. *et*) Rivkah his wife," precisely, which alludes to the Shechinah that was with Rivkah, BECAUSE *ET* ('WITH'), AS WE KNOW, IS THE NAME OF THE SHECHINAH. Another explanation asks if we could possibly conceive of Isaac performing his marital duties during the daytime. We have learned that the children of Yisrael are holy and abstain from cohabitation in the daytime. Therefore, how could Isaac, who was holy, cohabit during the day?

98. אֶלָּא, וַדַּאי אֲבִימֶלֶךְ חַכִּים הֲוָה, וְאִיהוּ אִסְתַּכַּל בְּאִצְטַגְנִינוּתָא דִּילֵיהּ, דְּאִיהוּ חַלּוֹן, כְּתִיב הָכָא בְּעַד הַחַלּוֹן, וּכְתִיב הָתָם בְּעַד הַחַלּוֹן נִשְׁקְפָה וַתְּיַבֵּב אֵם סִיסְרָא, מַה לְהַלָּן בְּאִצְטַגְנִינוּתָא, אוֹף ה"נ בְּאִצְטַגְנִינוּתָא, וְחָמָא, דְּלָא הֲוָה, כְּמָה דַהֲוָה אָמַר יִצְחָק, אֶלָּא וַדַּאי אִיהוּ מְצַחֵק עִמָּה, וְאִיהִי אִתְּתֵיהּ. וּכְדֵין וַיִּקְרָא אֲבִימֶלֶךְ לְיִצְחָק וַיֹּאמֶר וגו'. רִבִּי יוֹסֵי אָמַר, יָאוֹת הֲוָה אֲבִימֶלֶךְ לְמֶעְבַּד לְיִצְחָק, כְּמָה דַעֲבַד לְאַבְרָהָם, בַּר דְּהָא אוֹכַח לֵיהּ קוּדְשָׁא בְּרִיךְ הוּא בְּקַדְמֵיתָא.

98. HE ANSWERS: Assuredly Abimelech was wise and looked at the wisdom of the stars, that is called a 'window', as it is written here, "out at a window" (Beresheet 26:8), and elsewhere, "The mother of Sisra looked out at a window" (Shoftim 5:28). As THE WINDOW there REFERS TO astrology, so THE WINDOW here REFERS to astrology. And he saw there that it was not as Isaac said, but that he surely was sporting with her, and she was his wife. Then, "Abimelech called Isaac..." (Beresheet 26:9) Rabbi Yosi said that it would have befitted Abimelech to do this to Isaac AND TAKE HIS WIFE, as he did to Abraham, were it not for the Holy One, blessed be He, who

reproved him earlier FOR WHAT HE DID TO ABRAHAM, SAYING "BEHOLD, YOU ARE A DEAD MAN, BECAUSE OF THE WOMAN..." (BERESHEET 20:3).

99. תָּא חֲזֵי, כְּתִיב כִּי אָמַרְתִּי רַק אֵין יִרְאַת אֱלֹהִים בַּמָּקוֹם הַזֶּה, אֲמַר רָבִּי אַבָּא, בְּג״כ אָמַר אֲחוֹתִי הִיא, בְּגִין לְאִתְדַּבְּקָא בִּשְׁכִינְתָּא, דִּכְתִיב אֱמוֹר לַחָכְמָה אֲחוֹתִי אָתְ. מַאי טַעְמָא, בְּגִין דִּבְהוּ לָא הֲוָה מְהֵימְנוּתָא, דְּאִי מְהֵימְנוּתָא, אִשְׁתַּכַּח בֵּינַיְיהוּ, לָא הֲוָה אִצְטְרִיךְ, אֲבָל מִגוֹ דְּלָא הֲוָה בֵּינַיְיהוּ מְהֵימְנוּתָא, אֲמַר הָכִי, וּבְגִין כָּךְ אָמַר כִּי אָמַרְתִּי רַק אֵין יִרְאַת אֱלֹהִים בַּמָּקוֹם הַזֶּה, אֵין יִרְאַת אֱלֹהִים, דָּא מְהֵימְנוּתָא.

99. Come and behold: it is written, "Because I thought, 'Surely the fear of Elohim is not in this place'" (Beresheet 20:11). According to Rabbi Aba, this is the reason why he said, "She is my sister." He wanted to cleave to the Shechinah, as it is written, "Say to wisdom: [NAMELY, THE SHECHINAH] you are my sister." Why? Because they had no faith in them, for if they had faith, he would not have needed that. But because they had no faith, he said, 'SHE IS MY SISTER'. He therefore said, "Because I thought, 'Surely the fear of Elohim is not in this place." The fear of Elohim is Faith.

100. אֲמַר רָבִּי אֶלְעָזָר, בְּגִין דְּלָא שַׁרְיָא שְׁכִינְתָּא, לְבַר מֵאַרְעָא קַדִּישָׁא, וְעַל דָּא אֵין יִרְאַת אֱלֹהִים בַּמָּקוֹם הַזֶּה, דְּלָאו אַתְרֵיהּ הוּא, וְלָא שַׁרְיָא הָכָא, וְיִצְחָק אִתְתַּקַּף בֵּיהּ בִּמְהֵימְנוּתָא, דְּחָמָא דְּהָא שְׁכִינְתָּא גוֹ אִתְּתֵיהּ שַׁרְיָא.

100. Rabbi Elazar said that this is because the Shechinah does not live outside the Holy Land. Therefore, there is no fear of Elohim in this place, AS FEAR MEANS THE SHECHINAH. This is not Her place, and She does not dwell here. And Isaac was strengthened by the faith, WHICH IS THE SHECHINAH, when he saw the Shechinah dwelling in his wife.

13. "And Abimelech charged"

A Synopsis
We learn how the actions and conduct of the righteous people, such as the Patriarch Yitzchak, help to build and strengthen our physical dimension of Malchut. These acts of the righteous are mirrored in our own spiritually significant actions, as in the laying of Tfilin and the donning of Tzitzit.

The Relevance of this Passage
By drawing on the metaphysical power of righteous personages such as Isaac, and also on the spiritual forces released by laying Tfilin and wearing Tzitzit, we build and strengthen our souls. In this way, we ensure that our sojourn in this physical existence will be filled with spiritual growth and enlightenment.

101. וַיְצַו אֲבִימֶלֶךְ אֶת כָּל הָעָם לֵאמֹר הַנּוֹגֵעַ בָּאִישׁ הַזֶּה וּבְאִשְׁתּוֹ מוֹת יוּמָת. תָּא חֲזֵי, כַּמָּה אוֹרִיךְ לְהוּ קוּדְשָׁא בְּרִיךְ הוּא, לְרַשִׁיעַיָּיא, בְּגִין הַהוּא טִיבוּ דַּעֲבַד עִם אֲבָהָן קַמָּאי, דְּהָא בְּגִין דָּא לָא שַׁלִּיטוּ בְּהוּ יִשְׂרָאֵל, עַד לְבָתַר דָּרִין בַּתְרָאִין, יָאוֹת עֲבַד אֲבִימֶלֶךְ, דַּעֲבַד טִיבוּ עִם יִצְחָק, דְּאָמַר לוֹ הִנֵּה אַרְצִי לְפָנֶיךָ בַּטּוֹב בְּעֵינֶיךָ שֵׁב.

101. "And Abimelech charged all his people, saying, 'He that touches this man or his wife shall surely be put to death'" (Beresheet 26:11). Come and behold: how long had the Holy One, blessed be He, refrained from avenging the wicked, for as a result of the good Abimelech did with the first Patriarchs, the children of Yisrael did not rule over the Philistines until generations later. Abimelech did well to act properly toward Isaac, as he said TO ABRAHAM, "Behold, my land is before you: dwell where it pleases you" (Beresheet 20:15). THIS SAYING ALSO ENCOMPASSES THE DESCENDANTS OF ABRAHAM. THIS IS WHY HE KEPT HIS WORD WITH ISAAC AS WELL, AND RABBI ELAZAR PRAISES HIM FOR KEEPING HIS PROMISE.

102. רִבִּי יְהוּדָה אָמַר, חֲבַל עֲלַיְיהוּ דְּרַשִׁיעַיָּיא, דְּטִיבוּתָא דִּלְהוֹן לָאו אִיהוּ שְׁלִים, תָּא חֲזֵי, עֶפְרוֹן בְּקַדְמֵיתָא אָמַר, אֲדֹנִי שְׁמָעֵנִי הַשָּׂדֶה נָתַתִּי לָךְ וְהַמְּעָרָה אֲשֶׁר בּוֹ לְךָ נְתַתִּיהָ וגו'. וּלְבָתַר אָמַר, אֶרֶץ אַרְבַּע

מֵאוֹת שֶׁקֶל כֶּסֶף וגו', וּכְתִיב וַיִּשְׁקוֹל אַבְרָהָם לְעֶפְרוֹן וגו', עוֹבֵר
לַסּוֹחֵר. אוֹף הָכָא, כְּתִיב בְּקַדְמֵיתָא, הִנֵּה אַרְצִי לְפָנֶיךָ וגו'. וּלְבָתַר
אָמַר לוֹ, לֵךְ מֵעִמָּנוּ כִּי עָצַמְתָּ מִמֶּנּוּ מְאֹד. אָמַר לֵיהּ רִבִּי אֶלְעָזָר, דָּא
הוּא טִיבוּ דַּעֲבַד עִמֵּיהּ, דְּלָא נָסִיב מִדִּילֵיהּ אֲבִימֶלֶךְ כְּלוּם, וְשַׁדְּרֵיהּ
בְּכָל מָמוֹנֵיהּ, וּלְבָתַר אֲזַל בַּתְרֵיהּ, לְמִגְזַר עִמֵּיהּ קְיָים.

102. Rabbi Yehuda said: Woe to the wicked, whose generosity is not complete. Come and behold: Efron first said, "my lord, hear me: the field I give you, and the cave that is in it" (Beresheet 23:11). Later he said, "four hundred shekels" (Ibid. 14), and then, "and Abraham weighed to Efron...current money with the merchant" (Ibid. 16). Here too, it is written at first WHAT HE SAID TO ABRAHAM, "Behold, my land is before you," WHICH INCLUDES ISAAC. Then he said TO ISAAC, "Go from us; for you are much mightier than we" (Beresheet 26:16). Rabbi Elazar said to him: This is the benevolence Abimelech had for Isaac. He took nothing from him and sent him away with his money and possessions. Then, he went after him to make a covenant with him.

103. וְאָמַר רְבִּי אֶלְעָזָר, יָאוֹת עֲבַד יִצְחָק, דְּהָא בְּגִין דְּיָדַע רָזָא
דְּחָכְמְתָא, אִשְׁתַּדַּל וְחָפַר בֵּירָא דְּמַיִין, בְּגִין לְאִתְתַּקְּפָא בִּמְהֵימְנוּתָא
כִּדְקָא יָאוֹת, וְכֵן אַבְרָהָם, אִשְׁתַּדַּל וְחָפַר בֵּירָא דְּמַיָּא, יַעֲקֹב אַשְׁכַּח
לֵיהּ מִתְתַּקַּן, וְיָתִיב עֲלֵיהּ וְכֻלְּהוּ אַזְלוּ בַּתְרֵיהּ, וְאִשְׁתַּדָּלוּ, בְּגִין
לְאִתְתַּקְּפָא בִּמְהֵימְנוּתָא שְׁלֵימָתָא כִּדְקָא יָאוֹת.

103. And Rabbi Elazar said that Isaac did well because he knew the secret of wisdom. He strove and dug a well of water, THAT IS, HE FIXED THE NUKVA CALLED A 'WELL OF WATER', so as to be properly invigorated by Faith, WHICH IS THE NUKVA. Abraham also strove and dug a well of water. Jacob found it completed and settled by it. Everybody went after it and strove by it, so as to be strengthened by the true Faith, as is proper.

104. וְהַשְׁתָּא יִשְׂרָאֵל, אִתְתַּקְּפוּ בֵּיהּ בְּרָזֵי דְּפִקּוּדֵי אוֹרַיְיתָא, כְּגוֹן דְּכָל
יוֹמָא וְיוֹמָא אִתְתַּקַּף בַּר נָשׁ בְּצִיצִית, דְּאִיהוּ מִצְוָה, וּבַר נָשׁ אִתְעַטַּף
בֵּיהּ. הָכֵי נָמֵי בִּתְפִלֵּי, דְּמַנַּח אַרֵישֵׁיהּ וּבִדְרוֹעֵיהּ, דְּאִינּוּן רָזָא עִלָּאָה,

כִּדְקָא חֲזֵי, בְּגִין דְקוּדְשָׁא בְּרִיךְ הוּא אִשְׁתַּכַּח בֵּיהּ בְּבַר נָשׁ, דְּאִתְעַטַּר
בֵּיהּ בִּתְפִלּוֹי, וְאִתְעַטַּף בַּצִיצִית, וְכֹלָּא רָזָא דִמְהֵימְנוּתָא עִלָּאָה.

104. Presently, the children of Yisrael are strengthened by THE WELL OF
WATER, THE SECRET OF THE NUKVA, according to the secret of keeping
the commandments of the Torah; NAMELY, every day a man is strengthened
and enveloped by the commandment of the *Tzitzit* ('fringes'), as he also is
by the Tefilin he puts on his head and arm. This is as it should be, for they
are the supernal mystery. For the Holy One, blessed be He, dwells with the
man who is crowned by Tefilin and clothed with the fringes. All is in the
secret of high Faith, NAMELY, THE NUKVA, MEANING THAT SHE IS
AMENDED BY THE PRECEPTS A MAN FOLLOWS.

105. וְעַל דָּא, מַאן דְּלָא אִתְעַטַּף בְּהַאי, וְלָא אִתְעַטַּר לְאִתְתַּקְּפָא
בִּתְפִלֵּי בְּכָל יוֹמָא, דָּמֵי לֵיהּ דְּלָא שַׁרְיָא עִמֵּיהּ מְהֵימְנוּתָא, וְאִתְעֲדֵי
מִנֵּיהּ דְּחִילוּ דְּמָארֵיהּ, וּצְלוֹתֵיהּ לָאו צְלוֹתָא כִּדְקָא יָאוֹת. וּבְגִין כָּךְ
אֲבָהָן הֲווֹ מִתְתַּקְּפֵי גוֹ מְהֵימְנוּתָא עִלָּאָה, בְּגִין דְּבֵירָא עִלָּאָה דְרָזָא
דִמְהֵימְנוּתָא שְׁלֵימָתָא, שַׁרְיָא בֵּיהּ.

105. Therefore, whoever does not wear the fringes and is not invigorated by
the Tefilin daily, appears as if faith does not dwell with him. The fear of his
Master is removed from him, and his prayer is no proper prayer. For this
reason, the fathers were strengthened by the supreme faith, since within the
supernal well dwells whole faith, NAMELY, THE CORRECTED NUKVA.

14. "And he called the name of it Rechovot"

A Synopsis

Here, the Rabbis expound meaning of the Sfirot through a discussion of the World to Come. It is said that the Torah's more mundane verses possess hidden meanings pertaining to the spiritual processes that the patriarchs endured in Upper Worlds. With this insight, we see that the deeds of the righteous are performed in order to preserve our world. This is why they are able to draw down the Shechinah into our lower realm.

The Relevance of this Passage

If we are unaware of the meaning and metaphysical power concealed in the Torah's seemingly uninteresting verses, we are prevented from deriving immense Light and strength from Torah study. This passage offers us the opportunity to ignite sparks of Light by connecting to these veiled meanings. In so doing, we tilt our own actions towards the side of righteousness, thus helping to sustain this world by our very existence.

106. וַיַּעְתֵּק מִשָּׁם וַיַּחְפֹּר בְּאֵר אַחֶרֶת וגו', רִבִּי חִיָּיא פָּתַח וְאָמַר וְנָחֲךָ יי' תָּמִיד וְהִשְׂבִּיעַ בְּצַחְצָחוֹת נַפְשֶׁךָ וְעַצְמֹתֶיךָ יַחֲלִיץ וגו'. הַאי קְרָא אוֹקְמוּהָ וְאִתְּמַר. אֲבָל בְּהַאי קְרָא, בֵּיהּ אִתְתַּקְפוּ מָארֵי מְהֵימְנוּתָא, דְּאַבְטַח לוֹן לְעָלְמָא דְּאָתֵי. וְנָחֲךָ יי' תָּמִיד, בְּהַאי עָלְמָא, וּבְעָלְמָא דְּאָתֵי. וְנָחֲךָ יי', כֵּיוָן דַּאֲמַר וְנָחֲךָ יי', אַמַּאי תָּמִיד. אֶלָּא דָּא תָּמִיד דְּבֵין הָעַרְבָּיִם, דְּאִיהוּ אִתְתַּקַּף תְּחוֹת דְּרוֹעֵיהּ דְּיִצְחָק, וְדָא הוּא חוּלָקָא לְעָלְמָא דְּאָתֵי, מְנָלָן מִדָּוִד דִּכְתִיב יַנְחֵנִי בְּמַעְגְּלֵי צֶדֶק לְמַעַן שְׁמוֹ.

106. "And he removed from there, and dug another well..." (Beresheet 26:22). Rabbi Chiya opened the discussion with the verse, "and Hashem shall guide you continually, and satisfy your soul in drought, and make strong your bones" (Yeshayah 58:11). This verse had already been explained, but by this verse the faithful were strengthened, for it promises them the World to Come. "And Hashem shall guide you continually" in this world and the World to Come. "And Hashem shall guide you." HE ASKS: Because he said, "And Hashem shall guide you," why add the word "continually (Heb. *tamid*)?" For this hints at the daily offering (lit. 'continue') made at dusk that receives its strength from underneath

Yitzchak's arm, AS IT CORRESPONDS TO THE SERVICE OF MINCHAH, THAT ISAAC COMPOSED, WHO IS THE SECRET OF THE ILLUMINATION OF THE LEFT. It is the portion of the World to Come, NAMELY, THE NUKVA, THAT RECEIVES THE PORTION OF CHOCHMAH FROM YISRAEL-SABA AND TEVUNAH, CALLED 'THE WORLD TO COME'. How do we know that "HASHEM SHALL GUIDE YOU CONTINUALLY" REFERS TO THE ILLUMINATION OF THE LEFT? From David, as it is written, "He leads me in the paths of righteousness for His name's sake" (Tehilim 23:3). JUST AS THE WORD "LEADS," SPOKEN BY DAVID, MEANS THE ILLUMINATION OF THE LEFT, AS IT IS WRITTEN, "IN THE PATHS OF RIGHTEOUSNESS," WHICH IS A NAME OF THE NUKVA WHEN SHE SHINES FROM THE LEFT, HERE TOO WHEN IT SAYS "GUIDE," IT ALLUDES TO THE ILLUMINATION OF THE LEFT.

107. וְהִשְׂבִּיעַ בְּצַחְצָחוֹת נַפְשֶׁךָ, דָּא אַסְפַּקְלַרְיָא דְּנָהֲרָא, דְּכָל נִשְׁמָתִין אִתְהֲנָן, לְאִסְתַּכְּלָא וּלְאִתְעֲנָגָא בְּגַוָּוה. וְעַצְמֹתֶיךָ יַחֲלִיץ, הַאי קְרָא, לָאו רֵישֵׁיה סוֹפֵיה, אִי נִשְׁמָתֵיה דְּצַדִּיקָא, סָלְקָא לְעֵילָא מַאי וְעַצְמֹתֶיךָ יַחֲלִיץ. אֶלָּא הָא הָא אוּקְמוּהָ, דָּא תְּחִיַּית הַמֵּתִים, דְּזַמִּין קוּדְשָׁא בְּרִיךְ הוּא לְאַחֲיָיא מֵתַיָּא, וּלְאַתְקָנָא לוֹן לְגַרְמוֹי דְּבַר נָשׁ, לְמֶהֱוֵי כְּקַדְמֵיתָא, בְּגוּפָא שְׁלִים, וְנִשְׁמָתָא אִתּוֹסְפַת נְהוֹרָא גּוֹ אַסְפַּקְלַרְיָאה דְּנָהֲרָא, לְאִתְנַהֲרָא עִם גּוּפָא, לְקָיְימָא שְׁלִים כִּדְקָא חָזֵי.

107. "And satisfy your soul in drought (also: brightness)" (Yeshayah 58:11) refers to the shining lamp, NAMELY, ZEIR ANPIN, THE SECRET OF THE ILLUMINATION OF THE RIGHT, THE SECRET OF CHASSADIM, that all the souls delight in and take pleasure in beholding. The verse ends, "and make strong your bones" (Ibid.). The end does not suit the beginning, for if the soul of the righteous IS SATISFIED, AS SAID BEFORE "AND SATISFY YOUR SOUL IN BRIGHTNESS," WHICH SPEAKS ABOUT THE NEFESH AND NESHAMAH OF THE RIGHTEOUS, why does it now say "and make strong your bones," WHICH TALKS ABOUT THE BONES OF THE BODY? BUT HE ANSWERS that this has already been explained. It refers to the resurrection of the dead, the fact that the Holy One blessed be He, will revive the dead and fix man's bones as they were at first, in a whole body. And Light will be added from the shining lamp so the soul will be illuminated together with the body in a complete whole. THIS WAY, IT REFERS TO THE SOUL OF THE

RIGHTEOUS, TO WHICH THE HOLY ONE, BLESSED BE HE, WILL GIVE A
WHOLE BODY IN WHICH TO BE CLOTHED FOR ETERNITY.

108. וּבְגִּין כָּךְ כְּתִיב, וְהָיִיתָ כְּגַן רָוֶה. מַאי כְּגַן רָוֶה, דְּלָא פָּסְקוּ מֵימוֹי
עִלָּאִין, לְעָלַם וּלְעָלְמֵי עָלְמִין, וְהַאי גִּינְתָּא אִתְשַׁקֵי מִנֵּיהּ, וְאִתְרַוֵּי
מִנֵּיהּ תָּדִיר. וּכְמוֹצָא מַיִם, דָּא הַהוּא נָהָר, דְּנָגִיד וְנָפִיק מֵעֵדֶן, וְלָא
פָּסְקִין מֵימוֹי לְעָלְמִין.

108. For this reason, it is written, "you shall be like a watered garden, and
like a spring of water" (Yeshayah 58:11). HE ASKS: What is this watered
garden? AND HE ANSWERS: Its supernal water, THAT IS, THE ABUNDANT
YIELD OF BINAH, never ceases its eternal flow. This garden, MALCHUT,
always slakes its thirst from it. "a spring of water" refers to that river, which
emerges and flows out of Eden, which waters never cease flowing.

109. תָּא חֲזֵי, בֵּירָא דְּמַיִּין נָבְעִין, הַאי אִיהוּ רָזָא עִלָּאָה, בְּגוֹ רָזָא
דִּמְהֵימְנוּתָא, בֵּירָא דְּאִית בֵּיהּ מוֹצָא מַיִם, וְאִיהוּ בֵּירָא דְּאִתְמַלְיָא
מֵהַהוּא מוֹצָא מַיִם, וְאִינּוּן תְּרֵין דַּרְגִּין דְּאִינּוּן חַד, דְּכַר וְנוּקְבָא כַּחֲדָא
כִּדְקָא יָאוֹת.

109. HE THEN EXPLAINED THE DIFFERENCE BETWEEN THE WATERED
GARDEN AND THE SPRING OF WATER. Come and behold: A well of living
water is the supreme secret, WHICH IS BINAH, within the faith, WHICH IS
MALCHUT. THEN SHE IS a cistern, from where the spring of water, and a
cistern that is filled by that spring of water. These two grades are one,
namely, male and female properly as one.

110. וְתָא חֲזֵי, הַהוּא מוֹצָא מַיִם, וְהַהוּא בֵּירָא, אִינּוּן חַד, וְאִקְרֵי כֹּלָּא
בְּאֵר, דְּהָא הַהוּא מְקוֹרָא דְּעַיֵּיל, וְלָא פָּסִיק לְעָלְמִין, וּבֵירָא אִתְמְלֵי.
וּמַאן דְּאִסְתַּכַּל בְּבֵירָא דָּא, אִסְתַּכַּל בְּרָזָא עִלָּאָה דִּמְהֵימְנוּתָא, וְדָא
הוּא סִימָנָא דַּאֲבָהָן, דְּמִשְׁתַּדְּלֵי לַחְפּוֹר בֵּירָא דְּמַיָּא, גּוֹ רָזָא עִלָּאָה,
וְלֵית לְאַפְרְשָׁא בֵּין מְקוֹרָא וּבֵירָא, וְכֹלָּא חַד.

110. Come and behold: This spring of water and the cistern are one.

Together they are called 'a well'. FOR THE SPRING IS DERIVES FROM ALEPH, AND MALCHUT IS A CISTERN (HEB. *BOR*). TOGETHER THEY FORM THE WELL (HEB. *BE'ER*). For this spring flows INTO MALCHUT and never ceases, so the cistern is always filled. And whoever looks at the well, NAMELY, AT MALCHUT, looks on the supernal mystery of faith, NAMELY, BINAH. And this is the reasoning behind THE LABOR OF the Patriarchs, who strove to dig a well of water in the supernal secret, BINAH. There must be no division between the source, WHICH IS THE SPRING OF WATER, and the cistern itself, for all is one.

111. וַיִּקְרָא שְׁמָהּ רְחוֹבוֹת. (רָמִיז, דְּזַמִּינִין בְּנוֹי, לְמִפְלַח וּלְאַתְקָנָא הַאי בֵּירָא כְּדְקָא חָזֵי, בְּרָזָא דְקָרְבָּנִין וְעִלָּוָון. כְּגַוְונָא דָא, וַיַּנִּיחֵהוּ בְּגַן עֵדֶן לְעָבְדָהּ וּלְשָׁמְרָהּ, אִלֵּין קָרְבָּנִין וְעִלָּוָון) וּבְגִין דָא, יִתְפַּשְּׁטוּן מַבּוּעוֹי לְכָל סִטְרִין כְּדְבָר אַחֵר וְיָפוּצוּ מַעְיְנֹתֶיךָ חוּצָה בָּרְחֹבֹת פַּלְגֵי מָיִם, וּבְגִין כָּךְ וַיִּקְרָא שְׁמָהּ רְחוֹבוֹת.

111. THEN, "and he called the name of it Rechovot" (Beresheet 26:22). For this reason, its springs will spread on all sides, THAT IS, TO THE RIGHT AND THE LEFT, WHICH ARE CHOCHMAH AND CHASSADIM, as it is written, "So will your spring be dispersed abroad, and streams of water will flow in the broad places (Heb. *rechovot*)" (Mishlei 5:16). For this reason, "he called the name of it Rechovot."

112. רִבִּי שִׁמְעוֹן פְּתַח וַאֲמַר, חָכְמוֹת בַּחוּץ תָּרוֹנָה בָּרְחֹבוֹת תִּתֵּן קוֹלָהּ. הַאי קְרָא אִיהוּ רָזָא עִלָּאָה. מַאי חָכְמוֹת, אִלֵּין חָכְמָה עִלָּאָה, וְחָכְמְתָא זְעֵירָא דְּאִתְכְּלִילַת בָּהּ בְּעִלָּאָה, וְשַׁרְיָא בָהּ.

112. Rabbi Shimon began with the verse, "Wisdoms cry aloud in the streets; she utters her voice in the squares (Heb. *rechovot*)" (Mishlei 1:20). This verse contains a deep mystery. Why IS IT WRITTEN IN THE PLURAL, THAT IS, "wisdoms," AND NOT WISDOM? HE SAID: They are the upper wisdom, CHOCHMAH OF ARICH ANPIN, and the lower wisdom that is included and dwells within the upper one, THE LOWER CHOCHMAH, NAMELY, THE NUKVA.

113. בַּחוּץ תָּרוֹנָה. תָּא חֲזֵי, חָכְמָה עִלָּאָה, אִיהִי סְתִימָא דְּכָל סְתִימִין,

וְלָא אִתְיְידַע, וְלָאו אִיהִי בְּאִתְגַּלְיָא, כְּדָבָר אַחֵר לֹא יָדַע אֱנוֹשׁ עֶרְכָּהּ
וגו', כַּד אִתְפַּשְּׁטַת לְאִתְנַהֲרָא, אִתְנַהֲרָא בְּרָזָא דְעָלְמָא דְאָתֵי, וְעָלְמָא
דְאָתֵי אִתְבְּרֵי מִנֵּיהּ, כִּדְתָנָן עַלְמָא דְאָתֵי אִתְבְּרֵי בְּיוּ"ד, וְאִתְכַּסְיָא הַאי
חָכְמָה תַּמָּן, וְאִינּוּן חַד, בְּזִמְנָא דְאִתְעַטַּר כֹּלָּא בְּרָזָא דְעָלְמָא דְאָתֵי,
כְּדְקָאַמְרָן, כְּדֵין הוּא חֶדְוָה, לְאִתְנַהֲרָא, וְכֹלָּא בַּחֲשַׁאי, דְּלָא אִשְׁתְּמַע
לְבַר לְעָלְמִין.

113. "Cry aloud in the streets": Come and behold: The upper Chochmah OF ARICH ANPIN is the most concealed of all. It is not to be known or revealed, as it is written, "Man cannot know its price" (Iyov 28:13), for when it was diffused in order to illuminate, it shone on the secret of the World to Come. This World to Come was created from it, ARICH ANPIN, as we learned, that the World to Come was created by the Yud, in which Chochmah was covered. And they became one WITH THE HEAD OF ARICH ANPIN, when everything was adorned with the secret of the World to Come. Everything then is joyfully luminous, everything is silent, never heard outside.

114. תּוּ בָּעְיָא לְאִתְפַּשְּׁטָא, וְנָפֵיק מֵהַאי אֲתַר, אֶשָׁא וּמַיָא וְרוּחָא, כְּמָה
דְאִתְּמַר, וְאִתְעֲבֵיד חַד קָלָא, דְּנָפְקָא לְבַר וְאִשְׁתְּמַע, כְּמָה דְאִתְּמַר,
כְּדֵין מִתַּמָּן וּלְהָלָן אִיהוּ חוּץ, דְּהָא לְגוֹ בַּחֲשַׁאי אִיהוּ, דְּלָא אִשְׁתְּמַע
לְעָלְמִין, הַשְׁתָּא דְאִשְׁתְּמַע רָזָא, אִקְרֵי חוּץ, מִכָּאן בָּעֵי בַּר נָשׁ
לְאַתְקְנָא בַּעֲבִידְתֵּיהּ וּלְשָׁאֲלָא.

114. It wanted to illuminate further. Thus, from this place came fire, water, and wind, as we have learned. And they became one voice that went out and was heard. From then on, it assumed the aspect of "out." For inside it is silent, SOUNDLESS, never to be heard. Now that the secret is heard, it is called "out." From here on, it behooves a man to improve his deeds and ask, NAMELY TO PRAY AND ELEVATE FEMALE WATER AND DRAW CHOCHMAH. THIS IS LIKE ASKING FOR RAIN.

115. בָּרְחוֹבוֹת, מַאן רְחוֹבוֹת, דָּא הַהוּא רְקִיעָא, דְּבֵיהּ כָּל כֹּכְבַיָּא
דְּנָהֲרִין וְאִיהוּ מַבּוּעָא דְמֵימוֹי לָא פָסְקִין, כְּדָבָר אַחֵר, וְנָהָר יוֹצֵא מֵעֵדֶן
לְהַשְׁקוֹת אֶת הַגָּן, וְאִיהוּ רְחוֹבוֹת, וְתַמָּן תִּתֵּן קוֹלָהּ, עֶלָאָה וְתַתָּאָה,

וְכֹלָּא חַד.

115. "In the squares (Heb. *rechovot*)." HE ASKS: What is the meaning of squares? HE REPLIED, this is the firmament where all the stars are shining, YESOD OF BINAH IN WHICH ARE SUSPENDED THE ENTIRE MOCHIN OF MALE AND FEMALE, AND THE SOULS, WHICH ARE CALLED 'STARS'. It is a spring "whose waters fail not" (Yeshayah 58:11), as it is written, "And a river went out of Eden to water the garden" (Beresheet 2:10). It is called 'Rechovot'. There "she utters her voice," the upper, BINAH, and the lower, MALCHUT. And all is one.

116. וּבְגִין דָּא אֲמַר שְׁלֹמֹה, הָכֵן בַּחוּץ מְלַאכְתֶּךָ וְעַתְּדָהּ בַּשָּׂדֶה לָךְ וְגוֹ'. הָכֵן בַּחוּץ, כְּמָה דְאִתְּמַר. דִּכְתִיב בַּחוּץ תָּרוֹנָה, דְּהָא מִכָּאן קַיְימָא עֲבִידָא לְאִתְתַּקְּנָא, וּמִלָּה לְשָׁאֲלָה, דִּכְתִיב, כִּי שְׁאַל נָא לְיָמִים רִאשׁוֹנִים וְגוֹ', וּלְמִקְצֵה הַשָּׁמַיִם וְעַד קְצֵה הַשָּׁמָיִם.

116. For that reason Solomon said, "Prepare your work outside, and make it fit for yourself in the field" (Mishlei 24: 27). "Prepare...outside" MEANS, as it is written, "cry aloud in the streets," FOR CHOCHMAH IS NOT REVEALED UNTIL IT IS REMOVED FROM INSIDE OUT. For here, IN ZEIR ANPIN, CALLED 'OUTSIDE', work, THE SECRET OF THE NUKVA, can be corrected. And this may be sought, as it is written, "For ask now of the days that are past...and from the one side of heaven to the other" (Devarim 4:32).

117. וְעַתְּדָהּ בַּשָּׂדֶה לָךְ, דָּא שָׂדֶה אֲשֶׁר בֵּרֲכוֹ יְיָ'. וּבָתַר דְּיִנְדַּע בַּר נָשׁ רָזָא דְחָכְמְתָא, וְיִתְקִּין גַּרְמֵיהּ בָּהּ, מַה כְּתִיב אַחַר וּבָנִיתָ בֵיתֶךָ, דָּא נִשְׁמָתָא דְבַר נָשׁ בְּגוּפֵיהּ, דְּיִתְתַּקַן וְיִתְעֲבֵיד גְּבַר שְׁלִים, וְעַל דָּא, כַּד חָפַר יִצְחָק וְעָבַד בֵּירָא בִּשְׁלָם, לְהַהוּא שְׁלָם קָרֵי לֵיהּ רְחוֹבוֹת, וְכֹלָּא כְּדְקָא יָאוֹת. זַכָּאִין אִינוּן צַדִּיקַיָּא, דְּעוֹבָדֵיהוֹן לְגַבֵּי קוּדְשָׁא בְּרִיךְ הוּא לְקַיְּימָא עָלְמָא. דִּכְתִיב כִּי יְשָׁרִים יִשְׁכְּנוּ אָרֶץ, יַשְׁכִּינוּ אָרֶץ. וְהָא אוֹקְמוּהָ.

117. "And make it fit for yourself in the field." This is THE NUKVA CALLED "a field which Hashem has blessed" (Beresheet 27: 27). After learning the mystery of wisdom and perfecting himself therein, it is then written, "and afterwards build your house" (Mishlei 24: 27). A HOUSE IS a man's soul, that he will then fix within his body, to become a whole man. Therefore, when Isaac dug and formed the well peacefully, he called that "peace" Rechovot. And all was properly done. Happy are the Righteous, whose deeds before the Holy One, blessed be He, are to preserve the world, THAT IS, TO BUILD AND MAINTAIN THE NUKVA CALLED 'WORLD', as it is written, "For the upright shall dwell in the land" (Mishlei 2:21), which should be read as, 'cause to dwell' WHICH MEANS THAT THEY WILL DRAW THE SHECHINAH CALLED 'LAND', UPON THE LOWER BEINGS, as was already explained.

15. "his eyes were dim, so that he could not see"

15. "his eyes were dim, so that he could not see"

A Synopsis

Rabbi Shimon and his son Rabbi Elazar discuss differences in the eyesight of Abraham, Isaac, and Jacob as they grow older, and the significance of this for our realm of Malchut and the supernal mysteries. The patriarchs were connected to Left Column, which denotes judgement and darkness. This is the secret meaning behind the concept of blindness in the Torah. Isaac embodied a complete connection to the Left Column; therefore, were are told that he is totally blind. Ya'akov's connection to both the Right and Left Columns is indicated by his only partial blindness.

The Relevance of this Passage

Our physical bodies are directly affected by our connection to the Light during our lives. These effects can be both positive and negative. Illness and health are merely expressions of how we balance the Right and Left Columns – sharing and receiving – throughout our lives. We are often judgmental [Left Column] during moments when we should be merciful [Right Column] and vice-versa. The wisdom to balance these two Columns is awakened within us.

118. וַיְהִי כִּי זָקֵן יִצְחָק. אָמַר רִבִּי שִׁמְעוֹן כְּתִיב, וַיִּקְרָא אֱלֹהִים לָאוֹר יוֹם וְלַחשֶׁךְ קָרָא לָיְלָה, הַאי קְרָא אוּקְמוּהָ וְאִתְּמָר. אֲבָל תָּא חֲזֵי, כָּל עוֹבָדוֹי דְקוּדְשָׁא בְּרִיךְ הוּא, כֻּלְּהוּ אִינוּן מִלִּין דִּקְשׁוֹט, וְכֹלָּא בְּרָזָא עִלָּאָה, וְכָל מִלּוֹי דְאוֹרָיְיתָא, כֻּלְּהוּ מִלֵּי מְהֵימְנוּתָא, וְרָזִין עִלָּאִין, כִּדְקָא יָאוּת.

118. "And it came to pass, that when Isaac was old" (Beresheet 27:1). Rabbi Shimon said: It is written, "And Elohim called the light Day, and the darkness he called Night" (Beresheet 1:5). This verse had already been explained; nevertheless come and behold: All the actions that the Holy One, blessed be He, performs, are true, and in the secret of the upper world. And all the words of the Torah are words of faith, WHICH IS THE SECRET OF THE NUKVA, and supernal mysteries, WHICH ILLUMINATE IT as they should.

119. וְתָא חֲזֵי, לָא זָכָה יִצְחָק כְּאַבְרָהָם, דְּלָא סָמוּ עֵינוֹי, וְלָא כְּהוּ. אֲבָל רָזָא עִלָּאָה אִיהוּ הָכָא, רָזָא דִּמְהֵימְנוּתָא, כְּמָה דְאִתְּמָר, דִּכְתִיב

וַיִּקְרָא אֱלֹהִים לָאוֹר יוֹם, דָּא אַבְרָהָם, דְּאִיהוּ נְהוֹרָא דִּימָמָא, וּנְהוֹרָא דִּילֵיהּ אָזֵיל וְנָהֵיר, וְאִתְתַּקַּף בְּתִקּוּנָא דְּיוֹמָא.

119. Come and behold: Isaac did not have the merit of Abraham, whose eyes were not blinded or dimmed. Here, however, is a supernal secret, the secret of faith. For we have learned that "And Elohim called the light Day" refers to Abraham, the light of day, THE SECRET OF THE RIGHT COLUMN, whose light grows stronger as the day advances, THE SECRET OF THE LIGHT OF CHASSADIM.

120. וּבְגִין כָּךְ, מַה כְּתִיב, וְאַבְרָהָם זָקֵן בָּא בַּיָּמִים, בְּאִינּוּן נְהוֹרִין דְּנָהֲרִין, וְאִיהוּ סִיב, כִּדְבָר אַחַר הוֹלֵךְ וְאוֹר עַד נְכוֹן הַיּוֹם, וּבְגִין כָּךְ, וַיִּקְרָא אֱלֹהִים לָאוֹר יוֹם. וְלַחֹשֶׁךְ קָרָא לָיְלָה, דָּא יִצְחָק, דְּאִיהִי חֹשֶׁךְ, וְאִיהוּ אָזֵיל לְקַבְּלָא לֵילְיָא בְּגַוֵּויהּ, וּבְגִין כָּךְ, אִיהוּ כַּד סִיב, מַה כְּתִיב, וַיְהִי כִּי זָקֵן יִצְחָק וַתִּכְהֶיןָ עֵינָיו מֵרְאוֹת. הָכֵי הוּא וַדַּאי, דְּבָעֵי לְאִתְחַשְּׁכָא, וּלְאִתְדַּבְּקָא בְּדַרְגֵּיהּ כַּדְקָא יָאוֹת.

120. Thus, it is written, "And Abraham was old, advanced in age" (Beresheet 24:1), that is, in the shining lights OF CHASSADIM. And he is old, as it is written, "that shines ever more brightly until the height of noonday" (Mishlei 4:18). Therefore IT IS WRITTEN OF HIM, "And Elohim called the light Day." "And the darkness he called Night." This is Isaac, who is dark, and gets DARKER to receive the night within him. Therefore, when he grew older, it is written, "And it came to pass, that when Isaac was old, and his eyes were dim, so that he could not see" (Beresheet 27:1). FOR HE BECAME COMPLETELY DARK. Assuredly he had to be COMPLETELY dark, to cleave well to his grade.

121. אָתָא רַבִּי אֶלְעָזָר בְּרֵיהּ, וְנָשֵׁיק יְדוֹי. אָמַר לוֹ שַׁפִּיר. אַבְרָהָם נָהֵיר, מִסִּטְרָא דְּדַרְגָּא דִּילֵיהּ, יִצְחָק אִתְחֲשַׁךְ, מִסִּטְרָא דְּדַרְגָּא דִּילֵיהּ, יַעֲקֹב אֲמַאי? דִּכְתִיב וְעֵינֵי יִשְׂרָאֵל כָּבְדוּ מִזֹּקֶן. אָמַר לוֹ הָכֵי הוּא וַדַּאי, כָּבְדוּ כְּתִיב, וְלֹא כָּהוּ. מִזֹּקֶן כְּתִיב, וְלָא מִזִּקְנוּ, אֶלָּא מִזֹּקֶן, מִזֹּקֶן דְּיִצְחָק, מֵהַהוּא סִטְרָא כָּבְדוּ. לֹא יוּכַל לִרְאוֹת, לְאִסְתַּכְּלָא כַּדְקָא חָזֵי,

אֲבָל לֹא כָהוּ. אֲבָל יִצְחָק, כָּהוּ וַדַּאי מִכֹּל וָכֹל, וְאִתְעֲבֵיד חֹשֶׁךְ, דְּהָא
כְּדֵין אִתְאֲחֵיד בֵּיהּ לַיְלָה, וְאִתְקַיָּים וְלַחֹשֶׁךְ קָרָא לָיְלָה.

121. Rabbi Elazar, his son, kissed his hands and said: This is well. Abraham shines on the side of his grade, and Isaac is darkened on the side of his grade. But why did Jacob GROW DARKER, as it is written, "Now the eyes of Yisrael were dim (lit. 'heavy') from age" (Beresheet 48:10). He answers: Assuredly it is AS I SAID, for it is written, "heavy," and not dim, AS WAS WRITTEN OF ISAAC; It is written "from age", not 'his age'. "from age" is to be interpreted as the age of Isaac, FOR HE INCLUDED BOTH ABRAHAM AND ISAAC. THEREFORE on the side OF ISAAC his eyes "were heavy...so that he could not see" (Ibid.), not properly, but he was not absolutely blind. But Yitzchak's eyes were completely dim, and it became darkness, for night, WHICH IS THE NUKVA, clove to him and it was fulfilled, "and the darkness he called Night."

16. "And he said, Behold now, I am old, I know not the day of my death"

A Synopsis

The events leading to Yitzchak's 'mistaken-identity' blessing of Jacob are discussed by Rabbi Elazar, as he expounds upon the significance of trust in the story of the fiery furnace. In the story, three righteous people are tossed into a fire. The men possess unshakable trust in The Creator, and have no regard for their survival or destruction. For this reason, these righteous men miraculously avoid injury.

Through this story, Rabbi Elazar shows, in great depth, that only complete trust in the Light of The Creator can bring forth Divine assistance. There must be no expectation or desire for a specific result – as is written, "according to his need." We're told of the importance of being prepared, and of dwelling on the Name of The Creator, and of how these qualities are intricately related to Torah study. Such study, we learn, requires a profound intention to extol The Creator. Our efforts must be for the sake of the whole world, not for ourselves, so the earth shall be full of the Knowledge of The Creator. The Rabbis then return to the story of the blessing, its significance for future generations, and its relation to both the Shechinah and this mundane realm of Malchut.

The Relevance of this Passage

People may unknowingly embark on a spiritual path for selfish reasons. They have hidden expectations of self-serving gain. Though this is not always their conscious intention, it's the reality. We can know if our desires and efforts are pure when we ask the Light for what we need and not just what we want. We then trust in the spiritual path, regardless of any tests and obstacles we encounter. These verses increase our level of trust in The Creator. They invoke certainty in times of distress, strength during times of strife. We can embrace whatever life brings, certain of the spiritual purpose behind it.

122. וַיִּקְרָא אֶת עֵשָׂו בְּנוֹ הַגָּדוֹל, דְּאִתְכְּלַל מִסִּטְרֵיה דְּדִינָא קַשְׁיָא וַיֹּאמֶר הִנֵּה נָא זָקַנְתִּי לֹא יָדַעְתִּי יוֹם מוֹתִי. רִבִּי אֶלְעָזָר פָּתַח וַאֲמַר, אַשְׁרֵי אָדָם עוֹז לוֹ בָךְ וגו', זַכָּאָה בַּר נָשׁ, דְּאִתְתַּקַּף בֵּיה בְּקוּדְשָׁא בְּרִיךְ הוּא וְיַשְׁוֵי תּוּקְפֵיה בֵּיה.

16. "And he said, Behold now, I am old, I know not the day of my death"

122. "He called Esau his eldest son..." This means that he was included within strict Judgment, WHICH IS THE ASPECT OF ESAU. THEREFORE HE CALLED ESAU. "And he said, Behold now, I am old, I know not the day of my death." Rabbi Elazar opened the discussion with the verse, "Happy is the man, whose strength is in You..." (Tehilim 84:6), happy is the man who is strengthened by the Holy One, blessed be He, and puts his trust in Him.

123. יָכוֹל כַּחֲנַנְיָה מִישָׁאֵל וַעֲזַרְיָה, דְּאִתְתַּקְפוּ וַאֲמְרוּ, הֵן אִיתַי אֱלָהָנָא דִּי אֲנַחְנָא פָּלְחִין, יָכִל לְשֵׁיזָבוּתַנָא מִן אַתּוּן נוּרָא יָקָדְתָּא וּמִן יְדָךְ מַלְכָּא יְשֵׁיזָב. תָּא חֲזֵי, דְּאִי לָא יְשֵׁזִיב, וְלָא אִתְקַיַּים עֲלַיְיהוּ קוּדְשָׁא בְּרִיךְ הוּא, אִשְׁתַּכַּח שְׁמֵיה דְּקוּדְשָׁא בְּרִיךְ הוּא, דְּלָא יִתְקַדַּשׁ בְּעֵינַיְיהוּ דְכֹלָּא, כְּמָה דַּאֲמָרוּ. אֶלָּא, כֵּיוָן דְּיָדְעוּ דְּלָא אֲמְרוּ כְּדְקָא יָאוֹת, אַהֲדְרוּ וַאֲמְרוּ, וְהֵן לָא יְדִיעַ לֶהֱוֵא לָךְ מַלְכָּא וגו'. בֵּין יְשֵׁזִיב בֵּין לָא יְשֵׁזִיב יְדִיעַ לֶהֱוֵי לָךְ מַלְכָּא וגו'. וְתָנֵינָן דְּמִלָּה דְּאוֹדַע לְהוּ יְחֶזְקֵאל, וְשָׁמְעוּ וְקַבִּילוּ מִנֵּיה, דְּקוּדְשָׁא בְּרִיךְ הוּא לָא אִתְקַיַּים עֲלַיְיהוּ, בְּגִין דִּיקַבְּלוּן אַגְרָא. וּכְדֵין אַהֲדְרוּ וַאֲמְרוּ, וְהֵן לָא יְדִיעַ לֶהֱוֵי לָךְ מַלְכָּא וגו'.

123. This trust could be interpreted as the trust that Hananiah, Mishael, and Azariah put in Him when they said, "Behold, our Elohim whom we serve is able to deliver us; He can deliver us from the burning fiery furnace, and out of your hand, king..." (Daniel 3:17), MEANING, THAT THEY TRUSTED THAT THE HOLY ONE, BLESSED BE HE, WOULD SURELY SAVE THEM FROM THE FIERY FURNACE. HE SAYS THAT THIS IS NOT SO, ONLY come and see, if He would not save them and be with them, it would come to pass that the name of the Holy One, blessed be He, would not be sanctified before the eyes of everyone, as they said. But when they realized they did not speak properly, they spoke again, saying "But if He does not, be it known to you, king..." (Ibid. 18), THAT IS, whether He will save them or not, let it be known to you that we will not worship an image. It was made known to them by Ezekiel, whom they heard and believed, that the Holy One, blessed be He, would not be with them, TO SAVE THEM. AND HE TOLD THEM THAT, so that they would SURRENDER THEIR SOULS AND be rewarded. Then they spoke again, saying, "be it known to you, King..."

124. אֶלָּא לָא יִתְתַּקַּף בַּר נָשׁ, דְּיֵימָא קוּדְשָׁא בְּרִיךְ הוּא יְשֵׁזְבִינַנִי, אוֹ אִיהוּ עָבֵיד לִי כָּךְ וְכָךְ, אֲבָל יְשַׁוֵּי תּוּקְפֵּיהּ בֵּיהּ בְּקוּדְשָׁא בְּרִיךְ הוּא, דִּיסַיֵּיע לֵיהּ, כַּד אִיהוּ אִשְׁתַּדַּל בְּאִינּוּן פְּקוּדִין דְּאוֹרַיְיתָא, וּלְמֵיהַךְ בְּאֹרַח קְשׁוֹט, דְּכֵיוָן דְּאָתֵי בַּר נָשׁ לְאִתְדַּכָּאָה, מְסַיְיעִין לֵיהּ וַדַּאי, וּבְדָא יִתְתַּקַּף בֵּיהּ בְּקוּדְשָׁא בְּרִיךְ הוּא, דְּאִיהוּ יְסַיֵּיע לֵיהּ, וְיִתְתַּקַּף בֵּיהּ, דְּלָא יַשְׁוֵּי תּוּקְפֵּיהּ בְּאָחֳרָא, וּבְגִין כָּךְ עֹז לוֹ בָךְ. מְסִלּוֹת בִּלְבָבָם, דְּיַעֲבֵיד לְבֵיהּ כַּדְקָא יָאוֹת, בְּלָא הִרְהוּרָא אָחֳרָא, אֶלָּא כְּהַאי מְסִלָּה, דְּאִיהִי מְתַיַּישְׁבָא, לְאַעֲבָרָא בְּכָל אֲתַר דְּאִצְטְרִיךְ, הָכֵי נָמֵי.

124. A man should not assume and think, the Holy One, blessed be He, will save us, or, that the Holy One, blessed be He, will do such and such for me. However, it behooves man to place his trust in the Holy One, blessed be He, to help him ACCORDING TO HIS NEED, as long as he strives to keep the precepts of Torah and to walk the path of truth. When a man wishes to be purified, he is surely helped, and he should trust the Holy One, blessed be He, to help him in this. And he should put his trust in Him, and not in another. Therefore, it is written, "whose strength is in you." "In whose heart are your highways" (Tehilim 84:6) MEANS that it behooves him to prepare his heart as fit, so that no strange thoughts will come into it, but to be as a mended way to pass through, where ever one needs to, EITHER RIGHT OR LEFT. THUS WHETHER THE HOLY ONE, BLESSED BE HE, DOES GOOD FOR HIM OR NOT, HIS HEART SHOULD BE READY AND PREPARED, AND NOT HARBOR STRANGE THOUGHTS IN ANY CASE WHATSOEVER.

125. דָּבָר אַחֵר אַשְׁרֵי אָדָם עוֹז לוֹ בָךְ, עֹז: כְּדִבָּר אַחֵר יְיָ' עֹז לְעַמּוֹ יִתֵּן, בְּגִין דְּאִצְטְרִיךְ לֵיהּ לְבַר נָשׁ, דְּיִתְעַסַּק בְּאוֹרַיְיתָא לִשְׁמֵיהּ דְּקוּדְשָׁא בְּרִיךְ הוּא, דְּכָל מַאן דְּאִתְעַסַּק בְּאוֹרַיְיתָא, וְלָא אִשְׁתַּדַּל לִשְׁמָהּ, טַב לֵיהּ דְּלָא אִתְבְּרֵי. מְסִלּוֹת בִּלְבָבָם, מַאי מְסִלּוֹת בִּלְבָבָם, כְּדִבָּר אַחֵר סֹלּוּ לָרֹכֵב בָּעֲרָבוֹת בְּיָהּ שְׁמוֹ. דָּא הַהִיא אוֹרַיְיתָא, דְּאִיהוּ אִשְׁתַּדַּל בָּהּ, לְאַרְמָא לֵיהּ לְקוּדְשָׁא בְּרִיךְ הוּא, וּלְמֶעְבַּד לֵיהּ חֲטִיבָא בְּעָלְמָא.

125. Another explanation for, "Happy is the man, whose strength is in

16. "And he said, Behold now, I am old, I know not the day of my death"

You." Strength as in "Hashem gives strength to His people" (Tehilim 29:11), MEANS THE TORAH. AND "WHOSE STRENGTH IS IN YOU" MEANS that it is incumbent on a man to be occupied in studying Torah for the name (sake) of the Holy One, blessed be He, NAMELY, THE SHECHINAH, THAT IS CALLED 'NAME'. For whoever is occupied in the Torah, but does not care for its name, would have been better never born. What is meant by the verse, "in whose heart are Your highways (Heb. *mesilot*)?" It is as in the verse, "extol (Heb. *solu*) Him who rides upon the clouds; Yah is His name" (Tehilim 68:5), WHICH REFERS BOTH TO EXTOLLING THE RIDER ON THE CLOUDS AND THE HIGHWAYS IN THEIR HEARTS. THIS MEANS that when he studies the Torah, HE SHOULD BE INTENT UPON extolling the Holy One, blessed be He, and glorifying and extoling Him throughout the world. THUS STUDYING TORAH FOR ITS OWN SAKE (NAME) IS FOR THOSE "IN WHOSE HEART ARE YOUR HIGHWAYS." THIS MEANS THAT ONE MUST BE INTENT WHEN STUDYING TORAH TO DRAW THE BOUNTY OF KNOWLEDGE FOR ONE AND FOR THE WHOLE WORLD, SO THAT THE NAME OF THE HOLY ONE, BLESSED BE HE, WILL GROW IN THE WORLD, AS IT IS WRITTEN, "FOR THE EARTH SHALL BE FULL OF THE KNOWLEDGE OF HASHEM" (YESHAYAH 11:9) AND "HASHEM SHALL BE KING OVER ALL THE EARTH" (ZECHARYAH 14:9).

126. תָּא חֲזֵי, יַעֲקֹב כָּל עוֹבָדוֹי הֲווֹ לִשְׁמָא דְקוּדְשָׁא בְּרִיךְ הוּא, וּבְגִין כָּךְ, קוּדְשָׁא בְּרִיךְ הוּא עִמֵּיהּ הֲוָה תָּדִיר, דְּלָא אַעֲדֵי מִנֵּיהּ שְׁכִינְתָּא, דְּהָא בְּשַׁעֲתָּא דְּקָרָא לֵיהּ יִצְחָק, לְעֵשָׂו בְּרֵיהּ, יַעֲקֹב לָא הֲוָה תַּמָּן, וּשְׁכִינְתָּא אוֹדָעַת לָהּ לְרִבְקָה, וְרִבְקָה אוֹדָעַת לֵיהּ לְיַעֲקֹב.

126. Come and behold: Jacob, all that he did was for the sake of the Holy One, blessed be He, and for that reason the Holy One, blessed be He, was with him always, by that the Shechinah never moved from him. For when Isaac called for Esau, his son, Jacob was not there. The Shechinah told this to Rivkah, who informed Jacob.

127. רִבִּי יוֹסֵי אָמַר, תָּא חֲזֵי, אִי ח"ו בְּהַהוּא זִמְנָא יִתְבָּרַךְ עֵשָׂו, לָא יִשְׁלוֹט יַעֲקֹב לְעָלְמִין. אֶלָּא מֵעִם קוּדְשָׁא בְּרִיךְ הוּא הֲוָה, וְכֹלָּא בַּאֲתְרֵיהּ אָתָא, כִּדְקָא חָזֵי. תָּא חֲזֵי, וְרִבְקָה אוֹהֶבֶת אֶת יַעֲקֹב כְּתִיב,

וְהָא אִתְּמַר. וּבְגִין כָּךְ, שַׁדְּרַת בְּגִינֵיהּ דְּיַעֲקֹב, הִנֵּה שָׁמַעְתִּי אֶת אָבִיךְ מְדַבֵּר אֶל עֵשָׂו אָחִיךְ לֵאמֹר.

127. Rabbi Yosi said, come and behold: If, heaven forbid, Esau would have been blessed at that time, Jacob would not have ruled over the world, BUT STAYED, HEAVEN FORBID, IN EXILE ALWAYS. But it was decreed by the Holy One, blessed be He, THAT JACOB WILL BE BLESSED, and everything happened as it should. Come and behold: It is written, "but Rivkah loved Jacob" (Beresheet 25:28), as has been explained. Therefore, she sent for Jacob and said to him "Behold, I heard your father speak to Esau your brother" (Beresheet 27:6).

128. וְעַתָּה בְנִי שְׁמַע בְּקוֹלִי וְגוֹ'. בְּהַהוּא זִמְנָא, עֶרֶב פֶּסַח הֲוָה, וּבָעֵי יֵצֶר הָרָע לְאִתְבַּעֲרָא וּלְשַׁלְטָאָה סִיהֲרָא. רָזָא דִּמְהֵימְנוּתָא. וְעַ"ד עֲבַדַת תְּרֵי תַבְשִׁילִין.

128. "Now therefore, my son, obey my voice..." (Beresheet 27:8): It was then Pesach (Passover) eve, and the Evil Inclination had to be exterminated from the world, and the moon, the secret of faith, NUKVA, had to govern. Therefore, Rivkah cooked two dishes.

129. רִבִּי יְהוּדָה אֲמַר, רָמַז הָכָא, דְּזַמִּינִין בְּנוֹי דְּיַעֲקֹב, לְקָרְבָא שְׁנֵי שְׂעִירִים, חַד לַיְיָ', וְחַד לַעֲזָאזֵל בְּיוֹמָא דְכִפּוּרֵי. וּבְגִין כָּךְ, קְרֵיבַת שְׁנֵי גְדָיֵי עִזִּים, חַד בְּגִין דַּרְגָּא דִלְעֵילָא, וְחַד בְּגִין לְכַפְיָיא דַרְגֵּיהּ דְּעֵשָׂו, דְּלָא יִשְׁלוֹט עֲלֵיהּ דְּיַעֲקֹב, וְעַ"ד שְׁנֵי גְדָיֵי עִזִּים, וּמִתַּרְוַויְיהוּ טָעִים יִצְחָק וְאָכִיל.

129. Rabbi Yehuda said that this alludes to the descendants of Jacob, who in the future offered two goats on Yom Kippur, one for Hashem and one to Azazel. For this reason, Rivkah offered "two kids of the goats," one for the supernal grade and one to subjugate the grade of Esau, so he would not rule over Jacob. Thus, there were two kids of the goats. From both, Isaac tasted and ate.

130. וַיָּבֵא לוֹ יַיִן וַיֵּשְׁתְּ, וַיָּבֵא לוֹ יַיִן, רֶמֶז רָמִיז, מֵאֲתַר רָחִיק קָרִיב

16. "And he said, Behold now, I am old,
I know not the day of my death"

לֵיהּ. רִבִּי אֶלְעָזָר אֲמַר, רֶמֶז, מֵהַהוּא יַיִן דְּכָל חֶדוּ אִשְׁתְּכַח בֵּיהּ, בְּגִין לְחַדְתָּא לֵיהּ לְיִצְחָק, דְּבָעֵי חֶדְוָה, כִּדְקָא בָּעֲיָין חֶדְוָה, לְחַדְתָּא סִטְרָא דִּלְוָאֵי, וְעַל דָּא וַיָּבֵא לוֹ יַיִן וַיֵּשְׁתְּ.

130. It is written, "and he brought him wine, and he drank" (Beresheet 27: 25), AND NOT, "AND HE SERVED HIM WINE." By this he hints that he served him wine from afar. According to Rabbi Elazar, this means that he brought him wine in which there is complete joy, THAT IS, THE WINE "WHICH CHEERS ELOHIM AND MAN" (SHOFTIM 9:13), to gladden Isaac, for he needed cheering, as the side of the Levites needs cheering, TO WIT, THE LEFT SIDE. FOR SINCE JUDGMENTS TAKE HOLD OF THE LEFT SIDE, THEREFORE, SADNESS DWELLS IN IT, AND THERE IS NEED OF HEARTENING ALL THOSE WHO ARE DRAWN FROM IT: THE LEVITES AND ISAAC AS WELL. Therefore, "he brought him wine, and he drank."

17. "The best clothes of her eldest son Esau"

A Synopsis

In this section the Rabbis continue their analysis of events leading to Yitzchak's "mistaken" blessing of Jacob. They explain the origin of Esau's clothing, which was given by Rivkah to Jacob. In truth, Isaac was not deceived into believing Jacob was actually Esau. Ya'akov's clothing radiated a scent direct from the Garden of Eden. Isaac blessed Jacob because the garments emitted this holy aroma – not because he was deceived. Isaac realized that this fragrance could only accompany someone worthy of the blessing. Thus, we learn that Jacob embodied the power and soul of Adam. Rabbi Elazar describes the relationship of Jacob to Adam in terms of Ya'akov's beauty. This also illuminates his relationship to the realm of Binah.

The Relevance of this Passage

Adam originally wore the garments mentioned above in the Garden of Eden, thus, the garments' Divine scent when Jacob wore them. Jacob, we are told, is the embodiment of Adam, and his original clothes are returned to him by Rivkah. The Zohar is evolving a lesson concerning a natural law: all things eventually return to their rightful owners. Nothing that truly belongs to us can ever really leave us. Whatever we lose, we never really had. This enlightened view of life is awakened within us. The scent of the Garden of Eden is infused within us, so that we emit this fragrance [Light] in our lives, wherever we go. People around us will sense this Light.

131. וַתִּקַּח רִבְקָה אֶת בִּגְדֵי עֵשָׂו וְגו', אִלֵּין אִינוּן לְבוּשִׁין דְּרָווַח עֵשָׂו מִנִּמְרוֹד, וְאִלֵּין לְבוּשֵׁי יְקָר, דַּהֲווֹ מִן אָדָם הָרִאשׁוֹן, וְאָתוּ לְיָדָא דְּנִמְרוֹד, וּבְהוּ הֲוָה צָד צֵידָה, נִמְרוֹד, דִּכְתִיב הוּא הָיָה גִּבּוֹר צַיִד לִפְנֵי יי' וְגו', וְעֵשָׂו נָפַק לְחַקְלָא, וְאַגַּח בֵּיהּ קְרָבָא בְּנִמְרוֹד, וְקָטַל לֵיהּ, וּנְסַב אִלֵּין לְבוּשִׁין מִנֵּיהּ, הה"ד וַיָּבֹא עֵשָׂו מִן הַשָּׂדֶה וְהוּא עָיֵף, וְאוֹקְמוּהָ, כְּתִיב הָכָא וְהוּא עָיֵף, וּכְתִיב הָתָם כִּי עָיְפָה נַפְשִׁי לְהֹרְגִים.

131. "And Rivkah took the best clothes of her eldest son Esau" (Beresheet 27:15). These are the garments Esau took from Nimrod. They are the precious garments from Adam, which came to the hands of Nimrod, who used them when he hunted, as it is written, "He was a mighty hunter before

Hashem" (Beresheet 10:9). And Esau went into the field, where he fought with and killed Nimrod, removing the garments from him. This is the meaning of "and Esau came the field, and he was faint" (Beresheet 25:29). It has already been explained why it is here written, "and he was faint," and elsewhere, "for my soul faints before the slayers" (Yirmeyah 4:31). THESE ARE ANALOGOUS. THERE IT IS WRITTEN "FAINT" TO REFER TO KILLING. HERE TOO, THERE IS KILLING, BECAUSE ESAU MURDERED NIMROD.

132. וְעֵשָׂו הֲוָה סָלִיק לוֹן לְאִינוּן לְבוּשִׁין, לְגַבָּה דְּרִבְקָה, וּבְהוּ הֲוָה נָפִיק וְצָד צֵידָה, וְהַהוּא יוֹמָא לָא נָטַל לוֹן, וּנְפַק לְחַקְלָא, וְאִתְעַכַּב תַּמָּן. וְכַד הֲוָה לָבִישׁ לוֹן עֵשָׂו, לָא הֲווֹ סָלְקִין רֵיחִין כְּלָל, כֵּיוָן דְּלָבִישׁ לוֹן יַעֲקֹב, כְּדֵין תָּבַת אֲבֵדָה לְאַתְרָהּ, וּסְלִיקוּ רֵיחִין, בְּגִין דְּשׁוּפְרֵיהּ דְּיַעֲקֹב, שׁוּפְרֵיהּ דְּאָדָם הֲוָה. וּבְגִין כָּךְ אַהֲדָרוּ בְּהַהִיא שַׁעֲתָּא לְאַתְרַיְיהוּ, וּסְלִיקוּ רֵיחִין.

132. Esau hid these garments with Rivkah and wore them when he went hunting. On the day, WHEN ISAAC SENT FOR HIM TO RECEIVE THE BLESSINGS, he did not take them to the field and was therefore late. When Esau wore them, they put forth no scent at all, but when Jacob wore them, the lost object was restored AS THEY RETURNED TO THE ASPECT OF ADAM. For the beauty of Jacob was the beauty of Adam. They therefore returned to their place and emitted fragrance.

133. אָמַר רַבִּי יוֹסֵי, שׁוּפְרֵיהּ דְּיַעֲקֹב דְּאִיהוּ שׁוּפְרֵיהּ דְּאָדָם אֵיךְ אֶפְשָׁר, וְהָא תָּנֵינָן, תַּפּוּחַ עֲקֵבוֹ דְּאָדָם הָרִאשׁוֹן, מַכְהֵה גַּלְגַּל חַמָּה, וְאִי תֵּימָא דְּכָךְ הֲוָה יַעֲקֹב. אָמַר לוֹ רַבִּי אֶלְעָזָר, וַדַּאי הָכִי הֲוָה, בְּקַדְמֵיתָא עַד לָא חָב אָדָם הָרִאשׁוֹן, לָא הֲווֹ יַכְלִין כָּל בִּרְיָין לְאִסְתַּכְּלָא בְּשׁוּפְרֵיהּ, כֵּיוָן דְּחָטָא, אִשְׁתַּנֵּי שׁוּפְרֵיהּ, וְנִתְמָאַךְ רוּמֵיהּ, וְאִתְעֲבֵיד בַּר מֵאָה אַמִּין. וְתָא חֲזֵי, שׁוּפְרֵיהּ דְּאָדָם הָרִאשׁוֹן, רָזָא אִיהוּ, דִּמְהֵימְנוּתָא עִלָּאָה תַּלְיָא בְּהַהוּא שׁוּפְרָא, וּבְגִין כָּךְ, וִיהִי נֹעַם יְיָ' אֱלֹהֵינוּ עָלֵינוּ. וּכְתִיב לַחֲזוֹת בְּנֹעַם יְיָ', וְדָא הוּא שׁוּפְרֵיהּ דְּיַעֲקֹב וַדַּאי, וְכֹלָּא רָזָא עִלָּאָה אִיהוּ.

133. Rabbi Yosi said: YOU SAY THAT Jacob's beauty was the beauty of Adam. How could this be? We learned that the apple of Adam's heel eclipsed the orb of the sun. Could you say that for Jacob? Rabbi Elazar replied, assuredly before Adam sinned no creature could behold his beauty. But after he sinned, his beauty changed, his stature diminished, and he was a hundred cubits high. BUT BEFORE THE SIN, HIS HEIGHT WAS FROM EARTH TO HEAVEN. THE BEAUTY OF JACOB WAS LIKE THE BEAUTY OF ADAM AFTER HE SINNED. Come and behold: Adam's beauty is a mystery on which supernal faith, BINAH, stems. THAT IS, HE ACHIEVED THE LIGHT OF BINAH AND THERE ATTAINED THIS BEAUTY. Of this, the scripture says "And let the beauty of Adonai our Elohim be upon us" (Tehilim 90:17), AS THE LIGHT OF BINAH IS CALLED 'BEAUTY'. It is also written, "to behold the beauty of Hashem" (Tehilim 27:4). This is, assuredly, the beauty of Jacob, THAT IS, HE ACHIEVED THE LIGHT OF BINAH, AS DID ADAM. And all is in the supernal mystery.

134. וַיָּרַח אֶת רֵיחַ בְּגָדָיו וַיְבָרֲכֵהוּ. תָּא חֲזֵי, וַיָּרַח אֶת רֵיחַ הַבְּגָדִים לא כְּתִיב, אֶלָּא רֵיחַ בְּגָדָיו, כְּדָבָר אַחֵר עוֹטֶה אוֹר כַּשַּׂלְמָה נוֹטֶה שָׁמַיִם כַּיְרִיעָה. דָּבָר אַחֵר וַיָּרַח אֶת רֵיחַ בְּגָדָיו וַיְבָרֲכֵהוּ. דְּכֵיוָן דְּאַלְבִּישׁ לוֹן יַעֲקֹב, סְלִיקוּ רֵיחִין בְּהַהִיא שַׁעְתָּא, וְעַד דְּלָא אָרַח רֵיחִין דִּלְבוּשׁיֵהּ, לָא בָּרֲכֵיהּ, דְּהָא כְּדֵין יָדַע דְּאִתְחֲזֵי הוּא לְאִתְבָּרְכָא, דְּאִי לָא אִתְחֲזֵי לְאִתְבָּרְכָא, לָא סְלִיקוּ כָּל הַנֵּי רֵיחִין קַדִּישִׁין בַּהֲדֵיהּ, הה"ד וַיָּרַח אֶת רֵיחַ בְּגָדָיו וַיְבָרֲכֵהוּ.

134. "And he smelled the smell of his garments, and blessed him" (Beresheet 27:27). Come and behold: It is not written, "and he smelled the smell of the garments" but "the smell of his garments." This is according to the verse, "Who covers Himself with light as with a garment: who stretches out the heavens like a curtain" (Tehilim 104:2). Another explanation is that once Jacob wore them, they emitted an aroma. As long as Isaac did not smell the aroma of the garments, he did not bless him. But then, WHEN THEY EMITTED AN AROMA, he knew that the wearer was worthy of being blessed. For if he did not deserve to be blessed, no holy aroma would be put forth. This is the meaning of the verse "and he smelled the smell of his garments, and blessed him."

135. וַיֹּאמֶר רְאֵה רֵיחַ בְּנִי כְּרֵיחַ שָׂדֶה אֲשֶׁר בֵּרְכוֹ יְיָ'. וַיֹּאמֶר: מִלָּה
סְתִים הוּא. אִית דְּאַמְרֵי שְׁכִינְתָּא הֲוַת, וְאִית דְּאַמְרֵי יִצְחָק הֲוָה. כְּרֵיחַ
שָׂדֶה אֲשֶׁר בֵּרְכוֹ יְיָ', מַאן שָׂדֶה, דָּא שָׂדֶה דְּתַפּוּחִים. שָׂדֶה דַּאֲבָהָן
עִלָּאִין סְמִיכוּ לֵיהּ וּמְתַקְּנִין לֵיהּ.

135. "And said, See, the smell of my son is like the smell of a field which Hashem has blessed" (Beresheet 27:27). The meaning of "and said" is not clear, FOR IT IS NOT KNOWN WHO SAID IT. Some say it is the Shechinah; some say it was Isaac who said "like the smell of a field which Hashem has blessed." HE ASKS: What is this field? AND HE ANSWERS: This is a field of apple trees, NAMELY, THE NUKVA CALLED 'THE FIELD OF HOLY APPLES', which the supernal Patriarchs, CHESED, GVURAH AND TIFERET OF ZEIR ANPIN support and cultivate.

18. "In my distress I cried to Hashem, and He heard me"

A Synopsis

We learn why Jacob's cunning in receiving Isaac's blessing was actually necessary to save the world from the same serpent that had earlier caused the fall of Adam. The Rabbis next give counsel on the meaning for all Yisrael of the multiple blessings given to Jacob and those given to Esau, both for the present and for the time of the coming of Messiah. The blessings given to Jacob are explained with respect to their meaning throughout history. These blessings act as portals through which particular blends of energy flow to mankind at the appropriate periods.

We also learn the central meaning of Jacob for Yisrael in a spiritual, historical context. Jacob, as the embodiment of Adam, encompasses the entire story of man. Jacob represents the complete drama of human existence, represented by the Sfirah of Tiferet. Specifically, this refers to the bringing together, in one place, of all that has happened and that will happen from the time of Adam, to the final coming of the Messiah.

The section concludes with an apportioning of the blessings, each one in its appropriate time, in relation to the history of Yisrael and the coming of the end of the Correction of the souls of man.

The Relevance of this Passage

Through the story of the children of Yisrael, we learn that the threads of the Torah are spiritually woven into the history of the world. We secure a powerful connection to Jacob, and in turn, to the ancient and timeless blessings that we presently need in order to hasten the final redemption. We awaken our awareness of the role and significance our lives play in the overall spiritual plan.

136. וְיִתֶּן לְךָ הָאֱלֹהִים מִטַּל הַשָּׁמַיִם וּמִשְׁמַנֵּי הָאָרֶץ וְרֹב דָּגָן וְתִירוֹשׁ. אָמַר רִבִּי אַבָּא, הַאי קְרָא אוּקְמוּהָ, אֲבָל תָּא חֲזֵי, שִׁיר הַמַּעֲלוֹת אֶל יְיָ' בַּצָּרָתָה לִי קָרָאתִי וַיַּעֲנֵנִי. כַּמָּה שִׁירִין וְתוּשְׁבְּחָן, אָמַר דָּוִד מַלְכָּא קַמֵּי קוּדְשָׁא בְּרִיךְ הוּא, וְכֹלָּא בְּגִין לְאַתְקָנָא דַרְגֵּיהּ, וּלְמֶעְבַּד לֵיהּ שְׁמָא, כִּדְבָּר אַחֵר וַיַּעַשׂ דָּוִד שֵׁם, וְשִׁירָתָא דָּא אָמַר כַּד חָמָא עוֹבָדָא דָּא לְיַעֲקֹב.

136. "Therefore the Elohim give you of the dew of heaven, and the fatness

of the earth, and plenty of corn and wine" (Beresheet 27:28). Rabbi Aba said: This verse has already been explained. Nevertheless, come and look at the verse, "A song of ascent. In my distress I cried to Hashem, and He heard me" (Tehilim 120:1). How many songs and praises did David say before the Holy One, blessed be He, all in order to fix his grade, THE SECRET OF THE NUKVA, and to make himself a name, NAMELY, TO DRAW MOCHIN UPON IT, as it is written, "And David got him a name" (II Shmuel 8:13). This song he said when he saw what Jacob accomplished, THAT HE WAS ANSWERED AND RECEIVED THE BLESSINGS. HE SAID: "IN MY DISTRESS I CRIED TO HASHEM, AND HE HEARD ME." IF IT WERE NOT FOR JACOB, WHO RECEIVED THE BLESSINGS, THE SECRET OF THE WHOLE MOCHIN TO CONSTRUCT THE NUKVA, DAVID COULD NOT HAVE MADE HER A NAME.

137. רִבִּי אֶלְעָזָר אָמַר, יַעֲקֹב אָמַר שִׁירָתָא דָא, בְּשַׁעְתָא דַּאֲמַר לֵיהּ אֲבוֹי, גְּשָׁה נָא וַאֲמֻשְׁךָ בְּנִי הַאַתָּה זֶה בְּנִי עֵשָׂו אִם לֹא, כְּדֵין הֲוָה יַעֲקֹב בְּעָאקוּ סַגִּי, דְּדָחִיל דַּאֲבוֹי יָדַע לֵיהּ, וְאִשְׁתְּמוֹדַע קַמֵּיהּ. מַה כְּתִיב וְלֹא הִכִּירוֹ כִּי הָיוּ יָדָיו כִּידֵי עֵשָׂו אָחִיו שְׂעִירוֹת וַיְבָרֲכֵהוּ. כְּדֵין אָמַר, אֶל יְיָ בַּצָּרָתָה לִי קָרָאתִי וַיַּעֲנֵנִי.

137. Rabbi Elazar said: It was Jacob who sang this song, when his father said to him, "Come near, I pray you, that I may feel you, my son, whether you are really my son Esau or not" (Beresheet 27:21). Then was Jacob in great distress, for he feared that his father will recognize and know him. Then it is written, "and he recognized him not, because his hands were hairy, as his brother Esau's hands: so he blessed him" (Beresheet 27: 23). So he said: "In my distress I cried to Hashem, and He heard me."

138. יְיָ הַצִּילָה נַפְשִׁי מִשְּׂפַת שֶׁקֶר מִלָּשׁוֹן רְמִיָּה, דָּא הוּא דַּרְגָּא, דְּעֶשָׂו שַׁרְיָא בֵּיהּ, דְּאִיהוּ שְׂפַת שָׁקֶר. שְׂפַת שֶׁקֶר, בְּשַׁעְתָא דְּאַיְיתֵי הַהוּא חִוְיָא, לְוָוטִין עַל עָלְמָא, וּבְעָקִימוּ, אַיְיתֵי לְוָוטִין, דְּאִתְלַטְיָא עָלְמָא.

138. "Deliver my soul, Hashem, from lying lips, from a deceitful tongue" (Tehilim 120:2). This is the portion where Esau is, NAMELY, THE SERPENT, who has lying lips. What are the lying lips OF HIS GRADE? When the

serpent brought curses upon the world, BY INCITING ADAM TO EAT OF THE TREE OF KNOWLEDGE, he brought them deceitfully and crookedly.

19. The Blessings

A Synopsis

The Zohar expounds upon the blessings that were originally intended for Esau but deceitfully appropriated by Jacob.

Like all stories in scripture, this one is imbued with deeper meaning. In truth, the episode of "The Blessings" concerns the establishment of the universal spiritual system that mankind would utilize in its quest for transformation. The Patriarchs represent the various spiritual components that comprise the system. At this particular point in its development, a critical moment is at hand. The battle for dominion over the dimension of physicality is being determined. Thus, we learn that Ya'akov's "stealing" of the blessing away from his brother Esau, signifies the victory of the Light over the forces of darkness.

The Zohar then explicates upon the secret behind the blessing: Some blessings are to be utilized in the age before the End of Days, while other blessings are designated for the Final Redemption.

The Relevance of This Passage

The power to triumph over dark forces within us, and those in our midst, is given to us through the Light of the Blessings that shine in the verses, revealing deeper, mystical truths.

139. תָּא חֲזֵי, בְּשַׁעֲתָּא דַּאֲמַר יִצְחָק לְעֵשָׂו, וְצֵא הַשָּׂדֶה וְצוּדָה לִי צֵידָה, בְּה"א, וְאוֹקְמוּהָ, וְנָפַק עֵשָׂו, בְּגִין דְּיִתְבָּרֵךְ מִיִּצְחָק, דְּקָאֲמַר לֵיהּ, וַאֲבָרֶכְכָה לִפְנֵי יְיָ', דְּאִלּוּ אֲמַר וַאֲבָרֶכְכָה, וְלָא יַתִּיר, יָאוֹת. כֵּיוָן דַּאֲמַר לִפְנֵי יְיָ', בְּהַהִיא שַׁעֲתָּא, אִזְדַּעְזַע כָּרְסֵי יְקָרָא דְּקוּדְשָׁא בְּרִיךְ הוּא, אָמְרָה, וּמַה דְּיִפּוֹק חִוְיָא מֵאִינּוּן לְוָטִין, וְיִשְׁתָּאַר יַעֲקֹב בְּהוּ.

139. Come and behold: When Isaac said to Esau "and go out to the field, and catch me some venison (Heb. *tzeidah*)" (Beresheet 27:3), with a *Hei*, INSTEAD OF USING *TZAYID*, WITHOUT A *HEI*. This has already been explained. And Esau went HUNTING to be blessed by Isaac, who said to him "and bless you before Hashem" (Ibid. 7). It would have been well to say just "and I will bless you," but since he added "before Hashem," the Throne of Glory of the Holy One, blessed be He, then trembled and said: Could it be, that the serpent is freed from these curses, and Jacob remains subject to them?

140. בְּהַהִיא שַׁעְתָּא, אִזְדַּמַן מִיכָאֵל, וְאָתָא קַמֵּיה דְּיַעֲקֹב, וּשְׁכִינְתָּא בַּהֲדֵיה, וְיָדַע יִצְחָק, וְחָמָא לְגַן עֵדֶן, בַּהֲדֵיה דְּיַעֲקֹב, וּבְרָכֵיה קַמֵּיה, וְכַד עָאל עֵשָׂו, עָאל בַּהֲדֵיה גֵּיהִנֹּם, וְעַל דָּא וַיֶּחֱרַד יִצְחָק חֲרָדָה גְדוֹלָה עַד מְאֹד, דְּחָשַׁב דְּלָא הֲוָה עֵשָׂו בְּהַהוּא סִטְרָא, פָּתַח וְאָמַר, גַּם בָּרוּךְ יִהְיֶה.

140. At that time Michael came before Jacob with the Shechinah. Isaac knew that and saw that the Garden of Eden is with Jacob, so he blessed him. When Esau entered, Gehenom entered with him. Therefore: "And Isaac trembled very much" (Beresheet 27:33), because he had previously thought that Esau was not of that side. Therefore he said "AND HAVE BLESSED HIM? Moreover, he shall be blessed."

141. בְּגִין כָּךְ, אִזְדַּמַן יַעֲקֹב, בְּחָכְמְתָא וּבַעֲקִימוּ דְּאַיְיתֵי בִּרְכָאן עֲלֵיה דְּיַעֲקֹב, דְּאִיהוּ כְּגַוְונָא דְּאָדָם הָרִאשׁוֹן, וְאִתְנְטָלוּ מֵהַהוּא חִוְיָא דְּאִיהוּ שְׂפַת שֶׁקֶר. דְּכַמָּה שִׁקְרָא אָמַר, וְכַמָּה מִלֵּי דְּשִׁקְרָא עָבַד, בְּגִין לְאַטְעָאָה וּלְאַיְיתָאָה לְוָוטִין עַל עָלְמָא, בְּגִין כָּךְ, אָתָא יַעֲקֹב בְּחָכְמָה, וְאַטְעֵי לַאֲבוּי, בְּגִין לְאַיְיתָאָה בִּרְכָאן עַל עָלְמָא, וּלְנַטְלָא מִנֵּיה, מַה דְּמָנַע מֵעָלְמָא, וּמִדָּה לָקֳבֵל מִדָּה הֲוָה, וְעַ"ד כְּתִיב וַיֶּאֱהַב קְלָלָה וַתְּבוֹאֵהוּ וְלֹא חָפֵץ בִּבְרָכָה וַתִּרְחַק מִמֶּנּוּ. עֲלֵיה כְּתִיב, אָרוּר אַתָּה מִכָּל הַבְּהֵמָה וּמִכָּל חַיַּת הַשָּׂדֶה. וְאִשְׁתָּאַר בֵּיה לְדָרֵי דָרִין, וְאָתָא יַעֲקֹב וְנָטִיל מִנֵּיה בִּרְכָאן.

141. For that reason Jacob behaved with cunning and guile, and brought blessings on Jacob, who resembled Adam, that were taken from the serpent of the lying lips, who talked and acted deceitfully, in order to incite ADAM TO EAT FROM THE TREE OF KNOWLEDGE and bring curses upon the world. For that reason, Jacob behaved with cunning and misled his father, so as to bring blessings upon the world and snatch from the serpent what he withheld from the world, THAT IS, THE BLESSINGS HE WITHHELD FROM THE WORLD. This was measure for measure, of which it is written, "For he loved cursing, and it came to him: and he delighted not in blessings, and it was far from him" (Tehilim 109:17). About him, the verse reads, "you are cursed above all cattle, and above every beast of the field" (Beresheet 3:14).

He stayed accursed forever more, and Jacob came and took the blessings from him.

142. וּמִן יוֹמוֹי דְּאָדָם, אִזְדַּמַּן יַעֲקֹב, לְנַטְלָא מֵהַהוּא חִוְיָא, כָּל הַנֵּי בִּרְכָאן, וְאִשְׁתָּאַר אִיהוּ בִּלְוָוטִין, וְלָא נָפַק מִנַּיְיהוּ. וְדָוִד אָמַר בְּרוּחַ קוּדְשָׁא, מַה יִּתֵּן לְךָ וּמַה יּוֹסִיף לָךְ לָשׁוֹן רְמִיָּה חִצֵּי גִבּוֹר שְׁנוּנִים. מַה אִיכְפַת לֵיהּ לְהַהוּא חִוְיָא בִּישָׁא, דְּאַיְיתֵי לְוָוטִין עַל עָלְמָא, כְּמָה דַאֲמָרוּ, נָחָשׁ נוֹשֵׁךְ וּמֵמִית, וְלֵית לֵיהּ הֲנָאָה מִנֵּיהּ.

142. From the time of Adam, Jacob was destined to take from the serpent all these blessings, and the serpent was to remain accursed, NEVER to be released from them. And David, inspired by the Holy Spirit, asked, "What shall be given to you? Or what shall be done to you, you false tongue? Sharp arrows of the mighty" (Tehilim 120:3-4). What causes this evil serpent to bring curses upon the world, when he is, as they said, a serpent that bites and kills, but draws no pleasure from it?

143. לָשׁוֹן רְמִיָּה: דְּרָמֵי לֵיהּ לְאָדָם וּלְאַתְּתֵיהּ, וְאַיְיתֵי בִּישָׁא עֲלֵיהּ, וְעַל עָלְמָא. לְבָתַר אָתָא יַעֲקֹב, וְנָטִיל מִדִּילֵיהּ כָּל אִינּוּן בִּרְכָאן. חִצֵּי גִבּוֹר שְׁנוּנִים, דָּא עֵשָׂו דְּנָטַר דְּבָבוּ לְיַעֲקֹב, עַל אִינּוּן בִּרְכָאן, כְּדְבַר אַחֵר וַיִּשְׂטֹם עֵשָׂו אֶת יַעֲקֹב עַל הַבְּרָכָה וְגו'.

143. "...False tongue." For the serpent deceived Adam and his wife and brought evil on him and the world. Then came Jacob, who took the blessings that were his own. "Sharp arrows of the mighty" refers to Esau, who harbored hatred toward Jacob on account of the blessings, as it is written, "and Esau hated Jacob because of the blessing" (Beresheet 27:41).

144. וְיִתֶּן לְךָ הָאֱלֹהִים מִטַּל הַשָּׁמַיִם וּמִשְׁמַנֵּי הָאָרֶץ, הָא מִלְּעֵילָא וּמִתַּתָּא בְּחִבּוּרָא חֲדָא. וְרוֹב דָּגָן וְתִירוֹשׁ, הָא אוּקְמוּהָ, אֲבָל כְּדִכְתִיב וְלֹא רָאִיתִי צַדִּיק נֶעֱזָב וְזַרְעוֹ מְבַקֶּשׁ לָחֶם. תָּא חֲזֵי, נַעַר הָיִיתִי וְגו' וְאוּקְמוּהָ, הַאי קְרָא שָׂרוֹ שֶׁל עוֹלָם אֲמָרוֹ וכו'. וּבְגִין כָּךְ אָמַר וְרוֹב דָּגָן וְתִירוֹשׁ.

144. "Therefore the Elohim gives you of the dew of heaven, and the fatness of the earth" (Beresheet 27:28), NAMELY, from above and below, ZEIR ANPIN AND NUKVA, joined together, AS HEAVEN IS ZEIR ANPIN AND THE EARTH IS THE NUKVA. "...and plenty of corn and wine" (Ibid.) has already been explained. It is similar to the verse, "yet I have not seen a just man forsaken, and his seed begging bread" (Tehilim 37:25). Come and behold: "I have been young, and now am old" (Ibid.). This verse was said by the minister of the world, NAMELY, METATRON. And therefore he said "and plenty of corn and wine."

145. יַעַבְדוּךָ עַמִּים בְּזִמְנָא דְּשַׁלִּיט שְׁלֹמֹה מַלְכָּא בִּירוּשָׁלֵם, דִּכְתִיב וְכָל מַלְכֵי הָאָרֶץ וגו' מְבִיעִים אִישׁ מִנְחָתוֹ וגו'. וְיִשְׁתַּחֲווּ לְךָ לְאוּמִים, בְּזִמְנָא דְיֵיתֵי מַלְכָּא מְשִׁיחָא, דִּכְתִיב וְיִשְׁתַּחֲווּ לוֹ כָל מְלָכִים. רַבִּי יְהוּדָה אָמַר, כֹּלָּא בְּזִמְנָא דְיֵיתֵי מַלְכָּא מְשִׁיחָא, כִּדְכְתִיב וְיִשְׁתַּחֲווּ לוֹ כָל מְלָכִים כָּל גּוֹיִם יַעַבְדוּהוּ.

145. "Let peoples serve you" (Beresheet 27:29). THIS WAS when king Solomon reigned in Jerusalem, as it is written, "And all the kings of the earth...brought every man his present" (II Divrei Hayamim 9:23-24). "...and nations bow down to you" at the advent of Messiah, according to the verse, "And may all Kings fall down before him." Rabbi Yehuda said: all this will occur with the coming of the King Messiah, as written: "And may all kings fall down before him; all nations serve him" (Tehilim 72:11).

146. הֱוֵה גְבִיר לְאַחֶיךָ, הֱוֵה, וְלֹא אָמַר הֱיֵה, אוֹ תִהְיֶה. אֶלָּא דָּא רָזָא עִלָּאָה דִּמְהֵימְנוּתָא, דְּאִלֵּין אַתְוָון אִנּוּן רָזֵי דִמְהֵימְנוּתָא, ה' לְעֵילָּא, וא"ו בְּאֶמְצָעִיתָא, ה' לְבָתַר. וּבְגִין כָּךְ אָמַר, הֱוֵה גְבִיר לְאַחֶיךָ, לְשַׁלְטָאָה עֲלַיְיהוּ, וּלְרַדָּאָה לוֹן, בְּזִמְנָא דְּאָתָא דָוִד מַלְכָּא. רַבִּי יוֹסֵי אָמַר, כֹּלָּא אִיהוּ בְּזִמְנָא דְיֵיתֵי מַלְכָּא מְשִׁיחָא, דְּהָא בְּגִין דַּעֲבָרוּ יִשְׂרָאֵל עַל פִּתְגָּמֵי אוֹרַיְיתָא, כְּדֵין וּפָרַקְתָּ עֻלּוֹ מֵעַל צַוָּארֶךָ.

146. "Be lord over your brethren" (Beresheet 27:29). HE ASKS: WHY DOES SCRIPTURE USE *Heveh* (be), instead of the more accepted *Heyeh* or *Tih'yeh*? HE ANSWERS: This is a supernal mystery of faith, for these letters, *HEI-VAV-HEI* are mysteries of faith. The upper *Hei* above IS BINAH, *Vav* in the middle IS TIFERET, and the last *Hei* IS MALCHUT. Therefore he said "*Heveh* (be) a lord over your brethren," rule over them, and govern them BY THE POWER OF THESE LETTERS, when king David will appear. Rabbi Yosi said that all that will happen when Messiah will come, THAT IS, ALL THESE BLESSINGS ALLUDE TO THE TIME OF THE END OF CORRECTION AND AFTER THE ADVENT OF MESSIAH, AND NOT BEFORE. For AS LONG AS Yisrael transgress the words of the Torah, then, IT IS WRITTEN, "you shall break his yoke from off your neck" (Ibid. 40). THEREFORE, BLESSINGS WILL PREVAIL ONLY AFTER THE ADVENT OF MESSIAH, WHEN THEY WILL REPENT AND SIN NO MORE.

147. וְיִתֶּן לְךָ הָאֱלֹהִים רִבִּי יוֹסֵי אָמַר, כָּל הַנֵּי בִּרְכָאן, מִסְּטְרָא דְּחוּלָקֵיהּ דְּיַעֲקֹב הֲווֹ, וּמִדִּילֵיהּ נָטַל, וְאִלֵּין בִּרְכָאן, הֲוָה קָא בָּעֵי יִצְחָק לְבָרְכָא לֵיהּ לְעֵשָׂו, וּבְגִין כָּךְ עֲבַד קוּדְשָׁא בְּרִיךְ הוּא, וְגָרַם לֵיהּ לְיַעֲקֹב, לְנַטְלָא מִדִּילֵיהּ.

147. "Therefore the Elohim give you" (Beresheet 27:28). Rabbi Yosi said that all these blessings on the side of Ya'akov's portion were his, and he took his own. And Isaac wanted to bestow the blessings THAT BELONGED TO JACOB upon Esau. Therefore, the Holy One, blessed be He, caused them to revert to Jacob, that he may take that which is his own.

148. תָּא חֲזֵי, בְּשַׁעְתָּא דְּהַהוּא נָחָשׁ, אַיְיתֵי לְוָוטִין עַל עַלְמָא, וְאִתְלַטְיָא אַרְעָא, מַה כְּתִיב, וּלְאָדָם אָמַר כִּי שָׁמַעְתָּ לְקוֹל אִשְׁתְּךָ וְגוֹ', אֲרוּרָה הָאֲדָמָה בַּעֲבוּרֶךָ וְגוֹ', דְּלָא תְּהֵא עָבְדָא פֵּירִין וְאִיבִּין כְּדְקָא יָאוֹת, לָקֳבֵל דָּא, וּמִשְׁמַנֵּי הָאָרֶץ. בְּעִצָּבוֹן תֹּאכְלֶנָּה, לָקֳבֵל דָּא מִטַּל הַשָּׁמָיִם. וְקוֹץ וְדַרְדַּר תַּצְמִיחַ לָךְ, לָקֳבֵל דָּא, וְרֹב דָּגָן וְתִירוֹשׁ. בְּזֵעַת אַפֶּךָ תֹּאכַל לֶחֶם, לָקֳבֵל דָּא, יַעַבְדוּךָ עַמִּים וְיִשְׁתַּחֲווּ לְךָ לְאוּמִּים, דְּאִינּוּן יַעַבְדוּן אַרְעָא, וְיִפְלְחוּן בְּחַקְלָא, כְּדִבּר אַחֵר וּבְנֵי נֵכָר אִכָּרֵיכֶם וְכוֹרְמֵיכֶם. וְכֹלָּא נָטַל יַעֲקֹב, דָּא לָקֳבֵל דָּא, וּמִדִּילֵיהּ נָטַל. וְקוּדְשָׁא בְּרִיךְ הוּא גָּרֵים לֵיהּ לְיַעֲקֹב, דְּיִטֹּל הַנֵּי בִּרְכָאן, לְאִתְדַּבְּקָא בְּאַתְרֵיהּ וְחוּלָקֵיהּ, וְעֶשָׂו לְאִתְדַּבְּקָא בְּאַתְרֵיהּ וְחוּלָקֵיהּ.

148. Come and behold: Of the time when the serpent brought curses upon

the world, and the land was accursed, it is written, "And to the man he said: Because you have hearkened to the voice of your wife...cursed is the ground for your sake" (Beresheet 3:17), for it will not produce fruit nor vegetation in a proper measure. Correspondingly JACOB WAS GIVEN BLESSINGS FOR THE TIME AFTER THE ADVENT OF MESSIAH, WHEN THE SIN OF THE TREE OF KNOWLEDGE WILL HAVE BEEN ATONED FOR: "...and the fatness of the earth" MEANS THAT THE EARTH WILL BE WHOLE AGAIN; AGAINST THE CURSE "in sorrow shall you eat of it" (Ibid.), HE WAS BLESSED "of the dew of heaven"; CORRESPONDING TO THE CURSE "thorns and thistles shall it bring forth to you," HE WAS BLESSED accordingly with "plenty of corn and wine." In opposition to THE CURSE "in the sweat of your face shall you eat bread," HE WAS BLESSED, AS IT IS WRITTEN, "let peoples serve you, and nations bow down to you," as they will cultivate the land and till the field, as it is written, "and the sons of the alien shall be your plowmen and your vinedressers" (Yeshayah 61:5). Jacob took it all measure for measure, EACH BLESSING CORRESPONDING TO ONE CURSE OF THE RREE OF KNOWLEDGE, and of his own he took. The Holy One, blessed be He, caused Jacob to receive these blessings and cleave to his place and portion, while Esau cleaved to his own place and portion. RABBI YOSI SUPPORTS WHAT WAS SAID, THAT THE BLESSINGS WERE VALID FOR THE END OF CORRECTION, BY SAYING THAT THEN WILL THE SIN OF THE TREE OF KNOWLEDGE BE ATONED FOR, AND IT WOULD BE POSSIBLE TO MERIT A BLESSING INSTEAD OF A CURSE, WHICH WAS NOT TRUE BEFORE ATONING FOR THE SIN OF THE TREE OF KNOWLEDGE.

149. אָמַר ר' חִזְקִיָּה, וְהָא חָמֵינָן, דְּמִשְׁמַנֵּי הָאָרֶץ וְטַל הַשָּׁמַיִם, אִינוּן בִּרְכָאן נָטַל עֵשָׂו לְבָתַר, כִּדְבָר אַחֵר הִנֵּה מִשְׁמַנֵּי הָאָרֶץ יִהְיֶה מוֹשָׁבֶךָ וְטַל הַשָּׁמַיִם מֵעָל.

149. Rabbi Chizkiyah said: We see that the fatness of the earth and the dew of heaven were the blessing Esau later received, as it is written, "of the fatness of the earth, and of the dew of heaven from above" (Beresheet 27:39). CAN YOU SAY THAT THESE CORRESPOND TO THE CURSES OF THE TREE OF KNOWLEDGE AFTER THE PENITENCE AT THE ADVENT OF MESSIAH?

150. אָמַר רִבִּי שִׁמְעוֹן, לָאו הַאי כְּהַאי, וְלָא דָּא כְּדָא, כַּמָּה אִתְפָּרְשָׁאן

דַּרְגִּין, בְּיַעֲקֹב כְּתִיב, וְיִתֶּן לְךָ הָאֱלֹהִים, וּבְדָא כְּתִיב יִהְיֶה. בְּיַעֲקֹב
כְּתִיב, מִטַּל הַשָּׁמַיִם וּמִשְׁמַנֵּי הָאָרֶץ, בְּעֵשָׂו כְּתִיב מִשְׁמַנֵּי הָאָרֶץ וְטַל
הַשָּׁמַיִם, דְּהָא לָאו דָּא אִיהוּ כְּדָא.

150. Rabbi Shimon said: The one is not like the other; ESAU IS NOT LIKE
JACOB, and this does not resemble that. THE BLESSING OF ESAU DOES
NOT RESEMBLE THE BLESSING OF JACOB. How different are the grades!
of Jacob, it is written, "Therefore the Elohim give you." And of Esau, it is
written, "YOUR DWELLING shall be." ELOHIM IS NOT MENTIONED IN THIS
BLESSING, SO IT WILL NOT COMPRISE HOLINESS. It is written of Jacob,
"of the dew of heaven, and the fatness of the earth," and of Esau, "of the
fatness of the earth, and of the dew of heaven," WITH THE EARTH
PRECEDING HEAVEN, for there is no resemblance between them.

151. וְדַרְגִּין אִתְפָּרְשָׁן כַּמָּה וְכַמָּה. בְּגִין דִּבְדָא דְּיַעֲקֹב כְּתִיב בֵּיהּ, וְיִתֶּן
לְךָ הָאֱלֹהִים מִטַּל הַשָּׁמַיִם, דָּא טַל עִלָּאָה דְּנָגִיד מֵעַתִּיק יוֹמִין, דְּאִקְרֵי
טַל הַשָּׁמַיִם, הַשָּׁמַיִם דִּלְעֵילָא, טַל דְּנָגִיד בְּדַרְגָּא דִּשְׁמַיָּא, וּמִתַּמָּן לַחֲקַל
תַּפּוּחִין קַדִּישִׁין. וּמִשְׁמַנֵּי הָאָרֶץ, הָאָרֶץ: דָּא אֶרֶץ הַחַיִּים דִּלְעֵילָא,
וְיָרִית לַהּ בְּאַרְעָא דִּלְעֵילָא, וּבַשָּׁמַיִם דִּלְעֵילָא. וּלְעֵשָׂו בְּאַרְעָא דְּהָכָא
לְתַתָּא, וּבַשָּׁמַיִם דְּהָכָא לְתַתָּא. יַעֲקֹב לְעֵילָא לְעֵילָא. עֵשָׂו לְתַתָּא
לְתַתָּא.

151. Their grades differ considerably from each other. It is written of Jacob,
"Therefore the Elohim give you of the dew of heaven" (Beresheet 27:28).
This is the supernal dew drawn from Atik Yomin, which is called 'the dew
of heaven', THAT IS, THE DEW FROM ABOVE, drawn from the grade called
'heaven', ZEIR ANPIN, from which it flows into the field of holy apple trees,
MALCHUT, ABOUT WHICH IT IS THEN WRITTEN, "of the fatness of the
earth." The earth refers to the land of the living above, THAT IS, MALCHUT,
WHILE ATTIRING THE SFIRAH BINAH CALLED 'LIVING ELOHIM', IS THEN
CALLED 'THE LAND OF THE LIVING'. And Jacob inherited THE BLESSING in
the upper earth, MALCHUT, and upper heaven. THE BLESSING OF Esau was
in the lower land here and in the lower heaven here IN THIS WORLD. Jacob
WAS BLESSED high above, IN THE HEAVEN AND EARTH OF ATZILUT, and
Esau down below, IN THE HEAVEN AND EARTH OF THIS WORLD.

152. תּוּ, יַעֲקֹב לְעֵילָא וְתַתָּא, וְעֵשָׂו לְתַתָּא. וְאַף עַל גַּב דִּכְתִיב וְהָיָה כַּאֲשֶׁר תָּרִיד וּפָרַקְתָּ עֻלּוֹ מֵעַל צַוָּארֶךָ. מֵהַאי דְּהָכָא לְתַתָּא, אֲבָל לְעֵילָא לָא כְּלוּם, דִּכְתִיב כִּי חֵלֶק יְיָ' עַמּוֹ יַעֲקֹב חֶבֶל נַחֲלָתוֹ. תָּא חֲזֵי, בְּשַׁעְתָּא דְּשָׁרוּ לְנַטְלָא בִּרְכָאן דִּלְהוֹן, יַעֲקֹב וְעֵשָׂו. יַעֲקֹב נָטַל חוּלָקֵיהּ דִּלְעֵילָא, וְעֵשָׂו נָטִיל חוּלָקֵיהּ לְתַתָּא.

152. Also, Jacob WAS BLESSED above and below IN THE UPPER HEAVEN AND EARTH, AND IN THIS WORLD AT THE ADVENT OF MESSIAH. And Esau only below IN HEAVEN AND EARTH OF THIS WORLD. And though it is written, "and it shall come to pass when you shall have the dominion, that you shall break his yoke from off your neck" (Beresheet 27:40), WHICH MEANS THAT IF YISRAEL WILL SIN, THE BLESSINGS WILL BE ANNULLED, this was SAID CONCERNING HEAVEN AND EARTH here IN THIS WORLD, but up above, nothing IS CANCELED, as it is written, "For Hashem's portion is his people: Jacob is the lot of His inheritance" (Devarim 32:9). Come and behold: When Jacob and Esau started to avail themselves of the blessings, Jacob received his share from above, and Esau took his share below.

153. רִבִּי יוֹסֵי בְּרִבִּי שִׁמְעוֹן בֶּן לָקוּנְיָא אָמַר לְרִבִּי אֶלְעָזָר, כְּלוּם שָׁמַעְתָּ מֵאָבִיךָ, אַמַּאי לָא אִתְקַיְּימוּ בִּרְכָאן, דְּבָרְכֵיהּ יִצְחָק לְיַעֲקֹב, וְאִינוּן בִּרְכָאן דִּבְרִיךְ יִצְחָק לְעֵשָׂו, אִתְקַיְּימוּ כֻּלְּהוּ.

153. Rabbi Yosi, the son of Rabbi Shimon, son of Lakunia, asked Rabbi Elazar, has your father explained why the blessings with which Isaac blessed Jacob did not prevail, while the blessings Isaac bestowed on Esau all did?

154. א"ל, כָּל אִינוּן בִּרְכָאן מִתְקַיְּימֵי, וּבִרְכָאן אַחֲרָנִין דְּבָרְכֵיהּ קוּדְשָׁא בְּרִיךְ הוּא לְיַעֲקֹב. אֲבָל מִיָּד, יַעֲקֹב נָטַל לְעֵילָא, וְעֵשָׂו נָטִיל לְתַתָּא. לְבָתַר, כַּד יָקוּם מַלְכָּא מְשִׁיחָא, יִטּוֹל יַעֲקֹב לְעֵילָא וְתַתָּא, וְיִתְאֲבֵיד עֵשָׂו מִכֹּלָּא, וְלָא יְהֵא לֵיהּ חוּלָקָא וְאַחְסָנָא וְדוּכְרָנָא בְּעָלְמָא, כְּדָבָר אַחֵר , וְהָיָה בֵית יַעֲקֹב אֵשׁ וּבֵית יוֹסֵף לֶהָבָה וּבֵית עֵשָׂו לְקַשׁ וְגו'. בְּגִין דְּיִתְאֲבֵיד עֵשָׂו מִכֹּלָּא, וְיָרִית יַעֲקֹב תְּרֵין עָלְמִין, עָלְמָא דֵין

וְעָלְמָא דְאָתֵי.

154. He replied that all these blessings prevailed, along with other blessings that the Holy One, blessed be He, gave to Jacob. But at first, Jacob received ALL HIS BLESSINGS above only, FROM THE UPPER HEAVEN AND EARTH. THEY WERE THEREFORE INCOMPLETE, UNTIL HE ALSO RECEIVED THE BLESSINGS FROM BELOW. And Esau received below. After King Messiah will arise, Jacob will receive above and below, THAT IS, FROM THE LOWER HEAVEN AND EARTH AS WELL, and Esau will lose everything. He will have no portion and inheritance or remembrance in the world. This is the meaning of the verse, "And the house of Jacob shall be fire, and the house of Joseph flame, and the house of Esau for stubble" (Ovadyah 1:8), for Esau will lose everything, and Jacob will inherit both worlds, this world, NAMELY, THE LOWER HEAVEN AND EARTH, and the World to Come, NAMELY, THE UPPER HEAVEN AND EARTH. IT GOES WITHOUT SAYING THAT EVEN BEFORE THE ADVENT OF MESSIAH, JACOB RECEIVES BLESSINGS FROM THE LOWER HEAVEN AND EARTH, THAT IS, WHEN THE TEMPLE EXISTED, ON SHABBATOT AND HOLIDAYS AND ALSO THROUGH PRAYERS. BUT BECAUSE THEY ARE NOT CONSTANT, IT IS NOT CONSIDERED RECEIVING. BUT IN THE FUTURE IT SHALL BE PERMANENT.

155. וּבְהַאי זִמְנָא כְּתִיב וְעָלוּ מוֹשִׁיעִים בְּהַר צִיּוֹן לִשְׁפּוֹט אֶת הַר עֵשָׂו וְהָיְתָה לַיְיָ' הַמְּלוּכָה. הַהוּא מַלְכוּ דְעֵשָׂו, דְּנָטַל בְּהַאי עַלְמָא, יְהֵא לֵיהּ לְקוּדְשָׁא בְּרִיךְ הוּא בִּלְחוֹדוֹי. וְכִי הַשְׁתָּא לָאו אִיהִי מַלְכוּ מְקוּדְשָׁא בְּרִיךְ הוּא אֶלָּא אַף עַל גַּב דְּשַׁלִּיט קוּדְשָׁא בְּרִיךְ הוּא לְעֵילָא וְתַתָּא, הָא יָהַב לוֹן לִשְׁאָר עַמִּין, לְכָל חַד וְחַד, חוּלָק וְאַחְסַנְתָּא בְּהַאי עַלְמָא, לְאִשְׁתַּמְּשָׁא בֵּיהּ, וּבְהַהִיא זִמְנָא, יִטּוֹל מִכֻּלְּהוּ מַלְכוּתָא, וּתְהֵא דִילֵיהּ כֹּלָּא, דִּכְתִיב וְהָיְתָה לַיְיָ' הַמְּלוּכָה, לֵיהּ בִּלְחוֹדוֹי, דִּכְתִיב וְהָיָה יְיָ' לְמֶלֶךְ עַל כָּל הָאָרֶץ בַּיּוֹם הַהוּא יְיָ' אֶחָד וּשְׁמוֹ אֶחָד.

155. At that point, it is written, "And liberators shall ascend upon mount Zion to judge the mountain of Esau; and the kingdom shall be Hashem's" (Ibid.). The kingdom that Esau received in this world shall be for the Holy One, blessed be He, alone. HE ASKS IF this kingdom did not already belong to the Holy One, blessed be He? AND HE ANSWERS: Although the Holy

One, blessed be He, rules above and below, He lets other peoples rule, giving each a part and inheritance in this world for their use. At that time He will take the kingdom from them all, and it will be solely His, as it is written, "And Hashem shall be king over all the earth: on that day Hashem shall be one, and His name One" (Zecharyah 14:9).

156. וַיְהִי אַךְ יָצֹא יָצָא יַעֲקֹב וְגו'. רִבִּי שִׁמְעוֹן אָמַר, אַךְ יָצֹא יָצָא, תְּרֵי יְצִיאוֹת הַלָּלוּ לָמָה. אֶלָּא חַד דִּשְׁכִינְתָּא, וְחַד דְּיַעֲקֹב, דְּהָא כַּד עָאל יַעֲקֹב, שְׁכִינְתָּא עָאלַת עִמֵּיה, וְקַמֵּי שְׁכִינְתָּא אִתְבָּרֵךְ, דְּיִצְחָק הֲוָה אָמַר בִּרְכָאן, וּשְׁכִינְתָּא אוֹדֵי לְהוֹ עֲלַיְיהוּ. וְכַד נָפַק יַעֲקֹב, שְׁכִינְתָּא נָפְקַת עִמֵּיה, הֲדָא הוּא דִכְתִיב אַךְ יָצֹא יָצָא יַעֲקֹב, תְּרֵי יְצִיאוֹת כְּחַד.

156. "And Jacob was scarce gone out (lit. 'went out going')" (Beresheet 27:30): Rabbi Shimon said: "...went out, going" refers to two goings out. Why? Because one is of the Shechinah and one of Jacob. For when Jacob entered, the Shechinah came in with him, and he was blessed before the Shechinah. Isaac said the blessings and the Shechinah approved. Therefore, when Jacob went out, the Shechinah went out with him. This is the hidden meaning of the phrase "and Jacob went out going," which mentions two goings out together.

157. וְעֵשָׂו אָחִיו בָּא מִצֵּידוֹ. מִן הַצַּיִד לָא כְּתִיב, אֶלָּא מִצֵּידוֹ, דְּאִיהוּ צֵידָה דִּילֵיה, דְּלָא הֲוָה בֵּיה בְּרָכָה, וְרוּחַ הַקֹּדֶשׁ צָוְוחָה וְאָמְרָה, אַל תִּלְחַם אֶת לֶחֶם רַע עַיִן.

157. "Esau his brother came in from his hunting" (Ibid.): HE ASKS: Why is it written "his hunting", and not "the hunting." HE SAYS THAT THIS INDICATES THAT it is Esau's hunting that contains no blessing. And the holy spirit cried out, "Do not eat the bread of him who has an evil eye" (Mishlei 23:6).

158. וַיַּעַשׂ גַּם הוּא מַטְעַמִּים וְגו'. יָקוּם אָבִי, דְּבוּרֵיה, הֲוָה בְּעַזּוּת, בִּתְקִיפוּ רוּחָא, מִלָּה דְּלֵית בָּהּ טַעֲמָא, יָקוּם אָבִי. תָּא חֲזֵי, מַה בֵּין יַעֲקֹב לְעֵשָׂו, יַעֲקֹב אָמַר בְּכִסּוּפוֹ דַּאֲבוֹי, בַּעֲנָוָה, מַה כְּתִיב וַיָּבֹא אֶל אָבִיו וַיֹּאמֶר אָבִי. מַה בֵּין הַאי לְהַאי, אֶלָּא, דְּלָא בָּעָא לְאִזְדַּעְזְעָא

-259-

לֵיהּ, מַלִּיל בְּלִשׁוֹן תַּחֲנוּנִים, קוּם נָא שְׁבָה וְאָכְלָה מִצֵּידִי. וְעֵשָׂו אָמַר, יָקוּם אָבִי, כְּמַאן דְּלָא מַלִּיל עִמֵּיהּ.

158. "And he also had made savory food...Let my father arise" (Beresheet 27:31). His speech was impertinent, rough, and impolite. Come and behold the difference between Jacob and Esau. Jacob talked to his father humbly, with humility. It is written, "And he came to his father, and said, My father" (Ibid. 18). The difference between the language of Esau and Jacob is that Jacob did not want to frighten him. Thus, he spoke humbly, saying "arise, I pray you, sit and eat of my venison." Esau, however, said "Let my father arise," as if he was not speaking to him, BUT TO HIMSELF.

159. תָּא חֲזֵי, בְּשַׁעְתָּא דְּעָאל עֵשָׂו, עָאל עִמֵּיהּ גֵּיהִנָּם, אִזְדַּעְזַע יִצְחָק, וְדָחִיל. דִּכְתִיב וַיֶּחֱרַד יִצְחָק חֲרָדָה גְּדוֹלָה עַד מְאֹד. כֵּיוָן דִּכְתִיב וַיֶּחֱרַד יִצְחָק חֲרָדָה גְּדוֹלָה דַּי מַהוּ עַד מְאֹד. אֶלָּא, דְּלָא הֲוָה דְּחִילוּ וְאֵימָתָא. דְּנָפַל עֲלֵיהּ דְּיִצְחָק, רַבְּתָא, מִיּוֹמֵי דְּאִתְבְּרֵי, וַאֲפִי' בְּהַהִיא שַׁעְתָּא, דְּאִתְעֲקַד יִצְחָק עַל גַּבֵּי מַדְבְּחָא, וְחָמָא סַכִּינָא עֲלֵיהּ, לָא אִזְדַּעְזַע, כְּהַהִיא שַׁעְתָּא, דְּעָאל עֵשָׂו, וְחָמָא גֵּיהִנָּם דְּעָאל עִמֵּיהּ, כְּדֵין אָמַר, בְּטֶרֶם תָּבֹא וָאֲבָרֲכֵהוּ גַּם בָּרוּךְ יִהְיֶה, בְּגִין דְּחָמֵית שְׁכִינְתָּא דְּאוֹדֵי עַל אִינוּן בִּרְכָאן.

159. Come and behold: When Esau entered, Gehenom came with him, and Isaac trembled with fear, as it is written, "And Isaac trembled very much" (Beresheet 27:33). HE ASKS: Why is "very much" used to describe "trembled." HE SAID: Isaac never felt such fear and terror during his life. Even when he was strapped upon the altar and saw the knife, he did not tremble as when Esau entered and brought Gehenom with him. Then he said: "before you came, and have blessed him? moreover, he shall be blessed." For I saw the Shechinah approving those blessings.

160. דָּבָר אַחֵר, יִצְחָק אָמַר וָאֲבָרֲכֵהוּ, נָפַק קָלָא וְאָמַר, גַּם בָּרוּךְ יִהְיֶה, בָּעָא יִצְחָק לְמֵילַט לֵיהּ לְיַעֲקֹב, אָמַר לֵיהּ קוּדְשָׁא בְּרִיךְ הוּא, יִצְחָק, גַּרְמָךְ אַנְתְּ לַיי', דְּהָא כְּבָר אֲמָרִת לֵיהּ, אֹרֲרֶיךָ אָרוּר וּמְבָרֲכֶיךָ בָּרוּךְ.

160. There is another explanation: Isaac said, "and have blessed him." A voice came forth, saying "moreover, he shall be blessed." Isaac wanted to curse Jacob, but the Holy One, blessed be He, said to him, Isaac, it is you whom you curse, for you have said to him "cursed be those that curse you, and blessed be those that bless you" (Beresheet 27:29).

161. תָּא חֲזֵי כֹּלָּא אוֹדוּ עַל אִינּוּן בִּרְכָאן, עִלָּאֵי וְתַתָּאֵי, וַאֲפִילוּ אִיהוּ חוּלָק עֲדְבֵיהּ דְּעֵשָׂו, אוֹדִי עֲלַיְיהוּ, וּבָרְכֵיהּ אִיהוּ, וְאוֹדֵי עַל אִינּוּן בִּרְכָאן, וְסַלְקֵיהּ עַל רֵישֵׁיהּ לְעֵילָּא.

161. Come and behold: Everyone acknowledged these blessings, the upper and lower, and even he, NAMELY, SAMAEL, THE MINISTER OF ESAU, the part and portion of Esau, acknowledged them. And he blessed him and approved of the blessings, and raised him above his head, THAT IS, HE WAS SUBMISSIVE TO HIM.

162. מְנָלָן, דִּכְתִיב וַיֹּאמֶר שַׁלְּחֵנִי כִּי עָלָה הַשַּׁחַר וַיֹּאמֶר לֹא אֲשַׁלֵּחֲךָ כִּי אִם בֵּרַכְתָּנִי. וַיֹּאמֶר שַׁלְּחֵנִי, בְּגִין דְּאַתְקִיף בֵּיהּ יַעֲקֹב. וְכִי הֵיךְ יָכִיל בַּר נָשׁ דְּאִיהוּ גּוּפָא וּבִשְׂרָא, לְאִתְתַּקְפָא בֵּיהּ בְּמַלְאָכָא, דְּאִיהוּ רוּחַ מַמָּשׁ, דִּכְתִיב עוֹשֶׂה מַלְאָכָיו רוּחוֹת מְשָׁרְתָיו אֵשׁ לוֹהֵט.

162. From where do we know this? From the verse, "And he said, Let me go, for the day breaks. And he said, I will not let you go, unless you bless me" (Beresheet 32:27). It is written, "And he said, Let me go" because Jacob had seized him. HE ASKS: How can a man, flesh and blood, take hold of an angel, which is pure spirit, as it is written, "who makes the winds His messengers; the flames of fire His ministers" (Tehilim 104:4)?

163. אֶלָּא, מִכָּאן דְּמַלְאֲכֵי שְׁלִיחֵי דְּקוּדְשָׁא בְּרִיךְ הוּא, כַּד אִינּוּן נָחֲתִין לְהַאי עָלְמָא גְּלִימִין, וְאִתְגְּלִימוּ, וּמִתְלַבְּשִׁין בְּגוּפָא, כְּגַוְונָא דְּהַאי עָלְמָא, בְּגִין דְּהָכִי אִתְחֲזֵי, דְּלָא לְהַשְׁנָאָה מִמִּנְהָגָא דְּהַהוּא אֲתָר דְּאָזִיל תַּמָּן.

163. HE ANSWERS: It is understood from this that when angels, the messengers of the Holy One, blessed be He, descend into this world, they are clothed in a body in the likeness of this world, for it is not seemly to deviate from the custom of the place one visits.

164. וְהָא אִתְּמֵר, דְּמֹשֶׁה כַּד סָלֵיק לְעֵילָּא, מַה כְּתִיב וַיְהִי שָׁם עִם יְיָ' אַרְבָּעִים יוֹם וְאַרְבָּעִים לַיְלָה לֶחֶם לֹא אָכַל וּמַיִם לֹא שָׁתָה, בְּגִין מִנְהֲגָא, דְּלָא לְהַשְׁנָאָה מֵהַהוּא אֲתַר דְּאָזֵיל לְתַמָּן, וְאִינּוּן מַלְאָכִין כַּד נַחֲתוּ לְתַתָּא כְּתִיב וְהוּא עוֹמֵד עֲלֵיהֶם תַּחַת הָעֵץ וַיֹּאכֵלוּ. וְכֵן הָכָא, הַאי מַלְאָכָא, כַּד נָחַת לְתַתָּא, לָא אִתְאָבַק עִמֵּיהּ דְּיַעֲקֹב, אֶלָּא מִגּוֹ דַּהֲוָה אִתְלַבַּשׁ בְּגוּפָא כְּגַוְונָא דְּהַאי עָלְמָא. וְעַל דָּא אִתְאָבַק יַעֲקֹב בַּהֲדֵיהּ, כָּל הַהוּא לֵילְיָא.

164. We have learned that when Moses went up, "he was there with Hashem forty days and forty nights; he did neither eat bread, nor drink water" (Shemot 34:28) in order not to deviate from the custom of the place he went to. And of the angels, WHO VISITED ABRAHAM when they descended, it is written, "and he stood by them under the tree, and they ate" (Bereshit 18:8). Here also, the descending angel could not struggle with Jacob unless clothed in a body, as is done in this world. Therefore Jacob wrestled with him the whole night. But if he were not clothed (in human form), Jacob could not have wrestled with him.

165. תָּא חֲזֵי, בְּגִין דְּשַׁלְטָנוּתָא דְּהַנֵּי, לָאו אִיהוּ אֶלָּא בְּלֵילְיָא וַדַּאי, וּבְגִין כָּךְ, שַׁלְטָנוּתָא דְעֵשָׂו, לָאו אִיהוּ אֶלָּא בְּגָלוּתָא, דְּאִיהוּ לַיְלָה, וְעַל דָּא בְּלֵילְיָא אִתְתַּקַּף עִמֵּיהּ דְּיַעֲקֹב, וְאִתְאָבַק עִמֵּהּ. וְכַד אֲתָא צַפְרָא, אִתְחֲלָשׁ חֵילֵיהּ, וְלָא יָכֵיל, וּכְדֵין אִתְתַּקַּף יַעֲקֹב, בְּגִין דְּיַעֲקֹב, שַׁלְטָנוּתֵיהּ בִּימָמָא

165. Come and behold: Because this those OF THE OTHER SIDE dominate only during the night, assuredly this is why Esau rules only in exile, which is night, WHEN IT IS DARK FOR US. Hence, THE ANGEL wrestled and struggled with Jacob during the night. But when morning came, the strength of the angel failed, and he did not prevail. Then Jacob got stronger, as the dominion of Jacob is during the day.

166. וּבְגִין כָּךְ, כְּתִיב מַשָּׂא דּוּמָה אֵלַי קֹרֵא מִשֵּׂעִיר שֹׁמֵר מַה מִּלַּיְלָה

שָׁמַר מַה מֵּלִיל. דְּהָא כְּדֵין שׁוּלְטָנוּתֵיה דִּידֵיה דְּעֵשָׂו, דְּאִיהִי שָׂעִיר, בַּלַּיְלָה אִיהוּ, וּבְגִין כָּךְ אִתְחֲלָשׁ, כַּד אָתָא צַפְרָא, וּכְדֵין וַיֹּאמֶר שַׁלְּחֵנִי כִּי עָלָה הַשָּׁחַר.

166. Therefore, it is written, "The burden of Dumah. One calls to me out of Seir, Watchman, what of the night? Watchman, what of the night?" (Yeshayah 21:11), for the dominion of Esau, who is called 'Se'ir', is during the night. Therefore the angel weakened when morning came, and then "he said, Let me go, for the day breaks."

167. וַיֹּאמֶר לֹא אֲשַׁלֵּחֲךָ כִּי אִם בֵּרַכְתָּנִי, כִּי אִם בֵּרַכְתָּנִי, כִּי אִם תְּבָרְכֵנִי מִבָּעֵי לֵיה מַאי כִּי אִם בֵּרַכְתָּנִי. אִם אוֹדִית, עַל אִינוּן בִּרְכָאן דְּבָרְכַנִי אַבָּא, וְלָא תְהֵא מְקַטְרְגָא לִי בְּגִינַיְיהוּ, מַה כְּתִיב, וַיֹּאמֶר לֹא יַעֲקֹב יֵאָמֵר עוֹד שִׁמְךָ כִּי אִם יִשְׂרָאֵל וְגוֹ', אַמַּאי יִשְׂרָאֵל, אָמַר לוֹ בַּעַל כָּרְחִין אִית לָן לְשַׁמָּשָׁא לָךְ, דְּהָא אַנְתְּ אִתְעַטְּרַת בְּחֵילָךְ, לְעֵילָא בְּדַרְגָּא עִלָּאָה, יִשְׂרָאֵל יִהְיֶה שִׁמְךָ וַדַּאי.

167. "And he said, I will not let you go, unless you bless me" (Beresheet 32:27). HE COMMENTED, IT IS WRITTEN, "Unless you bless me," but it should have been "unless you will bless me", IN THE FUTURE TENSE. Why, therefore, is it written literally, "unless you have blessed me" IN THE PAST TENSE? THE REASON IS THAT HE TOLD HIM if you will acknowledge the blessings my father gave to me and not denounce me for them, THEN I WILL LET YOU GO. FOR THAT REASON, IT IS WRITTEN, "UNLESS YOU HAVE BLESSED ME" IN THE PAST TENSE, FOR IT REFERS TO THE BLESSINGS OF ISAAC. It is also written, "And he said, Your name shall be called no more 'Jacob', but Yisrael" (Beresheet 32:29). HE ASKS: Why did he call him Yisrael? AND HE ANSWERS that he told him, we are compelled to serve you, for through your exceeding might, you have been crowned above, in the highest grade. THEREFORE your name shall surely be Yisrael.

168. כִּי שָׂרִיתָ עִם אֱלֹהִים, מַאי עִם אֱלֹהִים, ס"ד דַּעֲלֵיה הֲוָה אָמַר, אֶלָּא אָמַר לֵיה, שָׂרִיתָ לְאִתְחַבְּרָא וּלְאִזְדַּוְּוגָא עִם אֱלֹהִים בְּחִבּוּרָא,

בְּזִוּוּגָא דְשִׁמְשָׁא וְסִיהֲרָא, וְע"ד לָא כְּתִיב אֶת אֱלֹהִים, אֶלָּא עִם אֱלֹהִים, בְּחִבּוּרָא וְזִוּוּגָא חֲדָא.

168. "For you have striven with Elohim." HE ASKS: What is the meaning of the phrase "with Elohim?" Could it be that he referred to himself WHEN HE SAID "FOR YOU HAVE STRIVEN WITH ELOHIM?" HE ANSWERS "have striven" to be joined and united "with Elohim," THE SHECHINAH, as the union of the sun and moon, WHICH ARE ZEIR ANPIN AND NUKVA. Hence it is not written "against Elohim," but rather "with Elohim," WHICH INDICATES JOINING TOGETHER WITH ELOHIM in a union.

169. דָּבָר אַחֵר , וַיֹּאמֶר: כְּדָבָר אַחֵר וַיֹּאמֶר אִם שָׁמֹעַ תִּשְׁמַע לְקוֹל יי' אֱלֹהֶיךָ, אוּף הָכָא, וַיֹּאמֶר לֹא יֵאָמֵר עוֹד שִׁמְךָ יַעֲקֹב כִּי אִם יִשְׂרָאֵל, כְּדֵין אִתְעַטַּר יַעֲקֹב בְּדַרְגֵּיהּ, לְמֶהֱוֵי כְּלָלָא דַּאֲבָהָן. מַה כְּתִיב, וַיְבָרֶךְ אוֹתוֹ שָׁם. מַאי וַיְבָרֶךְ אוֹתוֹ שָׁם, דְּאוֹדֵי לֵיהּ עַל כֻּלְּהוּ בִּרְכָאן, דְּבָרְכֵיהּ אֲבוֹי.

169. Another explanation of "And he said" has the same meaning as "and He said, If you will diligently hearken to the voice of Hashem your Elohim" (Shemot 15:26). AS "AND HE SAID" REFERS TO THE AWAKENING TO STRIVE TO HEARKEN TO THE VOICE OF HASHEM. Here too "And he said" MEANS THAT HE WOKE HIM AND SAID "Your name shall be called no more 'Jacob', but Israel." Then was Jacob crowned by his grade, FOR HE STROVE TO AND ROSE TO THE GRADE OF THE NAME ISRAEL, WHICH IS THE MOCHIN OF THE FIRST THREE SFIROT, ISRAEL BEING COMPOSED OF THE LETTERS OF 'LI ROSH (LIT. 'I HAVE A HEAD'), by which he will include all the Patriarchs, THAT IS, BE THE CENTRAL COLUMN, WHICH INCLUDES THE LEFT AND RIGHT COLUMNS, THE SECRET OF THE PATRIARCHS ABRAHAM AND ISAAC. It is written, "And he blessed him there" (Beresheet 32:30). WHY IS THE CONTENT OF THE BLESSING NOT SPECIFIED? HE ANSWERS: It means that he acknowledged all the blessings with which his father blessed him.

170. רִבִּי שִׁמְעוֹן פָּתַח וְאָמַר, בִּרְצוֹת יי' דַּרְכֵי אִישׁ גַּם אוֹיְבָיו יַשְׁלִים אִתּוֹ, תָּא חֲזֵי, כַּמָּה אִית לֵיהּ לְבַר נָשׁ, לְאִתְתַּקְּנָא שְׁבִילוֹי, בֵּיהּ

בְּקוּדְשָׁא בְּרִיךְ הוּא, בְּגִין לְמֶעְבַּד פִּקּוּדֵי דְאוֹרַיְיתָא, דְּהָא אוּקְמוּהָ, דְּוַדַּאי תְּרֵין מַלְאָכִין שְׁלִיחָן, אִית לְבַר נָשׁ מִלְעֵילָּא, לְאִזְדַּוְּוגָא בַּהֲדֵיהּ, חַד לִימִינָא, וְחַד לִשְׂמָאלָא, וְאִינּוּן סָהֲדִין בֵּיהּ בְּבַר נָשׁ, בְּכָל מַה דְּאִיהוּ עָבֵיד, אִינּוּן מִשְׁתַּכְּחֵי תַּמָּן, וְקַרְיָינָן לוֹן יֵצֶר טוֹב וְיֵצֶר רָע.

170. Rabbi Shimon began the discourse with the verse, "When a man's ways please Hashem, He makes even his enemies to be at peace with him" (Mishlei 16:7). Come and behold: Man has much to do if he wants to improve his behavior toward the Holy One, blessed be He, by keeping the precepts of the Torah. For we have learned that assuredly man has two angels, who are messengers that join him from above. One is on his right and the other on his left. They observe man in everything he does. They are called 'the Good Inclination' and 'the Evil Inclination'.

171. אָתֵי בַּר נָשׁ לְאִתְדַּכָּאָה, וּלְאִשְׁתַּדְּלָא בְּפִקּוּדֵי דְאוֹרַיְיתָא, הַהוּא יֵצֶר טוֹב דְּאִזְדַּוָּוג בֵּיהּ, כְּבָר אִיהוּ אִתְתַּקַּף עַל יֵצֶר הָרָע, וְאִשְׁתְּלִים בַּהֲדֵיהּ, וְאִתְהַפִּיךְ לֵיהּ לְעַבְדָּא. וְכַד בַּר נָשׁ אָזִיל לְאִסְתַּאֲבָא, הַהוּא יֵצֶר הָרָע, אִתְתַּקַּף וְאִתְגַּבַּר עַל הַהוּא יֵצֶר טוֹב, וְהָא אוֹקִימְנָא, וַדַּאי כַּד הַהוּא בַּר נָשׁ אָתֵי לְאִתְדַּכָּאָה, כַּמָּה תְּקִיף אִתְתַּקַּף בַּר נָשׁ, כַּד אִתְגַּבְּרָא הַהוּא יֵצֶר טוֹב כְּדֵין אוֹיְבָיו יַשְׁלִים אִתּוֹ, דְּהַהוּא יֵצֶר הָרָע אִתְכַּפְיָא קַמֵּיהּ דְּיֵצֶר טוֹב. וְעַל דָּא אָמַר שְׁלֹמֹה, טוֹב נִקְלֶה וְעֶבֶד לוֹ, מַאי וְעֶבֶד לוֹ, דָּא יֵצֶר הָרָע. וּכְדֵין כַּד אָזִיל בַּר נָשׁ בְּפִקּוּדֵי אוֹרַיְיתָא, כְּדֵין גַּם אוֹיְבָיו יַשְׁלִים אִתּוֹ, דָּא יֵצֶר הָרָע, וְדַאֲתָא מִסִּטְרוֹי.

171. When a man wishes to be purified and strives to observe the precepts of the Torah, the Good Inclination that joined him overpowers the Evil Inclination and makes peace with it. As a result, the Evil Inclination becomes a slave to the Good Inclination. When a man wishes to be defiled, the Evil Inclination is strengthened and overpowers the Good Inclination. This has already been explained. Assuredly, when man wishes to be purified, he has much to overcome. When the Good Inclination is strengthened, then "He makes even his enemies to be at peace with him." For the Evil Inclination, WHICH IS HIS ENEMY, is submissive to the Good Inclination. Of this Solomon said: "Better is he that is lightly esteemed, and has a servant" (Mishlei 12:9). The servant is the Evil Inclination, WHICH BECOMES A SERVANT TO THE GOOD INCLINATION. Then, when a man walks by the precepts of the Torah, "he makes even his enemies to be at peace with him," including the Evil Inclination and its escorts.

172. תָּא חֲזֵי, בְּגִין דְּיַעֲקֹב, אַבְטַח בֵּיה בְּקוּדְשָׁא בְּרִיךְ הוּא, וְכָל אָרְחוֹי הֲווֹ לִשְׁמֵיה, עַל דָּא אוֹיְבָיו יַשְׁלִים אִתּוֹ. וְדָא סמאל, חֵילָא וְתוּקְפָּא דַּעֲשָׂו, דְּאַשְׁלִים עִמֵּיה דְּיַעֲקֹב, וּבְגִין דְּאַשְׁלִים עִמֵּיה דְּיַעֲקֹב, וְאוֹדֵי לֵיה עַל אִינוּן בִּרְכָאן, כְּדֵין אַשְׁלִים עִמֵּיה עֵשָׂו, וְעַד דְּלָא אִשְׁתְּלִים עִמֵּיה יַעֲקֹב, לְגַבֵּי הַהוּא מְמַנָּא דְּאִתְפַּקַּד עֲלֵיה, לָא אַשְׁלִים עִמֵּיה עֵשָׂו, בְּגִין כָּךְ, בְּכָל אֲתַר תּוּקְפָּא דִּלְתַתָּא, תַּלְיָא בְּתוּקְפָּא דִּלְעֵילָא.

172. Come and behold: Because Jacob put his trust in the Holy One, blessed be He, and all that he did was for His sake, his enemies made peace with him: specifically Samael, who is the strength and might of Esau, made peace with Jacob. Because Samael made peace with Jacob and acknowledged all his blessings, Esau made peace with Jacob. Yet, as long as Jacob did not make peace with SAMAEL, the minister in charge of Esau, then Esau did not have made peace with him. This is because strength below always depends on strength above. As long as the strength of the ministers in charge over them is not weakened above, it is not possible to weaken the strength in this world.

173. וַיֶּחֱרַד יִצְחָק חֲרָדָה גְּדוֹלָה עַד מְאֹד וַיֹּאמֶר מִי אֵיפֹה. מִי אֵיפֹה: מַאי מִי אֵיפֹה, מִי הוּא זֶה מִבָּעֵי לֵיה, אֶלָּא מִי אֵיפֹה, דְּקַיְימָא שְׁכִינְתָּא תַּמָּן, כַּד בְּרִיךְ לֵיה יִצְחָק לְיַעֲקֹב, וְעַל דָּא אָמַר, מִי אֵיפֹה, מַאן הוּא דְּקָאִים הָכָא, וְאוֹדֵי עַל אִינוּן בִּרְכָאן, דְּבָרְכֵית לֵיה, וַדַּאי גַּם בָּרוּךְ יִהְיֶה. דְּהָא קוּדְשָׁא בְּרִיךְ הוּא אִסְתַּכֵּם בְּאִינוּן בִּרְכָאן.

173. "And Isaac trembled very much, and said, Who then (Heb. eifoh) is he" (Beresheet 27:33). HE ASKS: What is the meaning of "Who then?" It should have been "Who is it?" FOR 'EIFOH' LITERALLY MEANS WHERE. HE ANSWERS: "Who then" is correct because the Shechinah stood there when Isaac blessed Jacob! Thus he said "Who then," WHICH MEANS where is he who stood here and approved the blessings, whom I blessed. Assuredly "he

shall be blessed," for the Holy One, blessed be He, approved these blessings.

174. רִבִּי יְהוּדָה אָמַר, בְּגִין הַהִיא חֲרָדָה דְּאַחֲרִיד יַעֲקֹב, לְיִצְחָק אֲבוֹי, אִתְעֲנַשׁ יַעֲקֹב, בְּעוֹנָשָׁא דְּיוֹסֵף, דְּחָרַד חֲרָדָה כְּהַאי, בְּשַׁעֲתָּא דְּאָמְרוּ לֵיהּ, זֹאת מָצָאנוּ. יִצְחָק אָמַר מִי אֵיפֹה. בְּאֵיפֹה אִתְעֲנַשׁ יַעֲקֹב, דִּכְתִיב אֵיפֹה הֵם רוֹעִים, וְתַמָּן יוֹסֵף אִתְאֲבֵיד, וְאִתְעֲנִישׁ יַעֲקֹב. וְאַף עַל גַּב דְּקוּדְשָׁא בְּרִיךְ הוּא אַסְתַּכַּם עַל יְדוֹי, בְּאִינוּן בִּרְכָאן, אִיהוּ אִתְעֲנַשׁ בְּאֵיפֹה, דִּכְתִיב אֵיפֹה הֵם רוֹעִים. וּמִתַּמָּן אִתְאֲבֵיד מִנֵּיהּ, וְאִתְעֲנַשׁ כָּל הַהוּא עוֹנָשָׁא.

174. Rabbi Yehuda said that for this trembling that Jacob brought upon Isaac his father, Jacob was punished by THE SELLING OF Joseph, and he trembled when they said to him "This we have found" (Beresheet 37:32). Isaac said "Who then (Heb. *eifoh*)." And by "*eifoh*," Jacob was punished. And although the Holy One, blessed be He, approved all the blessings, nevertheless he was punished by "*eifoh*" as it is written, "where (*eifoh*) they feed their flock" (Beresheet 37:6), where Joseph was lost to him, and he was thereby punished.

175. וַיֶּחֱרַד יִצְחָק חֲרָדָה גְדוֹלָה, מַאי גְדוֹלָה, כְּתִיב הָכָא גְדוֹלָה, וּכְתִיב הָתָם וְאֵת הָאֵשׁ הַגְּדוֹלָה הַזֹּאת וְגו', דְּעָאל עַמֵּיהּ גֵּיהִנֹּם. עַד מְאֹד. מַאי עַד מְאֹד. כְּתִיב הָכָא מְאֹד, וּכְתִיב הָתָם וְהִנֵּה טוֹב מְאֹד, דָּא מַלְאַךְ הַמָּוֶת, כְּדֵין אָמַר מִי אֵיפֹה.

175. "...and Isaac trembled very much (lit. 'trembled very great trembling')." HE ASKS: What is the meaning of the word "great" as used in the scripture? AND HE ANSWERS: It is written "great" here and elsewhere, as in "and this great fire" (Devarim 18:16). IN BOTH VERSES, IT REFERS TO A GREAT FIRE, MEANING that Gehenom entered with him. HE THEN ASKS: What does "very" mean? AND HE ANSWERS: It is written "very" here and elsewhere, as in "and, behold, it was very good" (Beresheet 1:31). AGAIN, BOTH REFER TO the Angel of Death; IN THIS CASE, IT IS AN ALLUSION TO THE ANGEL OF DEATH, WHO CAME IN WITH ESAU. He then said "Who then...MOREOVER, HE SHALL BE BLESSED" (Beresheet 27:33),

WHEN HE UNDERSTOOD THAT THE BLESSINGS BELONGED TO JACOB AND NOT ESAU.

176. כְּשְׁמוֹעַ עֵשָׂו אֶת דִּבְרֵי אָבִיו וְגוֹ'. אָמַר רִבִּי חִיָּיא, כַּמָּה בִּישִׁין עָבְדוּ אִינוּן דִּמְעִין, דְּבָכָה וְאַפִּיק עֵשָׂו קַמֵּי אֲבוֹי, בְּגִין דְּיִתְבָּרֵךְ מִנֵּיהּ, בְּגִין דַּהֲוָה חָשִׁיב מִלָּה דַּאֲבוֹי יַתִּיר. הֲכִי קָרָא שְׁמוֹ, יַעֲקֹב. הֲכִי קָרָא שְׁמוֹ, קָרָא שְׁמוֹ הַהוּא דְּקָרָא לֵיהּ, אַפִּיק צִיצָא דְּרוֹקָא, בְּגִין קְלָנָא. הֲכִי נִקְרָא שְׁמוֹ לָא כְּתִיב, אֶלָּא קָרָא שְׁמוֹ.

176. "And when Esau heard the words of his father..." (Beresheet 27:34). Rabbi Chiya said: These tears brought so much evil UPON YISRAEL, that Esau cried to be blessed before his father, whose words were very important to him. BECAUSE OF THEM, ACCUSATIONS WERE MADE THAT YISRAEL DID NOT HONOR THEIR FATHERS AS HE DID. "Is not he rightly named Jacob" (Ibid. 36) means, So He named him, He who did so," NAMELY, THE HOLY ONE, BLESSED BE HE. He uttered this as if spitting, to degrade HE WHO CALLED HIM 'JACOB'. It is not written, "Is not he rightly named," but literally "Did not He rightly named him." THIS INDICATES THAT HE DID NOT MEAN TO DEGRADE JACOB, BUT HE WHO NAMED HIM JACOB.

177. וַיַּעְקְבֵנִי זֶה פַעֲמָיִם. זֶה. מַהוּ זֶה, וַיַּעְקְבֵנִי פַעֲמַיִם מִבְעֵי לֵיהּ. אֶלָּא, מִלָּה חַד הֲוֵי תְּרֵי זִמְנֵי, בְּכוֹרָתִי, אַהֲדַר לֵיהּ זִמְנָא אָחֳרָא בִּרְכָתִי, זֶה הוּא תְּרֵי זִמְנִין. כְּגַוְונָא דָא, כִּי עַתָּה שַׁבְנוּ זֶה פַעֲמָיִם, מִלָּה חַד, תְּרֵין זִמְנִין. חַד דְּהָא אַהֲדַרְנָא לֵיהּ, וְלָא נֶהֱוֵי בְּכִסּוּפָא קַמֵּיהּ דְּהַהוּא בַּר נָשׁ. שַׁבְנוּ: בְּשִׁנּוּ. אֲנַן בְּכִסּוּפָא מִנֵּיהּ, וּכְבָר אַהֲדַרְנָא.

177. "For he has supplanted these (Heb. zeh; lit. 'this') two times." HE ASKS: Why ADD THE WORD Zeh to modify "supplanted two times?" HE ANSWERS: It means two matters are contained in one. The word bechorati (my birthright) became at another time birchati (my blessing), FOR THEY CONSIST OF THE SAME LETTERS two times, WHICH INDICATES THAT THE SAME MATTER WAS REPEATED TWICE. FOR THE BIRTHRIGHT BELONGS TO THE FIRSTBORN, AND BECAUSE HE TOOK HIS BIRTHRIGHT, HE ALSO TOOK HIS BLESSING. THUS, THE TWO DECEPTIONS ARE ONE. In the same manner, the verse "surely now we had returned this (Heb. zeh) second time"

(Beresheet 43:10) MEANS that two matters are in one: 1) we would have returned (Heb. *shavnu*) by now and not be put to shame (Heb. *boshnu*) by that man, and 2) LITERALLY, we would have been back already. THE HEBREW LETTERS OF SHAVNU ARE THE SAME AS OF BOSHNU.

178. כְּגַוְונָא דָא, אֲמַר אִיּוֹב, וְתַחְשְׁבֵנִי לְאוֹיֵב לָךְ, אֲהַדַר אִיּוֹב: אוֹיֵב. וְאוֹקְמוּהָ דִכְתִיב אֲשֶׁר בִּסְעָרָה יְשׁוּפֵנִי וְגוֹ', אָמַר לְפָנָיו, רבש"ע, שֶׁמָּא רוּחַ סְעָרָה עָבְרָה לְפָנֶיךָ. וְהָכָא בְּכוֹרָתִי לָקַח וְהִנֵּה עַתָּה אַהֲדַר מִלָּה וּנְטִיל בִּרְכָתִי.

178. Similarly, Job said, "and hold me for Your enemy" (Iyov 13:24). THE LETTER COMBINATION *Job* turned into *oyev* (enemy). This was explained according to the verse, "For He crushes me with a tempest" (Iyov 9:17). He said before Him, Master of the universe, "perhaps a tempest stormed at You," AND JOB TURNED INTO YOUR ENEMY. Here also, "he took away my birthright" (Heb. *bechorati*), and the combination turned INTO "MY BLESSING (HEB. *BIRCHATI*), as in "he has taken away my blessing."

179. הֵן גְּבִיר שַׂמְתִּיו לָךְ וְגוֹ', וּלְכָה אֵיפוֹא מָה אֶעֱשֶׂה בְּנִי. וּלְכָה אֵיפוֹא, לֵית קָיְימָא הָכָא, מַאן דְּמִסְתַּכַּם עֲלָךְ. מָה אֶעֱשֶׂה בְּנִי. כְּדֵין, בָּרְכֵיהּ בְּהַאי עָלְמָא, וְאִסְתַּכַּל בְּדַרְגֵּיהּ, וַאֲמַר וְעַל חַרְבְּךָ תִחְיֶה, דְּהָא הָכִי אִתְחֲזֵי לָךְ לְאוֹשָׁדָא דָמִין, וּלְמֶעְבַּד קְרָבִין, וְעַל דָּא אָמַר מָה אֶעֱשֶׂה בְּנִי.

179. "Behold, I have made him your lord...and what shall I do now for you, my son" (Beresheet 27:37). This means that there is no one present who gives consent THAT YOU WILL RECEIVE BLESSINGS. THEREFORE IT IS WRITTEN, "what shall I do now for you, my son." He then blessed him in this world. He looked at his grade and said to him "and by your sword shall you live," for it is fitting of you to shed blood and wage wars, SINCE YOU CLEAVE TO THE LEFT, WHICH IS OF JUDGMENTS. Therefore he said: "what shall I do now for you, my son," AS YOUR GRADE MERITS NO BLESSING.

180. רִבִּי אֶלְעָזָר אֲמַר, וּלְךָ אֵיפה מָה אֶעֱשֶׂה, כֵּיוָן דְּאָמַר הַאי, אֲמַאי

בְּנִי. אֶלָּא אָמַר לֵיהּ, וּלְךָ אֵיפֹה מָה אֶעֱשֶׂה, דְּאַנְתְּ בְּדִינָא וּבְחַרְבָּא וּבִדְמָא חֲזֵינָא לָךְ, וּלְאָחִיךָ בְּאֹרַח שְׁלִים. אֶלָּא בְּנִי, בְּנִי וַדַּאי, אֲנָא גָּרֵימְנָא לָךְ, בְּגִין דְּאַנְתְּ בְּנִי. וְעַל דָּא עַל חַרְבְּךָ תִחְיֶה וְאֶת אָחִיךָ תַּעֲבֹד. וַעֲדַיִין לָא אִתְקַיַּים, דְּהָא לָא פָּלַח לֵיהּ עֵשָׂו לְיַעֲקֹב. בְּגִין דְּיַעֲקֹב לָא בָּעָא לֵיהּ הַשְׁתָּא, וְאִיהוּ אַהֲדַר וְקָרָא לֵיהּ אֲדֹנִי כַּמָּה זִמְנֵי, בְּגִין דְּאִסְתַּכַּל לְמֵרָחוֹק, וְסָלִיק לֵיהּ, לְסוֹף יוֹמַיָּא, כִּדְקָאָמְרָן.

180. Rabbi Elazar discussed the verse, "what shall I do now for you." Why add "my son?" This is because he asked him "what shall I do now for you?" I have seen you in judgment, sword, and blood. And I have seen your brother walking the path of peace. He added "my son," for surely I brought all this upon you, as you are my son. Therefore "by your sword shall you live, and you shall serve your brother." This has not yet happened, for Esau is not yet a servant of Jacob. This is because Jacob has no need for him now. And he repeatedly called Esau "my master," because Jacob looked far ahead and saved it to the end of days, as we said above.

181. רַבִּי חִיָּיא וְרַבִּי יוֹסֵי הֲווֹ אָזְלֵי בְּאָרְחָא, עַד דַּהֲווֹ אָזְלֵי, חָמוּ לֵיהּ לְרַבִּי יוֹסֵי סָבָא, דַּהֲוָה אָזִיל בַּתְרַיְיהוּ יָתְבוּ, עַד דְּמָטָא לְגַבַּיְיהוּ. כֵּיוָן דְּמָטָא לְגַבַּיְיהוּ, אָמְרוּ הַשְׁתָּא אָרְחָא מִתְתַּקְּנָא קַמָּן, אַזְלוּ, אָמַר רַבִּי חִיָּיא עֵת לַעֲשׂוֹת לַיְיָ'. פָּתַח רַבִּי יוֹסֵי וַאֲמַר, פִּיהָ פָּתְחָה בְחָכְמָה וְתוֹרַת חֶסֶד עַל לְשׁוֹנָהּ. פִּיהָ פָּתְחָה בְחָכְמָה, דָּא כ"י, וְתוֹרַת חֶסֶד עַל לְשׁוֹנָהּ אִלֵּין אִינוּן יִשְׂרָאֵל, דְּאִינוּן לִישָׁנָא דְאוֹרַיְיתָא, דְּמִשְׁתַּדְּלֵי בָּהּ יוֹמֵי וְלֵילֵי.

181. As Rabbi Chiya and Rabbi Yosi were walking together, they noticed that Rabbi Yosi Saba was behind them. They sat down until he caught up to them. When he did, he said: 'now the path is readied before us,' and they went on. Rabbi Chiya quoted the verse, "It is time to act for Hashem" (Tehilim 119:126), while Rabbi Yosi began with the verse, "She opened her mouth with wisdom; and on her tongue is a Torah of steadfast love" (Tehilim 31:6). "She opened her mouth with wisdom" alludes to the Congregation of Yisrael, WHICH IS THE SHECHINAH; "and on her tongue is a Torah of steadfast love" refers to Yisrael, who are the tongue of the Torah, which is on their lips day and night.

182. פִּיהָ פָּתְחָה בְחָכְמָה, דָּא ב׳ דִּבְרֵאשִׁית, וְאוֹקְמוּהָ. וְתוֹרַת חֶסֶד עַל לְשׁוֹנָהּ דָּא אַבְרָהָם, דְּבֵיהּ בָּרָא עָלְמָא, וּבֵיהּ מִשְׁתָּעֵי תָּדִיר. ב׳ סָתִים מֵהַאי גִיסָא, וּפְתִיחָה מֵהַאי גִיסָא סְתִימָא מֵהַאי גִיסָא, כְּדִבְּבָר אֲחֵר וְרָאִיתָ אֶת אֲחוֹרָי. פְּתִיחָא מֵהַאי גִיסָא, בְּגִין לְאַנְהָרָא אַנְפָּהָא לְגַבֵּי עֵילָּא, וּפְתִיחָא מֵהַאי גִיסָא, בְּגִין לְקַבְּלָא מִלְּעֵילָּא, וְאִיהִי אַכְסַדְרָה לְקַבְּלָא. וּבְגִין כָּךְ קַיְימָא בְּרֵישָׁא דְּאוֹרַיְיתָא וְאִתְמַלְיָיא לְבָתַר, פִּיהָ פָּתְחָה בְחָכְמָה, בְּחָכְמָה וַדַּאי, דִּכְתִיב בְּרֵאשִׁית בָּרָא אֱלֹהִים, כְּתַרְגּוּמוֹ. וְתוֹרַת חֶסֶד עַל לְשׁוֹנָהּ, דְּהָא לְבָתַר מִשְׁתָּעֵי וַיֹּאמֶר אֱלֹהִים יְהִי אוֹר וַיְהִי אוֹר. פִּיהָ פָּתְחָה בְחָכְמָה, דָּא ה׳ דִּשְׁמָא קַדִּישָׁא, דְּכֹלָּא בָּהּ, וְאִיהִי סָתִים וְגַלְיָא, כְּלִילָא דְּעֵילָּא וְתַתָּא, רָזָא דְּעֵילָּא וְתַתָּא.

182. "She opened her mouth with wisdom." This is the letter *Bet* of Beresheet (Eng. 'In the beginning'). IT IS THE SECRET OF THE NUKVA, CALLED 'HOUSE' (HEB. *BAYIT*). "And on her tongue is a Torah of steadfast love (lit. 'Chesed')" refers to Abraham, THE SECRET OF THE COLUMN OF CHESED, with which He created the world, and he speaks always OF THE TORAH, WHICH IS THE DRAWING DOWN OF CHESED. THEREFORE, IT IS SAID "AND ON HER TONGUE IS A TORAH OF CHESED." HE FURTHER EXPLAINS THAT the letter *Bet* is closed on one side and open on the other. It is closed on one side, as it is written, "and you shall see My back" (Shemot 33:23). On the other side *Bet* is open, so that its face will shine upward TOWARD ZEIR ANPIN. It is also open to receive from ZEIR ANPIN above, AS WIDE OPEN as a foyer to receive BRIGHT LIGHT. FOR A FOYER RECEIVES MORE SUNSHINE THAN A HOUSE. For that reason, THE LETTER *BET* stands at the beginning of the Torah. THIS IS THE SECRET OF THE VERSE, "SHE OPENED HER MOUTH WITH WISDOM," and later was filled WITH ALL THE WORDS OF THE TORAH, WHICH IS THE SECRET OF "AND ON HER TONGUE IS A TORAH OF STEADFAST LOVE." Another explanation for the verse, "She opened her mouth with wisdom," IS THAT IT ALLUDES TO THE TORAH, which assuredly opens with wisdom, as it is written, "In the beginning Elohim created" (Beresheet 1:1), FOR "IN THE BEGINNING" IS

'WISDOM' in the Aramaic translation. Of the verse, "And on her tongue is a Torah of steadfast love (lit. 'Chesed')," the Torah later reads, "And Elohim said, Let there be light, and there was light" (Ibid. 3), WHICH IS THE LIGHT OF CHESED. ANOTHER EXPLANATION FOR THE VERSE, "She opened her mouth with wisdom," is that it is the first *Hei* of the holy name YUD HEI VAV HEI, WHICH IS BINAH, in which everything is contained. It is concealed and revealed, comprising both what is above and below!

183. פִּיהָ פָּתְחָה בְחָכְמָה, בְּגִין דְּאִיהִי סְתִימָא דְּלָא אִתְיְידַע כְּלַל, דִּכְתִיב וְנֶעֶלְמָה מֵעֵינֵי כָל חָי וּמֵעוֹף הַשָּׁמַיִם נִסְתָּרָה. וְכַד שָׁארֵי לְאִתְפַּשְּׁטָא, בְּחָכְמָה דְּאִתְדַּבַּק בָּהּ, וְאִיהִי בְּגַוָּוהּ, אֲפֵיקַת קָלָא, דְּאִיהִי תּוֹרַת חֶסֶד.

183. "She opened her mouth with wisdom" because it is concealed and utterly unrevealed, as it is written, "Seeing it is hidden from the eyes of all living, and kept close from the birds of the sky" (Iyov 28:21). When BINAH started to spread together with Chochmah that cleaved to it and was clothed in it, NAMELY, IN THE SECRET OF THE VERSE, "SHE OPENED HER MOUTH WITH WISDOM." IT COULD NOT SPREAD UNTIL it issued a sound, NAMELY, ZEIR ANPIN, THE CENTRAL COLUMN, which is "a Torah of Chesed," OF WHICH IT IS WRITTEN, "AND ON HER TONGUE IS A TORAH OF CHESED."

184. פִּיהָ פָּתְחָה בְחָכְמָה, דָּא ה"א בַּתְרָאָה, דְּאִיהוּ דִּבּוּר, וּמִלָּה תַלְיָא בְּחָכְמָה. וְתוֹרַת חֶסֶד עַל לְשׁוֹנָהּ. דָּא קוֹל דְּקַיְּימָא עַל דִּבּוּר, לְאַנְהָגָא לֵיהּ. וְתוֹרַת חֶסֶד, דָּא יַעֲקֹב, דְּאִיהוּ עַל לְשׁוֹנָהּ, לְאַנְהָגָא מִלָּה, וּלְאַחֲדָא לָהּ, דְּהָא לֵית דִּבּוּר בְּלָא קוֹל, וְאוֹקְמוּהָ.

184. STILL ANOTHER EXPLANATION OF THE VERSE, "She opened her mouth with wisdom" is that the last *Hei* OF THE NAME YUD HEI VAV HEI, NAMELY, THE NUKVA, refers to speech, which depends on wisdom. THIS MEANS THAT THERE IS NO SPEECH WITHOUT WISDOM AND THOUGHT. THEREFORE IT IS SAID OF THE NUKVA, "SHE OPENED HER MOUTH WITH WISDOM." THE VERSE, "and on her tongue is a Torah of Chesed" alludes to the voice, NAMELY, ZEIR ANPIN, which controls and conducts speech,

THE NUKVA. A FURTHER EXPLANATION OF "A Torah of Chesed love" is Jacob, NAMELY, ZEIR ANPIN CALLED 'TORAH', AND CHESED. He is "on her tongue," OVER THE SPEECH, to guide the word and be united with it, for there is no speech without sound.

185. פָּתַח רִבִּי חִיָּיא אֲבַתְרֵיה וַאֲמַר, אֲנִי חָכְמָה שָׁכַנְתִּי עָרְמָה וְדַעַת מְזִמּוֹת אֶמְצָא. אֲנִי חָכְמָה, דָּא כ"י. שָׁכַנְתִּי עָרְמָה, דָּא יַעֲקֹב, דְּאִיהוּ חַכִּים, וְדַעַת מְזִמּוֹת אֶמְצָא, דָּא יִצְחָק, דַּהֲוָה לֵיה דַעַת מְזִמּוֹת, לְבָרְכָא לֵיה לְעֵשָׂו. וּבְגִין דְּחָכְמָה אִשְׁתַּתַּף בַּהֲדֵיה דְּיַעֲקֹב, דְּאִיהוּ עָרְמָה, וְדַעַת מְזִמּוֹת אֶמְצָא, דְּאִתְבָּרַךְ יַעֲקֹב מֵאֲבוֹי, וְשָׁרוּ עֲלֵיה כָּל אִינּוּן בִּרְכָאן, וְאִתְקַיְּימוּ בֵּיה וּבִבְנוֹי, לְעָלַם וּלְעָלְמֵי עָלְמִין.

185. Rabbi Chiya then quoted the verse, "I, wisdom, dwell with prudence, and find knowledge in crafty schemes" (Mishlei 8:12). "I, wisdom" refers to the Congregation of Yisrael, NAMELY, THE NUKVA, CALLED 'THE LOWER CHOCHMAH'; "dwell with prudence" is Jacob, who is prudent BECAUSE HE TOOK THE BLESSINGS PRUDENTLY AND WITH CUNNING; AND "find knowledge in crafty schemes" alludes to Isaac, who used knowledge and stratagems to bless Esau. Wisdom, THE SHECHINAH CALLED 'WISDOM', was joined with Jacob, who dealt with prudence. Therefore Jacob WAS TO "find knowledge in crafty devices," by which he was blessed by his father, WHO HAD KNOWLEDGE OF STRATAGEMS TO BLESS ESAU, and all the blessings rested upon him and prevailed upon him and his descendents forever.

186. מֵאִינּוּן אִתְקַיְּימוּ בְּהַאי עָלְמָא, וְכֻלְּהוּ יִתְקַיְּימוּן, לְזִמְנָא דְמַלְכָּא מְשִׁיחָא, דִּכְדֵין יְהוֹן יִשְׂרָאֵל גּוֹי אֶחָד בָּאָרֶץ, וְעַם אֶחָד לְקוּדְשָׁא בְּרִיךְ הוּא, הה"ד וְעָשִׂיתִי אֹתָם לְגוֹי אֶחָד בָּאָרֶץ. וְיִשְׁלְטוּן לְעֵילָּא וְתַתָּא, דִּכְתִיב וַאֲרוּ עִם עֲנָנֵי שְׁמַיָּא כְּבַר אֱנָשׁ אָתֵה, דָּא מַלְכָּא מְשִׁיחָא, דִּכְתִיב וּבְיוֹמֵיהוֹן דִּי מַלְכַיָּא אִנּוּן יְקִים אֱלָה שְׁמַיָּא מַלְכוּ וְגוֹ'. וְע"ד בָּעָא יַעֲקֹב, דְּיִסְתַּלְּקוּן בִּרְכוֹי לְהַהוּא זִמְנָא דְּאָתֵי, וְלָא נָטַל לוֹן לְאַלְתָּר.

186. Some have prevailed in this world, and all will prevail at the advent of

King Messiah, when Yisrael will be "one nation in the land" (Yechezkel 37:22), one nation before the Holy One, blessed be He. This is the meaning of the verse "and I will make them one nation in the land," and they will reign above and below, as it is written, "and, behold, one like a son of man came with the clouds of heaven" (Daniel 7:13). This is King Messiah, as it is written, "And in the days of these kings shall the Elohim of heaven set up a kingdom..." (Daniel 2:44). Therefore, Jacob wanted his blessings to be postponed and did not take them at once.

187. פְּתַח רָבִּי יֵיסָא אֲבַתְרֵיה וַאֲמַר, וְאַתָּה אַל תִּירָא עַבְדִּי יַעֲקֹב נְאֻם
יי' וְאַל תֵּחַת יִשְׂרָאֵל וְגו'. הַאי קְרָא אוֹקְמוּהָ. אֲבָל בְּהַהִיא שַׁעֲתָא,
דְּנָפַק יַעֲקֹב מִקַּמֵּי אֲבוֹי, בְּאִינּוּן בִּרְכָאן, אִסְתַּכַּל בְּנַפְשֵׁיה, אֲמַר, הָא
אִלֵּין בִּרְכָאן, בָּעֵינָא לְסַלְּקָא לוֹן לְבָתַר, לְאָרִיכוּ יוֹמִין, וַהֲוָה דָּחִיל
וּמִסְתָּפֵי, נָפַק קָלָא וַאֲמַר, וְאַתָּה אַל תִּירָא עַבְדִּי יַעֲקֹב נְאֻם יי' כִּי אִתְּךָ
אָנִי, לָא אֶשְׁבּוֹק לָךְ בְּהַאי עָלְמָא. כִּי הִנְנִי מוֹשִׁעֲךָ מֵרָחוֹק, לְהַהוּא
זִמְנָא דְּאַנְתְּ סָלֵיק לוֹן, לְאִינּוּן בִּרְכָאן.

187. Rabbi Yosi then quoted the verse, "But fear not, O My servant Jacob, and be not dismayed, Yisrael" (Yirmeyah 46:27). This verse has already been explained. Nevertheless, after Jacob had received his father's blessings, he searched himself and said: I want these very blessings to be postponed for the time, so they will last. He was frightened LEST THE BLESSINGS DWELL UPON HIM NOW, FOR THEY MIGHT BE NEGATED IF YISRAEL SINNED. A voice resounded, saying "Fear not, O Jacob My servant, says Hashem: for I am with you" (Ibid. 28), and I will never leave you, for, "behold, I will save you from afar" (Ibid. 27) at the time for which the blessings were reserved.

188. וְאֶת זַרְעֲךָ מֵאֶרֶץ שִׁבְיָם, דְּאַף עַל גַּב דְּהַשְׁתָּא נָטִיל בִּרְכוֹי עֵשָׂו,
וְיִשְׁתַּעְבְּדוּן בִּבְנָךְ, אֲנָא אַפֵּיק לוֹן מִידוֹי, וּכְדֵין יִשְׁתַּעְבְּדוּן בָּנֶיךָ בֵּיה.
וְשָׁב יַעֲקֹב, לְאִינּוּן בִּרְכָאן, וְשָׁב יַעֲקֹב, דָּא שְׁכִינְתָּא. וְשָׁב יַעֲקֹב וַדַּאי.
וְשָׁקַט וְשַׁאֲנָן, כְּמָה דְּאוֹקְמוּהָ, מֵאִינּוּן מַלְכְּוָון: מִבָּבֶל, מִמָּדַי, וּמִיָּוָן,
וּמֵאֱדוֹם. דְּאִינְהוּ הֲווֹ דְּאִשְׁתַּעְבְּדוּ בְּהוּ בְּיִשְׂרָאֵל. וְאֵין מַחֲרִיד, לְעָלַם
וּלְעָלְמֵי עָלְמַיָּא.

188. The verse, "and your seed from the land of their captivity," means that although Esau now took the blessings and HIS CHILDREN will enslave your children, I will free them from his hands. Then, your children will enslave him. Then, "Jacob shall return," MEANING RETURN to these blessings, TO THE SHECHINAH THAT WILL BE WITH JACOB AGAIN. "And Jacob will return" assuredly "and be quiet and at ease," as has been explained THAT HE WILL HAVE REST from the kingdoms of Babylon, Media, Greece, and Edom, which were enslaving Yisrael." And none shall make him afraid" for ever and ever.

189. אָזְלוּ, עַד דַּהֲווֹ אָזְלֵי, אָמַר רָבִּי יוֹסֵי, וַדַּאי, כָּל מַה דַּעֲבֵיד קוּדְשָׁא בְּרִיךְ הוּא בְּאַרְעָא, כֹּלָא הֲוָה בְּרָזָא דְּחָכְמְתָא, וְכֹלָא בְּגִין לְאַחֲזָאָה חָכְמְתָא עִלָּאָה, לְהוּ לְבַר נָשׁ, בְּגִין דְּיִלְפוּן מֵהַהוּא עוֹבָדָא, רָזִין דְּחָכְמְתָא, וְכֹלָא אִינוּן כִּדְקָא יָאוֹת, וְעוֹבָדוֹי כֻּלְּהוּ, אוֹרְחֵי דְּאוֹרַיְיתָא, בְּגִין דְּאוֹרְחֵי דְּאוֹרַיְיתָא, אִינוּן אָרְחֵי דְּקוּדְשָׁא בְּרִיךְ הוּא, וְלֵית מִלָּה זְעֵירָא, דְּלֵית בָּהּ כַּמָה אוֹרְחִין וּשְׁבִילִין, וְרָזִין דְּחָכְמְתָא עִלָּאָה.

189. As they continued walking, Rabbi Yosi said: Assuredly, whatever the Holy One, blessed be He, does in the world is in the secret of wisdom. It is intended to teach the greatest wisdom to mankind, so man will learn from those acts the secrets of wisdom. And everything is as it should be. His works are all the ways of Torah, since the ways of Torah are the ways of the Holy One, blessed be He. And even in the smallest thing, there are ways and paths and secrets of high wisdom.

190. תָּא חֲזֵי, דְּהָא רְבִּי יוֹחָנָן בֶּן זַכַּאי הֲוָה אָמַר, תְּלַת מְאָה הֲלָכוֹת פְּסוּקוֹת, בְּרָזָא דְּחָכְמְתָא עִלָּאָה, בַּפָּסוּק וְשֵׁם אִשְׁתּוֹ מְהֵיטַבְאֵל בַּת מַטְרֵד בַּת מֵי זָהָב, וְלָא גָּלֵי לוֹן, אֶלָּא לְרִבִּי אֱלִיעֶזֶר, דַּהֲוָה עִמֵּיהּ, בְּגִין לְמִנְדַּע, דְּכַמָּה רָזִין עִלָּאִין אִינוּן, בְּכָל עוֹבָדָא וְעוֹבָדָא, דְּאִיהִי בְּאוֹרַיְיתָא, וּבְכָל מִלָּה וּמִלָּה, חָכְמְתָא אִיהִי, וְאוֹרַיְיתָא דִּקְשׁוֹט, בְּג״כ אִינוּן מִלִּין דְּאוֹרַיְיתָא, מִלִּין קַדִּישִׁין אִינוּן, לְאַחֲזָאָה מִינָהּ נִפְלָאוֹת, כִּדְבָר אַחֵר, גַּל עֵינַי וְאַבִּיטָה נִפְלָאוֹת מִתּוֹרָתֶךָ.

190. Come and behold: Rabbi Yochanan ben Zakai used to say that 300 legal decisions are derived from the verse, "and his wife's name was Mehetabel, daughter of Matred, daughter of Mezehab" (Beresheet 36:39). This he revealed only to Rabbi Eliezer, who was with him. That shows how many secrets of the Torah are in every deed in the Torah. In each word, there is wisdom and true doctrine. Therefore the words of the Torah are holy words, by which to conceive wondrous things, as it is written, "Open you my eyes that I may behold wondrous things out of Your Torah" (Tehilim 119:18).

191. תָּא חֲזֵי, בְּשַׁעְתָּא דַּעֲקִים הַהוּא חִוְיָא, לְאָדָם וּלְאִתְּתֵיה, דְּאַקְרִיב לְאִתְּתָא, וְאַטִּיל בָּהּ זוּהֲמָא, וְאִתְפַּתָּא בֵּיהּ אָדָם, כְּדֵין אִסְתָּאַב עַלְמָא, וְאִתְלַטְיָא אַרְעָא בְּגִינֵיה, וְגָרֵים מוֹתָא לְכָל עַלְמָא, וְקַיְימָא עַלְמָא לְאִתְפָּרְעָא מִנֵּיה, עַד דַּאֲתָא אִילָנָא דְּחַיֵּי, וְכָפֵי עַל אָדָם, וְכָפְיָיא לֵיה לְהַהוּא נָחָשׁ דְּלָא יִשְׁלוֹט לְעָלְמִין, עַל זַרְעָא דְּיַעֲקֹב.

191. Come and behold: When the serpent deceived Adam and his wife, when he approached her and injected impurity into her, Adam succumbed to temptation. Then the world was defiled and the land became accursed because of him. He brought death to the world. And the world was punished because of him, until the Tree of Life came, atoned for Adam, and subjugated the serpent, so that his seed will never rule the seed of Jacob.

192. דְּהָא בְּזִמְנָא דְּאַקְרִיבוּ יִשְׂרָאֵל שָׂעִיר, הֲוָה אִתְכַּפְיָא הַהוּא נָחָשׁ וְאִתְהַפַּךְ לְעַבְדָּא, כְּמָה דְּאִתְּמָר. וְעַ"ד אַקְרֵיב יַעֲקֹב לַאֲבוֹי, תְּרֵין שְׂעִירִין חַד, לְאִכְפַּיָא לְעֵשָׂו, דְּאִיהוּ שָׂעִיר, וְחַד, בְּגִין דַּרְגָּא דַּהֲוָה תָּלֵי בֵּיה עֵשָׂו וְאִתְדַּבַּק בֵּיה וְאִתְּמָר.

192. For when Yisrael offered a goat, the serpent was subdued and became a slave OF YISRAEL as we learned. Therefore, Jacob served his father two goats (Heb. *se'irim*), one with which to subjugate Esau, who is hairy (Heb. *sa'ir*), and the other for the grade upon which Esau depended and to which he cleaved. THIS WAS SAMAEL, THE MINISTER OF ESAU.

193. וּבְגִין כָּךְ קַיְימָא עַלְמָא, עַד דְּתֵיתֵי אִתְּתָא, כְּגַוְונָא דְּחַוָּה, וּבַר נָשׁ כְּגַוְונָא דְּאָדָם, וְיַעַקִימוּ וְיַחְכִּימוּ לֵיה לְהַהוּא חִוְיָא בִּישָׁא וְהַהוּא

דְּרָכֵיב עֲלֵיה וְכֹלָא אִתְּמַר.

193. Therefore the world is accursed until a woman comes, who resembles Eve, and a man, who resembles Adam. They will deceive and beguile the serpent and the one ruling him, NAMELY, SAMAEL. We have already learned this.

194. פָּתַח וַאֲמַר, וַיְהִי עֵשָׂו אִישׁ יוֹדֵעַ צַיִד אִישׁ שָׂדֶה, וְהָא אִתְּמַר וְיַעֲקֹב אִישׁ תָּם יֹשֵׁב אֹהָלִים. אִישׁ תָּם: גְּבַר שְׁלִים, כְּתַרְגּוּמוֹ. יָשַׁב אֹהָלִים, אַמַּאי אִיהוּ תָּם, בְּגִין דְּאִיהוּ יָשַׁב אֹהָלִים, דְּאָחִיד לִתְרֵין סִטְרִין, לְאַבְרָהָם וּלְיִצְחָק. וע״ד, יַעֲקֹב בְּסִטְרָא דְיִצְחָק אֲתָא לְגַבֵּי דְעֵשָׂו, כְּמָה דְאִתְּמַר, דִּכְתִיב, עִם חָסִיד תִּתְחַסָּד וְעִם עִקֵּשׁ תִּתְפָּל. וְכַד אֲתָא עִם בִּרְכָאן, בְּסִיּוּעָא דִלְעֵילָא קָא אֲתָא, בְּסִיּוּעָא דְאַבְרָהָם וְיִצְחָק, וּבְגִין כָּךְ בְּחָכְמְתָא הֲוָה, כְּמָה דְאִתְּמַר.

194. He opened the discussion with the verse, "and Esau was a cunning hunter, a man of the field: and Jacob was a plain man, dwelling in tents" (Beresheet 25:27). The phrase "a plain man" MEANS a whole man, according to the Aramaic translation, AS ILLUSTRATED BY THE FACT THAT HE WAS "dwelling in tents." He was plain because he dwelt in tents, WHICH MEANS THAT he held fast the two sides, RIGHT AND LEFT, WHICH ARE Abraham and Isaac, AND HE WAS FOUND WHOLE BOTH ON THE RIGHT, THE LIGHT OF CHASSADIM, AND THE LEFT, THE ILLUMINATION OF CHOCHMAH. Because HE COMPRISES OF BOTH SIDES, Jacob came to Esau from the side of Isaac THAT WAS INCLUDED IN HIM. THIS IS THE SECRET OF THE TWO HE GOATS HE SERVED ISAAC, WHICH CAME FROM THE ILLUMINATION OF THE LEFT, THE ASPECT OF ISAAC. As we learned from the verse, "With the merciful you will show yourself merciful...and with the perverse you will show yourself subtle" (Tehilim 18:26-27). When he came to receive the blessings, he came with support of Abraham and Isaac from above, NAMELY, SUPPORT FROM BOTH THE RIGHT AND LIEFT SIDES, and so all was done wisely.

195. תָּא חֲזֵי, כַּד יַעֲקֹב אִתְעַר, לְגַבֵּי סמא״ל, דַּרְגָּא דְעֵשָׂו, וְקַבֵּיל עֲלֵיה לְיַעֲקֹב, וְיַעֲקֹב נָצַח לֵיה, בְּכַמָה סִטְרִין, נָצַח לְחִוְיָה, בְּחָכְמְתָא,

וּבַעֲקִימוּ, וְלָא אִתְנְצַח, בַּר בְּשָׂעִיר. וְאַף עַל גַּב דְּכֹלָּא חַד, נָצַח כְּמוֹ כֵן לְסמא"ל, בְּנִצְחוֹנָא אָחֲרָא, וְנָצְחֵיהּ, הה"ד וַיֵּאָבֵק אִישׁ עִמּוֹ עַד עֲלוֹת הַשָּׁחַר. וַיַּרְא כִּי לֹא יָכוֹל לוֹ.

195. Come and behold: When Jacob arose against Samael, the grade of Esau, Samael fought and wrestled with him, but Jacob overpowered him in several ways. He conquered the serpent with cunning and subtlety, but he was only overpowered by the goat, THAT IS, BY THE TWO HE GOATS HE SERVED TO ISAAC HIS FATHER. WITH THESE, HE CONQUERED ESAU, THE GRADE OF THE SERPENT, AS HAS BEEN SAID. And though all is one, NAMELY, THE SERPENT AND SAMAEL, nevertheless he also conquered and overpowered Samael in another battle. This is derived from the verse, "and there wrestled a man with him until the breaking of the day. And when he saw that he did not prevail against him" (Beresheet 32:25-26).

196. תָּא חֲזֵי, זְכוּתֵיהּ דְּיַעֲקֹב כַּמָּה הֲוָה, דְּאִיהוּ אָתָא, וּבָעָא לְאַעְבָּרָא לֵיהּ מֵעַלְמָא, וְהַהוּא לֵילְיָא, הֲוַת לֵילְיָא דְּאִתְבְּרֵי בֵּיהּ סִיהֲרָא, וְיַעֲקֹב אִשְׁתְּאַר בִּלְחוֹדוֹי, דְּלָא הֲוָה עִמֵּיהּ אָחֳרָא, דְּתָנָן לָא יִפּוֹק בַּר נָשׁ יְחִידָאי בְּלֵילְיָא, וְכ"ש בְּלֵילְיָא דְּאִתְבְּרִיאוּ בֵּיהּ נְהוֹרִין, דְּהָא סִיהֲרָא אִיהִי חַסְרָא, דִּכְתִיב יְהִי מְאֹר"ת חָסֵר, וְהַהוּא לֵילְיָא, אִשְׁתְּאַר בִּלְחוֹדוֹי, בְּגִין דְּכַד סִיהֲרָא חַסְרָא, חִוְיָא בִּישָׁא אִתְתַּקַּף וְשָׁלְטָא, וּכְדֵין אָתָא סמא"ל, וְקַטְרֵיג לֵיהּ, וּבָעָא לְאוֹבָדָא לֵיהּ מֵעַלְמָא.

196. Come and behold: The merit of Jacob was such, that he, SAMAEL, wanted to exterminate Jacob from the world. That night was the night when the moon was created, THAT IS, WEDNESDAY EVE, A TIME OF DANGER. And Jacob stayed alone, and no one was with him, as we have learned that a man must not venture out alone at night. This is even more true on the night when the luminaries were created, for then the moon is defective, as it is written, "Let there be lights (Heb. *me'orot*)" (Beresheet 1:14), and the word Me'orot is spelled without THE LETTER VAV, WHICH IS A SIGN OF A CURSE. Because Jacob remained alone that night, HE WAS IN GREAT DANGER, because when the moon is defective, the evil serpent is strengthened and rules. Then Samael came and denounced Jacob and wanted him to perish from the world.

197. וְיַעֲקֹב הֲוָה תַּקִּיף בְּכָל סִטְרִין, בְּסִטְרָא דְיִצְחָק, וּבְסִטְרָא דְאַבְרָהָם, דְּאִינוּן הֲווֹ תְּקִיפוּ דְיַעֲקֹב. אָתָא לִימִינָא חָמָא לְאַבְרָהָם, תַּקִּיף בִּתְקִיפוּ דְיוֹמָא, בְּסִטְרָא דִימִינָא דְחֶסֶד. אָתָא לִשְׂמָאלָא, חָמָא לְיִצְחָק, תַּקִּיף בְּדִינָא קַשְׁיָא. אָתָא לְגוּפָא, חָמָא לְיַעֲקֹב, תַּקִּיף מִתְּרֵין סִטְרִין אִלֵּין, דְּסַחֲרָן לֵיהּ, חַד מִכָּאן, וְחַד מִכָּאן, כְּדֵין, וַיַּרְא כִּי לֹא יָכוֹל לוֹ וַיִּגַּע בְּכַף יְרֵכוֹ דְּאִיהוּ אֲתַר לְבַר מִגּוּפָא, וְאִיהוּ חַד עַמּוּדָא דְגוּפָא, כְּדֵין וַתֵּקַע כַּף יֶרֶךְ יַעֲקֹב בְּהֵאָבְקוֹ עִמּוֹ וְגוֹ'.

197. But Jacob was strong on all sides, on the side of Isaac and the side of Abraham. SAMAEL came to the right and saw Abraham strong with the vigor of day, namely, the right side, which is Chesed. He came to the left, and saw Isaac powerful with the strength of rigorous judgment. He came to the body, NAMELY, TO THE CENTRAL COLUMN, and saw Jacob strong on these two sides. ABRAHAM AND ISAAC surrounded him, one from here and one from there. Then "when he saw that he did not prevail against him, he touched the hollow of his thigh" (Beresheet 32:26), a place outside the body, the one pillar of the body ON WHICH THE WHOLE BODY IS SUPPORTED, NAMELY, NETZACH, THE PILLAR OF TIFERET, CALLED 'BODY'. Then "and the hollow of Ya'akov's thigh was put out of joint, as he wrestled with him..." (Ibid.).

198. כֵּיוָן דְּאִתְעַר צַפְרָא, וַעֲבַר לֵילְיָא, אִתְתַּקַּף יַעֲקֹב, וְאִתְחַלַּשׁ חֵילֵיהּ דְּסמא"ל, כְּדֵין אָמַר שַׁלְחֵנִי, דְּמָטָא זִמְנָא, לוֹמַר שִׁירָתָא דְצַפְרָא, וּבָעֵי לְמֵיזַל, וְאוֹדֵי לֵיהּ, עַל אִינוּן בִּרְכָאן, וְאוֹסִיף לֵיהּ בִּרְכָתָא אָחֳרָא, דִּכְתִיב וַיְבָרֶךְ אֹתוֹ שָׁם.

198. Once day broke and night departed, Jacob was strengthened, and the power of Samael diminished. Then he said: "Let me go" (Ibid. 27), for it was his time to say the morning hymns and he had to leave. He confirmed his blessings and added a blessing of his own, as it is written, "And he blessed him there" (Ibid. 30).

199. תָּא חֲזֵי, כַּמָּה בִּרְכָאן, אִתְבָּרֵךְ יַעֲקֹב, חַד דַּאֲבוֹי, בְּהַהוּא עֲקִימוּ, וְרָוַוח כָּל אִינוּן בִּרְכָאן. וְחַד דִּשְׁכִינְתָּא דְּבָרֵיךְ לֵיהּ קוּדְשָׁא בְּרִיךְ הוּא,

כַּד הֲוָה אָתֵי מִלָּבָן, דִּכְתִיב וַיְבָרֶךְ אֱלֹהִים אֶת יַעֲקֹב. וְחַד, דְּבָרְכֵיהּ לֵיהּ הַהוּא מַלְאָכָא, מִמַּנָּא דְעֵשָׂו. וְחַד, בְּרָכָה אַחֲרָא, דְּבָרְכֵיהּ לֵיהּ אֲבוּהָ, כַּד הֲוָה אָזֵיל לְפַדַּן אֲרָם, דִּכְתִיב וְאֵל שַׁדַּי יְבָרֵךְ אֹתְךָ וְגוֹ'.

199. Come and behold how many were the blessings Jacob received. The one from his father he earned through cunning, and that gained him all these many blessings; the one of the Shechinah he received from the Holy One, blessed be He, when he returned from Laban, as it is written, "And Elohim...blessed him" (Beresheet 35:9). He was given one by the minister of Esau and one from his father when he went to Paddan-Aram, as it is written, "And El Shadai bless you..." (Beresheet 28:3).

200. בְּהַהוּא זִמְנָא, דְּחָמָא יַעֲקֹב גַּרְמֵיהּ, בְּכָל הַנֵּי בִּרְכָאן, אָמַר, בְּמַאן בִּרְכָתָא דְּמִנַּיְיהוּ אֶשְׁתַּמֵּשׁ הַשְׁתָּא. אָמַר, בַּחֲלָשָׁא מִנַּיְיהוּ אֶשְׁתַּמֵּשׁ הַשְׁתָּא, וּמַאן אִיהוּ, דָּא בַּתְרַיְיתָא, דְּבָרְכֵיהּ אֲבוּהּ, וְאַף עַל גַּב דְּאִיהִי תַּקִּיפָא, אָמַר, לָאו אִיהִי תַּקִּיפָא, בְּשָׁלְטָנוּתָא דְּהַאי עַלְמָא כְּקַדְמָאָה.

200. At the time when Jacob saw himself with all these blessings, he said, Which shall I use now? He decided to use the weakest blessing of all. And which is that? It is the last blessing from his father. And although this too is a powerful blessing, it is not as strong for having power over the world as the first ones.

201. אָמַר יַעֲקֹב, אֶטּוֹל הַשְׁתָּא דָּא וְאֶשְׁתַּמֵּשׁ בַּהּ, וַאֲסַלֵּק כָּל אִינּוּן אַחֲרָנִין, לְזִמְנָא דְּאִצְטְרִיךְ לִי, וְלִבְנַאי בַּתְרָאי. אֵימָתַי, בְּזִמְנָא דְּיִתְכַּנְּשׁוּן כָּל עַמְמַיָּא, לְאוֹבָדָא בְּנֵי מֵעַלְמָא, דִּכְתִיב כָּל גּוֹיִם סְבָבוּנִי בְּשֵׁם יְיָ' כִּי אֲמִילַם. סַבּוּנִי גַם סְבָבוּנִי וְגוֹ'. סַבּוּנִי כִדְבוֹרִים וְגוֹ'. הָא הָכָא תְּלָתָא, לְגַבֵּי תְּלָתָא דְּאִשְׁתָּאֲרוּ. חַד, אִינּוּן בִּרְכָאן קַדְמָאֵי, דַּאֲבוּהּ. תְּרֵין, אִינּוּן בִּרְכָאן, דְּבָרְכֵיהּ קוּדְשָׁא בְּרִיךְ הוּא. תְּלַת, אִינּוּן בִּרְכָאן, דְּבָרְכֵיהּ הַהוּא מַלְאָכָא.

201. Jacob said: I will avail myself of this blessing and use it. The others I will reserve until the time when I and my children after me will need them. When WILL THIS BE? At the time the nations gather to exterminate my children from the world, as it is written, "All nations compassed me about: but in the name of Hashem I cut them off. They compassed me about; indeed, they compassed me...They compassed me about like bees..." (Tehilim 118:10-12). There are three VERSES that correspond to the three blessings THAT HE DID NOT USE. The one is the blessing from his father; the second is the blessing from the Holy One, blessed be He; and the third is the blessing he was given by the angel.

202. אֲמַר יַעֲקֹב, לְהָתָם אִצְטְרִיכוּ, לְגַבֵּי מַלְכִין וְכָל עַמִּין דְּכָל עָלְמָא, וְאֵסַלֵּיק לוֹן לְהָתָם, וְהַשְׁתָּא לְגַבֵּי דְּעֵשָׂו, דִּי לִי בְּהַאי. לְמַלְכָּא, דַּהֲווֹ לֵיהּ כַּמָּה לִגְיוֹנִין תַּקִּיפִין, כַּמָּה מָארֵי מַגִּיחֵי קְרָבָא, לַאֲגָחָא קְרָבִין, דִּזְמִינִין לְגַבֵּי מַלְכִין תַּקִּיפִין, לַאֲגָחָא בְּהוֹ קְרָבָא. אַדְהָכֵי שָׁמַע עַל לִסְטִים חַד קַפָּחָא, אֲמַר, הַנֵּי בְּנֵי תַּרְעֵי, יְהָכוֹן תַּמָּן. א״ל, מִכָּל לִגְיוֹנִין דִּילָךְ, לֵית אַנְתְּ מְשַׁדַּר הָתָם, אֶלָּא אִלֵּין. אֲמַר, לְגַבֵּי הַהוּא לִסְטִים, דִּי בְּאִלֵּין, דְּהָא כָּל לִגְיוֹנוֹתַי, וּמָארֵי קְרָבָא, אֶסְתַּלַּק לְגַבֵּי אִינוּן מַלְכִין תַּקִּיפִין, בְּיוֹמָא דִּקְרָבָא, דְּאִצְטְרִיכוּ לִי, לֶיהֱווּ.

202. Jacob said: At that time, I will need ALL THE BLESSINGS TO PROTECT ME from the kings and all the nations in the world THAT WILL SURROUND ME. THEREFORE, I will reserve these blessings for that time. And now, for Esau, this blessing should suffice, TO WIT, THE SECOND BLESSING HIS FATHER GAVE HIM. This is like a king, who had several battalions of mighty warriors and several qualified ministers of war capable of engaging in warfare against mighty kings. In the meantime, when he learned about a great robber, he sent his gatekeepers TO FIGHT HIM. When HIS SERVANTS asked him, why did you choose to send the gatekeepers when you have such strong battalions available, the king replied, these will suffice to cope with this robber. I will reserve the battalions and ministers for war against the mighty kings, so they will be available when I need them.

203. אוֹף הָכֵי, יַעֲקֹב אֲמַר לְגַבֵּי עֵשָׂו, דִּי לִי הַשְׁתָּא בְּאִלֵּין בִּרְכָאן. אֲבָל לְהַהוּא זִמְנָא, דְּאִצְטְרִיכוּ לִבְנַי, לְגַבֵּי כָּל מַלְכִין וְשַׁלִּיטִין דְּכָל עָלְמָא, אֲסַלֵּק לוֹן.

203. Jacob said the same: To cope with Esau, these blessings HE RECEIVED

FROM HIS FATHER WHEN HE WENT TO PADDAN-ARAM, will suffice. But THE REST OF THE BLESSINGS, I shall reserve for that time when my children will need them to fight the kings and rulers in the world, who will rise against them.

204. כַּד יִמְטֵי הַהוּא זִמְנָא, יִתְעָרוּן אִינּוּן בִּרְכָאן, מִכָּל סִטְרִין, וְיִתְקַיַּים עַלְמָא עַל קִיּוּמֵיהּ כַּדְקָא יָאוֹת, וּמֵהַהוּא יוֹמָא וּלְהָלְאָה, יְקוּם מַלְכוּתָא דָּא עַל כָּל שְׁאָר מַלְכוּ אַחֲרָא, כְּמָה דְּאוֹקִימְוּהָ, דִּכְתִיב תַּדִּק וְתָסֵף כָּל אִלֵּין מַלְכְוָתָא וְהִיא תְּקוּם לְעָלְמַיָּיא. וְהַיְינוּ הַהִיא אַבְנָא, דְּאִתְגְּזֶרֶת מִן טוּרָא דִי לָא בִידַיִן, כִּדְבָר אָחֵר מִשָּׁם רוֹעֶה אֶבֶן יִשְׂרָאֵל, מַאן אֶבֶן דָּא. דָּא כְּנֶסֶת יִשְׂרָאֵל, כְּמָה דְאַתְּ אָמַר וְהָאֶבֶן הַזֹּאת אֲשֶׁר שַׂמְתִּי מַצֵּבָה וְגוֹ'.

204. When that time arrives, all the blessings will be aroused on all sides TOWARDS YISRAEL, and the world will be properly established. From that day on, this kingdom shall rise, THAT IS, THE SUPERNAL KINGDOM, THE NUKVA OF ZEIR ANPIN, above all the other kingdoms, as was explained when discoursing on the verse, "but it shall break in pieces and consume all these kingdoms, and it shall stand forever" (Daniel 2:44). This is the stone that was cut out of the mountain and not by man, WHICH WAS MENTIONED IN THE SCRIPTURE, as it is written, "from thence from the shepherd, the Stone of Yisrael" (Beresheet 49:24). What is this stone? It is the congregation of Yisrael, THE NUKVA OF ZEIR ANPIN, as written, "and this stone, which I have set for a pillar..." (Beresheet 28:22), WHICH IS THE NUKVA.

205. ר' חִיָּיא אָמַר, מֵהָכָא שְׁאָר יָשׁוּב שְׁאָר יַעֲקֹב, אִלֵּין בִּרְכָאן אַחֲרָנִין, דְּאִשְׁתָּאֲרוּ, וּכְתִיב, וְהָיָה שְׁאֵרִית יַעֲקֹב בְּקֶרֶב עַמִּים רַבִּים בַּגּוֹיִם כֻּלְּהוּ, וְלֹא בְּעֵשָׂו בִּלְחוֹדֵיהּ, וּכְתִיב וְהָיָה שְׁאֵרִית וְגוֹ', כְּטַל מֵאֵת יי'.

205. Rabbi Chiya said that from this IT IS UNDERSTOOD THAT THE REST OF THE BLESSINGS OF JACOB REMAIN FOR YISRAEL TO USE IN THE FUTURE, as it is written, "A remnant shall return, even the remnant of Jacob" (Yeshayah 10:21). About these remaining blessings, IT HAS BEEN

WRITTEN, "A REMNANT SHALL RETURN," MEANING THAT THEY WILL RETURN TO YISRAEL. It is also written, "And the remnant of Jacob shall be in the midst of many peoples" (Michah 5:6), THAT IS, among all the nations, not Esau alone, FOR THEN THE REST OF THE BLESSINGS WILL BE AROUSED, as it is written, "And the remnant...like dew from Hashem."

206. פְּתַח ר' יֵיסָא וַאֲמַר בֵּן יְכַבֵּד אָב וְעֶבֶד אֲדוֹנָיו, בֵּן: דָּא עֵשָׂו דְּלָא הֲוָה בַּר נָשׁ בְּעָלְמָא, דְּיוֹקִיר לַאֲבוֹי, כְּמָה דְּאוֹקִיר עֵשָׂו לַאֲבוֹי. וְהַהוּא יַקִּירוּ דְּאוֹקִיר לֵיהּ אַשְׁלֵיט לֵיהּ בְּהַאי עָלְמָא.

206. Rabbi Yisa quoted the verse, "A son honors his father, and a servant his master" (Malachi 1:6). "A son" refers to Esau, for in the whole world there was no man who respected his father as Esau did; the homage he paid him made him ruler of the world.

207. וְעֶבֶד אֲדוֹנָיו: דָּא אֱלִיעֶזֶר עֶבֶד אַבְרָהָם וְאוֹקְמוּהָ, דְּהָא בַּר נָשׁ דַּהֲוָה אָתֵי לְחָרָן, בְּכַמָּה עוֹתְרָא, וְכַמָּה מַתְּנָן וּנְבַזְבְּזִין, וּגְמַלִּין טְעִינָן, דְּלָא אָמַר לִבְתוּאֵל וְלָבָן, דְּאִיהוּ רְחִימוֹי דְּאַבְרָהָם, אוֹ בַּר נָשׁ אָחֳרָא, דְּאָתֵי בִּפְיוּסָא דְּאַבְרָהָם, אֶלָּא עַד לָא יְמַלֵּל מִלּוֹי מַה כְּתִיב, וַיֹּאמֶר עֶבֶד אַבְרָהָם אָנֹכִי, וּלְבָתַר אֲדֹנִי אֲדֹנִי, בְּגִין דְּיוֹקִיר לֵיהּ לְאַבְרָהָם, הַהוּא יְקָרָא, וְהַהוּא טִיבוּ, אוֹרִיךְ לֵיהּ לְכַמָּה זִמְנִין.

207. "...and a servant his master" refers to Eliezer, the servant of Abraham. This has been explained. The man came to Charan with great wealth and camels loaded with many gifts to lavish, yet he did not say to Betu'el and Laban, that he is Abraham's friend, or any other man, who came at Abraham's request, but when he started his speech, it is written, "And he said, I am Abraham's servant" (Beresheet 24:34). Later, he repeated SEVERAL TIMES, 'my master'. Because he respected Abraham with honor and kindness, they were patient with him for some time.

208. כָּךְ עֵשָׂו, הַהוּא יְקָרָא דְּאוֹקִיר לֵיהּ לַאֲבוֹי, אוֹרִיךְ לֵיהּ כָּל הַנֵּי זִמְנִין דְּיִשְׁלוֹט בְּעָלְמָא דָּא, וְאִינּוּן דְּמֵעִין, אוֹרִידוּ לוֹן לְיִשְׂרָאֵל בְּשַׁעְבּוּדָא דִּילֵיהּ עַד דְּיִתּוּבוּן יִשְׂרָאֵל לְקוּבְּ"ה, בִּבְכִיָּה וּבִדְמָעִין, דִּכְתִיב בִּבְכִי יָבֹאוּ וְגו', וּכְדֵין כְּתִיב, וְעָלוּ מוֹשִׁיעִים בְּהַר צִיּוֹן לִשְׁפֹּט אֶת הַר

עֲשָׂו וְהָיְתָה לַיי׳ הַמְּלוּכָה.

208. By right of that honor that he showed to his father, the Holy One, blessed be He, was forbearing with him when he ruled this world. And these are the tears that Yisrael shed under his yoke, until Yisrael will return to the Holy One, blessed be He, with crying in tears and weeping, as it is written, "They shall come with weeping..." (Yirmeyah 31:8) and then, "And liberators shall ascend upon mount Zion to judge the mountain of Esau; and the kingdom shall be Hashem's" (Ovadyah. 1:21).

בָּרוּךְ יי׳ לְעוֹלָם אָמֵן וְאָמֵן.

Blessed be Hashem for ever and ever. Amen and Amen.

NOTES

NOTES

NOTES

NOTES

NOTES

NOTES

NOTES

NOTES

NOTES

NOTES

NOTES

NOTES

NOTES

NOTES

NOTES

NOTES